ORDNANCE SURVEY MEMOIRS OF IRELAND

Volume Eighteen

PARISHES OF COUNTY LONDONDERRY V
1830, 1833, 1836–7

Published 1993.
The Institute of Irish Studies,
The Queen's University of Belfast,
Belfast.
In association with
The Royal Irish Academy,
Dawson Street,
Dublin.

Reprinted 2021 by Ulster Historical Foundation

Grateful acknowledgement is made to the Economic and Social Research Council and the Department of Education for Northern Ireland for their financial assistance at different stages of this publication programme.

Copyright 1993.

All rights reserved. No part of this publication may be reproduced, stored in a retrieval system or transmitted, in any form or by any means, electronic, mechanical, photocopying, recording or otherwise, without the prior permission of the publisher.

Paperback ISBN 13: 978-0-85389-441-4
Hardback ISBN 13: 978-0-85389-440-7

Printed in Ireland by SPRINT-print Ltd.

Ordnance Survey Memoirs of Ireland
VOLUME EIGHTEEN

Parishes of County Londonderry V
1830, 1833, 1836–7

Maghera and Tamlaght O'Crilly

Edited by Angélique Day and Patrick McWilliams.

The Institute of Irish Studies
in association with
The Royal Irish Academy

EDITORIAL BOARD

Angélique Day (General Editor)
Patrick S. McWilliams (Executive Editor)
Nóirín Dobson (Assistant Editor)
Dr B.M. Walker (Publishing Director)
Professor R.H. Buchanan (Chairman)

CONTENTS

	Page
Introduction	ix
Brief history of the Irish Ordnance Survey and Memoirs	ix
Definition of terms used	x
Note on Memoirs of County Londonderry	x

Parishes in County Londonderry

Maghera	1
Tamlaght O'Crilly	82

List of selected maps and drawings

County Londonderry, with parish boundaries	vi
County Londonderry, 1837, by Samuel Lewis	viii
Great Standing Stone of Swatragh	11
Door lintel of Maghera old church	38
James II brass money	60
Church of Tamlaght O'Crilly	93
Giant's chair from Timaconway townland	113
Landscape view near Tamlaght village	127

List of O.S. maps, 1830s

Maghera	2
Swatragh	76

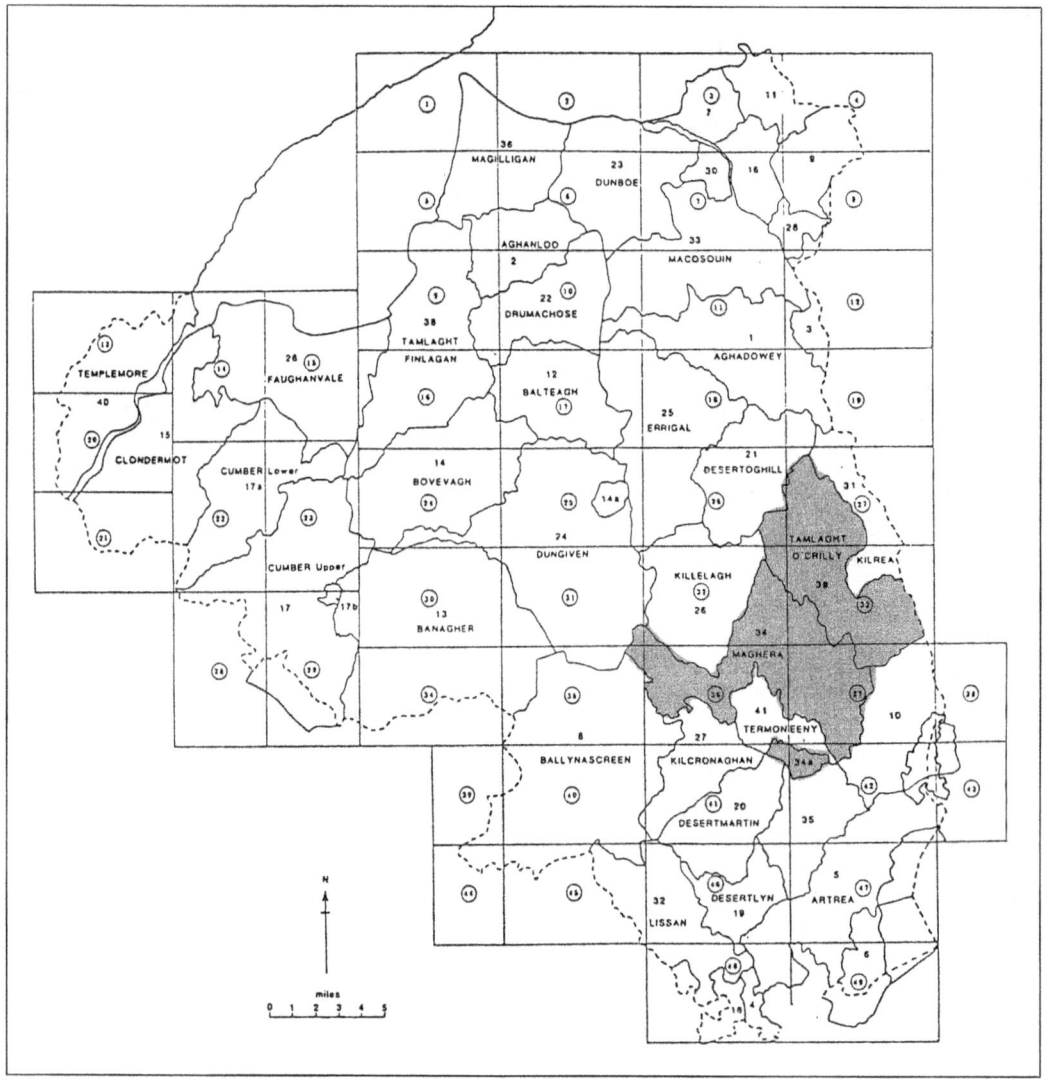

ACKNOWLEDGEMENTS

During the course of the transcription and publication project many have advised and encouraged us in this gigantic task. Thanks must first be given to the Royal Irish Academy, particularly former librarian Mrs Brigid Dolan and her staff, for making the original manuscripts available to us. We are also indebted to Siobhán O'Rafferty for her continuing help in deciphering indistinct passages of manuscript. We are grateful to Mrs Fay of Knockcloghrim for letting us see her invaluable transcription of Tamlaght O'Crilly.

We should like to acknowledge the following individuals for their special contributions. Dr Brian Trainor led the way with his edition of the Antrim Memoir and provided vital help on the steering committee. Dr Ann Hamlin also provided valuable support, especially during the most trying stages of the project. Professor R.H. Buchanan's unfailing encouragment has been instrumental in the development of the project to the present. Without Dr Kieran Devine the initial stages of the transcription and the computerising work would never have been completed successfully: the project owes a great deal to his constant help and advice. Dr Kay Muhr's continuing contribution to the work of the transcription project is deeply appreciated. Mr W.C. Kerr's interest and expertise have been invaluable. Professor Anne Crookshank and Dr Edward McParland were most generous with practical help and advice concerning the drawings amongst the Memoir manuscripts. We would like to thank the Director of the Ordnance Survey, Dublin and the keepers of the fire-proof store, among them Leonard Hines. Finally, all students of the nineteenth century Ordnance Survey of Ireland owe a great deal to the pioneering work of Professor J.H. Andrews, and his kind help in the first days of the project is gratefully recorded.

The essential task of inputting the texts from audio tapes was done by Miss Eileen Kingan, Mrs Christine Robertson, Miss Eilis Smyth, Miss Lynn Murray, and, most importantly, Miss Maureen Carr.

We are grateful to the Linen Hall Library for lending us their copies of the first edition 6" Ordnance Survey Maps: also to Ms Maura Pringle of QUB Cartography Department for the index maps showing the parish boundaries. For providing financial assistance at crucial times for the maintenance of the project, we would like to take this opportunity of thanking the trustees of the Esme Mitchell trust and The Public Record Office of Northern Ireland.

Left:
Map of parishes of County Londonderry. The area described in this volume, the parishes of Maghera and Tamlaght O'Crilly, has been shaded to highlight its location. The square grids represent the 1830s 6" Ordnance Survey maps. The encircled numbers relate to the map numbers as presented in the bound volumes of maps for the county. The parishes have been numbered in all cases and named in full where possible, except those in the following list: Agivey 3, Arboe 4, Ballinderry 6, Ballyaghran 7, Ballyrashane 9, Ballyscullion 10, Ballywillin 11, Bovevagh 14a, Coleraine 16, Derryloran (no Memoir) 18, Kildollagh 28, Killowen 30, Maghera 34a, Magherafelt 35.

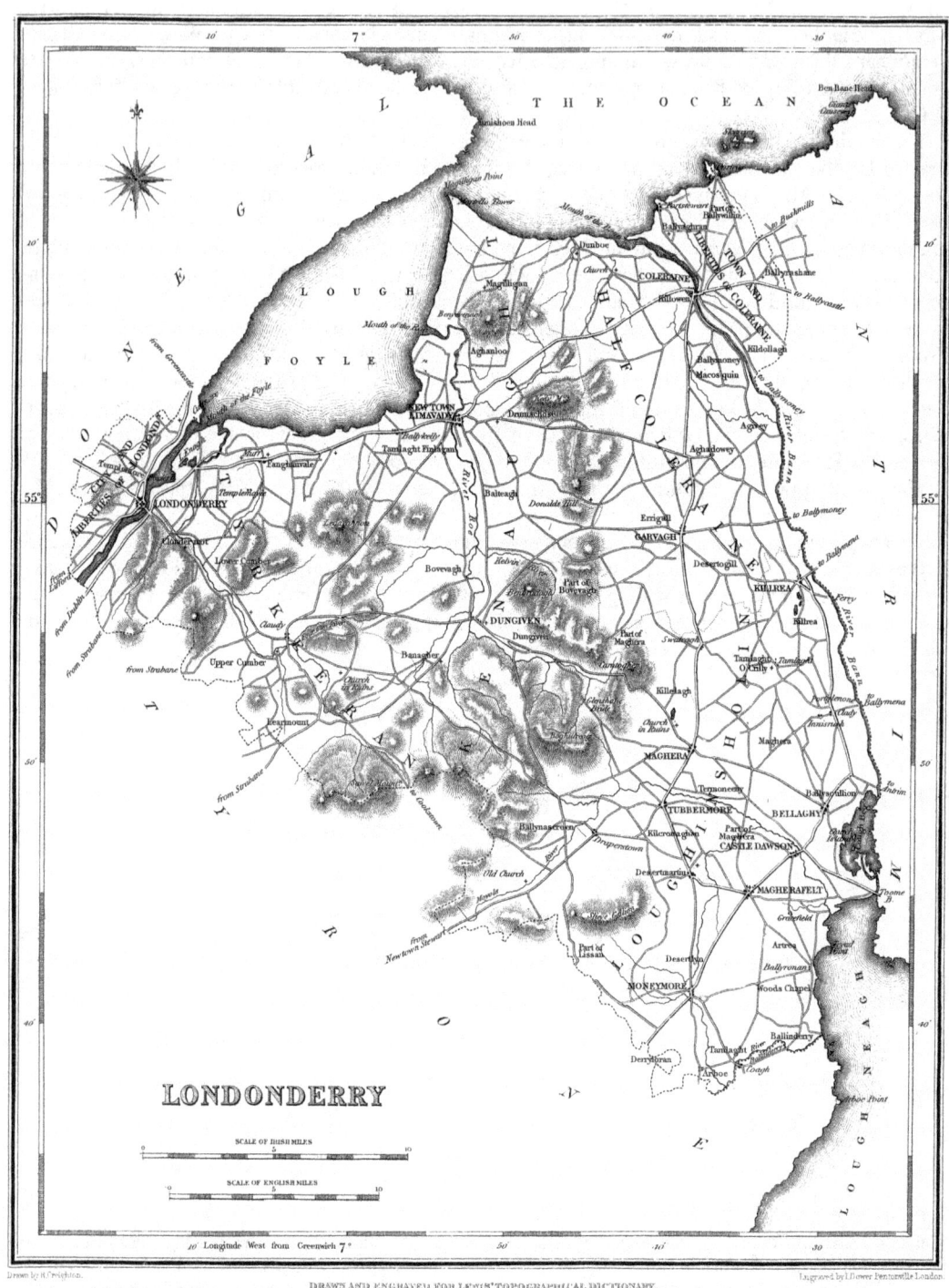

Map of County Londonderry, from Samuel Lewis' *Atlas of the counties of Ireland* (London, 1837)

INTRODUCTION AND GUIDE TO THE PUBLICATION OF THE ORDNANCE SURVEY MEMOIRS

The following text of the Ordnance Survey Memoirs was first transcribed by a team working in the Institute of Irish Studies at The Queen's University of Belfast, on a computerised index of the material. For this publication programme the text has been further edited: spellings have been modernised in most cases, although where the original spelling was thought to be of any interest it has been retained and is indicated by angle brackets in the text. Variant spellings for townland and lesser place-names have been preserved, although parish and major place-names have been standardised and the original spelling given in angle brackets. Names of prominent people, for instance landlords, have been standardised where possible, but original spellings of names in lists of informants, emigration tables and on tombstones have been retained. We have not altered the Memoir writers' anglicisation of names and words in Irish.

Punctuation has been modernised and is the responsibility of the editors. Editorial additions are indicated by square brackets: a question mark before and after a word indicates a queried reading and tentatively inserted information respectively. Original drawings are referred to in the text, and some have been reproduced. Manuscript page references have been omitted from this series. Because of the huge variation in size of Memoirs for different counties, the following editorial policy has been adopted: where there are numerous duplicating and overlapping accounts, the most complete and finished account, normally the Memoir proper, has been presented, with additional unique information from other accounts like the Fair Sheets entered into a separate section, clearly titled and identified; where the Memoir material is less, nothing has been omitted. To achieve standard volume size, parishes have been associated on the basis of propinquity.

There are considerable differences in the volume of information recorded for different areas: counties Antrim and Londonderry are exceptionally well covered, while the other counties do not have quite the same detail. This series is the first systematic publication of the parish Memoirs, although individual parishes have been published by pioneering local history societies. The entire transcriptions of the Memoirs made in the course of the indexing project can be consulted in the Public Record Office of Northern Ireland and the library at the Queen's University of Belfast. The manuscripts of the Ordnance Survey Memoirs are in the Royal Irish Academy, Dublin.

Brief history of the Irish Ordnance Survey in the nineteenth century and the writing of the Ordnance Survey Memoirs

In 1824 a House of Commons committee recommended a townland survey of Ireland with maps at the scale of 6", to facilitate a uniform valuation for local taxation. The Duke of Wellington, then prime minister, authorised this, the first Ordnance Survey of Ireland. The survey was directed by Colonel Thomas Colby, who had under his command officers of the Royal Engineers and three companies of sappers and miners. In addition to this, civil assistants were recruited to help with sketching, drawing and engraving of maps, and eventually, in the 1830s, the writing of the Memoirs.

The Memoirs were written descriptions intended to accompany the maps, containing information which could not be fitted on to them. Colonel Colby always considered additional information to be necessary to clarify place-names and other distinctive features of each parish; this was to be written up in reports by the officers. Much information about parishes resulted from research into place-names and was used in the writing of the Memoirs. The term "Memoir" comes from the abbreviation of the word "Aide-Memoire". It was also used in the 18th century to describe topographical descriptions accompanying maps.

In 1833 Colby's assistant, Lieutenant Thomas Larcom, developed the scope of the officers' reports by stipulating the headings or "Heads of Inquiry" under which information was to be reported, and including topics of social as well as economic interest. By this time civil assistants were writing some of the Memoirs under the supervision of the officers, as well as collecting information in the Fair Sheets.

The first "Memoirs" are officers' reports covering Antrim in 1830, and work continued on the Antrim parishes right through the decade, with special activity in 1838 and 1839. Counties Down and Tyrone were written up from 1833 to 1837, with both officers and civil assistants working on Memoirs. In Londonderry and Fermanagh research and writing started in 1834. Armagh was worked on in 1835, 1837 and 1838. Much labour was expended in the Londonderry parishes. The plans to publish the Memoirs commenced with the parish of Templemore, containing the city and liberties of Derry, which came out in 1837 after a great deal of expense and effort.

Between 1839 and 1840 the Memoir scheme collapsed. Sir Robert Peel's government could not countenance the expenditure of money and time on such an exercise; despite a parliamentary commission favouring the continuation of the writing of the Memoirs, the scheme was halted before the southern half of the country was covered. The manuscripts remained unpublished and most were removed to the Royal Irish Academy, Dublin from the Ordnance Survey, Phoenix Park. Other records of the Ordnance Survey, including some residual material from the Memoir scheme, have recently been transferred to the National Archives, Bishop Street, Dublin.

The Memoirs are a uniquely detailed source for the history of the northern half of Ireland immediately before the Great Famine. They document the landscape and situation, buildings and antiquities, land-holdings and population, employment and livelihood of the parishes. They act as a nineteenth century Domesday book and are essential to the understanding of the cultural heritage of our communities. It is planned to produce a volume of evaluative essays to put the material in its full context, with information on other sources and on the writers of the Memoirs.

Definition of descriptive terms

Memoir (sometimes Statistical Memoir): an account of a parish written according to the prescribed form outlined in the instructions known as "Heads of Inquiry", and normally divided into three sections: Natural Features and History, Modern and Ancient Topography, Social and Productive Economy.

Fair Sheets: "information gathered for the Memoirs", an original title describing paragraphs of information following no particular order, often with marginal headings, signed and dated by the civil assistant responsible.

Statistical Remarks/Accounts: both titles are employed by the Engineer officers in their descriptions of the parish with marginal headings, often similar in layout to the Memoir.

Office Copies: these are copies of early drafts, generally officers' accounts and must have been made for office purposes.

Ordnance Survey Memoirs for County Londonderry

This volume, containing the Memoirs for the parishes of Maghera and Tamlaght O'Crilly in east Londonderry, is the fifth publication for the county and the eighteenth in the present series. It describes the scenery and life of this rural area, focusing on the linen town of Maghera, and local centres including Clady, Curran, Gulladuff, Knockcloghrim, Swatragh, Tamlaght and Upperlands, detailing the trades and occupations of the people, their traditions and entertainments, as well as the provision of charity and health care. The accounts provide some particularly valuable information on emigration from the area; both Bleakly's Fair Sheets for Maghera and Fagan's for Tamlaght O'Crilly contain lists of emigrants for the years 1834 and 1835, while Stokes' Maghera Memoir contains a number of vividly descriptive and deeply moving letters from recent emigrants.

There is no complete Memoir for either parish but the main accounts by John Stokes, normally responsible for Antiquities, are fluent and detailed, and have been supplemented by material from the Fair Sheets. The Fair Sheets for this area are particularly rich in detail for customs, folklore and antiquities. John Bleakly, the lowest paid civil assistant, uses a somewhat condensed style in contrast to the vivid vernacular of his more senior colleague Thomas Fagan, and between them, they describe the area in great depth. John Stokes' accounts for both parishes make for very entertaining and informative reading.

There are also brief additional notes on townland names and orthography by Larcom, O'Donovan and Dalton which, in some measure, reflect the fundamental importance of place-name research to the whole Memoir project and the degree of personal interest that Larcom, as head of the project, invested in the work at local level.

Drawings in the Memoir papers are listed below and are cross-referenced in the text; some are illustrated. The manuscript material is to be found in Boxes 44 and 46 of the Royal Irish Academy's collection of Ordnance Survey Memoirs, and section references are given beside each parish below in their printed order.

Maghera: Box 44 I 3, 7 with 2 and 4, 6, and parts of 2, 8, 5 and 4.

Tamlaght O'Crilly: Box 46 I 6 with 1, 2, 3, 4 and 5.

Drawings

Maghera (sections 6, 1, 8 and 4):

Stone with groove cut across the centre.

Maghera old church; view of steeple and entrance; detail drawings of bishop, door lintel with dimensions [illustrated], and head of saint in steeple wall.

Maghera old church, ground plan with annotations and dimensions; views of windows.

Maghera old church, 3 windows in tower and south entrance to tower [by C.W. Ligár].

Monuments of Knockoneill, plan of casiol and section of wall; ancient fences and cairns [by J. Stokes].

North view of artificial island and old fort in Ballymacpeake townland.

Artificial island and old fort in Ballymacpeake townland, scaled plan with orientation; fireplace in fort with dimensions.

Part of canoe found in lake in Ballymacpeake, view of side and section with dimensions [by C.W. Ligar].

Great Standing Stone of Swatragh, with dimensions and figure to give scale [illustrated] [by J. Stokes].

Brass sword from Drumlamph townland, 2 section drawings, full size [by C.W. Ligar].

Ancient quern from Mr Knox's collection, end, top and side views with dimensions; another quern from Mr Knox's collection, side and top views with dimensions.

Stone font of monastery of Maghera, bottom and top view and section with dimensions.

Copper spearhead from Maghera with section and dimensions.

Stone hatchets with section of each and dimensions.

Flint arrowheads, back, front and edge of each with dimensions.

Silver medal from Maghera, both faces, full size.

Spearheads from Maghera, side view and section of each [by J. Stokes].

Stone hatchet from Drumard, view and section with dimensions; fragment of clay urn, view and section with dimensions.

Old tobacco pipes called "Danes pipes", side and bottom views.

Coins from Maghera, both faces of each [by C.W. Ligar ?].

James II brass money; coin of 1689, both faces with tokens and Latin inscriptions [illustrated].

Dungleady Fort, view, scaled plan and section with dimensions [by J. Stokes].

Stone sledge, outline and section.

Brass battleaxe from Fallagloon, full size; stone hatchet.

Ancient quern from Drumlamph townland, overview; stone slab with figure of the cross on it, full size.

Flint arrowhead from Gulladuff, full size; ancient axe from Drumard, 2 views; arrowheads and stone hatchet from Drumard.

Ancient iron axe from Drumard, view and section.

Flint arrowheads from Ballymacpeake.

Brass halbert from Dreenan townland.

Brass halbert from Toberhead townland, full size.

Flint arrowhead found between Fallagloon and Falgortrevy.

Stone hatchet, or "thunderbolt", from Fallagloon.

Brass halbert from Craigmore, full size.

Outline of stone hatchets and flint arrowheads from Danish fort in Ballymacross [by T. Fagan].

Brass spear from Culnagrew.

Artificial cave in Drumard townland, with orientation and dimensions [by J. Bleakly].

Tamlaght O'Crilly (sections 2 and 3):

Part of corn mill from Black lough in Inishrush townland.

Church of Tamlaght O'Crilly, view of door and gravestones [illustrated].

Hatchet from fort in Ballynian townland, side view and section with dimensions; stone axe from same fort, full view, side view, frontal view with dimensions [by J. Stokes].

Landscape view near Tamlaght village [illustrated] [by C.W. Ligar].

Mithoe from Black lough, full view and section with dimensions.

Ancient spade and iron ball from Timaconway townland with dimensions.

Giant's chair from Timaconway townland with dimensions [illustrated] [by J. Stokes].

Outline of wooden spade from Timaconway with dimensions.

Part of corn mill from Black lough.

Outline of brass halbert from Drumnacarman [by T. Fagan].

Parish of Maghera, County Londonderry

Statistical Account by Lieutenant R.J. Stotherd, April 1830, with notes by Another

NATURAL STATE

Situation and Name

In the barony of Loughinsholin and county of Londonderry. It is a rectory in the province of Armagh and diocese of Derry, the right of presentation being in the bishop of that see.

The ancient and modern name of this parish is compounded of Magher-na-dra [3 short and 1 long stress] i.e. "the field of vespers."

Boundaries, Extent and Divisions

It is bounded on the north by the parishes of Errigal and Desertoghill <Desertoghil>, on the east by Tamlaght O'Crilly and Ballyscullion, on the south by Magherafelt, Termoneeny, Desertmartin and Kilcronaghan, and on the west by Ballynascreen, Dungiven and Killelagh. It is a very straggling parish, almost surrounding the 2 parishes of Killelagh and Termoneeny, and its extent can therefore scarcely be defined, varying in breadth from east to west from [blank] to [blank] miles. [Insert marginal note: This information must be obtained from the plan]. Its length from north to south is about 2 miles and it contains about 24,000 English acres. It is divided into 41 townlands, the properties of the Mercers', the Drapers' and the Vintners' Companies, and of the see of Derry.

NATURAL FEATURES

Surface

The principal part of this parish consists of whinstone hills, whose gentle undulations are very generally under cultivation and are frequently divided from each other by flat or flow bogs. The 2 long necks of land which extend up the face of Carntogher mountain and nearly surround the parish of Killelagh are also under tillage for a considerable height up the face of the mountain, when the mountain bog and heather commences which terminates its summit.

Soil

The soil is as various as its surface: towards the east it is light and gravelly; the centre and principal parts of the parish consists of a light stony soil common to the basaltic country east of Carntogher, which is tolerably productive; on the banks of the Moyola there is some good strong clay land descending the face of the mountain on the south west of the parish. The soil is shallow but tolerably good, reposing on the sandstone which requires a great succession of manure.

Produce, Fuel and Turbary

Potatoes, oats and flax succeed each other in general, sometimes the potatoes are followed by 2 crops of oats and then potatoes again. The farmers are too poor to fallow barley and some wheat is also grown.

The parish is well supplied with turbary from the numerous bogs which intersect it.

NATURAL HISTORY

Limestone

This parish depends on the Desertmartin quarries for its supply of limestone for agricultural and other economical purposes. A small quarry, high up the mountain in the boundary watercourse between Corlacky townland in parish Killelagh and Knockoneil townland in parish Maghera, was opened and the supply for a short period led to the hope that it would prove extensive. A road was formed to it at a considerable expense but, the bed proving very small, it was shortly exhausted.

Freestone

On the east face of Carntogher mountain beds of freestone of every variety, from the coarse conglomerate to the finest freestone for building purposes, abound and quarries of considerable extent have been opened on the banks of the Moyola and Fallylea rivers.

MODERN TOPOGRAPHY AND PRODUCTIVE ECONOMY

Town of Maghera

Maghera is the only post and market town in the 3 parishes Maghera, Killelagh and Termoneeny. Tuesday is the general market day, Friday the corn market, of which there is generally a good supply. There are also 2 fairs held in the year, chiefly for cattle and a few horses, the latter of a very bad description. [Insert marginal note: The tolls of the town have been recently purchased from the proprietor by the inhabitants and 12 fairs

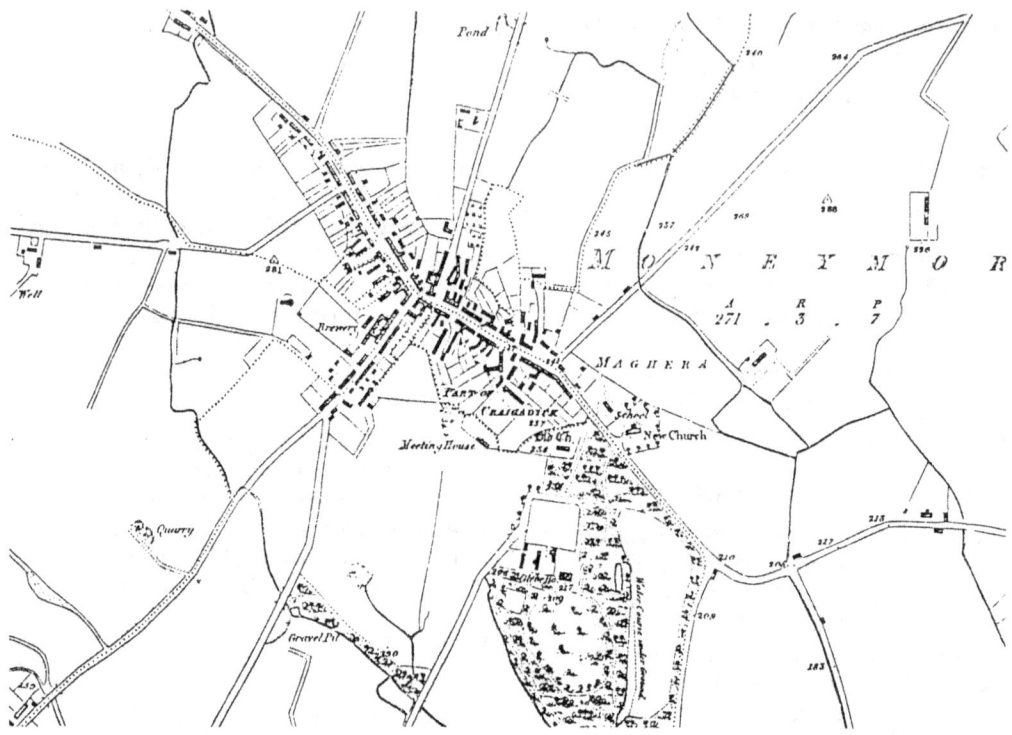
Map of Maghera from the first 6" O.S. maps, 1830s

are henceforward to be held in the year on the last Tuesday in every month]. The town contains but one public building, a wretched market house. [Insert marginal note: A new market house on a small scale is now building. There is also a corn market and a neat schoolhouse].

A plain church has lately been built on the road to Castledawson <Castle Dawson>, [insert addition: cost 1,600 pounds], the ancient church being allowed to fall into ruins. [Insert marginal note: The chapel is a plain but extensive edifice, capable of receiving 5,000 persons, and a Presbyterian meeting house in the town and a second of smaller size in the village of Swatragh. There is also a meeting house in the village of Coolnady].

Village of Swatragh

A dirty straggling village, which takes its name from the townland Swatragh in which it is situated, is the only other assemblage of houses of any extent in the parish. 4 fairs are held in the year for cattle.

Manufactures

A small quantity of coarse linen is made in this parish for the Maghera market, and yarn is spun by those who have no other employment. [Insert marginal note: An extensive bleach green at Upperlands, belonging to Mr Alexander Clark]. The peasantry are, however, chiefly engaged in agricultural pursuits.

In the town of Maghera is a large brewery belonging to Mr Alexander Clark. Near the Moyola river, on the road to Tobermore, is an extensive bed of blue clay, much used in brick-making. [Insert marginal note: The bricks are sold from 5s to 8s per 1,000].

Roads

The high road from Belfast and Antrim by Toomebridge thro' Dungiven to Derry, passing thro' the town of Maghera, as also the direct road from Dublin and Coleraine, west of Lough Neagh, traverses this parish; they are both kept in bad repair, particularly the latter, the laying out of which might also be very much improved by avoiding the hills. The by-roads, of course, are in general in very bad order.

NATURAL FEATURES

Rivers

The Moyola and Clady are the principal rivers which, with their numerous tributary streams, water this parish. The former has its source in the Ballynascreen mountains, running thence east, intersecting the barony of Loughinsholin and falling into Lough Neagh. Its course is marked by the fertility and richness of its banks: when rocky being productive of the finest freestone, when flat its immediate holmes being capable of the highest cultivation. It was formerly celebrated for its trouts, but the mill-dam at Castledawson prevents the salmon and sea trout from Lough Neagh getting higher up the river. It would otherwise be as fine a fishing river as any in Ireland.

The latter, the Clady, is a small tributary stream to the Bann, having its source near to the summit of the Carntogher ridge. After dividing the 2 parishes of Maghera and Killelagh, it turns eastward through the former parish, being the boundary to several townlands in its passage. After receiving the Grillagh river, the 2 united fall into the Bann near Portglenone. It abounds in trouts, salmon and pike.

SOCIAL ECONOMY

Population

The country is thickly covered with the cottages of the farmers and peasantry, some of which are tolerably comfortable. 2 or 3 families with that of the rector are the only respectable people in the parish. [Insert marginal note: The rectory is the only demesne in the parish].

Subjoined is a copy of the return furnished to the House of Commons in 1821: [table contains the following headings: houses, persons, occupations, schools].

2,077 inhabited houses, 2,436 families, 59 uninhabited houses, 3 building; 5,505 males, 6,085 females, total 12,590; 2,677 chiefly employed in agriculture, 4,681 in trades and manufactures, 357 in occupations not comprised in preceding classes, total number occupied 7,715; schools: 281 males, 210 females, total 491. [Signed] R.J. Stotherd, Lieutenant Royal Engineers, 15th April 1830.

Memoir by J. Stokes, January 1837, with sections by C.W. Ligar

NATURAL FEATURES

Hills

The parish chiefly consists of whinstone hills, with a substratum of freestone in the western part, where in many places it crops out. They rise gradually from the east towards the summit of the Carntogher and Ballynascreen ridge, of which they contribute to make the base and side. The eastern division of these hills varies in height from 200 to 300 feet above the sea and may be said to form a part of the broad valley of the Bann. At its western extremity, where the inclined plain becomes steeper, it is 1,100 feet above the sea. There is a nearly detached portion of the parish separated by Killelagh which is yet more elevated.

Lakes

There are no lakes, unless a sheet of water which is partly in the townland of Drumard and partly in Moyagall deserves that name. It is shallow, in the middle of a bog and comprehends about 5 acres.

Rivers

The Moyola and Clady are the principal rivers.

These rivers rise very suddenly and subside quickly. The overflowing of the Moyola, the bed of which in the parish is soft and sandy, rather benefits than injures the soil. But from the other streams which flow chiefly on rocky beds, the floods often prove detrimental, and by embankments endeavours have been made to remedy that disadvantage.

There are no good falls on the Moyola; it is otherwise with the Clady. The best fall on the latter river is in Upperlands <Upperland>.

The parish is remarkbly well supplied with water from rivulets and springs. The latter are in general copious and of an excellent quality.

Bogs

Throughout the parish the soil in the valleys is in general composed of flow bogs. The surface of the ground being much broken with hollows, the bogs are in consequence numerous but small. Timber occurs imbedded in them and in great quantities. It is, however, of little value, being much injured to all appearance by fire. The red oak and the fir are the only species of trees to be met with, but it is remarkable that they seldom occur mixed indiscriminately together. When oak is found there is very little fir and vice versa. Where, however, they are in the same bog, the oak lies on the borders, the fir in the centre. Here we may state that the substratum, except where the base rocks appear, varies from light sand to heavy clay. The trees are almost all broken at the same height, a little above the roots, the stumps in every case remaining upright. Much the greater number of the trees lie towards the east, or that quarter of the compass. It is not unusual to meet in deep places 2 stumps, one directly above the other, and perhaps a tree stretched below them. The bog at the edges becomes shallower, owing to the shape of the basin it is in, but chiefly to the drainage having caused it to sink considerably. In other parts it is deep, commonly from 8 to 10 feet. It is even found to reach 16.

In Ballynahonebeg and other bogs piles have been found sunk perpendicularly and supporting beams laid horizontally on them, thus forming a road. Whenever such have been discovered, the timber has immediately been taken up for profit, and none such are now known to exist.

Woods

[Insert addition: There is yet in Drumlamph a small portion of land covered with the stunted remains of a natural wood; they consist principally of oak and hazel. There is no trace of it having been connected with a large forest, as that small planting about a mile to the northward, in the townland of Ballymacpeake Upper, is of a comparatively recent date. This also is now in a stunted state. The only artificial wood or planting in the parish is in that which forms the part of the ornamental grounds belonging to the house of the Rev. Spencer Knox near Maghera].

Remains of Natural Wood

In the townland of Drumlamph there are of the remains of natural wood, consisting of oak, ash, birch, alder, wild cherry tree and a little elm, 28 acres.

In Tigarvil there are of hazel, oak, birch, alder and whitethorn, 4 acres.

In Upperlands there are of oak, birch, hazel and alder, thinly mixed with ash, 4 and a half acres.

In Culnady there are of hazel and thorn trees, 20 acres.

Around the parapets of Dunglady Fort there are of hazel, with black and whitethorn, 1 acre.

In Upper Ballymacpeake there are of oak, ash, alder, birch and hazel, 1 acre; the same in Ballymaul, 1 acre, making in all a total of 59 and a half acres. There are about 20 acres more in the course of being destroyed by reclaiming, making altogether 79 and a half acres.

Climate

The climate in the lower part of the parish is mild, but the higher you ascend on the side of the mountain, the less genial it becomes. However, as cultivation has as yet only reached to the height of 700 feet, the crops are not much affected by the change. At that elevation they are about a fortnight later than in the low grounds. It may be said in general that the wheat is ripe towards the beginning of September, oats the beginning of October and barley about the end of August. Potatoes are dug in November.

MODERN TOPOGRAPHY

Village of Maghera

The village of Maghera is [blank] miles from Dublin and on the high road between Dublin and Coleraine. It consists of 1 street, with 3 small lanes. The principal street is half a mile long and stands in a bleak dreary situation. It is probably as old as the foundation of the church and monastery adjacent to it (see Ancient Topography). No part of the original houses or any vestige of them remain. The only ancient building is the old church. The parish church stands at the east end, but it contains no chapel.

The public buildings are the old and new market houses and 2 hotels, both indifferent. The market houses are small and plain, and stand at the eastern and western ends of the street. The new market house was built in 1832 at the cost of 300 pounds; the old one in 1824 for the same sum. In the first flax is sold, in the latter meal and grain. In the latter also the court house is held. The general style of the houses is one of meanness and discomfort. They are, however, improving.

The main street is 40 feet wide, the 2 lanes 19 and a half and 27 respectively. They were formerly paved but are now covered with broken stone. The main street is flagged in some parts. There are 229 houses, of which 76 are 2-storey high and the remainder 1-storey. In the last 8 years 26 houses of stone and brick have been rebuilt. In the last 5, 13 new ones of stone have been built. The most respectable is occupied by Alexander Clark Esquire and was rebuilt in 1832.

Schoolhouse

There is a good schoolhouse at the eastern end of the village nearest the church. It is a good 2-storey house, slated, standing upon the glebe land of the parish. There is 1 acre attached, granted by deed for the purpose of education. It was built in 1821 at the cost 400 pounds, viz. 100 pounds from the Kildare Street Society, 125 pounds from the Mercers' Company and 175 pounds from private subscription.

Parish of Maghera

SOCIAL AND PRODUCTIVE ECONOMY

Habits of the People

There are no local laws or customs. The people are all petty shopkeepers and do not hold much intercourse with one another. They are improving in their domestic habits. There are no libraries or reading rooms among them, but there has been lately established among the tradesmen a small debating club upon historical subjects. There had been a news room at Falls' Hotel, but it was given up for want of support.

See appendix for a table of occupations.

Banks

A branch of the Agricultural and Commercial Bank formerly attended every Tuesday from Garvagh. That bank has at present (January 1837) stopped payment. There are no savings banks.

Markets

There is a market every Tuesday and a fair on the last Tuesday of every month. There are no tolls or customs. That burthen was shaken off in December 1832 by a meeting of the gentlemen and merchants of the town and vicinity, in which it was resolved that they should be purchased from the proprietor, Alexander Clark Esquire of Upperlands, for 270 pounds, the sum taken.

An important staple in this market at present is flax. The annual quantity sold appears to be increasing. That of corn is diminishing on account of a preference that exists for the Magherafelt market. The butter market, though introduced only in 1832, is doing pretty well. See [Fair Sheets] for a table of the quantities sold at market.

The butter market was established through the instrumentality of Mr Clark of Upperlands and the principal shopkeepers of the village. An attempt was made at the same time to set up a pork market, which failed by the greatness of the weekly export of pork that takes place from the village and neighbourhood through the hands of several farmers and residents. It is believed that about 200 pounds worth of pork leaves it every week for Belfast. There is also a good export of eggs to Scotland.

Fairs

In the fair held on the 27th day of December 1836 there were sold: horses 7, black cattle 217, from 3 pounds to 40 pounds each; sheep 57, from 10s to 40s each; pigs 263, various prices. This was a smaller fair than usual, from the extreme cold and severity of the weather.

Supply of Food

The village is well supplied with meat, but not with fruit, vegetables, milk or butter. Beef is 4d the lb and prime mutton 5d. A great part of the mutton is from small mountain sheep at an inferior price. The cattle are not stall fed or grazed about the town.

Building Materials

Memel timber from Coleraine at 1s 8d per foot is chiefly used. Lime is brought from Desertmartin and laid down for 1s 6d per barrel of 3 bushels. Stone is found near the town and laid down for 6d per load of 15 cwt. Brick is from Ballynahone, 1 and a half miles distant; is laid down on the ground at from 1s to 1s 6d per 100 of 5 score. Queen ton slates from Coleraine are laid down for 3 pounds 13s per ton. Countesses 5 pounds 15s per 1,000. The carriage from the town is 6d per cwt.

Insurance and Employment

There are 2 houses insured from fire. There are no combinations at present to deprive workmen of the liberty of working as they please, and at any prices, nor are there any seasons in particular at which artisans and labourers are in considerable numbers unemployed.

Coaches

The coach from Dungannon to Coleraine passes every day at twelve, meeting at the same time the return coach from Coleraine to Dungannon. A coach from Londonderry to Belfast also formerly passed through at that hour, but it was given up January 1837 by the proprietor for want of support, after having been for some time replaced by a car.

Dispensary

There is a dispensary, see Dispensaries, Social Economy for further particulars, and the appendix for the number and nature of the diseases. See appendix also for the schools.

Conveyances

There are 5 part cars for hire and 1 chaise. The chaise and 2 of the cars are kept by Falls' Hotel. The other 3 cars are kept by different publicans. There are also 12 private ones.

Amusements

The general habits as to amusement of the people are quite of a domestic character. There is no place of public amusement.

Progress of Improvement

The village is improving. 50 years ago it was about the same size as it is now, but the houses were then all thatched cabins, which have since been enlarged and altered according as the circumstances of the inhabitants improved. In doing so, they generally raised them 1 storey. The oldest part is roundabout the well, called Tober Lowrie i.e. the eastern end.

MODERN TOPOGRAPHY

Village of Swatragh

Swatragh is a small village situated on the high road from Maghera to Garvagh and at the distance of 4 and a half miles statute from the former town. It contains 42 houses, of which 36 are 1-storey high and 6 are 2-storey high. The former are all cabins. A collection of houses has existed here for at least 200 years. In 1778 there were but 9 of them, all thatched hovels.

Its improvement may be attributed to the exertions of James Henry Esquire, than agent to Alexander Stewart Esquire of Ards in the county Donegal, who in that year gave great encouragement to John Reynolds and his brother Manus to build. Soon after, Mr Henry conjointly with Hugh Lyle Esquire of Coleraine revived the old quarterly fair, the patent for which, it is said, had been granted 200 years ago. It has now passed from the Stewart family to the Mercers' Company, under whose fostering care it will no doubt speedily improve. It is rather stationary at present in the progress of improvement. The new dwelling house of Doctor Mooney, the surgeon, will, however, be an ornament.

SOCIAL AND PRODUCTIVE ECONOMY

Trades in Swatragh

The following are the trades and occupations of this village: carpenters 2, blacksmiths 1, [crossed out: linen weavers 2], shoemakers 1, nailors 1, wheelwrights 1, publicans 3, publican and grocer 1, schoolmaster 1, schoolmistress 1, grocers 5, farmers 16, dressmakers 1, surgeon 1, miller 1, kiln man 1, linen weavers 2, bailiffs 1, [total] 40 and 2 schoolhouses.

Swatragh became a station for constabulary police in the year 1827; they were withdrawn in 1834.

Fairs

There are 4 fairs held annually in Swatragh, viz. on the 5th March, 18th May and 17th August, for the sale of horses, cows, pigs, sheep, goats and yarn. They are not large and are toll free.

Mail and Dispensary

The mail between Dungannon and Coleraine passes every day.

The physician of the Kilrea dispensary is bound to attend at the Swatragh dispensary every Saturday to assist in difficult cases. About 100 cases a week are dispensed to. For tables of this dispensary, see appendix.

General Remarks

This village has a very poor mean look and is scattered in an irregular double row on both sides of the high road.

Village of Curran

Curran is a small village in the townland of Curran. It contains 31 houses, 4 of which are 2-storeys high and the other 27 1-storey high. It forms a straggling street in a bleak cold situation. 60 years ago it was but a "clachan" of 6 cabins, including 1 public house and a smith's forge, and inhabited by 2 families called Marlin and Kent. There are now 2 annual fairs held in it, one on the 22nd of November, the other, on the 23rd of June, for the sale of cows, goats, pigs, sheep, yarn, soft goods and hardware. These fairs are not large. On the last fair day i.e. 23rd of November 1826 [1836], only 20 cows and 1 pig were exhibited.

The following are the trades and occupations: publicans 3, publicans and grocers 1, grocers 3, shoemakers 1, tailors 1, carpenters 1, hacklers 1, wheelwrights 1, weavers 16, stonemasons 1, poor widows 1, dealers in rags, flax, eggs and feathers 1, [total] 31. The weavers are also all labouring cottiers and have each an acre of land and a cow's grass.

Curran is 4 and a half statute miles south east of Maghera and on the old road from it to Magherafelt.

Village of Gulladuff

Gulladuff is a small cluster of [insert addition: 14 houses, one of which is 2-storey high, all in pretty good repair], situated in the townland of Gulladuff and at the distance of [blank] miles statute from

Parish of Maghera

Maghera. There are, April 1836: 2 blacksmiths, [insert addition: 6 weavers, 2 carpenters, 3 shoemakers], 1 wheelwright [insert addition: 1 wheelwright and turner], 1 butcher, 2 publicans [insert addition: 2 publicans and grocers], 1 surgeon, 1 schoolmaster, 1 schoolmistress. The houses are of stone and thatched.

Grain Market

A grain market was established here in 1829 by its landlords.

In 1829 there were sold: oats, 90 sacks containing 2,160 stones; barley, 9 sacks containing 180 stones.

In 1830: oats, 96 sacks containing 2,304 stones; barley, 10 sacks containing 200 stones.

In 1831: oats, 100 sacks containing 2,400 stones; barley, 10 sacks containing 200 stones.

In 1832: oats, 100 sacks containing 2,400 stones; barley, 10 sacks containing 200 stones; wheat, 86 sacks containing 8 tons 12 cwt.

In 1833: oats, 100 sacks containing 2,400 stones; barley, 10 sacks containing 200 stones; wheat, 96 sacks containing 9 tons 12 cwt.

In 1834: oats, 120 sacks containing 2,880 stones; barley, 12 sacks containing 240 stones; wheat, 112 sacks containing 11 tons 4 cwt.

In 1835: oats, 150 sacks containing 3,600 stones; barley, 12 sacks containing 240 stones; wheat, 120 sacks containing 12 tons.

[Insert addition: In 1836: oats 200 sacks, barley 20 sacks, wheat 34 sacks].

It is considered that the prosperity of this market will not be permanent, as it is not only too near the great market of Maghera and Magherafelt but also is chiefly supported by the purchases made by the Messrs Gaussen of Ballyronan, who have given their commission to one of the inhabitants. This village is increasing in size, see appendix for a table of its state for January 1837.

MODERN TOPOGRAPHY

Maghera Church

The parish church, a plain Gothic building, stands at the southern end of the town. It is 67 and a half feet by 33 on the outside, with a steeple 17 feet square. It is lighted by 4 Gothic windows and an east window, elegantly ornamented with a stained glass representation of the Last Supper. The interior is in excellent order, with a flagged aisle and accommodation for 200 adults. There is also a gallery and vestry room. It was built in 1820 at the cost of 1,500 pounds from the Board of First Fruits.

Presbyterian Meeting Houses

The Presbyterian meeting house of Swatragh was built by subscription in the year 1829 and cost 1,260 pounds. It is 52 feet by 21 feet in the inside. Of the above sum, the Mercers' Company gave 150 pounds. The interior is in good order, is lighted by 11 windows and can accommodate a congregation of 230 adults. The house is slated.

There is a very small Presbyterian congregation at the village of Curran. They meet in the national schoolhouse at that place.

The new Presbyterian meeting house at Maghera is built on the site of the old one and at the south eastern end of the town. It was begun in the year 1835. The following persons contributed towards its erection: the Irish Society 50 pounds, the Mercers' Company 50 pounds, the Drapers' Company 30 pounds, Alexander Clark Esquire of Maghera 25 pounds, Henry Barre Beresford Esquire 10 pounds, Sir Robert Bateson Baronet 10 pounds, Captain Jones 10 pounds, Rev. James Spencer Knox (rector) 5 pounds, Mr Matthew Lytle (Maghera) 5 pounds, Mr James Lytle (farmer) 5 pounds, Mr A.J. Campbell (merchant at Glasgow) 5 pounds, collected in Belfast by the minister of the congregation the Rev. Charles Kennedy 35 pounds, collected by the same in Glasgow 50 pounds, [total] 290 pounds, with smaller contributions collected from the inhabitants of this and the adjoining parishes.

This meeting house is near the old church and on the estate of Alexander Clark Esquire of Maghera, who gave the ground rent free. It measures 75 feet by 45 in the clear outside. The estimate of what the erection would cost was 800 pounds. It has cost more than that already, but the interior is not complete, a gallery being still to be erected. It is lighted by 8 windows and will accommodate in the interior a congregation of 320 adults. The land attached amounts to 1 rood and 10 perches Cunningham measure and is situated in the townland of Largantogher.

Seceding Meeting House

The Seceding meeting house of Culnady was built in 1801 at the cost of 350 pounds. It is 63 feet by 30 in the clear, is lighted by 11 windows and contains sittings for 300 adults. The interior and exterior are in good repair. A good iron gate in front, value 5 pounds, was given by the lord of the soil Barre Beresford Esquire.

Roman Catholic Chapels

The Roman Catholic chapel at Moyagall was

built by subscription in the year 1802. It is 88 feet by 27 feet in the inside, all galleried except where the altar and pulpit stands. It is lighted by 8 windows on the southern wall. There are no forms or seats in the gallery or on the floor. Altogether it can hold about 2,000 people. This chapel is built of stone and lime and slated. It is all in good repair. There is a graveyard, well walled except in part on the northern side.

The new Roman Catholic chapel in Fallagloon, commonly called the Glenn chapel, was commenced in 1825 and finished for public service in 1828. The cost was 1,600 pounds, obtained by subscription. It is not galleried. It is 110 feet by 40 feet inside.

The Rev. J. Spencer Knox, rector gave 10 pounds, Alexander Clark Esquire, Maghera 8 pounds, Drapers' Company 20 pounds, Captain LaMont (deceased) 12 pounds, Peter Henry, surgeon R.N. 14 pounds, Thomas McKenna, publican 16 pounds, Michael Logan (publican) 16 pounds, Alexander Falls, hotelkeeper 14 pounds, Daniel McKenna, farmer 8 pounds, John McCloskey (publican) 8 pounds, Charles McKenna (farmer) 8 pounds, John Kelly (blacksmith) 8 pounds, Bernard Fairis (farmer) 8 pounds, John McKenna (farmer) 8 pounds, Neill Diamond (farmer) 8 pounds, Pat Hessan, farmer 7 pounds 10s, Pat Henry (grocer) 7 pounds 10s, Hugh Bradley (publican) 7 pounds 10s, Pat Cassidy (farmer) 7 pounds 10s, Pat McNamee, farmer 7 pounds 10s, Andrew Conroy 7 pounds 10s, James McKenna (farmer) 7 pounds 10s, James Bradley, farmer 7 pounds 10s, Arthur Hessan, farmer 7 pounds 10s, Thomas Conroy, farmer 7 pounds 10s, John Morisson (roadmaker) 7 pounds 10s, Patrick McKenna (farmer) 7 pounds 10s; with 88 others who gave each 5 pounds for their seat and others who gave smaller contributions.

The chapel is slated. The building is lighted by 16 arched windows. The 2 windows on each side of the altar are ornamented with stained glass, as well as the lights over the doors. The altar is ornamented with 4 fluted columns of wood. Behind it there is a room for the priest to change his vestments in, as is usual. This chapel is not yet consecrated. There is accommodation for 2,000 persons. There is a bell and belfry, the former of which was purchased in Dublin at the cost of 50 pounds. There is also a graveyard attached to the south west side.

Gentlemen's Seats

The Glebe House, the residence of the Rev. James Spencer Knox, is situated at the eastern end of the town and near to the parish church. It was built in 1820 and cost 4,000 pounds, the half of which was granted by the Board of First Fruits. There are 84 acres Cunningham measure of excellent land attached as a farm, 10 acres of which are under ornamental planting. The greater part of this was put down in 1820. It is laid out in walks tastefully disposed and upon the whole does credit to the taste of the proprietor. This house is 3-storey high, with excellent office houses and a well-walled garden. The avenue gate is opposite to the church gate.

Grillagh alias Gracefield Cottage, the seat of Mrs Patterson, widow, is situated on the road from Maghera to Garvagh, at the distance of 1 and a half miles statute from the former town. It was built about the year 1806. It is a neat thatched cottage with a garden.

Upperlands, the seat of Alexander Clark Esquire, is situated on the road from Maghera to Kilrea, at the distance of 3 miles statute from the former town. It is a small thatched cottage, built about the year 1813 and surrounded with a plantation of fir.

The 2 latter seats are but third rate. The rector's is much the most important. It adds greatly to the appearance of the town of Maghera. Mr Clark of Maghera is about to build one at the foot of Carntogher mountain.

Communications: Roads

The high road from Belfast and Antrim by Toomebridge through Dungiven to Londonderry passes through the town of Maghera, as also the direct road from Dublin to Coleraine. They are both in good repair. Of the first there are 6 miles, of the second 5 miles.

The leading or high road from Maghera to Bellaghy is 21 feet wide, clear of drains and fences and partly in good repair. In 1831, that part of the road which passes through the townland of Beagh Spiritual was, at a hill, cut down through a solid rock about 6 feet deep. The coach from Londonderry to Belfast was obliged to avoid this road in consequence of the bad state of that part of it which passes through the townland of Ballymacross. Of it, there are 5 and a quarter miles.

The repair of the high road from Maghera to Tobermore is contracted for for 7 years at 8d per perch. The high road from Magherafelt to Kilrea is kept in repair by presentment. The road from Maghera to Kilrea through Upperlands is kept in repair by presentment. The high road from

Maghera to Dungiven is kept in repair by a contract for 7 years at 7d per perch.

The old Carn road on the same line is 21 feet wide, clear of drains. It is in very bad repair. The road from Maghera to Portglenone is in bad order. It is kept in repair by presentment.

The breadth of the road from Dublin to Coleraine has been lately enlarged by the county from 20 to 30 feet, it being a mail coach line. The breadth of the Londonderry and Belfast line is 21 feet.

Not the slightest care to avoid hills has been taken in the laying out of any line in the parish.

The road from Dungannon to Coleraine passing through from south to north; this, with the Bellaghy road, are the only two of importance. The others are in fact by-roads.

Communications: Bridges

The Milltown bridge, in the townland of Craigadick, was built about 36 years ago. It has 2 arches, one 14 feet in span, the other 18. The parapets are 4 feet high and the roadway is 19 and a half feet broad. All is in good repair.

The bridge in the townland of Craigadick, and on the new road from Maghera to Tobermore, has 1 arch, 18 feet in span. The roadway is 26 feet broad. The parapets are 3 feet high and in bad repair. It was built in 1827.

The bridge which divides Culnady from Tirnageeragh has 4 arches, the central ones each 16 feet in span, the others 8 feet. The roadway is 18 and a half feet wide, but the parapets quite dilapidated.

The bridge in Dreenan has 1 arch, 13 feet in span. The roadway is 20 feet wide, the parapets 4 feet high; all is in very bad repair.

The bridge in Dunglady has 2 arches, which are 17 feet in span each. The roadway is 18 feet wide, the parapets 2 feet high and in bad repair.

The bridge in Upperlands has 1 arch, 29 feet in span. The roadway is 21 feet broad, the parapets 2 and a half feet high; all is in good repair.

The bridge at Swatragh has 2 arches, each 15 feet in span. The roadway is 18 and a half feet and the parapets 3 feet high; all is in good repair.

The bridge at Curran, in the townland of Curran and over the Moyola, has 4 arches, each 21 feet in span. The roadway is 14 feet broad. The parapets are 3 and a half feet high; all is in bad repair.

The bridge in Curran has 2 arches, each 14 feet in span; the roadway is 21 feet broad.

There is nothing to prevent any further improvement in bridges or communications.

General Appearance and Scenery

The scenery in the parish itself is cold and dreary. The features of the country are not sufficiently bold to please or compensate for the deficiency of high cultivation or of wood, which, if judiciously disposed even in small portions on a surface so varied by abrupt hills, would appear to great advantage. The eye therefore turns with eagerness to the magnificent chain of mountains that bounds the view to the westward and by a low connecting neck guides it more towards the south, where it rests upon Slieve Gullion, which appears more picturesque from its being almost isolated.

ANCIENT TOPOGRAPHY

Ecclesiastical: Old Church of Maghera

In the mountainous parts of the parish the tradition is that the old church of Maghera was, together with an abbey in its immediate neighbourhood, [founded] by St Columbkille. It is one of the 9 churches said to have been founded by that saint in a circle roundabout that of Ballinascreen. In drawing[s], there is a general view of the steeple, the only part perfect. The rest of the building is in complete dilapidation. The stones are not large or carefully fitted, except in some parts of the steeple. From the manner in which the steeple is inserted into the gable end of the church, it would appear that the whole building was not erected at the same time. [Insert footnote: The families buried in the chancel and graveyard are detailed at large in the appendix. The yard is an extensive one]. The most ancient tomb in the graveyard is that which is attributed to St Lawrence. It is a plain block of stone, quite uncarved, standing to the west of the church. There are no crosses visible anywhere.

As to the interior, [the] drawings represents the ground plan and the architectural peculiarities. In drawing[s] the doorway is represented. The carved work is much decayed, the stonework not being of good quality. The sides seem to have been once beautifuly ornamented with carved flowers. As to the bishop on the right hand side, his name is uncertain among the old inhabitants. The majority consider him as St Peter. Some call him St Lawrence, others St Columbkille.

It is remarkable that there is the head and shoulders of some saint built into the wall of the steeple and appearing on the outside. It is 2 feet wide and exhibits a round fat face. In the general view of the steeple it is marked by the point "A." There was another formerly beside it, but the stone split from frost and fell off.

Whether it was actually intended for an object of adoration to those who came in at the door below, or whether it is the ornamental fragment of some other church accidentally built in, is hard to say. For there are, among the masonry in 3 different places, ornamented stones apparently brought there from the same cause as those that were observed in the old church of Ballynascreen. 2 are in the arch of the northern door of the steeple, each containing a slight groove cut in its face, as it is in the drawing in the margin. [Rough representation of a stone with groove cut across the centre]. Nothing of the kind is in the southern door. The third is in the bottom of the northern angle of the gable, and exhibits in that part of it which can be seen, a regularly turned cylindrical face evidently produced by the chisel.

This church ceased to be used in the year 1819, when it was dismantled and part of the stones used to build the new church. The east end is quite modern. It was built about the year 1790 at the expense of the parish of Killelagh, which at that time was united to Maghera. The ruin seems [to be] decaying rapidly. A stone has fallen out of the doorway since the drawing of the 12 apostles was made by Mr Ligar, which, though commonly called by that name, is in reality the Crucifixion.

Vesper Field

The piece of ground now under the rector's garden was formerly known by the name of the Vesper Field, from its having been the site of an abbey said to have been founded by St Lowrie, or first presided over as abbot by him. The foundations of a building thought to be a church, of the usual dimensions, were discovered in it about 50 years ago.

Well: Tober Lowrie

It is said also that the monks, being disturbed at their devotions by the frequency with which the inhabitants of the neighbouring village of Maghera, composed at that time of the huts inhabited by the serfs and retainers of the abbey, went to their well for water, applied to St Lowrie who opened for them in a miraculous manner the well in the town still known by the name of Tober Lowrie. It is a good clear spring and emits all the year round a plentiful supply.

Old Abbey

According to tradition an abbey also stood in the townland of Grillagh, on the site of the house now occupied by Mrs Patterson. It was founded by the O'Crillys. The townland is still called by the old Irish Munnisther-na-Crillagh. The founder of this abbey was also the founder of the church and abbey of Tamlaght O'Crilly. The bank on which it stood has a cheerful southern aspect, with a stream pouring along at the foot of it.

Old Burial Ground

In making a new line of road through the townland of Fallagloon about 48 years ago, there were discovered beneath the surface coffin boards, skulls <sculls> and other human bones, indicating the site of an old burial ground. They were reinterred in the same place.

Pagan: Military Remains

There are no military remains.

Ancient Monument

In the townland of KnockO'Neill, and on an eminence in a secluded part of the mountain, there stands an ancient casiol of loose stones, represented in drawing[s]. The surrounding [wall ?] varies in height from 3 and a half to 5 feet and in breadth at the base from 3 to 5 feet. In the interior there are the ruins of a number of ancient graves, enclosed by large stones varying in height above the surface from 1 to 4 feet. They are of the usual form of what are called giant's graves. On the north eastern side there are 2 Danish fences and the obscure remains of what had been apparently a building of some kind. 2 small cairns are also to be seen close to the casiol. It is locally said that the above obscure traces were once a well-defined building with walls 5 feet thick.

The tradition about the whole place is that it was a monument raised over the bodies of Neil McLaughlin and his followers, who were killed in the townland of Slaught Neill in the parish of Killelagh, in a battle with a son of a prince of the O'Neills, who wished to revenge the death of his father by the said McLaughlin.

This monument has been greatly dilapidated by the country people within the last 50 years. Only 1 grave is at present distinctly visible. Many years ago a sword was found in one of them.

The townland is very wild and secluded. It includes the heathy and boggy slopes at the foot of the mountain Carntogher. The ground round about is very rocky and desolate, and contains scarcely any inhabitants.

Old Island and Fort

[C.W. Ligar] There is in the townland of

Parish of Maghera

Ballymacpeak a small lake containing the remains of what was once a well-constructed artificial island, but was nearly destroyed about 40 years since by a person who had an idea that treasures were concealed in it. From the ruins now to be seen the island appears to have been about 20 or 30 feet in diameter. It was formed by upright oak stakes driven into the ground and mortised into a series of horizontal ones, which formed a floor or platform on which was laid earth mixed with bog. This is the account given of it by persons who live in the vicinity and who remember when it stood undisturbed, and who say that there was formerly a narrow footway leading from the island to the shore of the lake opposite to the old fort situated on its borders. The footpath was formed of stakes similar to the island.

The waters of the lake have been drained and vegetation is rapidly encroaching into it, and to all appearance will very soon replace the water with a kind of soft bog. A few of the stakes which formed the island still remain standing.

In the lake on the north side a boat was found measuring 15 or 16 feet in length and turned up at the ends like a canoe. It was constructed out of a solid oak tree and a series of holes of half an inch in diameter were pierced through the bottom at nearly equal distances along it. The breadth of the boat was about 3 feet and the sides about 1 foot high. Nothing now remains of it but a piece 5 and a half feet long and of half the original breadth, in the possession of John O'Hara, townland of Drumlamph, and is used by him for a part of a bedstead. See drawing of the island, fort and the part of the boat.

The fort or rather mound resembles in construction many others in the county. It consists of a mound of earth surrounded by a fosse, which is again surrounded by a parapet. In the fosse on the north west side there is a collection of stones sunk in the ground, which appear to have been a fireplace measuring 2 feet every way.

Forts

[J. Stokes] See a [later] report for a description of the fort of Dungleady. There are no others worth mentioning.

Standing Stones

In Drumconready, and near the River Moyola, there are 2 standing stones called the Stockans. One of them stands upright and is 4 feet high, 3 and a half broad and 2 and a half thick. The other is in a reclining position, supported partly on the top of the first and is 6 feet long, 5 feet broad and 3 feet thick. It is the opinion of the inhabitants that these stones had been originally designed for a druid's altar.

There is a remarkable standing stone in the townland of Culnagrew near Swatragh. It is on the top of a hill near the Kilrea road and is commonly called the Great Standing Stone of Swatragh. It has been already noticed in a former report on Ancient Topography (see map of standing stone boundaries), but has been there erroneously described as being 12 feet high. See drawing in which a view of it is given for the actual dimensions. See also the above-mentioned report for further particulars relating to the standing stones in the neighbourhood of that village.

Grave in Culnagrew

In the same townland there was found in 1816 beneath a cairn of stones a "grave" 6 feet long and 2 feet wide, enclosed with flat stones and roofed with the same. It contained an earthen urn filled with black ashes. It is more than probable that all giant's graves were originally built for the pur-

Great Standing Stone of Swatragh

pose of containing, like this, an urn of ashes and were then covered up with cairns of stones.

Caves

There are but 2 caves known to exist at present in the parish. One is in the townland of Drumard, disposed in the form of a "T" and built in the usual manner. The other is in Rocktown, but closed up. The first is 4 feet high and 5 feet wide. The top of the "T" is 24 feet long; the upright part is but 10.

Graves

In the townland of Craigadick there was found in 1835, upon the top of a hill called Silver hill, a grave 2 feet below the surface, about 5 feet long, 2 and a half feet broad and 2 feet deep. It was floored, enclosed and roofed by long flat stones and in it there stood several small earthen pans containing calcined bones and ashes. They mouldered down on removal. Several other graves of a similar description have been found beneath the surface of the same hill, at different periods preceding the above date. They all contained vessels of bones and ashes.

It is more than probable that this was a Danish or heathen burial ground. The hill received its name from silver coins having been found in it.

Miscellaneous Discoveries

In the townland of Beagh Spiritual there was found in 1829, about 2 feet below the surface, a small earthen crock containing about 1 quart measure of flints of various sizes and shapes. All was destroyed and lost.

A pair of quern-stones were found in Drumard, the lower one supported on 3 short feet about 1 inch in height each. The stone was circular, 14 inches in diameter.

Ancient Name of Maghera

It is said that the ancient name of Maghera was Maghera Entriah or "the plain of seasons." The tract of ground now occupied by the rector's house and farm intervened between the monastery of Maghera and that of Mullagh in Termoneeny (now the old church). It was used by the monks of both places as a spot for their morning and evening seasons of meditation, and thus gave name to the village.

Ancient Cave

In the townland of Brackaghgreilly, within about 150 yards of a Danish fort, there was discovered in 1832, at some depth beneath the surface, a cave 16 feet long by 7 wide and about 4 feet high in the interior. The sides were made of an oak frame and the floor covered with long planks of oak. It is not known what the roof was composed of, as it had fallen in before the place was discovered. There is a beam from the framework and one of the planks of the floor at present in Henry O'Neill's house in the above townland. The beam is 16 feet 10 inches broad and 8 inches thick, and quite sound. This cave is now destroyed and the rest of the timber converted to other uses.

Oval Vessel

John Logue of the townland Craigmore, while cutting turf in Tamnymullen in 1820, found 8 feet beneath the surface an ancient oval vessel 15 by 12 inches across the top and about 12 feet deep. It was supported on 3 small feet and appeared to have been carved out of a solid piece of timber. It soon fell to pieces.

Stone Circle and Urn

In the townland of Swatragh there was found in 1831, at the depth of 1 and a half feet beneath the surface, some stones set round in a circle, in which was deposited an ancient earthen urn containing a quantity of burned bones and ashes. It was covered on the mouth with a flat stone. The vessel was very thick and rudely constructed but soon fell to pieces.

Old Butter

Much bog butter has been found in the bogs of the parish, contained in rudely formed vessels hollowed out of a single piece of timber. These were all so old that they mouldered away on being taken up.

Brass Sword and Stakes

The brass sword now in the possession of Mr David Henderson of Drumlamph is in pretty good preservation and was discovered in 1831, 11 feet under the surface of the flow bog in that townland. It rested on the clay bottom. Near the place a number of hazel stakes were found with their points, which seemed regularly formed with a sharp-edged tool, set in the ground. See drawing for a representation of the sword.

Wooden Vessels

2 ancient wooden vessels were found in the year 1834 under a flow bog in the townland of Dreenan.

Parish of Maghera

Nothing but small fragments now remain. They were hollowed from the trunk of a tree. They were about 1 foot broad and 1 foot deep, covered with circular lids having a small hole through the centre of each.

Quern-stones

[A] drawing represents a remarkable quern-stone now in the rector's cabinet and found under very peculiar circumstances. In extracting a large stick of timber from the bottom of a bog, it was found under the stick and resting on the substratum, and from its position evidently appeared to have been there before the fall of the tree. See drawing for another of the rector's [querns].

Many other quern-stones were found in the parish, generally in pairs; some were ornamented.

Ancient Font

An ancient font of freestone, supposed to have belonged to the Maghera monastery, is now in the possession of John Morrison, reedmaker in that town. It is rudely formed, see drawing.

Spearhead, Hatchets and other Discoveries

[A] drawing represents a remarkable specimen of a spearhead in the rector's cabinet, found in this parish.

Drawings [also] exhibit specimens of stone hatchets and arrowheads of remarkably rude and primitive form. The breaks visible in several of the hatchets or "thunderbolts" appear to have been produced when the instrument was first made.

[Insert footnote: [Other drawings represent the following:] a silver medal found in Maghera in 1837; several very rudely shaped spearheads found at different times in the parish; a rudely formed stone hatchet and a fragment of an urn that had contained bones and ashes; a full size representation of a "peh pipe" from this parish; some remarkable coins and a specimen of James II's brass money].

SOCIAL ECONOMY

Early Improvements

The parish of Maghera, owing to its being not so mountainous, is better situated in favour of the worldly circumstances of its inhabitants than the parish of Ballynascreen, the inhabitants of which are in general poorer and less independent. It has been more colonized by Scotch and English settlers. The circumstances of the inhabitants of the more mountainous parts of this parish have been greatly improved since they left off illicit distillation, which occurred within the last 20 years. Before that time potatoes formed nearly the whole of the commodities sent by them to the Maghera market. The circumstances of the inhabitants of the lowlands, consisting chiefly of Scotch, have on the other hand deteriorated in consequence of the decline of the linen trade during the same time. The habits also of the Irish have as much accelerated their increase of wealth as those of the other race have hastened its diminution: the former being content with much the least respectable exterior appearance. From these circumstances the Irish inhabitants are not now as formerly so much behind the Scotch and English settlers in the progress of improvement.

No causes deeper than the general and gradual improvements that are naturally taking place throughout the country have appeared to influence it in this parish. There are no agricultural societies or shows in it, nor have the landlords particularly exerted themselves. There is a great want of resident gentlemen. [Next line cut off].

Townlands and Prevailing Names

The wealthiest townlands in the parish are Slaghtybogy, Ballymacross, Curran, Curragh and Drumlamph. In the first the names of the families are Graham, Crockett, Elliot, Miller, Johnstone, Given, Anderson and Pool. There are 5 middlemen with their undertenants, the middlemen paying 1 pound 10s per acre, the others 2 pounds. The largest farm, one of 50 acres, has been obtained, piece by piece, from the farmer's neighbours, in payment of debt from them to him.

In Ballymacross the names are Grey, Elliot, Lesley, Fleming, Scott, Lockhart, McKeown, Lamon, Johnstone, Crawford, Martin and McCahey. The houses here are more comfortable than in Slaghtybogy and the people more industrious. They were more wealthy 30 years ago.

In Curragh the names are Anderson, McKeown (10 families), McClellan, Campbell, Armour, Fulton and Aull. The largest farm is 21 acres, the smallest 2. The houses are more comfortable and the inhabitants more industrious than in Ballymacross. The land is better and the growth of wheat more extensive.

In Curran the names are Cavin, Downing, Paterson, McClellan, Mewhinny, Stone, Forbes, Harbeson, Johnstone, Henry and Marlin. The houses here are more comfortable but not cleaner than in Ballymacross. The townland has increased in wealth since the year 1798. In all the above townlands the names only of landholders are mentioned.

Drumlamph appears to be wealthier than any of them, but then its social economy is involved in that of the parish of Ballyscullion, on the edge of which it lies. These are at present the wealthiest townlands. Whether in the progress of improvement they will continue so is uncertain. There is little actual capital among them.

The McKennas, Bradleys and McWilliams abound in the western parts of the parish and the Lyttles and Converys in the eastern, especially in Falgortrevy and Gulladuff. The names, however, given in the appendix, as copied from the tombs in the old churchyard, which was up to 1819 the general burying place for all sects and denominations, will give a clearer idea of the amount of Scotch and English blood that has been introduced into the district.

Importance of Maghera Fair

The foundation of its present state and condition may be said to have been laid in Charles II's reign. In that period the patent for the fair of Maghera was granted, from which it would seem that its improvement had in that period only just commenced. It would have been at the present time greater if they had kept up the market of linen cloth formerly held at that village. It ceased about the year 1806, in consequence of a disturbance which broke out among the sellers and buyers about a fraudulent web. An attempt was made to rescue it from the inspector and vitriol was thrown upon the clothes of the merchants, who of course would not attend again. Fine webs were chiefly sold. An attempt was made about 9 years ago to revive it, but without success from the want of purchasers.

The inhabitants of the extreme east of the parish seem to prefer bringing their produce to the fairs and markets of Magherafelt, which is now a formidable rival to Maghera. It has a linen market, the profits and advantages of which that village might have shared, perhaps monopolized, but for the quarrelsome disposition of its inhabitants. They are in no want of market towns in every direction to which to carry their agricultural produce.

Obstructions to Improvement

There is a disputed boundary between the Rev. James Spencer Knox and John Stevenson Esquire of Fortwilliam in the parish of Kilcronaghan. The River Moyola <Mayola> is their mearing between the townland of Ballynahone in Maghera and the opposite bank. The river has changed its course several times and has thus produced the uncertainty. The parish of Maghera is said to have gained 10 acres, of which, however, one-half is but gravel and sand. Mr Stevenson has made a strong embankment to prevent its further progress.

Local Government

The following tables of offences exhibit a great decrease in their number from 1834 to 1835. The cause of this is not the improved disposition of the people but the refusal of the magistrates to grant a summons unless the alleged offence is really of importance. The falling off there visible of nearly one-half in the criminal offences and one-third in the civil shows in a strong light the quarrelsome disposition of the plaintiffs. An offence frequently committed is turf-stealing. This circumstance may be attributed to the great number of poor that surround and reside in the town and the large quantity of turf bog on the road from it to Tobermore.

[C.W. Ligar] The following is a register of the proceedings in criminal matters at the petty sessions held in Maghera from 1st January to 31st December in the years 1834 and 1835, extracted from the sessions books.

1834: settled or no appearance 271, dismissed 128, fined in different sums 102, referred to arbitration 29, informations taken 11, bound over to keep the peace 10, postponed 14, settled by the court 12, no jurisdiction 6, total number of cases during the year 583.

1835: settled or no appearance 82, dismissed 80, fined in different sums 76, referred to arbitration 14, informations taken 18, bound over to keep the peace 2, postponed 12, settled by the court 14, no jurisdiction 6, total number of cases during the year 304.

The following is a register of the civil cases for the same time.

1834: decreed 69, dismissed 35, settled or no appearance 114, settled in court 0, referred to arbitration 2, postponed 4, no jurisdiction 3, total 227.

1835: decreed 74, dismissed 28, settled or no appearance 36, settled in court 6, referred to arbitration 10, postponed 2, no jurisdiction 1, total 157.

[J. Stokes] In the Maghera books for registering the offences at petty sessions, the name of the townland in which the defendant resided is not always given.

Parish of Maghera

Manor Court

There is a manor court held monthly in the court house by John Savage, surgeon, who is seneschal. 5 pounds Irish currency is the greatest sum recoverable.

Magistrates and Constabulary

The 2 magistrates are John Stevenson Esquire of Tobermore and James Clark Esquire, Maghera. They are both within convenient distances. There is in the town a chief constable of police with 8 men. The greater part of the offences tried are assaults. The Drunkards' Act produces a considerable number of cases. There is little or no illicit distillation. Coining of base money is a crime strongly suspected to be practised here. The counterfeit money is well known. [Insert footnote: Note the delinquents have as yet escaped detection].

Party Feeling

There is a great deal of party feeling in this parish and it has several times been the cause of ferocious party fights. The firmness of the magistracy, however, has of late suppressed all attempts of the kind. The people are fond of intricate and vexatious litigations with one another.

Dispensaries

See tables. It is hard to say what effect they may have had on the general health of the people. At present there is much fever in the mountains.

Education

The schools of Maghera appear at present to be increasing in number. The parishioners are anxious for instruction and knowledge. A resident in the parish bears the following testimony in favour of Sunday schools:

"Sunday schools here as elsewhere have been found efficient means of providing religious improvement. The teachers are for the most part selected from among persons competent to bestow in Scripture, and such as evidence by their lives and conduct their own convictions. It is plain that seminaries for education based on this foundation must act usefully and powerfully in forming pious principles and practice in the minds of youth. In this way Sunday schools operate, and probably not with less effect because their recurrence is but once in 7 days. That day being the sabbath, which thus habitually becomes the object of reverence, Sunday so appropriated assumes the character of a religious armoury, from which the weapons of spiritual resistance to sin during the week are properly drawn. This habit persevered in during the period of boyhood and youth will and does necessarily produce a corresponding amelioration of character in the pupils, and through them it is communicated to the parents, of which I am acquainted with many gratifying instances coming fairly under the class of facts enquired after.

The above answer serves also as a reply to the question put, for if Sunday schools influence a large class beneficially and produce religious and moral conduct, as well in parent as child, it follows that they commend themselves to public opinion and become progressively more popular. Their general extension gives the best testimony in favour of this valuable fact. Every year witnesses an increase and improvement in the system according to which they are conducted. In many places they have materially superseded the daily schools: parents in indigent circumstances or whose children cannot conveniently be dispensed with from domestic or agricultural employments rest content with such education as these periodical opportunities supply."

Adults in the winter season attend evening schools (see the tables). This shows how anxious they are for instruction and improvement. These peculiar schools are chiefly attended by Presbyterians.

Poor Shop

There was a poor shop in the lane leading to the old church which had been established in 1824 through the instrumentality of Mrs Knox. It had been superintended by her and its establishment had been liberally subscribed to by the late Bishop of Derry and the Drapers' Company. Like other poor shops the applicants came recommended by a ticket, in which the person who recommended him became security for the repayment in small instalments of the value of the goods given. It relieved the wants of the parishes of Kilcronaghan, Termoneeny and Killelagh, as well as the one it was held in. It continued its course of usefulness until the year 1836, when its object was defeated by the people for whose benefit it was intended. In that year the number of defaulters in the payment expected for the goods amounted to 120. The total sum due by them was 40 pounds, in smaller items from 1s to 4 pounds. 7 ran away and the remainder were sued at law. From these circumstances a suspension of the poor shop has ensued.

Liberality of Mr Clark

There are 3 houses in the town free of rent given to 16 poor persons who are unable to work. They are the property of Alexander Clark Esquire. [Insert marginal note: By the late Alexander Clark Junior, son to this gentleman, the interest of 200 pounds has been bequeathed to the parish. His family are the executors].

Bequest

Nesbitt Downing of the townland of Dreenan bequeathed 5 pounds as a provision for the poor of the parish. The interest of it was to have been annually distributed with the poor's money on Easter Sunday. The principal is deposited in the hands of Robert Elliot of Slaghtybogy but none of the interest has been paid since the 20th of April 1832. 25s of it was paid, both principal and interest, but the remainder is not forthcoming. It has been sued for at law by the churchwardens but without success.

Poor on Church List

There are 20 poor persons or paupers whose names are on the church list. Of these, 12 at present are of the Established Church, 3 are Catholics and 5 Presbyterians. Old age and infirmity has been the general causes of their poverty.

Poor-box Collection

The amount of the poor-box collection as given by the churchwarden was, for the year ending Easter 1836, 11 pounds 4s 6d, but from the benevolence of the rector's family the actual amount was 20 pounds. This sum, including what is given by the congregation themselves, is distributed every year among the poor. The average number of annual applications for a place on the church list is 30. It is not increasing.

Charity of Rector and Mr Clark

As has been remarked in several other parishes, the rector's house is the great source of charitable relief. Clothing and fuel are always given gratis by him in severe seasons to all deserving objects. The actual value of this is not included in the sum above mentioned, nor is the assistance given at the door of the Glebe House included.

Neither is Mr Clark deficient in the same laudable anxiety to relieve the wants and distresses of the poor of every denomination. Much food and clothing is distributed by his family, and on every Wednesday, which [remainder blank].

Spinning Fund

The spinning fund was instituted by the rector's family in 1831. Flax is given out to 12 poor housekeepers who are employed to spin it, and they receive at the same time wages one-third higher than what they would get anywhere else. A pauper is employed also in hackling the flax at an advanced price. By this addition to the price they receive the benefit both of employment and charity. The tow is sold to the poor of the neighbourhood at the lowest market price. A fund or capital, as it were, was first raised by subscription.

Lying-in Basket

There is another excellent charity, namely the "lying-in basket", for the accommodation of poor lying-in married females of respectable character. It was established by Mrs Knox in 1825 and is supported and conducted by her. The basket contains 1 entire suit of bed and body linen, of which there are 2 changes for each woman, and there are also 2 entire suits for each child. The poor woman has the use of the above articles for 1 month and they are then returned clean. There is no particular form of application for them. Any well-conducted female who is recommended by some of the most respectable farmers, or who is already known to Mrs Knox, will receive a supply upon private application.

Since the departure of that benevolent lady to the Continent, no applications have of course taken place. It should be added that a suit of clothes is presented to each infant. Dating from the month of January 1837, it may be added that the last application for the lying-in basket took place on the 23rd December 1836 and that the last flax was given out from the spinning fund in the previous month of November.

Catholic Charity

It should be added also that the Catholic clergy appear to have exerted themselves in some degree to relieve the poor here, but it was found difficult to ascertain precisely and with certainty the manner and extent of that relief.

Charity: "Helping Day"

40 paupers attend once a week at the "helping day" in Maghera. Of these, most are from distant parts of the country. 10 paupers reside in the village itself. The money which they receive from the wealthy is spent upon what are to them luxuries, such as tea, sugar, tobacco, snuff and whis-

Parish of Maghera

key. The greater part of their real support is borne by the farming and labouring class who give them meal and potatoes.

Drumard Townland

The poorest townland (as to the circumstances of its inhabitants) in the parish is Drumard. It contains 81 farmhouses. There are no cottiers, the agent not allowing any cottier to live in it on account of its being scantily supplied with bog. There is but 1 farm of 15 acres, the rest are of 6 acres at an average. Dirt and indolence are everywhere visible.

Remarks on Illicit Distillation

As has been noticed in another head, the removal of illicit distillation from the mountainous townlands has diminished the amount of poverty in them.

Seceders

Another congregation, in opposition to the above [in Curran] and in connection with the Synod of Ulster, was set up about 6 weeks after the formation of the first. It is held in the national schoolhouse and supplied by their own clergy. Their hour of meeting is 5 p.m.

Methodists

The Methodists appear to be rather stationary in this parish. At Maghera they were in a dormant state and had neglected the peculiarities of their discipline until they were roused and reformed by the activity of their monthly preacher, who visits them periodically. An itinerant preacher also visits, once a month, the village of Curran and preaches in a private house opposite the barn belonging to the Seceder. The class consists of the usual number, 12, and has been established about 8 years.

Income of the Clergy

The annual income of the rector, the Rev. James Spencer Knox, is derived from 1,100 pounds per annum of tithe composition, with glebe land.

The annual income of the Presbyterian clergyman, the Rev. Charles Kennedy, is 75 pounds regium donum in Irish currency, with 64 pounds of stipend British currency.

The annual income of the Rev. James Sloan, minister of the Seceding congregation at Swatragh, is 50 pounds regium donum in Irish currency and 30 pounds stipend in British currency.

The annual income of the Rev. Alexander Mulligan, Seceding minister of the congregation at Culnady, is 50 pounds regium donum of Irish currency with 45 pounds British of stipend. That of the Rev. John McKenna, master of the Glenn chapel, is 110 pounds, one-third of which goes to pay his curate.

That of the Rev. Charles McCann is also 110 pounds, one-third of which goes to pay his curate.

Extent of Congregation

The congregation under Mr Kennedy is attached to the Synod of Ulster and comes from the parishes of Maghera, Killelagh, Termoneeny and a few from Tamlaght O'Crilly.

Mr Sloan's congregation comes from Maghera, Desertoghill, Tamlaght O'Crilly and Killelagh.

Mr Mulligan's comes from Maghera, Termoneeny and Tamlaght O'Crilly.

Mr Kennedy's is the largest and consists of 3,500 persons.

The Catholic congregations appear to be increasing. About 80 years ago the same priest was jointly sufficient for both Ballyscullion and this parish.

The moral and religious feelings of the people appear to be improving.

Houses

The general style of the cottages is upon the whole inferior in this parish to what it is in Kilcronaghan or Desertmartin. It improves at the eastern side. Along the high road from Maghera to Swatragh they are small, mean and dirty, but not so much so as some that had been observed in the parish of Ballynascreen. Few, if any, contain any mud in the walls. All are of 1-storey except three, one in Grillagh, one in Slaghtybogy and one in Curragh.

They all belong to farmers i.e. the 2-storey houses. As for their comfort or cleanliness, but little can be said favourably. Not having any examples before them to look up to or imitate, the inhabitants do not seem to understand what it is. In the townland of Slaghtybogy, one of the wealthiest in the parish, the richer tenants have their houses as dirty as the poorest. They say that the houses occupied by their ancestors are good enough for them. In the whole of it there are but six that have the appearance of being whitewashed outside. However, in Ballymacross, another rich townland inhabited by English settlers, Jacob Johnstone and a few others have the front of their houses ornamented with a little flower ground. It is worthy of remark that but few, comparatively speaking, of the names in Slaghtybogy are English.

Habits of the People

The food, fuel and dress of the parishioners are similar to those of the surrounding parishes. Longevity is considerable, the age of 100 being not uncommon. No remarkable instances of early marriages have been heard of.

Amusements

As for their amusements and recreations, the few that still exist are chiefly confined to the young. The old smoke tobacco, or gossip at a public house.

Games and Amusements

On Easter Monday the young parishioners resort to a field in the vicinity of Maghera and spend the greater part of the day in a play called "wink and follow." A ring is formed by the young of both sexes, when a young man winks at a female and immediately runs and touches her. She as immediately runs after him till taken. Both then return, kiss and place their feet upon a stone called "the priest." In the end of the day they repair to the public houses, where much of the night is spent in dancing and drinking. Many clandestine and imprudent marriages are the consequences of this amusement, which is similar in nature to that which has been under this head described in the Memoir of Tamlaght O'Crilly as taking place at the village of Inisrush.

A play called "bullet" is practised in the summer by the parishioners. The bullet is of lead, from 1 and three-quarter to 2 lbs weight, and is hurled along some level road for a wager of either money or whiskey upon the best throw.

Dog-fighting

The villagers of Maghera were formerly very fond of fighting their dogs with one another. This disposition indeed is common to the whole parish but is decreasing. They kept many large bulldogs, and the quarrels of these animals frequently produced quarrels among their masters also.

Religious Societies

The following is a detail of some societies which have an indirect influence on the habits of the people. Though two of them are located in the village of Maghera, they are in this view connected with the parish at large.

The bible depository was established in the year 1831 through the agency of Mrs Knox and Mrs Clark. It is at present conducted by a committee of 9 clergymen of the Established Church. The patroness is Mrs Knox. It is supported by voluntary contribution. The following persons contributed largely to its support: Mrs Knox, Mrs Clark, Miss Patterson, Miss Inch, Miss Crossley, Miss Beresford, Miss Clark of Rockfield.

A temperance society was set up in the year 1832 by 2 of the shopkeepers. It consists at present of 143 members.

2 religious meetings are held weekly, the one in Crew, the other in Swatragh, by the laymen of the Presbyterian congregation.

The last meeting of the Church Missionary Society was held in Maghera on the second day of September 1836.

Traditions

Fires on St John's Eve are still slightly kept up. There are no remarkable customs, legendary tales, poems or ancient music.

Notes on Letters of Emigrants

The following extracts from emigrants' letters, which have been added to this head, have been thought interesting as specimens of rustic literature. These kind of letters frequently bring to view and exhibit the domestic feelings of the people. The first given is an entire one. In them all the orthography is copied literally. The common run (to which they are superior) have all a remarkable similiarity to the conclusion of MD's letter.

Letter from a Female Emigrant

Philadelphia, 9th July 1836. My Dear Uncle,

An opportunity has at length arrived of writing to you, and I gladly avail myself of it in order, though late, to redeem my pledge or promise which I made you before I left home that I would write to you. If you were angry at me I understand because of this neglect. Indeed, I can offer no apology for it unless the very reasonable one that I was angry at you for not coming to see me before I left home. However, I forgave you long ago and I trust you will forgive me when you get this. We are all tolerably well, thank heaven, and have no reason to complain of our lot of this world's gear. From my brother's letters and others, you already know all interesting that we have to communicate. The country is in a prosperous condition, good wages and high prices for everything. Indeed markets are higher this season than ever they were in America. You were anxious to know how I thought America would suit cousin Henry. I will leave it to my brother who is here to state our views on this matter, as he has more time to say than I have. I have only to say that we all concur in his views of the matter.

Be pleased to remember me to all my friends, present my best compliments to Nelly, to all the children, Mr and Mrs Crilly, Owen McLead and his wife. Remember me to all of the Hagan family, to the Thompson family and to every friend who will think it worthwhile to enquire about me. Give my respects to Mary Laverty and tell her that her 2 fine boys come to see me every Saturday evening. They are in genteel employment and promise fair to be graceful and sober citizens. I am proud to say that they are a credit to themselves and a comfort to their friends. How glad I would be to see all my young countrymen so. Farewell, yours affectionately [signed] M.D.

Letter on Emigration

Extracts from the letter of an emigrant schoolmaster on emigration. Philadelphia, 9th July 1836. Dear Uncle Daniel.

Having an opportunity of sending a letter by hand, I am tempted to write to you a few weeks sooner than I intended, as it not many weeks since I wrote a very long letter to the Rev. John McKenna, which I hope he has got ere now, and I like so to measure my intervals that I may always have something new to communicate. But I have filled my unconscionably long letters with such variety of matter that I now have little new to communicate.

Having given a short vacation to my pupils during the hay-making, I came into town yesterday week and will leave it tomorrow, and right glad am I to get out to the green country again, for the heat is intolerable in this city. Yesterday the thermometer stood at 90 degrees in the shade, not far from the river. The rays of the sun pouring fiercely on the buildings and brick pavements of this city renders it like a tolerably heated oven, so that what with the roasting and frying heat of the day, the myriad of flies in clouds in every house, on every table and, I might say, in every dish, not only in the city but in the country, then the sweating and stewing by night, delightfully enlivened by the tickling bite of mosquitoes or bugs which the utmost cleanliness cannot sufficiently guard against, all render a summer's residence here in America truly *delightful.*

In my letter I make it a point to devote a paragraph to the state of the weather, but the peculiarites of this climate, its extreme and sudden transitions are known to you by hearsay at least. Indeed these evils of this climate are a serious drawback to the happiness of its inhabitants.

If it were asked me if I had yet to emigrate would I with my present experience do it, I would answer that under such circumstances as I had at home I would emigrate. I would say so without the least hesitation, and I say more, that if I had the means, as I hope to have through time, of bringing my father and his family here and placing them in a comfortable place in a healthy part of the country, I would for the sake of my own happiness, to be near them, for sake of theirs to be with us, and for their children's sake who never will rest in Ireland with much contentment, I would bring them all here, although I am as fully convinced as that I hold this pen in my fingers that the family that has a good comfortable way of living, together or near each other at home that is in Ireland, have more real heartfelt enjoyment in that home than they ever can have by coming to this country, unless they can bring with them strength of sinews, much of determination and plenty of money to bear them inland and establish them on a farm.

But our family early met with tyranny and misfortune. We were the children of circumstances and I think we did well to emigrate. Your sons have all a tolerable prospect of doing well at home, and the more I see of this troublesome game of life, the more I am convinced of the truth of that maxim that we should be content with a moderate share of the wealth of this world and should not be led away by avarice or what is as bad, by a foolish romantic ambition. Men but very seldom duly value the blessings of health, peace of mind and the society of those they love, till after they have lost them, and then their regret is enhanced by the reflection that they have left these invaluable blessings behind them in pursuit of shadows or of filthy trash.

Thousands are coming yearly to this country: there is room for all, employment for all and success for many. And those who are young and strong and qualified by a good trade and a disposition to do well ought to come if they have not a tolerable prospect at home, but it is a poor prospect which cannot be made tolerable by dint of industry, and the dint of industry must be used here.

In conclusion, if H. is resolved to come, you ought not to hinder him. Do your part with him as long as he is with you, as I know you will let him learn to be expert in keeping his own accounts.

Every American can keep his own accounts, and it is a pity of him who cannot. Let him not bother his head with grammar: it's of no use to him here, it is never looked [at] unless from professional men. If he stays long enough in Ireland to learn a trade, he will be nothing worse of it. If he comes without any trade he must set to one here, which is the best thing he could do if he must come out. The wealthiest men in the community teach their sons trades, and their daughters too. No matter how early or late a boy goes to serve as an apprentice, he is free when his one and twentieth year is completed. Whatever money he brings here can be placed in the savings institution for him, where it will accumulate.

I have given the above advice under the supposition that he is anxious to come out, but if he does not feel strongly inclined to come, do not urge him. He would feel like one transported. I have, as far as my limits would permit, stated my views as I would for my brother. Decide for yourselves. Farewell [signed] FD.

Emigrant's Letter

Extracts from a letter by the same [schoolmaster] on his first going out. To Mr D.M. Sandyhill, 12 August 1835. Dearly beloved parents, brothers and sisters,

I sit me down at length to enjoy a luxury which I have long looked forward to but which circumstances prevented me from enjoying till now, namely, the luxury of conversing with you in spirit, though separated by the immense space that lies between us. I wrote to you in Lewis Cassidy's letter which I hope has ere this reached you. Your fair enquiry will naturally be how we are in health. Glory be to the Omnipotent for his protection: we are all well except Margaret's little daughter, whom they did not expect to live any time when I left home last Sunday evening.

On Thursday the last day of April we sailed out of Lough Foyle. Having a stout north easterly breeze in our teeth, we had to tack every 10 minutes almost and the rolling of the ship sickened almost every passenger. As most of the active hands among the passengers were required to assist in tacking, I was not idle till we got fairly off the land and this knocking about I think kept me from seasickness. We lost sight of land that night and went on prosperously with a fair wind till Sunday evening, when every appearance of sea and sky gave indications of a disagreeable change. That morning we had seen a porpoise wedding, as the seamen called it, which we viewed with delight and astonishment, thousands of these fishes gambolling about in all directions. Some of our old seamen, as they looked soberly on, turned their quid and predicted a gale and so it came to pass.

That night continued pretty calm till next morning, then the wind chopped round to the south west and blew very hard all day. Night came on but brought no calm. We went to bed wth anxious hearts, having commended ourselves to the protection of the Most High. After a disturbed sleep of about 2 hours, we were awakened by the dash of a tremendous breaker that streamed like a torrent down every hatchway. It was then past midnight and the horrors of darkness were added to the horrors natural to young voyagers on their first experiencing a storm.

The gale had by that time risen to a storm and the sea, lashed and goaded into rage by the strong wind of the preceding day, now roared in tremendous concert with the wind, and its furious billows, urged along by the storm which now blew right ahead of us, broke like thunder against our bows, till our stout ship reeled and quivered like an aspen bough. Aloft the voice of our brave captain and his gallant crew pealed amid the war of elements, he issuing his orders with a firmness and precision that bespoke the intrepid seamen and they encouraging each other by their loud shouting as if in defiance of the tempest. All our sails were taken down. Not a rag could be kept up, only a triple-reefed fore topsail and mainstay sail to keep her steady. Below, the sounds were of a more distressing character, owing to some hundred tons of pig iron that was in the hold.

Our ship lurched heavily on her side, so much so that her main chains were completely immersed in water i.e. she was completely on her one side. This lurching which I have described put in pretty quick motion all little articles that lay between decks, and did not happen to be lashed firmly, so that pots, pans, delph, day boxes, barrels, water kegs and dirty buckets all flew about with tremendous fury and noise as our floating habitation turned almost upside down, 200 or 300 times in the course of the night. The noise of these mingled with the groans of the seasick, who cared little whether the ship sank or swam, and the audible supplications for mercy uttered by the more timid or more devout, in short the noise above and the noise below might give one a pretty neat idea of the place of infernal torments. I certainly prayed very stoutly, for in truth I had no hope that I should have the pleasure of describing the scene to you. How comfortable would be a bed of rushes any place on land that night.

However, the morning that we never expected to see dawned upon us, but brought no calm. Our ship was laid to and kept advancing backwards like mine uncle's old horse, at the rate of one mile an hour till Tuesday morning, when we got again under way. It is a desolate spectacle to see a ship laid to, her sails down and placed at the mercy of the wind, and when you see yourself confined together with near 200 of your fellow creatures within the narrow limits of a barque, no land within 400 miles, the ship sometimes lying between 2 mountainous waves, sometimes perched on the top of one, on each side a yawning hissing gulf <gulph> threatening to swallow her up, you are compelled to look up to Him alone who can say to the winds and waves "Peace, be still", and they are at peace.

We had many nights almost as bad as the one I have described, but we learned to laugh at dangers which at first we startled at. Our passage indeed was cold and boisterous throughout. We saw some whales on our passage and other large fish. We saw one morning more than 1,000 acres of sea literally covered with porpoises bounding along in our direction.

We entered the mouth of the Delaware on the 7th of June. The river and the banks present a strange yet beautiful appearance to the eye of a European: the river, crowded with innumerable sails of small craft, mostly oyster boats, the dark woods on either side, with here and there a rising settlement, a thriving town or a solitary farmhouse emerging from and diversifying their dark and almost unbroken gloom, furnish at once a novel and refreshing repast to eyes which for 6 long weeks before have been accustomed to gaze only on brickless fields of ocean. Your neighbours roundabout you enjoy more ease and sleep, and many of them too could command more ready cash than many of the farmers roundabout here, although these have dwellings like so many villas and eat and drink well.

I have now to inform you, my dear mother, that I received a letter from Mr Brannan of Washington, stating the number and situation of my Aunt Mary's family. There were 5 of them left, 2 girls and 3 boys. The eldest boy learned to be a painter and, on leaving his apprenticeship, went to New Orleans and has not since been heard of. The other 2 boys are labourers and are living somewhere in the state of Delaware. The eldest girl is married to a respectable shoemaker in Washington. The youngest is living with one Mrs Murray since she was a child, having been adopted by that lady at that time. She is very comfortable.

It is thus, my dear mother, that families are scattered and I know you will feel anxious and grieve at being separated from us, but be of good cheer. I trust that if the Almighty grants us health we will soon be able to assist you in buying that farm or some one else as good, for it was my earnest wish coming out to this country to procure a home for you in it, if I say that you could procure anything like happiness in it and, if not, to assist you at home and endeavour to make you comfortable in your old age. It grieved me very much to hear from Mr Mulholland that you were cast down with sorrow, though we do not wonder at it.

Now, my dear parents, for God's sake and for ours, endeavour to shake off sorrow and do not leave us to accuse ourselves of bringing down your grey hairs with sorrow to the grave, by leaving you when we should have staid by you. Our intentions were good and still continue so, and if God prosper our endeavours, we will soon be able to assist you and cheer you. I have no fear of it and many years will not pass, if we are all spared, till we see you all again, when our meeting will be as joyful as our parting was sorrowful.

I must now take my leave of you, my revered parents, my dear brothers and my innocent little sisters, and my loving friends who will come to drop a kind enquiry after me. I must bid you again another farewell. This hour is a severe one on me whilst I am closing this letter, this very long letter, though too confined for what I would say. 'Tis like a second parting and I would prolong it if I could. Remember me to Aunt Biddy and Uncles Hugh and Daniel and Michael, and to all my friends. It is a foolish custom, but I cannot get over it, but the truth is my friend, we remember you but too well; for if it be possible that the soul can disembody itself and take to flight whilst its prison of clay is asleep, mine is often with you, but I linger. Farewell, may the peace of God rest with you and may He preserve you in health and prosper your endeavours is the constant prayer of your anxious son [signed] FD.

Emigration and Migration

The reason why the emigration of 1835 is so much less than that of 1834 is the dullness of the linen trade throughout the latter year. The accounts from America by former emigrants were then tolerably good and, by the hopes they raised, acted as an additional incentive. There was also a good supply of vessels at the seaports.

In 1835 the linen trade looked better. The demand was brisk and prices advancing, all which circumstances gave employment to those persons who would otherwise have been obliged to emigrate. The accounts from America too became unfavourable, which greatly retarded the progress of emigration. The cost of the voyages became also a little higher.

In 1835 2 males between 20 and 30 years of age emigrated to Van Diemen's Land.

167 males migrate annually from the parish to Glasgow and Liverpool from the townlands of Culnagrew, Keady, Fallagloon, Drummuck, Gorteade, Drumard, Gulladuff, Dreenan, Macknagh, Lisnamuck, Drumconready, Bracknagrilly, Kirley, Moyagall, Crew, Dunglady, Swatragh and Culnady. Of the whole number, there are 3 of the Established Church and 4 Presbyterians, the rest all Catholics.

The following are the numbers from each townland: Drummuck 37, Moyagall 27, Dreenan 24, Culnagrew 16, Fallagloon 14, Keady 9, Gorteade 8, Swatragh 6, Drumard 6, Macknagh 5, Culnady 2, Dunglady 2, Drumconready 2, Lisnamuck 2, Gulladuff 2, Bracknagrilly 1, Crew 1, Kirley 3.

Fallagloon is the townland from which the greatest quantity of emigration took place. With the exception of 10, all the migrants went to Glasgow. They leave their families to support themselves by spinning, begging and various other shifts. They are cottiers.

Remarkable Character: Hermaphrodite in Curran

[C.W. Ligar] There is at present a curious instance of an hermaphrodite residing in a small cabin in the village of Curran, where she was born. Her name is Fanny Marlin; she wears the dress of a female principally, with a man's shirt and sometimes a coat. Her voice is manlike and she has a strong beard, which she keeps cut close to the skin. Her stature is small and her whole appearance masculine. She is now about 50 years of age and was a reputed fighter with a stick at fairs and quarrels.

Remarkable Men

[J. Stokes] The birthplace of Doctor Adam Clarke is situated in the townland of Moneymore, one quarter of a mile east of the town of Maghera. Nothing remains to mark the spot but 16 feet of a wall which stands 3 feet in height.

The birthplace of Doctor Henry Cooke, the celebrated leader of the Presbyterians, is situated in the townland of Grillagh. The house in which he was born is on the farm of Mr Isaac Fleming, but is nearly in ruins.

The parish also gave birth to Sir James Murray, consulting physician to one of the lords lieutenant.

Party Fights

Since the last rebellion no remarkable circumstances worthy of record have taken place in this district, except that on June 12th 1823 a party fight took place at Maghera, begun by an ordinary squabble between a grocer and a countryman who would not pay for his tobacco. It was so serious that 4 men were killed and 17 severely wounded. A party of cavalry and infantry were immediately stationed in the town. Preparations for a fight were made on 12th July 1830 but was suppressed by the rector and magistrates.

Office Copy of Part of Memoir, with letter by J. Stokes, November 1833

ANCIENT TOPOGRAPHY

Standing Stones

A standing stone in Swatragh <Swatrea>, parish of Maghera, 12 foot high. There are also 2 in one of the gardens of the village. They have very much the appearance, on being examined, of having been squared by a tool. They are each 4 feet high and are separated by an interval of 3 paces. The line on which they stand points nearly to the north east. At the town of Maghera the stone on Seefin hill is called Finn McCoul's Finger Stone.

Discovery of a Crock

About 14 years ago a farmer between Swatragh and Maghera broke accidentally into a cove. He found a horizontal grate of iron extending across the cove from one side to the other, and on this there was a "crock full of buttons." It was situated about 2 miles from Swatragh, a little way off from the right hand side of the road. My narrator had another [no other ?] name for the contents of the crock than that of "buttons." She was travelling from Swatragh to Maghera at the time, and the place was pointed out to her by a man called Diamond who related to her the story.

Letter by J. Stokes on Dungleady Fort

[Plan, vertical section and view of Dungleady Fort, breadth 330 feet, scale 1 inch to 200 feet, with dimensions of all ditches]. Maghera, November 2 1833. Dear Sir,

The fort of Dungleady is on the tip of a very high round hill at 3 and a half miles from Maghera, on the old road to Kilrea. It is at a short distance from the road and the approach to it is through fields <feilds>. The fort is of a slightly oblong form. It is not larger than the usual size of a Danish fort, but is surrounded by a triple rampart which makes the diameter of the whole to be 330 feet. The central part affords a small patch of grazing to the farmer who owns it. The tops and sides of the ramparts are covered with old blackthorn trees and stunted brushwood. The entrance to the fort which passes through them all is a paved causeway which is level throughout and owes its elevation above the bottoms of the ditches by being piled up with great stones.

The interior of the fort is slightly hollow, as you may see by the vertical section. This has been caused by a layer of stones having been originally laid round the brim. This was ascertained by violently thrusting a sharp walking-stick at different places into the ground. By the same method it appears probable that the ramparts are throughout made of regularly built stones at the bottom and of a mixture of clay and stones towards the top.

The rectangular space marked "c" was formed by a peasant who scooped it out and thatched it as a residence for himself and his family. They lived there for some time until at length after some heavy rains the end gave way and, falling inwards, very nearly smothered them. He then faced it with stone. This has not been many years ago. When he lived in it he took out much mud from the ditches as manure and he found the depth of the soil in the first ditch to be 6 feet. The dotted lines in the section mark out the probable depth of each ditch below their present bottoms. The peasantry have in many parts made gaps and passages through the ramparts for the purpose of gaining the interior, where in some parts they find good switches for basket-making. This has been the origin of all the passages excepting the paved causeway. One very deep cut was made by a farmer to obtain water for his malt kiln.

At the place where the paved causeway crossed the first rampart there formerly stood 2 long blocks of stone standing upright as pillars, and about 4 feet high. They were overturned by treasure seekers. One of them is still lying overturned and the other is overgrown with brambles. It is the opinion or idea of the country people that these were once posts of a gate. The paved causeway or passage does not appear to have been coeval with the erection of the fort, for when the 3 entrances are examined they look as if they had been torn through the ramparts. The stones taken out are laid out of the way on each side and in one part many of them are tumbled irregularly into the ditch. Neither are they cut in a regular manner, but very irregularly, and the whole causeway is slightly crooked. From an inspection of the place the idea presents itself that the entrances were once narrow passages not broader than a man's body, similar to those in Glenkeen Fort. There was once a draw-well in the middle of this fort. The predecessor of the farmer who at present owns it filled it up.

The sect of Quakers used it also as a burial ground. A suit of chain armour was found many years ago at a little bog not far off. The bridge marked "B" appears to be built with blocks of stone. There never has been any cave or chamber known under it or near it.

Appendix to Memoir by J. Stokes and J. Bleakly

ANCIENT TOPOGRAPHY

Drawings

Maghera old church: general view of the steeple; entrance to the body of the church (with carved door lintel); figure of a bishop carved in doorway; lintel of doorway, larger scale drawing with dimensions; head of a saint in the wall of the steeple; 4th May 1836 by C.W. Ligar.

Maghera old church: ground plan with annotations and orientation, main dimensions 75 feet by 26 and half feet; inside and outside views of the window by C.W. Ligar.

Maghera old church: 3 windows in the tower; south entrance to the tower by C.W. Ligar.

Monuments of Knockoneill, plan of casiol with section of wall, also 2 ancient fences and 2 cairns by J. Stokes.

North view of the artificial island and old fort, townland of Ballymacpeake; 30th April 1836 by C.W. Ligar.

Plan of artificial island formed with stakes, and of old fort, townland of Ballymacpeake, with orientation, scale 40 yards to 1 inch; enlarged plan of what appears to have been a fireplace [in fort], main dimensions 2 feet by 2 feet; 1st May 1836 by C.W. Ligar.

Part of the canoe which was found in the lake in which the artificial island is situated, in the townland of Ballymacpeake, now in the possession of John O'Hara of that townland; full view, originally 15 or 16 feet long, breadth 1 foot 10 inches, which is only half the original breadth;

section, 3 inches thick: the sides were 1 foot high when the canoe was found but have since been cut away; 30th April 1836 by C.W. Ligar.

Great standing stone of Swatragh with figure to give scale, dimensions 7 and a half feet by 3 feet; by J. Stokes.

Brass sword, full size, found in the townland of Drumlamph, resting in the clay 11 inches under the surface of a bog; in possession of Mr Henderson, Drumlamph; 2 section drawings; 2nd May 1836 by C.W. Ligar.

Ancient quern from Mr Knox's collection; end, top view and side views, dimensions 1 foot 5 inches by 8 inches; by J. Stokes.

Ancient quern from Mr Knox's collection, side and top views, dimensions 1 foot 2 inches, by 1 foot 1 inch by 6 and a half inches; by J. Stokes.

Stone font of the monastery of Maghera, formerly belonging to Mr Barnard, late rector of the parish; bottom and top views with section, dimensions 7 inches by 6 and half inches, and full drawing; by J. Stokes.

Copper spearhead from Maghera (drawn from Mr Knox's collection); full view and section, dimensions 9 and half inches by 2 and quarter inches; by J. Stokes.

5 stone hatchets, drawing and section of each with dimensions: 3 inches long, 4 inches, 2 and three-quarter inches, 3 and three-quarter inches, 4 inches; by J. Stokes.

7 flint arrowheads of rude form, back, front and edge of each, with dimensions: 1 and three-quarter inches long, 2 inches, 1 and half inches, 2 and half inches, 3 inches, 1 and half inches, 2 inches; by J. Stokes.

Silver medal found in Maghera, both faces, full size, with tokens and Latin inscriptions; by J. Stokes.

3 spearheads from Maghera, side view and section of each; by J. Stokes.

Stone hatchet, Drumard, view and section, 4 inches long; fragment of an urn of baked clay, view and section, 3 and half inches long.

One of the old tobacco pipes called by the peasantry "Danes' pipes", side and bottom views. 11th June 1836 by C.W. Ligar.

3 coins, both faces, one of James I, one probably of Elizabeth. The above coins were found in the parish of Maghera and are in the possession of Mr Moore, grocer, Maghera; by C.W. Ligar.

James II's brass money: both faces of a coin, 1689, with tokens and Latin inscriptions.

Coins

A quantity of silver coins of Elizabeth, bearing date 1575, were found in the townland of Drumlamph. They were equivalent to the sum of 4 pounds of our present money.

Social Economy

Persons buried at Old Church of Maghera

The following names appear upon the tombstones of the old church of Maghera.

English: Anderson, Brown, Clark, Collins, Drips, Clarnon, Cunningham, Forbes, Geaton, Hughes, Hull, Kyle, Miller, Marlin, Richardson, Wilson, Young, Harrell, Higgins, Ruddle, Cuddy, Morris, Lemon.

Scotch: Barklie, Campbell [crossed out: Cuddy], Dunlop, Dougall, McCrackin, Getty, Graham, Johnston, Kilmay, Keelt, McKee, [crossed out: Morris], Manolly, [crossed out: Lemon], McCready, Patterson, Stewart, Thompson, McCook.

Irish: Bradley, Brevolaghan, McCluskey, O'Donnelly, O'Dougherty, Diamond, Crilly, Convery, McCollaugh, McCann, McGuire, McGlade, Hassin, Hendy, [crossed out: Higgins], O'Kendry, Kelly, McKenna, Hagan, Lagan, Manelly, Mulholland, O'Neill, McPake, McKeigney, Sheil.

Trades and Occupations in Maghera

The following are the trades and occupations of Maghera.

Publicans 22, grocers 15, woollendrapers 4, haberdashers 9, apothecaries 5, carpenters 9, shoemakers 16, tailors 6, watchmakers 2, blacksmiths 5, whitesmiths 2, coopers 2, bakers 2, butchers 4, brewers 1, stonemasons 5, wheelwrights and farmers 5, painters and glaziers 3, saddlers 2, nailers 3, schoolmasters 3, schoolmistresses 1, dressmakers 8, dress and bonnetmakers 2, bonnetmakers 7, labourers 2, resident paupers 10, weavers 1, lodging houses 13, doctors 2, washerwomen 3, hucksters 7, dealer in rags, feathers and hair 1, dealer in eggs 1, flaxdressers, reedmakers 1, dealers in hardware 6, basket makers 1, skinners 1, houses waste 3, private houses 2, number of houses, total 229.

One of the hotels is classed as a private house. The other hotel is a public house.

Crime

List of criminal offences from the parish of Maghera decided upon from August 1832 to April 1836 by the magistrates at Kilrea petty sessions. [List with the following headings: date

Parish of Maghera

of information, offence, townland at which the defendant resides].

August 31, obtaining money under false pretences, Culnagrew.

September 3, stripping a house, Swatragh; September 12, assault, Keady.

October 2, assault, Dunglady.

November 2, waylaying and assault, 2 of Swatragh and Granaghan; November 21, assault, Granaghan; November 22, assault, 2 of Gorteade and Dunglady; November 26, assault, Gorteade; November 26, assault, Gorteade.

December 1, assault, Macknagh; December 6, forcible entry, Macknagh; December 19, stealing turf, Culnagrew.

January 2, assault, Gorteade.

March 4, assault, Slaghtybogy.

May 18, assault, Swatragh; May 9, assault, Gorteade; May 14, rescue, Beagh.

June 13, theft, Keady.

Cases at Maghera Dispensary in 1833

Alphabetical list of diseases in the Maghera dispensary from 13th January 1833 to 13th January 1834, with the number of cases.

Abscess 3, asthma 6, abortion 4, ascites 6, anasarca 4, aphtha 6, amenorrhoea 4, burns 6, bowel complaints 10, cough 4, cancer 50, croup 6, costiveness 20, cynanche 4, colic 10, catarrh 9, dyspepsia 20, diarrhoea 9, dropsy 4, debility 16, dysuria 4, eruptions 20, erysipelas 4, fever 120, flatulency 104, flux 6, foul stomach 10, fever typhus 10, gravel 3, gastrodynia 6, gonorrhoea 2, hurt 16, heartburn 10, hermorgia [haemorrhage?] 4, hepatitis 3, herpes 4, itch 10, inflamed eyes 6, indigestion 40, jaundice 4, lumbago 6, laxativeness 30, labour 6, measles 30, menorrhagia 20, pains 80, pneumonia 4, piles 6, paralysis 3, phthisis 2, pleuritis 6, pregnancy 30, prolapsus 2, quinsy 9, rheumatism 20, sore leg 3, swelled foot 2, swelled hands 4, swelled leg 2, sore eyes 26, suppression of menses 3, spasms 14, sprain 6, scurvy 4, spleen 4, sore heart 6, sore hand 7, tumours 6, ulcer 3, vomiting 6, worms 110, weed 6, white swelling 2.

Cases at Maghera Dispensary in 1834

Alphabctical list of diseases in the Maghera dispensary from the 13th of January 1834 to 13th January 1835, with the number of cases.

Amputations 3, anasarca 6, abortion 4, asthma 16, ascites 7, aphtha 4, bowel complaint 9, burns 4, boils 6, colic 6, costiveness 24, cough 60, catarrh 3, croup 2, cynanche 4, dyspepsia 24, diarrhoea 7, dropsy 2, debility 16, diseased stomach 6, deafness 6, dislocated shoulder 1, eruptions 10, erysipelas 4, fever 20, flatulency 60, foul stomach 20, flux 10, gastrodynia 4, gravel 6, gonorrhoea 6, hives 6, hepatitis 4, herpes 6, heartburn 9, hurt 20, haemoptysis 3, haemorroid 20, whooping <hooping> cough 16, itch 18, indigestion 6, inflamed eyes 9, inflamed glands 1, influenza 16, jaundice 6, labour 4, loss of appetite 3, measles 20, menorrhagia 3, nausea 6, neurosis 4, nervous debility 6, opthalmia 6, pains 90, paralysis 4, pleuritis 6, pregnancy 14, psora 3, piles 6, pneumonia 3, palpitation 9, prolapsus 6, quinsy 6, rheumatism 10, smallpox 10, swelling in leg 4, swelling in hand 6, swelling in foot 7, scurvy 4, sprain 14, sore mouth 4, scrofula 6, suppression of menses 4, tumour in tongue 4, typhus fever 30, ulcer 4, vomiting 6, worms 120, white scab 2, weed 3, white swelling 4.

Cases at Maghera Dispensary in 1835

Alphabetical list of diseases in the Maghera dispensary from the 13th January 1835 to the 13th January 1836.

Asthma 40, anasarca 6, ascites 9, abscess 4, abortion 3, burns 6, boils 9, bowel complaint 7, broken ribs 2, cough 40, confinement 60, croup 3, cut hand 4, catarrh 2, chronic rheumatism 40, costiveness 120, carbuncles 6, cynanche 6, cholera 6, diarrhoea 6, dyspepsia 20, dropsy 2, dysentery 10, dislocation 3, debility 20, erysipelas 6, eruptions 9, enlarged glands 2, epistaxis 2, fever 40, flatulency 120, foul stomach 14, gangrene 4, green scurvy 2, gonorrhoea 3, hurt 20, headache 60, haemoptysis 20, haematemesis 20, hemorrhoid 20, whooping cough 9, hives 6, itch 13, influenza 40, icterus 4, inflamed eyes 6, jaundice 4, lumbago 6, labour 60, measles 40, odontalgia 40, opthalmia 6, pains 16, pyrosis 26, pneumonia 4, psora 50, pregnancy 40, pleuritis 10, paralysis 6, piles 4, palpitation 10, quinsy 6, rheumatism 9, sprain 11, swelled leg 2, swelled feet 3, swelled hand 2, scurvy 6, scrofula 4, sore mouth 14, suppression of menses 16, tetanus 2, tumour 4, typhus fever 5, ulcer 6, vomiting 4, worms 110, weed 14, white swelling 6, white scab 6.

Cases at Maghera Dispensary in 1836

Alphabetical list of diseases in the Maghera dispensary from 13th January 1836 to 13th January 1837, with the number of cases.

Amputations 1, burns 20, broken arm 4, carbuncle 4, cough 300, diarrhoea 57, dropsy 20, enlarged glands 20, fever typhus 150, flatulency 300, fractured ribs 10, hurt 10, haemoptysis 10, indigestion 187, influenza 57, lumbago 60, psora 300, pleurisy 20, quinsy 50, rheumatic fever 20, suppression of menses 20, sore eyes 73, scrofula 20, Schiran's breast 16, sprain 10, toothache 100, worms 300.

Cases at Swatragh Dispensary in 1835

Alphabetical list of diseases in the Swatragh dispensary from the 7th of March 1835 to 7th of March 1836, with the number of cases.

Anasarca 20, asthma 27, ascites 10, abortion 20, burns 22, parturition 20, broken ribs 19, boils 30, bowel complaints 24, constipation 173, cough 100, catarrh 10, colic 21, cholera 10, costiveness 30, diarrhoea 40, deafness 30, dropsy 20, dislocation 26, erysipelas 50, fever 280, febrile diseases 73, flatulency 280, febries laetia 21, foul mouth 10, general debility 59, gravel 30, hurt 65, headache 50, heartburn 24, itch 80, indigestion 200, influenza 30, jaundice 20, measles 83, nervous debility 40, opthalmia 50, palpitation 100, pain in stomach 80, pain in back 50, pneumonia 20, pain in side 19, piles 20, quinsy 29, rheumatism 35, suppression of menses 59, suppression of urine 20, sore eyes 50, sprain 30, scrofula 18, toothache 36, ulcers 23, vomiting 30, whooping cough 80, weak stomach 57, worms 83, weed 11.

This dispensary opens from 9 to 11 a.m. on each day in the week, Wednesdays and Sundays excepted.

Cases at Swatragh Dispensary in 1836

Alphabetical list of diseases in the Swatragh dispensary from the 7th March 1836 to 1st January 1837, with the number of cases.

Asthma 80, burns and scalds 27, breast sore 16, broken ribs 30, carbuncle 30, cough 200, childbirth 7, cut in head 20, diarrhoea 57, dropsy 27, evil 19, fever 250, febrile diseases 180, flatulency 111, hurts from fall 47, headache 100, indigestion 187, itch 111, influenza 57, pleurisy 43, pneumonia 27, pain in back 60, quinsy 30, rheumatism 33, suppression of menses 53, sore eyes 73, sore arm 20, scorbutic affections 60, spitting of blood 11, swelled testicles 1, swelled gland in throat 11, sprains 30, toothache 48, vomiting 57, weakness in stomach 100, worms 160.

Maghera Dispensary Return

[Table for 8 years contains the following headings: number of patients relieved and dispensations of medicine (the same in each case), number of vaccinations (60 in each case), number of gratuitous visits, number of women delivered by midwife (none employed); expenditure: salary of surgeon and physician, salary of assistant and midwife (none employed), rent of dispensary (8 pounds per annum paid by the surgeon out of his salary), cost of medicine, repairs, other expenses; income: amount of subscription and county grant; number of committee].

[Remainder of appendix by J. Bleakly]

Year ending 13th January 1830: 2,000 patients relieved, 365 gratuitous visits; salary of surgeon or physician 30 pounds, cost of medicine 29 pounds 5s 9d, repairs 16s, other expenses 3 pounds 2s 10d ha'penny, total expenditure 71 pounds 4s 7d ha'penny; amount of subscription 33 pounds 3s 6d, county grant 33 pounds 3s 6d, total income 66 pounds 7s; 17 on committee.

Year ending 13th January 1831: 1,500 patients relieved, 400 gratuitous visits; salary of surgeon or physician 40 pounds, cost of medicine 20 pounds 12s 9d, other expenses 1 pound 6s 2d, total expenditure 61 pounds 18s 11d; amount of subscription 32 pounds 4s 8d, county grant 32 pounds 4s, total income 64 pounds 8s 8d; 16 on committee.

Year ending 13th January 1832: 4,000 patients relieved, 600 gratuitous visits; salary of surgeon or physician 50 pounds, cost of medicine 24 pounds 19s 6d ha'penny, repairs 15s, other expenses 10s 10d, total expenditure 84 pounds 5s 4d ha'penny; amount of subscription 35 pounds 10s, county grant 35 pounds 10s, total income 71 pounds; 15 on committee.

Year ending 13th January 1833: 2,500 patients relieved, 290 gratuitous visits; salary of surgeon or physician 50 pounds, cost of medicine 22 pounds 11s 5d ha'penny, other expenses 2 pounds 3s 7d ha'penny, total expenditure 82 pounds 15s 1d; amount of subscription 33 pounds 5s, county grant 30 pounds, total income 63 pounds 5s; 14 on committee.

Year ending 13th January 1834: 3,600 patients relieved, 320 gratuitous visits; salary of surgeon or physician 50 pounds, cost of medicine 41 pounds 13s 7d, other expenses 4s 7d, total expenditure 99 pounds 18s 2d; amount of subscription 33 pounds 17s, county grant 32 pounds 16s, total income 66 pounds 13s; 18 on committee.

Year ending 13th January 1835: 1,352 patients relieved, 334 gratuitous visits; salary of surgeon or physician 50 pounds, cost of medicine 10 pounds 2s 6d, other expenses 1 pound 2s 6d, total expenditure 69 pounds 5s; amount of subscription 36 pounds 1s, county grant 36 pounds 1s, total income 72 pounds 2s; 19 on committee.

Year ending 13th January 1836: 1,736 patients

relieved, 309 gratuitous visits; salary of surgeon or physician 50 pounds, cost of medicine 19 pounds 1s 8d, total expenditure 77 pounds 1s 8d; amount of subscription 33 pounds 9s, county grant 32 pounds 14s, total income 66 pounds 3s; 16 on committee.

Year ending 1st January 1837: 2,139 patients relieved, 234 gratuitous visits; salary of surgeon or physician 50 pounds, cost of medicine 25 pounds, total expenditure 75 pounds; amount of subscription 31 pounds, county grant 31 pounds, total income 62 pounds; 10 on committee.

Swatragh Dispensary Return

Year ending 7th March 1836: 2,677 patients relieved, 2,677 dispensations of medicine, 120 vaccinations, 780 gratuitous visits; number of women delivered by midwife: none employed; salary of surgeon or physician 80 pounds, salary of assistant and midwife: none employed; rent of dispensary: part of the surgeon's house, built by himself; cost of medicine 13 pounds; repairs: a new house; supported by the Mercers' Company, county grant none; superintended by the agent of the Mercers' Company.

Year ending 1st January 1837: 2,399 patients relieved, 2,399 dispensations of medicine, 100 vaccinations, 800 gratuitous visits; salary of surgeon or physician 80 pounds, cost of medicine 15 pounds 10s, total expenditure 95 pounds 10s.

Table of Mills

[Table contains the following headings: situation and description, date and cost of erection, proprietor, type and dimensions of wheel and machinery, date and cost of insurance, observations].

Craigadick corn mill is situated a quarter of a mile south west of Maghera, near the leading road from Maghera to Tobermore <Tobbermore>; the mill is built of stone and lime, thatched; proprietor Alexander Clark of Maghera; breast wheel, fall of water 10 feet, diameter of water wheel 14 feet, breadth 2 feet 4 inches, diameter of cog wheel 7 feet; single-geared <geered>, metal segments screwed on a wooden rim; this mill is situated on a stream which proceeds from Lough Bran in the parish of Killelagh, and is idle all the summer and part of the winter from want of water.

Curran corn mill is situated at the west end of the village of Curran, near the bridge and leading road from Castledawson to Tobermore, and built of stone and lime, thatched; George Rodgers rents the mill from the Right Honourable Lord Strafford; breast wheel, fall of water 3 feet 6 inches, diameter of water wheel 12 feet, breadth 4 feet 3 inches, diameter of cog wheel 7 feet 10 inches; single-geared, cast iron machinery; this mill is situated on a stream proceeding from Desertmartin and can work all seasons of the year; there are 2 corn kilns with tile heads attached.

Crew flax mill is situated at the foot of a hill, the house and machinery are in very bad repair, erected 1826; William Kissick rents the mill from [blank]; breast wheel, fall of water 14 feet, diameter of water wheel 12 feet, breadth 1 foot 8 inches, diameter of cog wheel 6 feet 6 inches; single-geared, wooden machinery; this mill is worked by a stream which proceeds from the Crew flow bog and has 2 berths or sets of scutchers, but idle all summer from want of water.

Swatragh corn mill is situated near the bridge at the end of the village; proprietor Alexander Clark Esquire of Upperlands; breast wheel, fall of water 20 feet, diameter of water wheel 14 feet, breadth 2 feet 6 inches, diameter of cog wheel 8 feet; single-geared, metal segments screwed on a wooden rim; this mill is worked by a stream which proceeds from Carntogher mountain and is idle in summer from want of water, and in bad repair.

Ballymacilcur flax mill is a small cabin thatched with shoves, and in very bad repair, erected 1826; proprietor William Huston; breast wheel, fall of water 6 feet, diameter of water wheel 11 feet, breadth 1 foot 6 inches, diameter of cog wheel 6 feet; single-geared, wooden machinery; this mill is worked by a stream which proceeds from Carntogher mountain and has 3 sets of scutchers, but idle in summer from want of water.

Tirgarvil corn mill is situated near the leading road from Maghera to Kilrea, a good house, slated, erected 1829 and cost 200 pounds; proprietor Alexander Clark Esquire of Upperlands; breast wheel, fall of water 6 feet, diameter of water wheel 12 feet, breadth 2 feet, diameter of cog wheel 9 feet; single-geared, cast iron machinery; the water which works the bleach mill works this mill also and can work at all seasons of the year; there are 2 good corn kilns attached.

Culnagrew flax mill near the leading road from Swatragh to Kilrea, built of stone, thatched with shoves and in bad repair, erected 6 months; Thomas McReynolds rents it from the Mercers' Company; breast wheel, fall of water 8 feet, diameter of water wheel 12 feet, breadth 2 feet 2 inches, diameter of cog wheel 6 feet 6 inches; single-geared, wooden machinery; this mill can work all seasons of the year and wrought by a stream proceeding from Desertoghill parish, and has 2 sets of scutchers.

Macknagh flax mill, a good house of stone, erected 1824 and cost 100 pounds; Alexander Moore rents it from the Mercers' Company; breast wheel, fall of water 4 feet, diameter of water wheel 14 feet, breadth 3 feet, diameter of cog wheel 8 feet; single-geared, metal segments screwed on a wooden rim; can work all seasons of the year and has 2 cog wheels of the same dimensions, one for scutching and the other for rolling <rooling>.

Upperlands tuck mill is on the opposite side of the stream with the corn mill, a small house in bad repair; Jacob Moore rents it from the Mercers' Company; breast wheel, fall of water 4 feet, diameter of water wheel 12 feet, breadth 2 feet; single-geared, wooden machinery; from the cheapness of the woollen cloth, the mill is not doing much work, as the people can have it from the shop cheaper than home-made; can work all seasons of the year.

Culnady corn mill is situated on the by-road from Culnady meeting house to Tirgarvil and is of stone, thatched; proprietor Alexander Clark Esquire of [Upperlands]; breast wheel, fall of water 9 feet 6 inches, diameter of water wheel 14 feet, breadth 2 feet 3 inches, diameter of cog wheel 9 feet; single-geared, cast iron machinery, water wheel is also of cast iron; this mill is worked by a stream which proceeds from Carntogher mountain and can work a little all seasons of the year; the machinery is in good repair.

Curragh flax mill, situated in the townland of Curragh, on the rocks near the mearing of Culnady, and is of stone, thatched and in bad repair, erected 2 years, a flax mill; William Dorrety rents the mill from John McKowen; breast wheel, fall of water 8 feet 6 inches, diameter of water wheel 12 feet 4 inches, breadth 1 foot 7 inches, diameter of cog wheel 6 feet 8 inches; single-geared, metal segments screwed on a wooden rim; this was a corn mill in 1833, but from want of custom it was converted into a flax mill, which last season was more profitable than corn, and is worked by a stream proceeding from Carntogher mountain and can work a little all seasons of the year.

Culnady flax mill is situated in the rear of the houses near the bridge and of stone and lime, slated, erected 1820, proprietor John Henry; breast wheel, fall of water 6 feet 4 inches, diameter of water wheel 12 feet, breadth 2 feet, diameter of cog wheel 9 feet; single-geared, cast iron cog wheel; this mill can work all seasons of the year, except 2 or 3 months in the summer, which is from want of water; 3 rollers attached, in good repair and on the stream which proceeds from Carntogher; 2 sets of scutchers attached.

Culnady flax mill is situated about 40 perches higher up on the stream and is of stone and lime, thatched, erected 1818; proprietor John Henry; breast wheel, fall of water 9 feet, diameter of water wheel 12 feet, breadth 2 feet, diameter of cog wheel 7 feet; single-geared, metal segments screwed on a wooden rim; this mill is on the same stream and can work at the same time, with 3 rollers attached and 3 sets of scutchers, all in good repair.

Drumlamph flax mill is situated near the leading road from Knockcloghrim <Knocklochram> to Castledawson and is built of stone, thatched, and cost 200 pounds, proprietor David Cunningham; breast wheel, fall of water 6 feet, diameter of water wheel 12 feet, breadth 4 feet, diameter of cog wheel 7 feet; single-geared, cast iron machinery; this mill has 12 berths or sets of scutchers, all in good repair, wrought by the Moyola water, and can work all seasons of the year. 4th July 1836.

SOCIAL ECONOMY

Sunday Schools in 1836

[Table contains the following headings: name, situation, when established, superintendent, number of teachers and number of scholars subdivided by religion and sex, hours of attendance, societies with which connected, observations].

Maghera, held in the day schoolhouse, established 1816, superintendents Rev J.S. Knox and Rev. George Vesey, curate; 6 male and 7 female teachers, total 13; number of scholars: 77 Established Church, 45 Presbyterians, 11 Roman Catholics, 3 other denominations, 50 males, 86 females, total 136, 38 exclusively Sunday school scholars; hours of attendance from 10 till half past 11 o'clock a.m.; Sunday School Society for Ireland give books; commences with singing and prayer and concludes with a public examination by the superintendent.

Ballynahonebeg, [held] in the houses through the townland, established 1830, superintendent William Lormer, schoolmaster; 3 male and 2 female teachers, total 5; number of scholars: 12 Presbyterians, 3 Roman Catholics, 35 other denominations, 30 males, 20 females, total 50, 21 exclusively Sunday school scholars; hours of attendance from 7 till 10 o'clock a.m.; Sunday School Society give books at a reduced price; commences with singing and prayer and concludes with the same.

Parish of Maghera

Beagh Spiritual, in a new schoolhouse on the road leading to Bellaghy, established 1834, superintendents William Crawford and James Graham; 2 male and 8 female teachers, total 10; number of scholars: 10 Established Church, 30 Presbyterians, 6 Roman Catholics, 33 other denominations, 43 males, 36 females, total 79, 59 exclusively Sunday school scholars; hours of attendance from half past 6 till half past 9 a.m. in the summer and from half past 8 till 10 a.m. in winter; Sunday School Society give books at a reduced price; commences with singing and prayer and concludes with the same.

Grillagh, held in a private house, established 1835, superintendent Mrs Sarah Patterson; 4 male and 2 female teachers, total 6; number of scholars: 64 Presbyterians, 11 other denominations, 16 males, 59 females, total 75, 16 exclusively Sunday school scholars; hours of attendance from 9 till 12 o'clock a.m. in winter and from 4 till 8 p.m. in summer; Sunday school Society give books free, except carriage; commences with singing and prayer and concludes with the same by the superintendent.

Curran, held in the barn where the Seceding congregation meets in the village, established 1828, superintendents Richard Cavin and George Rodgers; 5 male and 3 female teachers, total 8; number of scholars: 18 Established Church, 23 Presbyterians, 4 Roman Catholics, 10 other denominations, 20 males, 35 females, total 55; hours of attendance from 10 till 12 o'clock a.m.; [connected with] Sunday School Society; commences with singing and prayer and concludes with the same.

Moyagall Roman Catholic Sunday school, held in the Roman Catholic chapel, established 1835, superintendent Thomas McDavit, schoolmaster; 3 male and 3 female teachers, total 6; number of scholars: 86 males, 130 females, total 216, all Roman Catholics, 76 exclusively Sunday school scholars; hours of attendance from 9 till 12 o'clock a.m.; societies with which connected none; observations: none. Report for March 1836.

Tirnageeragh, held in the Seceding meeting house at Culnady, established 1824, superintendents Rev. Alexander Mulligan, Seceding minister and John McNaught, schoolmaster; 5 male and 2 female teachers, total 7; number of scholars: 10 Established Church, 9 Presbyterians, 1 Roman Catholic, 30 other denominations, 22 males, 28 females, total 50, 40 exclusively Sunday school scholars; hours of attendance from 8 till 10 o'clock a.m. and from 5 till 8 p.m.; Sunday School Society give books at a reduced price; commences with singing and prayer and concludes with the same.

Glenn Roman Catholic chapel Sunday school (female), held in the Roman Catholic chapel, established 1822, superintendent John Morrisson, reedmaker; 14 teachers, all female; number of scholars 150, all female and Roman Catholic, 50 exclusively Sunday school scholars; hours of attendance from 9 till 1 o'clock a.m.; societies with which connected: none.

Glenn Roman Catholic chapel (male) Sunday school, held in the Roman Catholic chapel, established 1822, superintendent Michael McKenna, schoolmaster; 8 teachers, all male; number of scholars 80, all male and Roman Catholic, 40 exclusively Sunday school scholars; hours of attendance from 9 till 1 o'clock a.m.; both Authorised and Douai <Douy> Version, and the children's day schoolbooks are used; societies with which connected none. Report for April 1836.

Public Schools in 1836

[Table contains the following headings: name, situation and description, when established, income and expenditure, physical, intellectual and moral education, number of pupils subdivided by age, sex and religion, name and religion of master or mistress].

Swatragh male school, situated near the corn mill at the south end of the town, a good house, slated, 39 and a half by 21 feet 10 inches, with 8 arched windows and 1 door, established 1826; income: from the Mercers' Company 3 pounds per annum, 6 pounds from pupils; expenditure: cost of building the schoolhouse 130 pounds, viz. 125 pounds from the Kildare Place Society and 5 pounds by subscription; intellectual education: books published by the Kildare Place Society with *Thompson's* and *Gough's Arithmetic*; moral education: visited by the clergy of all denominations, Authorised Version of Scripture is taught; number of pupils: males, 11 under 10 years of age, 15 from 10 to 15, 5 over 15, total 31; females, 13 under 10 years of age, 2 from 10 to 15, total 15; total number of pupils 46, 9 Protestants, 4 Presbyterians, 33 Roman Catholics; master John O'Neil, Roman Catholic.

Swatragh female school, situated at the end of the village on the Kilrea road, a good house, thatched, 16 by 14 feet, attached to the dwelling house, established in 1832; income: from the Mercers' Company 5 pounds, 6 pounds 12s from pupils; expenditure: house rent per annum paid by the Mercers' Company 5 pounds; intellectual education: *Manson's Primer and spelling book*, with the *Universal spelling book*, plain and fancy needlework is taught; moral education: visited by the clergy of all denominations, Authorised Version of Scripture is taught, and catechism on Mondays by mistress; number of pupils: 6 under 10 years of age, 20 from 10 to 15, 4 over 15, total 30, all female, 3 Protestants, 6 Presbyterians, 21 Roman Catholics; mistress Joanna Fanning, Roman Catholic.

Tirnageeragh, situated near the leading road from Maghera to Kilrea and held in a small cabin which is also the residence of the master, established in 1829; income: from the Mercers' Company 4 pounds, 9 pounds from pupils; expenditure: house rent with a garden and bog attached 2 pounds 15s; intellectual education: *Manson's Primer and spelling book*, with dictionary and *Gough's Arithmetic*; moral education: visited by the Protestant and Presbyterian clergy, Authorised Version of Scripture is taught and catechism; number of pupils: males, 10 under 10 years of age, 7 from 10 to 15, 1 over 15, total 18; females, 11 under 10 years of age, 2 from 10 to 15, 1 over 15, total 14; total number of pupils 32, 4 Protestants, 25 Presbyterians, 3 other denominations; master John McNaught, Presbyterian.

Dreenan, situated on the leading road from Maghera to Portglenone, a good room in a house, rented and thatched, 18 by 16 feet, established in 1816 and in 1832 it became connected with the London Hibernian Society; income: from the London Hibernian Society 4 pounds 10s, 3 pounds 10s from pupils; expenditure: house rent 2 pounds 10s; intellectual education: books published by the London Hibernian Society, with *Thompson's* and *Gough's Arithmetic*, *Jackson's Book-keeping* and *Murray's English grammar*; moral education: visited by the Protestant and Roman Catholic clergy, a Douai version is taught and catechism on Saturday; number of pupils: males, 10 under 10 years of age, 10 from 10 to 15, 10 over 15, total 30; females, 15 under 10 years of age, 9 from 10 to 15, 6 over 15, total 30; total number of pupils 60, 20 Protestants, 40 Roman Catholics; master James Cassidy, Roman Catholic.

Drummuck, on the leading road from Magherafelt to Kilrea, a small cabin 16 by 14 feet, established in 1826; income: from the London Hibernian Society 1 pound, 7 pounds 10s from pupils; expenditure: house rent paid by teacher's father; intellectual education: books published by the London Hibernian Society, *Thompson* and *Gough's Arithmetic* and *Lennie's English grammar*; moral education: visited by the Protestant and Roman Catholic clergy, Authorised Version and catechism is taught; number of pupils: males, 18 under 10 years of age, 10 from 10 to 15, 8 over 15, total 36; females, 7 under 10 years of age, 17 from 10 to 15, total 24; total number of pupils 60, 15 Protestants, 8 Presbyterians, 37 Roman Catholics; master James Boyle, Roman Catholic. Report for March 1836.

Drumard, situated on the leading road from Maghera to Bellaghy, a good house of stone and lime, thatched and 22 by 14 and a half feet, but no desk or seats, established in 1835; income: from the London Hibernian Society 8 pounds, 8 pounds from pupils; expenditure: cost of building the house 20 pounds, at the expense of the teacher; intellectual education: books published by the London Hibernian Society with *Universal* and *Manson's Spelling book and primer*, *Gough's Arithmetic*, *Murray's English grammar*; moral education: visited by the clergy of the Established Church, Authorised Version of Scripture is taught; number of pupils: males, 39 under 10 years of age, 39 from 10 to 15, total 78; females, 34 under 10 years of age, 10 from 10 to 15, total 44; total number of pupils 122, all Roman Catholics; master Bernard Kelly, Roman Catholic.

Moyagall, situated on the leading road from Maghera to Portglenone, held in the teacher's dwelling house which is a small thatched cabin, established in 1808; income: from the London Hibernian Society 4 pounds, 2 pounds 10s from pupils; intellectual education: books published by the London Hibernian Society, *Manson's Primer* and *Gough's Arithmetic*; moral education: visited by the clergy of the Established Church, catechism taught on Saturday; number of pupils: males, 14 under 10 years of age, 14 from 10 to 15, total 28; females, 10 under 10 years of age, 18 from 10 to 15, total 28; total number of pupils 56, 4 Protestants, 52 Roman Catholics; master Patrick McCloskey, Roman Catholic.

Curran, situated in the village of Curran, a thatched house 12 by 14 feet, attached to the dwelling house, established in 1832; income: from the London Hibernian Society 6 pounds, 12 pounds from pupils; expenditure: house rent 1 pound 10s; intellectual education: books published by the London Hibernian Society since 1833, with *Gough's Arithmetic* and *Jenning's Book-keeping*; moral education: visited by the clergy of the Established Church, Authorised Version of Scripture and catechism on Saturday; number of pupils: males, 14 under 10 years of age, 10 from 10 to 15, 6 over 15, total 30; females, 28 under 10 years of age, 10 from 10 to 15, 3 over 15, total 41; total number of pupils 71, 15 Protestants,

54 Presbyterians, 2 Roman Catholics; master Robert Marlin, Protestant.

Curran Irish national school, situated in the rear of the village, a good house of stone, thatched, 23 by 15 and a half feet with 4 good windows, each 10 feet of glass, in 1830 connected with the Kildare Society and since 1832 with the National Board; income: from the National Board 10 pounds, 6 pounds from pupils; expenditure: house rent 4 pounds; intellectual education: books published by the National Board; moral education: visited by the Roman Catholic clergy, Authorised Version of Scripture is taught and catechism on Saturday; number of pupils: males, 24 under 10 years of age, 10 from 10 to 15, 1 over 15, total 35; females, 25 under 10 years of age, 10 from 10 to 15, total 35; total number of pupils 70, 8 Protestants, 37 Presbyterians, 25 Roman Catholics; master Patrick Loughran, Roman Catholic.

Milltown, situated in the townland of Craigadick, on the leading road from Maghera to Tobermore, a good house, thatched, established in 1832; income: from the rector 1 pound, from Alexander Clark Esquire 2 pounds, 8 pounds from pupils: expenditure: cost of building 15 pounds; intellectual education: *Universal spelling book and primer, Thompson* and *Gough's Arithmetic*; moral education: visited by the Protestant clergy, Authorised Version and catechism is taught; number of pupils: males, 25 under 10 years of age, 4 from 10 to 15, 3 over 15, total 32; females, 7 under 10 years of age, 1 from 10 to 15, total 8; total number of pupils 40, 35 Presbyterians, 5 Roman Catholics; master Samuel Long, Presbyterian. Report for March 1836.

[Insert addition: Maghera parish school, situated at the east end of the town near the church, a good house, 2-storey high, built of stone and lime, slated, on the glebe land belonging to the present incumbent and in the townland of Moneymore; 1 acre of good land is attached, which was alienated by deed for the purpose of education; established in 1821 and cost 400 pounds, viz. from the Kildare Place Society 100 pounds, Mercers' Company 125 pounds and by local subscription 175 pounds; income: from the Rev. J. Spencer Knox, rector of the parish, 10 pounds, with a good house and garden. The grant from the Kildare Place Society ceased in 1832; from the commencement of the school till that period the master received 10 pounds per annum from the above society; from the Rev. George Vesey, curate of the parish, for teaching 6 poor children 1 pound; 9 pounds from pupils; expenditure: house rent free; intellectual education: books published by the Kildare Place Society, with *Thompson* and *Gough's Arithmetic, Murray's English grammar* and *Jackson's Book-keeping*; moral education: visited by the clergy of the Established and Presbyterian Churches, the Authorised Version of Scripture is taught; number of pupils: 66 under 10 years of age, 21 from 10 to 15, 2 over 15, total 89, all male, 38 Protestants, 27 Presbyterians, 2 Roman Catholics, 22 of other denominations; master Henry McHenry, a Protestant.

Situated at the suburbs of the town, a good house, slated, 19 by 16 and a half feet in the clear, with the teacher's apartment attached and 1 acre of garden, established in 1823; income: from the London Hibernian Society 9 pounds per annum, from the rector of the parish 2 pounds, from the curate 1 pound, 2 pounds from pupils; expenditure: house rent paid by the rector 2 pounds; intellectual education: books published by the London Hibernian Society, with *Thompson* and *Gough's Arithmetic*; moral education: visited by the clergy of the Established Church, Authorised Version of Scriptures is taught; number of pupils: males, 23 under 10 years of age, 24 from 10 to 15, total 47; females, 23 under 10 years of age, 13 from 10 to 15, total 36; total number of pupils 83, 6 Protestants, 33 Presbyterians, 40 Roman Catholics, 4 other denominations; master William Elliott, Independent.

Irish school, situated in the main street and held in the kitchen of the teacher's house, which is thatched and very small, established in 1834; income: from the Irish Society 5 pounds 5s per annum, persons from the age of 12 years to 65 years attend; expenditure: house rent 3 pounds per annum; intellectual education: books published by the Irish Society at a reduced price; moral education: visited once a quarter by the inspectors of the society; number of pupils: 62 from 10 to 15, 2 over 15, total 64, all male, 2 Protestants, 62 Roman Catholics; master Michael McKenna, Roman Catholic.

Maghera female parish school, held in the lower part of the male schoolhouse, established in 1827; income: from Mrs Knox 10 pounds, from the curate 10s for teaching 6 poor children; expenditure: house rent free and a garden; intellectual education: books published by the Kildare Place Society; moral education: visited by the clergy of the Established Church, Authorised Version is taught; number of pupils: 36 under 10 years of age, 14 from 10 to 15, 8 over 15, total 58, all female, 40 Protestants, 1 Presbyterian, 15 Roman Catholics, 2 other denominations; mistress Agness Elliott, Independent. Report for March 1836.

Fallagloon, situated on the road leading from Knockcloghrim to Dungiven, a good house of stone, slated, built by the Kildare Place Society and is 25 by 15 and a half feet in the clear, established in 1827; income: from the Rev. J.S. Knox 2 pounds, 4 pounds from pupils; until the year 1832 the master received 7 pounds per annum from the Kildare Place Society; expenditure: cost of building the schoolhouse 45 pounds and is kept in repair by Mr Knox; intellectual education: books published by the Kildare Place Society, with *Thompson* and *Gough's Arithmetic*, *Murray* and *Lennie's English grammar* and *Jackson's Book-keeping*; moral education: visited by the clergy of the Established Church, Authorised Version of Scripture is taught; number of pupils: males, 15 under 10 years of age, 5 from 10 to 15, total 20; females, 11 under 10 years of age, total 11; total number of pupils 31, 3 Protestants, 18 Presbyterians, 10 other denominations; master William Lormer, Independent.

Gorteade, situated at O'Kane's public house on the leading road from Maghera to Kilrea, a good house, thatched, 27 by 14 feet, established in 1831 and in 1834 it became connected with the London Hibernian Society; income: from the London Hibernian Society 4 pounds, from the Mercers' Company 3 pounds, 5 pounds from pupils; expenditure: house rent 3 pounds 10s, paid by the Mercers' Company; intellectual education: books published by the London Hibernian Society, with *Thompson* and *Gough's Arithmetic* and *Murray's English grammar*; moral education: visited by the Protestant and Presbyterian clergy, Authorised Version of Scriptures is taught and catechism on Saturday; number of pupils: males, 21 under 10 years of age, 10 from 10 to 15, 5 over 15, total 36; females, 11 under 10 years of age, 2 from 10 to 15, total 13; total number of pupils 49, 17 Presbyterians, 20 Roman Catholics, 12 other denominations; master William Thompson, Protestant.

Gorteade, situated near the leading road to Swatragh, a room in a dwelling house of the teacher, 10 by 14 feet, established in 1829; income: from the Mercers' Company 1 pound, 8 pounds from pupils; intellectual education: *Universal spelling book and primer*, *Knowles' Elocution*, *Thompson* and *Gough's Arithmetic*, *Jackson's Book-keeping* and *Murray's English grammar*; moral education: not visited by any [clergy], Authorised Version of Scripture is taught; number of pupils: males, 7 under 10 years of age, 19 from 10 to 15, 4 over 15, total 30; females, 3 under 10 years of age, 7 from 10 to 15, total 10; total number of pupils 40, 10 Presbyterians, 30 Roman Catholics; master Bernard Mellon, Roman Catholic.

Gorteade, near Mr Clark's bleach mill, situated near the bleach green and held in farmhouse, 12 by 14 [feet] (i.e. the room), thatched, established in 1824; income: from the Mercers' Company 1 pound, 4 pounds from pupils; intellectual education: *Universal* and *Manson's Spelling book and primer*, with *Thompson and Gough's Arithmetic*; moral education: not visited by any [clergy], Authorised Version of Scriptures is taught; number of pupils: males, 10 under 10 years of age, 14 from 10 to 15, 6 over 15, total 30; females, 6 under 10 years of age, 4 from 10 to 15, total 10; total number of pupils 40, 2 Protestants, 4 Presbyterians, 34 Roman Catholics; master Hugh Bradley, Roman Catholic. Report for April 1836].

Private Schools in 1836

[Table contains the following headings: name, situation and description, when established, income and expenditure, physical, intellectual and moral education, number of pupils subdivided by age, sex and religion, name and religion of master or mistress. No physical education].

Tirgarvil classical seminary, situated on the by-road leading from the Kilrea road to Culnady, a good room in a farmhouse which is also the teacher's dwelling, established 19th February 1829; income: supported by the parents of the children, 50 pounds from pupils; intellectual education: the usual college course; number of pupils: 5 from 10 to 15, 10 over 15, total 15, all male, 1 Protestant, 1 Presbyterian, 12 Roman Catholics, 1 Seceder; master Mr John McCloskey, Roman Catholic.

Crew, situated on the road leading from Maghera to Kilrea, a good house, of stone, thatched and 20 by 16 feet, established in 1822; income from pupils 30 pounds; expenditure: cost of building the house 15 pounds, by the teacher; intellectual education: *Knowles' Elocution*, *Manson's Spelling book* and dictionary and history, *Thompson's Arithmetic and geography*, *Murray's English grammar*; moral education: visited by the clergy of the Established Church, catechism and Authorised Version of Scripture on Saturday by the master; number of pupils: males, 10 under 10 years of age, 23 from 10 to 15, 7 over 15, total 40; females, 2 under 10 years of age, 25 from 10 to 15, 3 over 15, total 30; total number of pupils 70, 8 Protestants, 39 Presbyterians, 15 Roman Catholics, 8 other denominations; master David Paul, Presbyterian.

Parish of Maghera

Situated in the townland of Gulladuff, on the leading road from Maghera to Bellaghy, a small cabin attached to a dwelling house, established in 1833; income from pupils 4 pounds 10s; intellectual education: *Universal* and *Manson's Spelling book and primer* and natural history; moral education: visited by the clergy of all denominations, Authorised and Douai Version is taught; number of pupils: males, 10 under 10 years of age, 21 from 10 to 15, 10 over 15, total 41; females, 10 under 10 years of age, 7 from 10 to 15, total 17; total number of pupils 58, 14 Protestants, 1 Presbyterian, 43 Roman Catholics; master Thomas McDavit, Roman Catholic.

Curran night school, held in the national day schoolhouse at present, established in 1832; income from pupils 5 pounds; intellectual education: the day schoolbooks are used; number of pupils: males, 1 from 10 to 15, 17 over 15, total 18; females, 2 from 10 to 15, 6 over 15, total 8; total number of pupils 26, 3 Protestants, 15 Presbyterians, 8 Roman Catholics; master Patrick Loughran, Roman Catholic.

Situated at the foot of the mountain in the townland of Bracknagrilly, 70 perches west of the leading road to Dungiven, held in the barn of a farmhouse, 15 by 16 feet, established in 1833; income from pupils 20 pounds; expenditure: house rent 1 pound; intellectual education: *Universal* and *Manson's Spelling book, Thompson, Walkingham* and *Gough's Arithmetic* and *Knowles' Elocution*; moral education: not visited by any [clergy], Authorised and Douai Version of Scripture is taught; number of pupils: males, 16 under 10 years of age, 35 from 10 to 15, 11 over 15, total 62; females, 12 under 10 years of age, 7 from 10 to 15, total 19; total number of pupils 81, all Roman Catholic; master Michael McKenna, Roman Catholic. Report for April 1836.

Situated in the main street and held in the kitchen of the teacher's dwelling house, thatched and very small, established in 1831; income from pupils 13 pounds; expenditure: house rent 3 pounds; intellectual education: *Universal* and *Manson's Spelling book and primer, Knowles' Elocution, Thompson* and *Gough's Arithmetic, Murray's English grammar*; moral education: visited by the Roman Catholic clergy only, Authorised and Douai Version is taught by the master; number of pupils: males, 4 under 10 years of age, 21 from 10 to 15, 1 over 15, total 26; females, 26 under 10 years of age, 13 from 10 to 15, total 39; total number of pupils 65, all Roman Catholic; master Michael McKenna, Roman Catholic.

Night school, held in the day schoolhouse in the main street, established in 1831; income: each child pays 3s 4d per quarter and provides candles, [total] 3 pounds; intellectual education: the day schoolbooks are used; number of pupils: males, 6 from 10 to 15, 6 over 15, total 12; females, 4 from 10 to 15, 2 over 15, total 6; total number of pupils 18, all Roman Catholic; master Michael McKenna, Roman Catholic.

Gulladuff female school, situated in Gulladuff on the leading road from Maghera to Bellaghy, held in the upper room of a public house, established 2nd May 1836; income: for the present quarter 17 girls viz. 12 at 3s per quarter and 5 at 1s 6d per quarter, [total] 2 pounds 3s 6d for the present quarter; expenditure: the teacher is permitted to teach in the house rent free; intellectual education: *Universal spelling book and primer, Gough's Arithmetic*, with plain and fancy needlework; number of pupils: 5 under 10 years of age, 4 from 10 to 15, 8 over 15, total 17, all female, 1 Protestant, 1 Presbyterian, 15 Roman Catholics; mistress Elizabeth Loughran, Roman Catholic. Report for May 1836.

Beagh Spiritual, held in a good house which was built for a Sunday school in 1833, thatched and 25 by 17 feet inside, with 6 windows, viz. 3 on each side and a door on the end; situated on the leading road from Maghera to Bellaghy and built by subscription and cost 25 pounds, established 26th December 1836; income: 26 pupils at 1s 8d per quarter, [total] 2 pounds 2s 4d; expenditure: house rent free; intellectual education: the Sunday school books and London Hibernian Society books and primers; moral education: visited by none since its establishment; number of pupils: males, 8 under 10 years of age, 2 from 10 to 15, total 10; females, 13 under 10 years of age, 3 from 10 to 15, total 16; total number of pupils 26, 4 Protestants, 21 Presbyterians, 1 Roman Catholic; master William Baird, Presbyterian. Report for January 2nd 1837.

Grillagh evening adult class, held in the room of a farmhouse near the bridge, established December 1836; income: 14 pupils at 6d per quarter; expenditure: house rent free; intellectual education: writing only is taught; number of pupils: males, 5 from 10 to 15 years of age, 7 over 15, total 12; females, 2 over 15 years of age, total 2; total number of pupils 14, 1 Protestant, 10 Presbyterians, 3 Roman Catholics; master Joseph Daly, a Roman Catholic.

Held in the room of a small private house at the upper end of the town of Maghera, established November 1836; income: 2s 6d per quarter from each child; expenditure: house rent 10d per week;

intellectual education: *Universal spelling book, Manson's Primer, Gough's Arithmetic*, with plain and fancy needlework; moral education: the Roman Catholic priest, the Rev. [blank] McKenna, visited the school once only; number of pupils: males, 3 under 10 years of age, total 3; females, 4 under 10 years of age, total 4; total number of pupils 7, 2 Protestants, 5 Roman Catholics; mistress Martha Patterson, Roman Catholic. Report for January 1837.

Evening adult school, held in the day schoolhouse in the townland of Crew and only held during the winter quarter, one night in each week, established 20th December 1836; income from pupils 1 pound 4s per quarter; intellectual education: *Thompson's Arithmetic, Murray's English grammar* and *Knowles' Elocutionist*; moral education: not visited by any [clergy]; number of pupils: males 22, 2 females from 10 to 15 years of age, total 2; total number of pupils 24, 19 Presbyterians, 4 Roman Catholics, 1 other denomination; master David Paul, a Presbyterian.

Memoir by J.B. Williams [?], March 1836

MODERN TOPOGRAPHY AND SOCIAL ECONOMY

Town of Maghera

Maghera is the only post or market town in the 3 parishes of Maghera, Killelagh and Termoneeny. It has 2 market houses, one of which, in the east of the town, has been recently erected on the site of the old one thrown down. Both are small and plain, but in keeping with the general appearance of the town that presents but few good houses to the view. Mr Alexander Clark of Upperlands has built them both. The new one is the lint market, the other, the usual and grain market. In the latter also the sessions are held.

Dispensary

A dispensary was established in Maghera in 1827. It is supported by subscriptions and a grant from the county, each party paying one half. It includes the parishes of Maghera, Kilcronaghan, Termoneeny, Killelagh and part of Desertoghill.

Poor Shop

Every Tuesday is opened a poor shop, by which the poorer classes procure clothing, blankets, flax seed etc., which are paid up by 12 weekly instalments. This charitable institution was established in 1825 and is now managed by the ladies of the town. It is supported by local subscriptions. The parishes of Maghera, Kilcronaghan, Termoneeny and Killelagh have the benefit of this institution.

Book Depository

The Association for Discountenancing Vice have established in this town a depository for the sale of their bibles, testaments etc.

MODERN TOPOGRAPHY

School

The principal school in the parish is in the town of Maghera. It is built on glebe land, an acre of which has been alienated by deed by the present incumbent for the purpose of education. Its erection cost 400 pounds, which sum was raised as follows: grant from the Kildare Street Society 100 pounds, from the Mercers' Company 125 pounds, local subscriptions 175 pounds. It can accommodate 100 of each sex; the general attendance is 80 boys and 50 girls.

Village: Swatragh

The village of Swatragh is in the townland of the same name. It is a straggling place, but commencing to improve. In the year 1831 the Mercers' Company opened a dispensary which they support entirely themselves. The Kildare Street Society contributed principally to the erection of a very good schoolhouse in 1826 in this village. It cost 130 pounds and can accommodate 100 pupils; the average attendance is 60. A private school for girls was opened here in 1832. It is very successful, 50 attend regularly.

Public Buildings: Church

A plain church was built in 1820 on the road to Castledawson, close to the end of the town of Maghera, the ancient church being allowed to fall to ruins. It cost 1,600 pounds, which sum was advanced by the Board of First Fruits, to be paid by yearly instalments levied on the parish. It accomodates 500 individuals, but were the seats better disposed for that purpose, it could accommodate many more.

Presbyterian Meeting Houses

There are 3 Presbyterian meeting houses in the parish: one in Maghera, one in Swatragh, the third in Culnady. The first is a plain but extensive house capable of accommodating about 1,000 people. The exact date of its erection cannot be ascertained, as all documents relating to it were burned in the year 1798, when the house was occupied as a barrack. It is supposed, however, to have been built about the year 1780. It cost 800 pounds, raised by subscription.

The meeting house in Swatragh is small but very well finished. It was raised in 1830. It has cost altogether 300 pounds, raised by subscription, but to which the Mercers' Company contributed largely. The house accommodates 250 people.

The Culnady meeting house was built in 1804 by subscription; its exact cost cannot be ascertained. It is a little larger than Swatragh meeting house, but in bad repair.

Roman Catholic Chapels

There are 2 Roman Catholic chapels in the parish of Maghera: one in the townland of Fallagloon, the other in the townland of Moyagall. The first, however, is the best and most deserving of notice. It is built close to the road to Dungiven and stands almost due north and south. Its erection was commenced in 1825 and completed in 1827 at a cost of about 1,000 pounds, which sum was raised by subscription. The inside of the building is 110 feet long by 40 broad and a third part of it is galleried, which portion of the house is alone divided into seats. 4,000 people can be accommodated in it without difficulty, from the circumstance of the floor of the building not being divided into seats. The altar is to the west. Under it a very good room has been made to be used as a sacristy. There is a bell at the southern gable.

The Moyagall chapel was built in 1796 at the cost of 350 pounds, raised by subscription. It has no seats and, being galleried, may accommodate 1,500 people.

Schools

I have already mentioned 2 schools in connection with the Kildare Street Society; there is a third in Fallagloon which is not well attended.

There is a school in Curran, under the National Board of Education, which is not well attended.

Under the Hibernian Society there are 10 schools: viz. 1 in Curran, 2 in Drumlamph, 1 in Drumard, 1 in Drumuck, 1 in Moyagall, 1 in Dreenan, 1 in Tirgarvil, 1 in Craigmore in the town of Maghera and, lastly, 1 in Gorteade.

There are also several other schools kept by private teachers, but not of any note.

Gentlemen's Seats: Glebe House

The Glebe House of the Reverend Spencer Knox, rector of the parish, is adjacent to the town of Maghera. The house is simple but large and commodious. It was built in 1824. The Board of First Fruits advanced 1,500 pounds, which sum was to be paid in yearly instalments. More money was required for the completing of the building and it was given by the incumbent. The ornamental grounds are small and the planting, with the exception of a few fine trees, is young. But the grounds are tastefully laid out and kept in very good order. There is a good walled garden of about 1 acre and 1 rood.

Bleach Greens, Manufactories and Mills

There is only one bleach green in the parish, the property of Mr Alexander Clark of Upperlands. It is not extensive and comprehends 1 wash mill and 2 beetling engines. The wheels are all breast wheels; that which belongs to the wash mill is 14 feet by 5 feet 4 inches. Of the beetling engines one has a wheel 16 feet by 5, the other 19 feet by 4 feet 6 inches.

In the town of Maghera is a large brewery belonging to Mr Clark, also a grain store.

There are many mills in this parish. I shall enumerate them, stating first that they have all breast wheels viz. in Swatragh 1 corn mill, belongs to Mr Alexander Clark, wheel 14 feet by 2 and a half feet; in Craigadick 1 corn mill, belongs to Mr Clark; in Culnady 2 flax mills and 1 corn mill; in Crew 1 flax mill; in Fingarvil 1 corn mill; in Curragh 1 corn mill; in Upperlands 1 tuck mill; in Macknagh 1 flax mill. The diameter of the wheels belonging to these mills varies from 11 to 14 feet, their breadths from 2 to 3 feet.

Communications

The high road from Belfast and Antrim by Toome Bridge through Dungiven to Londonderry passes through the town of Maghera, as also the direct road from Dublin to Coleraine, west of Lough Neagh, which traverses the parish. They are both in good repair.

The first, from Belfast to Londonderry, was made and is kept in repair by the county; its breadth is 21 feet. The latter being now a mail coach line, the county propose <purpose> by degrees to bring to a breadth of 30 feet; they have already done so in some parts of it. This is much required, as in some places it is not even 20 feet wide.

The bridge over the Moyola <Mayola> near Fort William (an old one) is not more than 15 feet wide. The laying out of this road might also be very much improved by avoiding the hills.

The by-roads are generally in bad order. They also are repaired at the expense of the county, except those that are quite private.

Fair Sheets by Thomas Fagan, November 1836 to January 1837

ANCIENT TOPOGRAPHY

Standing Stones

In Drumconready and holding of Patrick Kerr, and on an eminence within a few yards of the Moyola, there stands 2 ancient standing stones locally called the Stuekan Stones, one of which stands upright, 4 feet above the surface, 3 and a half feet broad and 2 and a half feet thick. The other is in a reclining position, supported partly on the top of the upright column. This reclining stone is 6 feet long, 5 feet broad and 3 feet thick. It is the opinion of some of the local inhabitants that these stones were originally designed for a druid's altar.

Ancient Coin and Discoveries in Drumconready

In the above townland, and holding of Charles McKenna, there was discovered in 1811, in the arm or crevice <crevis> of a fir block that stood 6 feet beneath the surface of a bog, 4 pieces of ancient silver coin. They were of different sizes but of good substance. The largest of them was the size of a modern half-crown and the smallest the size of a shilling. They were secreted in the block by a stone that filled or closed the crevice outside, but, on being removed by the cutting of the block, the coin fell out. There was a double row of letters on each coin, together with a cross and bust <burst>, but the substance of the document or date of coinage could not be judged, though inspected by good scholars. This coin was sold in 1816 to a coiner of base money that passed through the neighbourhood.

There was found in the same place an ancient iron hatchet approaching to modern shape, also a row of sharp pointed stakes. The hatchet stands at present in the above McKenna's house. Informants Charless McKenna Junior and Senior and others. 18 November 1836.

Ancient Quern and Stone Sledge

There is at present in Drumconready, and dwelling house of Charles McKenna, 2 ancient quern <querin> stones found at some depth beneath the surface of a clay field in the above townland in the 17th century. They are 1 and a half foot in diameter each, but in all other particulars resemble others before described.

There was also found in the above townland, and above 100 years ago, under the surface a stone sledge shaped thus: [outline drawing and section]. On its flat and beneath on its side, it embraces the handle similar to a modern iron sledge or hammer. The black lines inside represents devices cut on its surface. The blank in the under draft embraced the handle. It is at present broken in the middle of the holes. Informants Charles McKenna and others. 23rd November 1836.

Ancient Name of Maghera

The ancient name of Maghera was Maghera Entrah, though subsequently changed to Maghera. The ancient name occurred under the following circumstances: at a former period there was a monastery in the neighbourhood of the ancient church and a second one on an eminence that stands at some distance from the church, which eminence is locally called Mullagh. That tract of ground now occupied by the Rev. Mr Knox's house and farm intervened between the 2 institutions and was allotted to the students for their morning and evening walk. It was in consequence called in the Irish language Maghera Entrah which means "the plain of seasons" or "certain hours of the day."

Lofty Eminence: Sie Fionn

That lofty eminence in the parish of Killelagh locally called Sie Fionn or "Fionn MaCuil's sitting place", got that name in consequence of being a site selected by the above chief [insert superscript: Balisarus ?] to sit on while on a hunting excursion in that neighbourhood, and from which eminence he had a full view of the hunt in the surrounding valleys. Informants Patrick Devlin and Charles McKenna.

Ancient Halbert and Old Butter

Paul McKenna of Brackaghgrilly, in making a fence in his holding in the above townland in 1831, got about 2 feet beneath the surface a brass battleaxe, the sides of which is neatly carved on the surface. It has been subsequently purchased by the Rev. Mr Knox of Maghera at 2s 6d.

There was found beneath the surface in the above townland in 1832 a large quantity of old butter contained in the bark of a tree. The bark was completely decayed, but the butter was found useful for various purposes.

Parish of Maghera

Axes

Francis Donnelly of Kirley, in cutting turf in the last-mentioned townland in 1832, got about 4 feet beneath the surface of the bog a brass halbert 6 inches in length and embracing the handles similar to a modern halbert. It was subsequently sold to a tinker.

There was found in the same bog an ancient iron pickaxe of very odd construction, and supposed to have been originally designed for raising iron mine, when the iron forges was in process of working in the neighbourhood.

Old Butter in Kirley

There was also found 4 feet beneath the surface of a bog in the above townland a quantity of old butter in the bark of a tree. Informants Paull McKenna, Francis Donnelly and others. 24th November 1836.

Ancient Cave

In Brackaghgrilly, within about 150 yards of the Danish fort in the holding of Henry O'Neill, there was discovered in 1832 at some depth beneath the surface a cave 16 feet long by 7 feet wide and about 4 feet high in the interior. It was constructed on an oak frame and floored with long flat planks of oak. It is not known what the roof was composed of, as it had fallen in before the cave was discovered. There is one of the oak beams occupied in the frame, and one of the planks used in the floor, at present at Henry O'Neill's in the above townland. The beam is 16 and a half feet long by 10 inches broad and 8 inches thick, and perfectly sound. The cave is now destroyed and the remainder of the timber occupied in its construction converted to other uses.

Ancient Battleaxe and Stone Hatchet

The annexed <annext> draft [drawing] represents the size and shape of a brass battleaxe found beneath the surface in Fallagloon at some former period, and now in the possession of Henery O'Neill of Brackaghgrilly. The blank embraced the handle.

The annexed draft [drawing] represents a stone hatchet locally called a thunderbolt. It was found beneath the surface in the above townland and is in Mr O'Neill's at present. Informants Henery O'Neill, Hugh McKenna and others. 25th November 1836.

Whinstone Font and Tradition

In Brackaghgrilly, and at Henery O'Neill's, there stands a whinstone 3 feet 8 inches long, 2 feet 2 inches broad and 1 and a half foot thick. There are 2 holes cut in it, one of which is oval, 15 by 12 inches and 10 inches in depth; the other is circular, 11 inches in diameter and 8 inches in depth. This stone was discovered at some former period at the roots of an ancient and extraordinary large yew tree that stood in the centre of a fort or ancient enclosure that stood in the above townland and farm of the above O'Neill. Catholic worship was performed beneath the shading branches of the above yew tree for a series <serious> of years, and the above stone is supposed to have been there employed for religious rites; the largest of the holes in it supposed to have been a font to contain holy water and the smaller hole a baptismal font. The stone is of a very hard quality, though the cutting of the holes are well executed.

It is likewise locally said that the ancient church of Maghera was originally commenced to be built in the above townland and neighbourhood of the aforesaid yew tree, but that at the request of the then neighbouring clergy of Killelagh and Mullagh, Maghera was subsequently selected as a more befitting site, as by such arrangements the 3 churches would stand within a short distance of each other and the clergy of the different places be able to assist each other in their spiritual duties. Informants Hugh McKenna, Henery O'Neill and others. 26th November 1836.

Copper Pan

James McKenna, in sinking a hill or some obstruction to a line of road in Tamnymullen in 1826, got about 3 feet beneath the surface an ancient copper pan, circular shape, about 12 inches in diameter and 14 inches in depth, and ornamented on the entire surface with the impressions of a small-faced hammer. It was bound near the mouth with an iron hoop which was corroded by rust and fell off as soon as the pan was removed, though the pan was perfectly sound and bright when cleaned. The Rev. Mr Knox of Maghera has subsequently procured the pan and has it in his cabinet.

Ancient Butter Stand

John Logue of Cragmore, in cutting turf in the above townland in 1820, got about 8 feet beneath the surface of the bog an ancient oval vessel 15 by 12 inches and about 2 inches in depth. It was supported on 3 feet, about 2 inches long each. The vessel was supposed to have been turned out of a solid piece of timber and to have been originally designed for a butter stand. After being removed and for some time exposed to the wind and heat of the sun, this vessel fell into small pieces. Informants John Logue and others. 29th November 1836.

Ancient Graves and Urns of Bones

Hugh Cassidy of Cragadick, in reclaiming the remains of scrag and ancient enclosures in that subdivision of the above townland locally called Silver hill, got in 1835 about 2 feet beneath the surface an ancient grave about 5 feet long, 2 and a half feet broad and 2 feet deep. It was floored, enclosed and roofed by long flat stones. In it was deposited small earthen pans containing calcined bones and ashes. The pans mouldered down by being removed from their original berth. The grave was subsequently destroyed and the stones converted to other uses.

Several graves of a similar description have been found beneath the surface of the above hill at different periods preceding the above date, all of which contained urns of bones. All these discoveries beneath the surface of the above hill induce the local inhabitants to believe that it was a Danish or heathen burial ground.

Derivation of Silver Hill

There was found beneath the surface of the above hill at different periods several pieces of ancient silver coin, also a small pan of gold. From these deposits being found beneath the surface of the eminence the local inhabitants have subsequently called it Silver hill. Informants John and Joseph McPeake and others. 30th November 1836.

Grillagh Abbey

Local tradition says that there was an ancient abbey in the townland of Grillagh, which was founded by the O'Crillys, subsequently dedicated to their name and called in the Irish language Munnisther-na-Crillagh, which name the townland gets in the Irish language by the old Irish residents to the present period. Clergy of the above name and stock is said to be very numerous in the above and neighbouring parishes at a former period, so much so that they are not only said to be the founders of Grillagh abbey but also of Tamlaght O'Crilly old church and abbey, and that they constituted the majority of the clergy of both institutions. Informants Henery McGuiggen and John O'Crilly.

Maghera Ancient Church

Tradition in the mountainous parts of the above parish says that Maghera ancient church was

Door lintel of Maghera old church

Parish of Maghera

founded, together with an ancient abbey that formerly stood in its neighbourhood, by St Columkille. This tradition is corroborated by the oldest and most respectable inhabitants in Ballynascreen <Ballinascreen>, though the more immediate residents of the town of Maghera would give St Laurence O'Quin or Bradley the credit of founding these institutions.

But tradition in the town of Maghera differs in a great measure regarding the church and abbey, for some assert on tradition that St Laurence was abbot in Maghera in the 12th century, and that about that period he caused that ancient spring well which is the chief support of the town in a miraculous manner to force or gush from the surface, as a great scarcity of water at that time prevailed in the town of Maghera, which obliged the inhabitants to solicit the saint's intercession in their behalf. However, the well is dedicated to his name and called in the Irish language Tobbar-nieve-Lourass or "St Laurence's well." But there is no local tradition to dedicate the church or abbey to his name, or call them St Laurence's church or abbey in the English or Irish language, but the supposed date of the church being built and the supposed period of the saint's governing. They differ to a great extent, as the former is supposed to have been built some time about the latter part of the fifth century. Besides, it will be found elsewhere mentioned as one of 9 churches dedicated to St Columkille as being founded by him in the above county and a portion [of] Tyrone.

On the right side of the door opening into the body of the church is in cut stone an image representing a bishop in full robes and wearing a mitre. It is not certain which of the above saints it represents. Also on cut stone on the north side of the tower, and at several feet in height above the door, stands 2 heads or faces, but one of them greatly destroyed. Informants John and Henery, Hugh and Patrick McKenna and others. 1st December 1836.

Old Butter

James Maloy, in cutting turf in Culnagrew in 1833, got 12 feet beneath the surface of the bog a cask of ancient butter. The vessel approached to the shape of a modern firkin <firken> but rudely constructed out of a solid piece of timber, but so decayed when found that it mouldered down and was cast into the remains of the bog. The butter was also rendered useless by time. All was found at the root of a block of wood. The lid of the cask stands at present in Widow Quin's in the above townland.

Brussell's Well

In the neighbourhood of the ancient standing stones which stand in Hugh O'Kane's garden in the village of Swatragh, there was an ancient spring well enclosed by stone columns. At some former period a woman washed some dirty clothes in it, which caused the spring to dry up in that place and start about 26 yards distance from it, in the same garden, and where it at present stands. It is locally called Brussell's Well.

Brass Battleaxe and Petrified Shell

Robert Courtnay, in cutting turf in the townland of Craigmore in 1832, got about 2 feet beneath the surface of the bog an ancient brass battleaxe of rare construction and in good preservation when found. It was subsequently procured by the Rev. Mr Knox of Maghera, in whose cabinet it at present stands.

There was also found in the same townland a petrified shell encrusted with flint on one side. Also in the same place 2 ancient querns similar in shape to others described. Informants James Maloy, Robert Courtnay and others. 5th December 1836.

Urn of Bones

Hugh Kenedy, in labouring in his holding in the townland of Swatragh in 1831, got about 1 and a half foot beneath the surface a circular stone building, in which was deposited an ancient earthen urn containing a quantity of calcined bones and ashes. It was covered on the mouth with a flat stone. The vessel was very thick but rudely constructed, and so decayed when found that it mouldered down on being removed from its original berth.

Old Butter

Ritchard Roe, in labouring the remains of a bog in Knockoneill in 1832, got beneath its surface a large quantity of old butter contained in a vessel rudely constructed out of a solid piece of timber, but in such a state of decay when found that it fell in pieces off the butter, though the butter was found useful for various purposes.

Ancient Carn and Buildings in Knockoneill

In the last-mentioned townland, and holding of Creighton Hutchenson, there stands the ruins of a very large carn of stones supposed to stand over a number of ancient graves. Also on the same site the ruins of large number of small houses, chiefly built of stones and supposed to have been Danish habitations; also the ruins of several Danish fences. On the same site stands, above the surface, a large number of whinstones seeming to stand at the heads of graves. The site altogether appears to the local inhabitants to have been a Danish burial ground, as well as their habitations. Informants Patrick Bradley, John O'Crilly and others. 6th December 1836.

Giant's Graves and Ancient Castle

In Knockoneill and holding of Creighton Hutchenson, and on an eminence in a secluded part of the mountain, there stands an enclosure about 90 by 85 feet. The fence is a stone wall; seems to be of ancient standing and varies in height from 3 and a half to 5 feet, and in breadth at the base from 3 to 5 feet. In the interior stands the ruins of a number of ancient graves varying in length and enclosed by large stones varying in height above the surface from 1 to 4 feet. These graves were canopied with stones of extraordinary size, many of which lie in and about the graves, and several others have been carried away to arch bridges. The ruins of these graves in all other particulars resemble giant's graves before described.

In the neighbourhood of the above enclosure it is locally said that there stood an ancient castle, the foundation of which has been raised at some former period and found to be as permanently built as any ancient castle or church known within this county. The walls were above 5 feet wide. Tradition also says that one of the above graves was explored by a Henery Kelly at some former period and that he discovered in it a sword and some other articles, but Kelly and family are now extinct and no account of what has become of the sword. Information obtained from Patt Bradley, Henery McGuiggen, Michael O'Crilly and others. 7th December 1836.

Derivation of Knockoneill and Slaughtneil

Local tradition says that Knockoneill got its name from a chief or petty prince called Neil McLoughlin, whose remains occupies one of the graves described [above] and who is said to be the first and principal buried in the enclosure, after which the hill on which the graves stands was dedicated to his name and called Knock Neil, but subsequently called Knockoneill. It is likewise said that the townland in Killelagh called Slaughtneil got its name from the above prince having been killed there under the following circumstances: that he and a neighbouring prince of the O'Neills were eternally at war with each other, but McLoughlin, in the course of these broils, became more popular than O'Neill and got more subjects to join in his cause, the result of which was that at a pitched battle he defeated and killed O'Neill and the greater part of his forces and banished the remainder of that illustrious family from their family residence and estates.

However, that in the course of some after years a son of the deceased <disceased> O'Neill, who was reared with his uncle in some part of the county Antrim, when arriving at maturity wished revenge for the murder of his father, mustered together a strong body of men and gave the above McLoughlin battle in the aforesaid Slaught Neil, where he killed McLoughlin and the greater part of his forces and put the remainder to flight, after which there was a monument raised on the spot where he was killed, which was dedicated to his name and called Slaught Neil and subsequently gave name to that townland. And that after the aforesaid monument was raised on the scene of action or murder of the aforesaid McLoughlin, that his remains was carried to the aforesaid Knockoneill and there interred with the bodies of some of his chief officers who fell in his cause. However, the killing of McLoughlin in the one townland and his being interred in the other gave name to both. Information obtained from Henery McGuiggen, Patrick Bradley, Michael O'Crilly and others. 8th December 1836.

Singular Occurrence

About 20 years ago a cow calved a calf in the townland of Beagh Spiritual that had 2 heads, 7 feet and 2 tails. The cow and calf died shortly after she calved. Informant John Slamon.

Ancient Grave

In Swatragh, and on an eminence in the holding of John Kenney, there stands a stone supposed to rest over a grave. It measures 7 feet in length, 5 feet in breadth and 4 and a half feet in thickness. Beneath it stands a long flat stone resembling a tombstone, on one end of which the above stone rests solid and the other end raised about 5 inches above the tombstone by 2 small stones evidently placed in that position by art. This stone and about it is said to have been gentle and often illuminated by night.

Human Skeleton

In making a line of by-road in Culnagrew in 1833, there was found about 3 feet beneath the surface

Parish of Maghera

the skeleton <skelleton> of a human body and beside it a small Danish pot. The skeleton was again buried on the site where found but the pot was corroded by rust. Informants John Kenny and John Slamon. 9th December 1836.

Ancient Halbert, Ancient Coin and Bones

Francis O'Kane, in cutting turf in the townland of Keady in 1828, got beneath its surface a brass halbert resembling ancient halberts. Already procured for the survey, it has a socket to embrace the handle and was in good preservation when found. It is still preserved by the above O'Kane for a friend.

James O'Crilly, in labouring in the above townland in 1826, got beneath the surface a piece of ancient silver coin about the size of a modern shilling, with a large head on one side of it and a cross on the other. There was also some inscription in very large letters, but could not be read by any persons who inspected it. This coin has been subsequently procured by the Rev. Corneilous O'Kane of Derry.

Edward Mallon, in labouring in the above townland in 1836, got about 3 feet beneath the suface a quantity of calcined bones contained in a stone building and covered on the top by a large stone.

Stone Columns and Ancient Carn

At arranged distances from the ancient standing stone in Culnagrew, in a western direction and in the holding of Andrew Slamons, there stands 2 ancient stone columns, one of which stands 4 feet high, 3 and a half feet broad and 2 feet thick. The second stands 2 and a half feet high, 2 and a half feet broad and 1 and a half feet thick. On the same line with these columns stands an ancient carn of stones, all which are locally believed to have belonged to the above standing stone and other stone buildings in its neighbourhood. Informants Patrick McAtamney and others.

Ancient Urn

Patrick Slamons, in demolishing an ancient carn of stones in his holding in the townland of Culnagrew in 1816, got beneath its ruins a grave 6 feet long and 2 feet wide. It was enclosed with flat stones and roofed with the same. It contained an earthen urn, in which was only some black ashes. The urn was in a tolerable state of preservation when found and remained in Slamons's house for some after years, but at length crumbled down. Information obtained from John Slamons and others.

Priest's Field and Old Abbey

In Craigmore, and holding of Alexander Heaslett, and stands as an angle into the townland of Grillagh, a field. It is called the Priest's Field, in consequence of a dispute that occurred between the landholders of both townlands at some former period, and in which dispute a priest interfered to settle the affair between the parties, but the result was that the priest was killed in the affray. Since that period the field is called the Priest's Field, but the cause of the dispute was which of the above 2 townlands should have the field.

It is likewise said that the above occurrence took place at the period that the old abbey stood in Grillagh. It is likewise said that the ancient name of Grillagh was Abbey Crilly or otherwise Ministher-na-Crillagh, and that such was the name inserted in all the old leases given of holdings in the townland. Information obtained from Robert Courtnay, one of the old lessees <leasees>. 10th December 1836.

Steel Coat

James Donnelly, in cutting turf in the townland of Tirnageeragh about 30 years ago, got beneath its surface a steel coat composed of small links or rings, much resembling those of a steel purse but of larger size. It was in full shape when found, but corroded to a mere skeleton by time and rust. It remained in the family for some subsequent years but was at length cut up in small pieces and taken away by Donnelly's neighbouring friends.

Old Butter and other Discoveries

There have been several articles of old butter got beneath the surface of the bogs of Drummuck and Dunglady, in cutting turf from time to time. Some of the butter was found in rudely constructed wooden vessels and more in earthen crocks. There have been also rows of sharp-pointed stakes got in the same bogs. Information obtained from Thomas Drips and others, 17th December 1836.

Ancient Dirk

John O'Connor, in labouring in the townland of Culnady in 1831, got beneath the surface an ancient steel dirk about 14 inches in length but greatly decayed by time and rust. It has been subsequently destroyed.

Ancient Meddar

Robert Drips of Culnady has in his house at present a meddar <madder> with 4 handles and carved or ornamented on the surface. It would hold about 1 British quart and is in a tolerable state of preservation.

Discoveries in Dunglady Fort

Hugh O'Connor, in labouring the interior of Dunglady Fort at some former period, found beneath its surface an eight-square beadstone, beautifully ornamented on the surface and about the size of a large nut. It has been subsequently lost by the family.

It is likewise said that the interior of the above fort was formerly occupied as a burial ground and that in labouring it at a former period many headstones were removed out of it.

Urn of Bones

In Ballymachileer, and holding of Willim Fleming, there was discovered beneath the surface at some former period an ancient earthen urn containing a quantity of calcined bones and ashes. The urn crumbled down shortly after being removed. Information obtained from John O'Connor, Hugh O'Connor and others.

Crock of Flints and Urn of Ashes

James Patterson Junior of Beagh Spiritual, in labouring in his holding in 1829, got about 2 and a half feet beneath the surface a small earthen crock containing about one quart of flints of various sizes and shapes. The crock was decayed when found and the flints subsequently destroyed.

James Patterson Senior of the above townland got beneath the surface in his holding at some former period an ancient earthen urn containing a quantity of ashes. It was covered on the mouth by a flat stone. The urn has subsequently crumbled down.

Ancient Coins and Instrument

Walter Grimes of Curragh got several pieces of ancient silver and copper coin beneath the surface of new land in his holding in 1831, one of which stands in his house at present, but greatly disfigured. They were supposed to have been coined in the reign of Queen Anne.

Peter Watt of Slaughtybogy got several pieces of ancient silver coin beneath the surface of a fort in his holding in 1832. These coins have been subsequently sold.

John McWilliams of the last-mentioned townland has in his house at present a three-pronged instrument, supposed to have been used in war, and found beneath the surface of a fort in his farm in 1826. Each of the prongs is about 6 inches in length. It is at present covered in a turf house. It embraced the handles through a socket. Informants Walter Grimes, John McWilliams and others. 19th December 1836.

Brass Halbert

The brass halbert now procured for the survey was found beneath the surface of a bog in the townland of Slaughtybogy by Walter Grimes in 1833.

Ancient Columns

In Fallagloon mountain, and holding of John McKenna and others, there stands a stone column 4 feet in height above the surface, 2 and a half feet in breadth and 1 foot in thickness. Within a few feet of it stands or rather lies 2 other columns that seems to have been standing at some former period, as they are on a range with the former. One of these stones is 5 feet long and 2 feet broad. The other is 4 feet long and 2 feet broad. Also, in its immediate neighbourhood stands several smaller columns varying in height above the surface from 1 to 2 and a half feet. These small columns stands at arranged distances one from the other and seems to have formed some irregular enclosure, though now in ruins and stands on the remains of a bog about 4 feet beneath the original surface, the cutting of which bog exposed the building to view. 20th December 1836.

Old Butter and Ancient Coin

Beneath the surface of a bog in Drumlamph in 1836 there was found an ancient meddar containing a quantity of old butter. The vessel was destroyed by the turf spade in raising it.

There was discovered, in sinking the foundations of a house in the above townland on the remains of an old wood in 1815, a quantity of ancient silver coin of various sizes; but the date of coinage could not be judged. The coin has been subsequently sold.

Ancient Meddar, Gold Coin and Wooden Halbert

Hugh Conery, in cutting turf in Rocktown at some former period, got beneath the surface a four-square vessel resembling a meddar. It was made

Parish of Maghera

of some kind of metal and stood on 3 feet, and covered with a lid. It was ornamented on the surface and contained a quantity of old butter when found, but it was reduced to a mere skeleton by time and rust, and has subsequently fallen to pieces.

James Mallon, in labouring in the last-mentioned townland in 1820, got beneath the surface an ancient gold coin said to have been coined in Queen Anne's reign. It was greatly decayed by time and has been subsequently lost.

Roger Conery, in reclaiming new land in the last-mentioned townland in 1821, got about 2 feet beneath the surface a wooden instrument about 2 feet in length and shaped like a halbert, with a gutter sunk in each side of it. It was sharp or rather thin in the point and sides. It was since destroyed. Informants James Mallon, John Hughes and others. 1st December 1836.

Ancient Querns

2 quern-stones, one of which the annexed draft [drawing] represents, was found about 1 foot beneath the surface of the remains of a bog in the townland of Drumlamph in 1832 by John Donnelly, on whose house they stand at present. The one represented above is the top one which stands in diameter 11 inches. The hole in the centre received the corn and stands 3 inches in diameter. The smaller holes seem to have embraced the handles by which it was wrought and the gutters leading from the centre hole to them are ornaments.

Cross and Ancient Coin

This cross [drawing] was found beneath the surface in Rocktown and is at present in James O'Neill's in the last-mentioned townland. The figure of the cross is sunk in a piece of stone slate of the above size and shape.

Bernard Mulholland of the last-mentioned townland got beneath the surface in his holding in 1826 an ancient silver coin, which he has subsequently sold to Mr Adams, watchmaker in Magherafelt, at 7s 6d. Informants John Donnelly, James O'Neill and others.

Ancient Quern

Alexander Downey of Drumard has in his house at present an ancient pair of quern-stones of very rare construction, and found beneath the surface of the remains of bog and near to an old spring well in the above townland in 1832. The lier is circular shape, 14 inches in diameter from out to out and stands 7 inches high, supported on 3 feet about 1 inch in height each. There is a rim round the top, inside of which the runner works. Inside the rim is 10 inches in diameter, with a small hole in one side to let the meal fall through. The runner is 9 inches in diameter, with a circular hole in centre, 3 inches in diameter, for receiving the corn. There is a smaller hole on one side to receive the handle by which it was wrought. The entire is well constructed and in a perfect state of preservation at present.

Ancient Burial Ground

There is a small island in the flow bog intervening between Drumard and Ballymcpeake, which island has been occupied by burials of young children for centuries back. The ruins of some of the graves still appear above the surface.

Brass Hatchet

James Bradley of Gulladuff got beneath the surface in 1831 an ancient brass hatchet resembling a butcher's meat hatchet. It has been subsequently given to a locksmith. Informants James Bradley, Owen McPeake and others. 22nd December 1836.

Arrowhead

The annexed draft [drawing] represents the size and shape of an elf <elve> stone or flint arrowhead found beneath the surface in Gulladuff, and is kept for curing cow cattle.

Ancient Iron Axe

The annexed draft [drawings] represents on the flat and on the side an ancient axe found under the surface 6 feet in Rocktown in 1835 by John McPeake, in whose house it stands at present in the townland of Drumard. The blank embraced the handle.

Arrowheads, Stone Hatchet and Ancient Axe

The drafts [drawings] represent 4 flint arrowheads and a stone hatchet locally called a thunderbolt, all found in Drumard beneath the surface. Informants Owen and John McPeake, from whom they are procured.

The above drafts [view and sections of axe] represents, on its flat and on its side, the size and shape of an ancient iron axe found beneath the surface in Drumard in 1830. The blank embraced the handles. It stands at present in James O'Neill's in the above townland. The 3 arrowheads and 5 stone hatchets this day procured was found beneath the surface in Drumard. Informants Owen and John McPeake.

Discoveries in Ballymcpeake

The annexed drafts [drawings] represents 3 flint arrowheads found beneath the surface in Ballymcpeake and are preserved at present by Patrick Keenan of the above townland, for curing cow cattle, for which purpose they are frequently used.

Thomas Keenan, in labouring in the above townland at some former period, got beneath the surface a quantity of ancient silver coin. The date of coinage could not be judged by any persons who saw it. It has been subsequently destroyed.

Patrick Keenan, in labouring in the above townland about 30 years ago, got beneath the surface 6 pieces of silver coin said to have been coined in the reign of Queen Anne. They have been subsequently given away to friends for pocket pieces.

John Mulholland, in cutting turf in the above townland in 1831, got beneath the surface of the bog an ancient meddar containg a quantity of old butter. The vessel was decayed when found and has subsequently fallen down.

In the same bogs there have been found from time to time in cutting turf several articles of old butter, some in wooden vessels and some in earthen vessels, also fire irons and rows of sharp pointed stakes. Informants Thomas and Patrick Keenan and others. 23rd December 1836.

James Keenan, in demolishing an ancient carn of stones in his holding in Ballymcpeake at some former period, got beneath its ruins an ancient urn containing a quantity of calcined bones and ashes. It was deposited in a circular stone building and covered on the mouth with a flat stone.

There was found in the neighbourhood of the above ancient carn a human skeleton at some depth beneath the surface. It was again buried on the site where it was found.

James Keenan, in labouring in the above townland about 20 years ago, got beneath the surface an ancient brass halbert about 15 inches in length and embraced the handle by a long tang, in which there was 3 holes for nails to fasten it on the handle. It has been purloined by some person unknown. Informants James and John Keenan and others.

Brass Halbert and Ancient Coins

The annexed draft [drawing] represents a brass halbert found about 1 foot beneath the surface in 1836 in Dreenan by Bernard O'Neill, in whose house it stands at present in the above townland.

Michael Denin of Dreenan, in labouring in his holding in the above townland in 1835, got about 1 foot beneath the surface 2 small pieces of ancient silver coin. They had on some document that could not be read by any who inspected them, as it was done in a language foreign to this country language. These coins have been subsequently destroyed.

Ancient Pike and Weapon

John Riddles of Drummuck, in demolishing an ancient carn of stones in his holding in 1832, got beneath its surface an ancient pike about 18 inches in length and raised along in the centre similar to a bayonet <baynot>, and having on a screwed tang to fasten it in the handle. He is said to preserve it for his own use.

Hugh Henery of the above townland, a whitesmith, got beneath the surface in his holding an ancient instrument of defence about 13 inches in length, with one side sharp, and handle attached to it 6 inches in length. It resembled those ancient weapons locally called skien fadtha or a "long fighting knife." He has subsequently made it into small knives. Informants Hugh Henery, Michael Denin and others. 24th December 1836.

Ancient Grave and Querns

On a small eminence in the townland of Dreenan, and holding of Stafford McCan, there stands an ancient grave composed of earth and stones and locally called a giant's grave. It is 12 feet long, 3 feet broad and about 6 inches above the surface, with a quantity of stones and a haw bush at one end of it. It was never explored.

In the neighbourhood of the above grave there was found beneath the surface at some former period 3 sets of quern-stones, some of which still remain in the townland and are similar to others before described.

Ancient Burial Ground and Querns

In making a new line of road through that part of Fallagloon now held by Widow Anderson about 48 years ago, there was discovered beneath the surface several coffin boards, skulls and other human bones, all which have been subsequently buried deeper on the same site where found.

There was found beneath the surface of the above site at the above period several quern-stones and forge dross. The querns were similar to others before described.

Parish of Maghera

Ancient Brass Ring

Hugh Cassidy, in raising an ancient grave in Craigadick in 1836, he found deposited along with earthen crocks that contained calcined bones and ashes, a small brass ring about 1 inch in diameter but greatly corroded by time and rust when found. It has been lost within the last few days.

Tooth of Large Size

In exploring one of the ancient graves in Knockoneill at some former period, there was discovered in it, together with a sword and some small bones, a tooth of more than ordinary size, which tooth has been preserved by John Maguiggin in Maghera many years for the inspection of the curious, many of whom report it to be the largest human tooth ever seen in this part of the country. It has been lost within the last few months.

Yew Tree

In Fallagloon, and holding of James McKenna, there stands a large yew tree said to be one of the oldest in the above county, though it is tolerably sound. Informants Hugh McKenna, Hugh Cassidy and others. 26th December 1836.

Brass Halbert and Old Butter

The annexed draft [drawing] represents the size and shape of a brass halbert found about 4 feet beneath the surface of a bog in the townland of Toberhead in 1826. It embraced the handles through a socket, as will be seen by the original. Informant Robert Sturgeon.

There was also found beneath the surface of the above bog in 1832 and in 1836 2 articles of old butter contained in bark of trees. The bark was decayed when found, but the butter was found useful for various purposes. A specimen of that found in 1836 is now procured for inspection.

Metal Implement and Ancient Well in Toberhead

John Thompson, in reclaiming new land in the above townland in 1826, got about 2 feet beneath the surface an ancient metal implement approaching to the shape of a smoothing iron, but not conjectured by the local inhabitants to have been originally designed for pressing clothes, as it was very thin. There was a handle on the back of it. This article was subsequently lost by children.

In the above townland, and holding of William Ferrier, there stands an ancient spring well locally called Toberhead Well, and gave name to the townland. Informants John Thompson and James McNichol. 28th December 1836.

Meddar Manufacturer

About 70 years ago there was a meddar maker brought from a neighbouring district by the inhabitants of Toberhead, to make them a supply of meddars out of some old alder and birch that stood in the remains of an old wood in that townland. It was asserted by the above tradesman, who was by name Maguiggen, that all ancient meddars was made of the aforesaid timbers and that no other timber would answer for the purpose.

Brass Weapon

John Quigly of Gulladuff got beneath the surface of a bog in the last-mentioned townland about 1817 a brass weapon approaching to the shape of a dagger. It has been subsequently given to the Rev. Mr Knox of Maghera. Informants James McNichol and John Quigly.

Flint Arrowhead

This flint arrowhead [drawing] was found 9 feet beneath the surface of that bog intervening between Fallagloon and Falgortrevy in 1828.

Old Butter and Ancient Dishes

Manases McGlade of Brockagh Reily got a vessel of old butter about 60 lbs weight beneath the surface of new land in the last-mentioned townland in 1832. It was contained in the bark of a tree which was utterly decayed when found. There was also a linen cloth round the butter inside the bark. The butter has been subsequently sold to a chandler.

In the above bog there was several rudely constructed wooden dishes found, in shape approaching to a tea tray, but quite decayed when found and subsequently fell to pieces.

Brass Halbert

John Lagan of Lisnamuck got an ancient brass halbert about 4 feet beneath the surface of new land in the above townland in 1830. It embraced the handle through a socket similar to others already described. This halbert has been subsequently lost by children.

Ancient Coin and Stone Hatchet

Michael Conery got 6 pieces of ancient silver coin about 3 feet beneath the surface of new land in

Fallagloon in 1816. The coin differed in size and was very thin. The document on them was in foreign language and could not be read. They have been subsequently sold in Belfast. Informants Michael Conery, John Lagan and others. 29th December 1836.

The annexed draft [drawing] represents the size and shape of a stone hatchet locally called a thunderbolt, which was found 8 feet beneath the surface of a bog in Fallagloon.

Ancient Chamber

Charles Cosker of Kirley got a circular chamber about 2 feet in diameter and 1 foot in depth, 3 feet beneath the surface of new land in 1818. It was enclosed by a stone building and contained a quantity of timber cinders, and was covered on the top by 5 flat stones of large size. There was also found beside it an ancient quern similar to others before described.

Ancient Yew

Manus Bradley got 4 pieces of yew timber varying in length from 1 to 3 feet and dressed by an axe for some particular purpose. There is some of this timber at present in the above Bradley's house in Fallagloon and is in sound state, and was found 4 feet beneath the surface of bog. Informants Charles Cosker, Manus Bradley and others. 31st December 1836.

Stone Font

In Kirley and holding of John Morrin, and within a few feet of the by-road leading from Glen chapel to the Forge bridge, there stands a stone 6 and a half feet long and 4 feet broad. In the middle of it is cut a circular hole 12 inches in diameter and 5 inches in depth. The original use of this hole is not conjectured by the local inhabitants.

Lissavishaludhan Fort and Urns of Bones

That fort in Drumconready, and holding of Patrick McKenna, locally called Lissavishaludhan took its name from a deep glen of mossy surface beneath it on the verge of the Moyola river, which glen is often inundated by the floods in the river and destroy the growing crop on it for a considerable distance. The glen is a three-angled space of ground surrounded by hills. Tradition says from some ancient prophecy that all that will repair to this glen in the event of some future war or rebellion will be secure from the relentless arms of a determined enemy.

Beneath the surface of the field in which the above fort stands, and within a few yards of the fort, there was discovered at some former period several earthen urns containing calcined bones and ashes. These urns were deposited in circular stone buildings and covered with flat stones. There was also found in the bottom of an ancient spring that stands near the fort a small noggin turned out of a solid piece of wood. Informants Andrew and Patrick McKenna and others. 2nd January 1837.

Brass Halbert

John Doherty of Drumard discovered beneath the surface of a bog, and within 15 yards of a lough which stands in the above townland, a brass halbert 20 inches in length and had on 2 wings by which it could be suspended on a cord. It was corroded by rust to a great extent when found in 1830 and has been since destroyed.

Earthen Urn and Old Building

Edward Hughes of Rocktown was repeatedly told by an old woman who pretended foreknowledge, that there was a crock of money deposited beneath a large flat stone at the root of an ancient thorn in his holding. However, in 1836 he explored round the thorn and found beneath the aforesaid stone an earthen urn about 8 inches in diameter and 9 inches in depth, and ornamented round the top. If it contained anything at any period it was decayed at the above date. The crock was enclosed in a circular stone building beneath the aforesaid stone. It has been since broken, but a specimen of it is procured for the survey.

James O'Neill discovered 2 feet beneath the surface in the above townland in 1833 the ruins of some ancient building which contained a quantity of old iron articles of odd construction. They have been since destroyed in a forge. Informants John Doherty, Edward Hughes and others. 4th January 1837.

Discoveries in Drumard

John Farrel of Drumard, in exploring an ancient cave that stands in his holding, discovered in the extreme end of it in 1820 a brass article resembling a watch-case but much deeper, and a small tube attached to it as if designed for melting some description of metal. This article is mislaid in the house and may be found at a future period.

There was a human skeleton found about 6 feet beneath the surface of a bog in the above townland

Parish of Maghera

in 1833. It was again buried on the site where found.

There was also found beneath the surface of the above bog at different periods several articles of old butter and pointed stakes, also old wooden vessels of rude construction, all which have been subsequently destroyed.

Ancient Urns

There was 3 earthen urns containing calcined bones and ashes got deposited beneath the surface of new land in Rocktown and farm now occupied by James O'Neill. They were enclosed in circular stone buildings and covered by flat stones. These urns have been found in 1805 and are subsequently destroyed. Informants John Hughes, John Doherty and others. 5th January 1837.

Brass Halbert and Brass Vessel

The annexed draft [drawing] represents the size and shape of a brass halbert found about 3 feet beneath the surface of new land in Craigmore in 1828. It is at present damaged to some extent and is procured for the survey.

Bernard Mulholland, in reclaiming new land in the above townland in 1806, got about 2 feet beneath the surface a brass vessel 10 inches in depth and 8 inches in diameter at the mouth, and in shape resembling a large bell. It was reduced to a mere skeleton by time and rust, and has subsequently fallen to pieces.

The above articles have been found on the neighbourhood of the ruins of some ancient building supposed to have been a Danes' mill.

Steel Weapon

Neil McGlade got a steel weapon about 2 feet in length, 4 inches in breadth and 2 inches thick in the back, and as sharp as a sword in the edge, about 6 feet beneath the surface of a bog in Ballynahonebeg in 1833. There was a wooden handle in it about 1 and a half foot in length but quite decayed when found. The weapon has been subsequently cut up and converted to other uses. Information obtained from Henery McKenna, Bernard Mulholland and others. 9th January 1837.

Antiques from Ballymacross

The under drafts [outline of stone hatchets and arrowheads] represent the size and shape of 2 stone hatchets and 7 flint arrowheads found beneath the surface of a Danish fort and its neighbourhood in Ballymacross, and some of which are rudely executed. There have been a steel weapon found in the above fort and 2 pieces of ancient silver coin. All the aforesaid articles except the coin is now procured for the survey. Informants Robert and John Lockart. 10th January 1837.

Productive and Social Economy

Maghera Fair

The following were the commodities offered for sale in the fair of Maghera held on the 27th day of December 1836, also the number of horse cattle, black cattle, sheep and pigs, also the prices brought by various commodities as enumerated on the above day.

Total horses 7, none bought. Young springers 6 to 10 pounds, strippers 3 to 5 pounds and some lower, total black cattle 217. Total sheep 57, from 10 to 40s according to quality. Total pigs 263, sold at various prices. Flax 5s to 7s per stone, tow per stone 3s to 5s. Spangles of fine yarn 1s 6d to 2s 6d, spangles of tow yarn 2s to 2s 8d. Flannel per yard 1s 2d, coarse linen per yard 8d, sacken cloth 7d ha'penny per yard. Wool per lb 1s 4d, woollen stockings 1s 6d per pair, cotton stockings 1s 8d per pair, woollen socks 8d per pair, cotton socks 7d per pair. Men's shoes 4s 6d per pair. Firkin of butter 10d per lb, fresh butter 8d ha'penny per lb. Good beef 3d ha'penny per lb, good mutton 4d ha'penny per lb, bacon <beacon> 7d per lb. Dulse 2d per lb, cheese 6d per lb, onions 1s 6d per stone. Water cans 1s 3d each, wash tubs 2 to 4s each. Kitchen chairs 1s each, kitchen stools 4d each. Noggins 4d each. Farm riddles 1s 8d each. Fir bed cords 8d per set. Scutching handles 8d each. Basket rods 8d per 120.

The following commodities were in abundant supply and sold at various prices: silks, callico, cottons, new and old, ready-made clothes for both sexes, delf, china, hardware, tinware, black and whitesmith work for farm and kitchen, glass windows, bread, gingerbreads. The above fairs and commodities brought to it was much more limited than usual, on account of the severity of the day, but cattle of every description, flax, butter and yarn met brisk sale at advanced prices. Informants Lewis McCan, Patrick Gormley and others. 27th December 1836.

Old Burial Ground of Maghera

The following are among the names of families who continue to bury in Maghera old graveyard and who have tombs and headstones: Anderson,

Bradley, Barkley, Brown, Brevlaghan, Clark, Campbell, Cudy, Collins, McCloskey, Dunlop, Dougall, O'Donelly, O'Dougherty, Drips, Diamond, Clainon, Crilley, McCook, Convery, Cunningham, McCracken, McCollough, McCann, Banef, O'Farrill, Forbes, McGuire, McGlade, Getty, Graham, Geaton, Gucking, Johnston, Hughes, Hasson, Hendy, Higins, O'Hendry, Hull, Kellmoy, Kyle, Keelt, Kelly, McKenna, McKee, Hagan, Logan, Morris, Miller, Manolly, Marlin, Mulholland, Linnon, O'Neill, Ruddle, McReady, Richardson, McPake, McKeigney, Patterson, Stewart, Sheil, Thompson, Willson, Young.

Nearly one-third of the tomb and headstones are grown over with fog, or letters so defaced as renders the names on them impossible to be made out, unless by much trouble. The names given are spelled as on the tomb and headstones. [Signed] Thomas Fagan, 11th January 1837.

Fair Sheets by John Bleakly, with sections by Thomas Fagan, July 1836 to February 1837

NATURAL FEATURES

Natural Wood

There are about 28 acres of a natural growth of wood, which consists chiefly of oak, ash, birch, alder, cherry tree and a little elm, in the townland of Drumlamph. The underwood consists of hazel and thorn only in the same townland, and locally called Johnstone wood, but at present nearly all reclaimed.

There are also about 4 acres of natural growth of underwood, consisting of hazel, oak, birch and alder with whitethorn, in the townland of Tirgarvil. There are also about 4 or 5 acres of natural wood in the townland of Upperlands, and consists of oak, birch, hazel and alder, thinly interspersed with ash, situated along the river which divides Tirgarvil from Upperlands, south of the road from Maghera to Kilrea near the corn mill. There are also about 20 acres of natural growth of underwood of hazel and thorn, chiefly in the townland of Culnady.

There is also 1 acre of natural wood of hazel, black and whitethorn around the trenches and parapets of Dunglady Fort. There are also about 1 acre of natural wood in Ballymackpeake Upper, consisting of oak, ash, alder, birch and hazel. There is also 1 acre of natural wood consisting of the same kind of natural wood, in the townland of Ballymacilcur, chiefly underwood.

ANCIENT TOPOGRAPHY

Discoveries: Old Wooden Ladle and Old Butter

An old wooden ladle cut out of the solid piece of black oak, 14 inches in diameter at the spoon part and 6 inches deep: the handle is 18 inches long and the ladle about 2 stone weight. Discovered in 1833 near the verge of Dreenan moss by Hugh O'Neil and is now in his possession, and is like a knob or knot <not> of oak.

Also a quantity of old butter deposited in a wooden vessel and found in 1833 in the moss in townland of Dreenan [by] Mrs McAtamney of Dreenan, see specimen. 28 October 1836.

SOCIAL ECONOMY

Superstition: Blinking Cattle

2 persons, the one a Presbyterian and the other a Covenanter and near relations: the accused was a woman, a Covenanter, the accuser a Presbyterian.

Both parties were brought before the Covenanting minister, the Rev. Mr Smith, in the meeting house at Knockcloghrim <Knocklockram> for the purpose of examining them. The woman was found guilty and expelled [from] the congregation. The woman was pursued from the cows of the Presbyterian into her own house almost breathless, and on further examination a large chest was opened, in which was deposited crocks of milk in a boiling state, as if occasioned by a very hot fire. Across the mouth of each crock was the form of a cross of wood. Attached to each point of the cross was a long hair, supposed to have been taken from the tails of the cows. Her husband, from the shame of his wife being accused and found guilty of so horrible a crime as her, found dead <died> the same night. It is said the cure was effected and the milk and butter restored, by taking a quantity of straw from the eave <eve> of the house of the person found guilty and burning it under the nostrils of the cow or cows blinked. The priests perform the cure by taking all the milk the cow gives and blessing it, and also blessing salt put into it. This to be given to the cow without letting a particle fall to the ground. This cure was given to the cow of a Presbyterian in parish of Termoneeny, but without effect. 28 July 1836.

Illicit Distillation

The years in which illicit distillation most prevailed are as follows: viz. 1803, 1804 and 1808 and 1809. Since the reduction of duty took place,

Parish of Maghera

very little illicit distillation is practised. From Doctor Barr.

Revenue Police

Maghera became a station for revenue police in 1829 and only remained 1 and a half years, from whence they were removed to Kilrea. From James Clark Esquire.

Mr Knox

Mr Knox came to the parish of Maghera in 1817. From Doctor Barr.

Mr Knox's Benevolence

The Rev. J. Spencer Knox this winter gave turf and sticks for fuel free to the poor of Maghera and also sold a quantity of turf to those who were able to pay. And also at Christmas gave a large quantity of beef and clothing to the poor, free.

Lying-in Basket

There is no regular form of application for the lying-in basket. Any well-conducted poor female who is recommended by some of the respectable farmers or known to Mrs Knox will receive a supply from the basket, but since Mrs Knox's absence, no applications have been made. From Miss Patterson, where the basket is deposited.

The last application for the lying-in basket was made on the 23rd of December 1836.

SOCIAL ECONOMY AND MODERN TOPOGRAPHY

Poor Shop

1st, There are 120 defaulters to Mr Knox's poor shop. 2nd, The total sum they are in default amounts to 40 pounds. 3rd, The highest sum due amounts to 4 pounds. 4th, The lowest sum due amounts to 1s. 5th, With scarcely any exceptions, those persons have paid the sums due, either through external influence or by compulsion of the law. 6th, Among the defaulters are many individuals habitually regular in their attendance on divine worship and ordinances. 7th, About 7 persons have absconded. Mr Knox came to the parish of Maghera in 1817. Information obtained from Mr Knox. 30 October 1836.

Bleach Mills

The machinery in the bleach mills at Upperlands contains 3 separate houses, viz. 2 beetling engines and 1 bleach house. One of the engine houses and one of the bleach houses are slated. The beetling house is thatched. All the houses are 2-storey high. The water wheel in the house at the road is 19 and a half feet in diameter and 4 and a half feet broad across the buckets; the other water wheel is 16 feet in diameter and 5 feet broad across the buckets; and the third water wheel is 12 feet in diameter and 5 feet broad across the buckets. The rims of 2 of the water wheels are of metal. The fall of water on the water wheel at the road is 15 feet and of the 2 upper water wheels each 6 feet. All the houses are in good repair, and a constant supply of water. There are 12 acres Irish plantation measure contained in the bleach field.

Residence of Mr Clark

Mr Clark's house is 1-storey high and thatched, built about 23 years ago. Information obtained from Alexander Clark Esquire, proprietor and James McCosker, lofts' man at the mills. 21 December 1836.

Bequest

There was 5 pounds of a bequest left by [blank] Downing of the townland of Dreenan, parish of Maghera, the interest of which was to be annually paid or distributed among the poor of the parish with the poor money on Easter Sunday. The principal is deposited in the hands of Robert Elliott of Slaghtyboggy, but none of the interest have been paid since 20th April 1832. At present only 3 pounds 15s is the principal at present in hands. The other 1 pound 5s was paid, both principal and interest. The churchwardens are now about to process for it, and which they have done twice before, but without success. Information obtained from Joseph Pettigrew, churchwarden. 2 December 1836.

SOCIAL AND PRODUCTIVE ECONOMY

Curran Village

Curran village about 60 years ago contained only 6 tolerable houses built of stone and lime, thatched, and a few cottiers' houses or cabins built of sods. The houses had no sash windows at that time. There was only 1 public house which was occupied by George Marlin, who had also a smith's forge. There was only 1 grocer or rather a huckster shop at that time, Charles McClane occupier, a house built on the site of the oldest house in the village. Part of the walls of the original house is still standing opposite the road leading to Knockcloghrim. Thomas Kent, a publican, occupies the next best house in the village and the house occupied by James Marlin nearly in the centre of the village was built in 1777 and on the site of one of the old houses. NB The Marlins and Kents were the original inhabitants.

Curran Fairs

There was only 20 head of black cattle (cows) and 1 pig in the last fair of Curran on the 23rd November 1836. From George Marlin, Thomas Kent, publican and Susan Marlin. 22 December 1836.

Occupations in Swatragh

There are 16 persons who live by farming alone in Swatragh. 31st December 1836.

Improvements in Swatragh

Swatragh <Swateragh>: swath signifies "jovial, merry." This name was given to it by a man travelling who became wearied or tired on horseback, and could find no house or place to stop at until he came to Swatragh, which was then only a few small houses, and from the hospitality and jovial manner in [which] the inhabitants received him, he called the place Swatragh. The old house in the town is that occupied by Thomas Hamilton, publican and John Reynold's house, farmer. In 1778 there was only 9 houses in the village, all thatched, and only 2 houses had sash windows.

Its improvement may be attributed to the exertions of James Henry Esquire, agent to the proprietor Alexander Stewart Esquire of Ards, county Donegal, who in 1778 gave encouragement to John Reynolds and Manus, his brother, to build. Stewart of Ards paid a chiefry to the Mercers' Company for it. The Mercers' Company received a chiefry out of Swatragh since the reign of James II. The first improvement of Swatragh was licensing a quarterly fair to it, which was done through the influence of [blank] Lyle Esquire, then mayor of Coleraine and [blank] Wilson, also of Coleraine, as it was then in their hands. It is upwards of 200 years since the patent was granted for a quarterly fair in Swatragh. [Blank] Stewart of Ards was bound to make more improvements in the village and also to build a market house in Kilrea, which he did not. Doctor Mooney built a fine house. Since it came into the hands of the Mercers' Company only 2 slated houses in the village and the meeting house at present, which is also slated. From Doctor Mooney, John Reynolds and Thomas Hamilton. 24 December 1836.

Provision for the Poor

The annual average collection of poor box money in Maghera parish church amounts to 20 pounds. There are 30 applicants annually for poor box money. There are at present 20 names of poor persons on the church list receiving the poor box money, viz. 12 of the Established Church, 5 Presbyterians and 3 Roman Catholics. Information obtained from the Rev. J. Spencer Knox, rector and Joseph Pettigrew, churchwarden. 26 December 1836.

There are 3 free houses containing 16 poor persons in the parish of Maghera and all supported through the benevolence of Mrs Clark, viz. the old windmill contains 9 poor persons, viz. 5 old women and 4 children. The house near the pound contains 4 poor persons, viz. 3 poor women and 1 child. The house on the roadside near the mill in the townland of Falgortreevy contains 3 poor persons, viz. 2 poor women and 1 child. Information obtained from the inmates of the houses. 27 December 1836.

Butter Market

The butter market was established by the unanimous consent of the respectable inhabitants of Maghera, who advertised for its establishment. Charles Harken, the weighmaster, was the first who introduced it and, in order to assist him, the following persons, Matthew Lyttle, David Thompson, William Allen, Michael Bradley and John Grey (now in America), commenced to purchase butter and pork in speculation, but not being competent judges purchased at a high rate and lost considerably. From Alexander Falls, Matthew Lyttle and Charles Harkin.

Spinning Fund

The principle of the spinning fund is chiefly to employ and support the respectable poor persons to clove, hackle and spin. Mr Knox's wages is one-third higher than the wages generally given, besides agent's fees. The yarn is sold in the market and the tow is also sold in the market. From the agent.

The last flax was given out from the spinning fund in November 1836.

Trades

There are 4 woollen drapers in Maghera. There are 2 bonnetmakers and 1 dressmaker who have houses of their own. The 2 clerks are lodgers. The ragman left the town, the dealer in eggs is a lodger.

Parish of Maghera

Flax, Butter and Grain Market

Flax sold in 1836, 170 tons; butter 20 cwt; pork limited, very little sold. Oats sold in 1836, 3,700 sacks containing 24 stone each. Oatmeal in 1836, 1,000 sacks containing 3 and a half cwt each. Barley, 200 sacks containing 28 stones each. From John McCloskey and Charles Harkin, weighmaster. 29 December 1836.

Labourers

There are 35 persons who are labourers and heads of families occupying houses of their own, and who live by labouring alone.

Butter Market

The quantity of butter sold in 1835 in the butter market of Maghera amounts to 30 cwt.

Cultivation of Wheat and Rye

The cultivation of wheat and rye was introduced so long ago that the oldest inhabitant does not remember it, and only in small quantities of 1 or 2 stones of each for their own use, which when ground at the mill was mixed and baked and was called mashlin bread. It is about 8 or 10 years since the farmers began to sow wheat and rye in larger quantities, in order to make sale of it to advantage at the Castledawson flour mills. At the above-mentioned period half an acre was supposed to have been a large sowing of wheat, but now every man whose farm will produce wheat will sow in proportion to size of his farm from half an acre to 10 acres.

Magherafelt is the market in which wheat is generally sold, as it is the longer established and the purchasers more numerous. Maghera, from want of influential persons to encourage the market and it being churchland property, no encouragement is given to establish a wheat, pork or butter market. From Alexander Falls, Charles Harkin, John McCloskey and Matthew Lyttle. 30 December 1836.

Schoolhouse at Beagh Spiritual

The schoolhouse at the Beagh Spiritual is on the leading road from Maghera to Bellaghy and is 25 by 17 feet inside, thatched, and was built in 1833 by subscription and cost 25 pounds. The Rev. J. Spencer Knox, rector gave 2 pounds 6s; Bellingim Mauleverer <Maulaverer> Esquire [insert superscript: proprietor] gave 1 pound; Robert Mauleverer Esquire gave 1 pound 1s; Alexander Clark Esquire gave 1 pound and the remainder from the inhabitants of the parish at large in smaller sums. The house was built for a Sunday school at first and is not yet finished for a day school, as there is nothing more than forms in it, no desks. From William and James Crawford and Henry Patterson, through whose instrumentality the schoolhouse was built and a singing and Sunday school was established. 3 January 1837.

Debating Society

A debating society commenced on last Wednesday (11th January 1837) in the house of Jonathan Graham, a publican in the town of Maghera, but have entered into no resolutions until Wednesday next, which will be the next night of meeting. The subjects on which they are [to] debate will be chiefly historical. The following are the members at present on the list: James McHenry, James Graham, Thomas Pettigrew, Hugh Morrisson, William Henry Hagan. The house or room is to be rented from James Graham, a member. 14 January 1837.

Gulladuff

Gulladuff contains 19 houses, one of which is not occupied and the others not yet finished. The following are the trades and occupations: blacksmiths 2, shoemakers 2, linen weavers 3, calico weaver (a female) 1, wheelwrights 1, carpenters 1, butcher 1, farmer 1, widow 1, schoolmistress 1, apothecary 1, publicans and grocers 2. The houses are all built of stone and thatched, one is a 2-storey house. The schoolmaster does not reside in the village. The male schoolhouse is a mere hut or cabin built of stone.

Grain Market in Gulladuff

The grain market is only from October till May 14th. John Downing states that the best part of the grain market is yet to come i.e. till May. From John Downing and James McQuillan, publicans and grocers, and James Drips, butcher and Thomas McDevit, schoolmaster. 16 January 1837.

Church Missionary Meeting

The last meeting of the Church Missionary Society was held in Maghera on the second day of September 1836.

Grain at Gulladuff Market

The following is the quantity of grain sold at the grain market of Gulladuff from the middle of October 1836 till the 16th of January 1837: oats

200 sacks, each sack containing 24 stone; wheat 34 sacks, each sack containing 24 stone; barley 20 sacks, each sack containing 24 stones. From John Downing and James McQuillan at Gulladuff.

MODERN TOPOGRAPHY AND SOCIAL ECONOMY

Presbyterian Meeting House

There are 2 roods of land Cunningham measure attached to the Presbyterian meeting house of Maghera, given by Alexander Clark Esquire of Maghera. From James Shannon, clerk of the church and Henry McHenry, schoolmaster and the Rev. Charles Kennedy, Presbyterian minister.

Materials for Building

Chiefly fir timber called Memel is used, which is procured at Coleraine and sold at 1s 8d per foot. Lime is brought from Desertmartin and laid down for 1s 6d per barrel of 3 bushels. Stone is found near the town and is laid down for 6d per load of 15 cwt. Brick from Ballynahone townland in the parish, 1 and a half miles distant and is laid down on the ground from 1s to 1s 4d per 100 of 5 score. Slates from Coleraine (queen ton) and is laid down for 3 pounds 13s per ton; (countesses) at 5 pounds 15s per 1,000, carriage 6d per cwt.

Bridge

The bridge on the new road a quarter of a mile from Maghera is in the townland of Craigadick.

Roman Catholic Chapel at Moyagall

The Moyagall Roman Catholic chapel is 88 by 27 feet inside. The gallery is mere steps and will hold as many persons as the lower part. There are 34 by 10 feet which is occupied by the altar, and will contain 2,036 persons.

Benevolence of Mr Clark

Alexander Clark Esquire of Maghera gave a quantity of turf free to the poor of Maghera this winter. From Matthew Lyttle, David Thompson, Doctor Barr and Alexander Falls of Maghera. 3 February 1837.

Instances of Longevity

Rose Devlin, a travelling pauper, died in this parish at the age of 107 years. In her 99th year a complete set of new teeth grew in her mouth.

In Macknagh townland Alice Mulholland, a widow, is 96 years of age. Denis Roe McKenna, a good Irish scholar, is now 95 years of age in the townland of Fallagloon. From Rev. J.S. Knox, rector.

Insured Houses

The only insured houses in the town of Maghera are 2 in number.

Health and Contagious Disease

Grillagh is said to be the most healthy townland in the parish.

Typhus fever at present prevails in the neighbourhood of the town of Maghera and also in part of the mountain district. From Doctor Barr, 19th January 1837.

Instance of good arising from Sunday Schools

A young woman residing at Craigadick named McCloskey, a Roman Catholic, who was a scholar attending Miss Clark's (now Mrs Stevenson) Sunday school, which was held in her father's house in Maghera, received a Bible from her teacher Miss Clark, as a token of merit for her good answering from the Scriptures and good conduct, which Bible she kept after leaving the school and carefully read at home, and committed a large portion of it to memory. The present Roman Catholic curate came into the house and saw the Bible on the dresser, and took it up and asked her why she kept such a book in the house and said she did not understand its meaning, and as it was not the right version she should not keep it. She said it was the right version and that Miss Clark had taught her to understand its meaning, and that she would not by any means part with her Bible.

Dispensary

Dispensary open from 9 to 11 o'clock a.m. on each day in the week, Wednesday and Sunday excepted, Daniel Mooney, surgeon. [Signed] John Bleakly, 10th May 1836.

TOWNLAND DIVISIONS

Slaghtyboggy Townland

The townland of Slaghtyboggy contains 23 farmhouses and 25 cottier houses. The size of the farms are from 50 acres to 2 acres Irish plantation measure. The heirs of the late Honourable Thomas Connolly are the proprietors, who receive from 2s to 5s per acre. The proprietors under them are: Mrs Johnstone, who holds the one-third of the townland and has 8 tenants under her who pay a

Parish of Maghera

rent of 30s per acre; James Courtney Esquire of Glenburn near Portglenone has 5 tenants who pay him a rent of 30s per acre each, and 3 tenants under them again who pay each 2 pounds per acre. Mrs Johnstone has 2 tenants who pay her each 2 pounds per acre. Robert Graham Senior, Robert Graham Junior, Robert Elliott, Mrs Crockett, Mrs Miller, Mrs John Johnstone, Lilly Given, James Anderson, Curragh, John Pool of Tamnymartin and Nesbitt Downing of Coleraine all hold from the head landlords.

Mrs Johnstone, who occupies the only 2-storey house in the townland, holds the largest farm in her own hands, which is about 50 acres, and has accumulated the most wealth of any in the townland, chiefly from industry and living sparingly. Her husband obtained all his land by purchase from his neighbours, many of whom were in debt to him and having no other means of clearing it than by disposing of their land and becoming undertenants to him, [they] who might have been as wealthy as their neighbours, but from indolence and drunkenness.

The richest man in the townland about 40 years ago was Robert Elliott, an old farmer, who from his wealth was called the Laird of Boggy, but from the extravagance of his wife and children became in debt and sold this property to Mrs Johnstone's husband (Robert Johnstone), whose ancestors have lived in the townland for upwards of 100 years. The Laird of Boggy occupied the only 2-storey house then in the parish, but is long since in ruins. It is about 20 years since his family lost the property.

Mrs Johnstone's house is the only slated house in the townland. All the other houses are of stone and thatched, and very few in good repair apparently outside, as they are not whitened and badly thatched. The inside is more comfortable, but none have that neat and comfortable appearance which might be expected from persons holding freehold property. There is little or no difference between [the] clean appearance of the houses of the middlemen and those of the undertenants: of the two the undertenants are the cleanest except Mrs Johnstone's house and a few others. There are only 6 houses which have the appearance of white outside in the townland. The inhabitants have little or no desire for making their houses comfortable, but say the houses occupied by their ancestors are good enough for them.

The townland is rather diminishing than increasing in wealth, chiefly owing to indolence. Information obtained from Mrs Johnstone, Andrew Miller, Robert Graham, Robert Elliott, James Anderson, Mrs John Johnstone, all freeholders in the townland. 6 January 1837.

Ballynacross Townland

Ballynacross contains 28 farmers and 6 cottiers. The average rent of the freeholds is 2s 6d per acre. The undertenants pay 35s per acre. The following are the tenants who hold under the head proprietors viz. Doctor Grey, Robert Elliott, Samuel Elliott, William Elliott, Ralph Lapsley, James Grey, Isaac Fleming, George Scott, Robert Lockart, John Lapsley, David McKowen, Francis Caskey, Hugh Lammon, Jacob Johnstone, Richard Johnstone, Robert Crawford (non-resident), Robert Martin, Charles McCahey, William Clark (non-resident), Hugh Marlin and James Marlin. There is no 2-storey houses in the townland but all the houses are built of stone and thatched, and in much better repair and more comfortable, both inside and outside, than those of Slaghtyboggy.

The townland is divided into Upper and Lower Ballynacross, as the houses are chiefly in 2 clusters. Jacob Johnstone and a few others in the upper half-town have the front of their houses ornamented with a little flower ground, which presents a neater appearance than the other houses. It is quite evident that the tenants are more industrious than the tenants of Slaghtyboggy. The inhabitants were more wealthy about 30 years ago. The decrease is owing to a failure in the linen trade, as many are weavers in the townland. The heirs of the Honourable Thomas Connolly are the proprietors. From Doctor Grey and some of the above freeholders. 7th and 8th January 1837.

Curragh Townland

There are 30 farmers and 4 cottiers in the townland of Curragh. The heirs of the right Honourable Thomas Connolly are the proprietors. The following are the freeholders under them: Alexander Kingston Fox Esquire, non-resident, James Anderson, resident, James Anderson Junior, John Anderson, William Anderson, Samuel Anderson, Robert McKowen, Robert McKowen Junior, William McKowen, John McKowen, James McKowen, William McKowen, Henry McKowen, Samuel McKowen, Joseph McKowen, Robert McKowen, John McClelland, Michael McClelland, John Campbell, John Armour, William Armour, Samuel Aull, James Aull, William Fulton, Thomas Fulton, Mrs Lowden, non-resident. The rest are undertenants. The average rent of the freeholders is 4s per acre, the undertenants pay 30s per acre.

The houses are all built of stone and thatched, and in pretty good repair; none slated but one which is a 2-storey house, occupied by James Anderson. The largest farm is 21 acres, the smallest 2 acres. The greater number are small farms, which is the cause of the townland not being more wealthy than it is. About 30 years ago the tenants were more wealthy than they are now, chiefly owing to the encouragement given to the linen trade, as many of the inhabitants were linen weavers. The houses are more comfortable both inside and outside than the houses of Slaghtyboggy or Ballynacross: the inhabitants are more industrious, the land of a better quality and the growth of wheat more extensive. As to the wealth of the inhabitants with reference to money, there is very little among them, as all the money they could gather in former times, when money was more plentiful, they expended in the purchase of land. Information obtained from James Anderson, William Anderson, Robert McKowen, John McClelland, John Armour and Thomas Fulton, farmers in the townland. 11th January 1837.

Curran Townland

There are 4 2-storey houses in the village, 2 of which are slated and 2 thatched. The houses in the country parts are all built of stone and lime, except 2 which are of brick, and all thatched except one. There are 7 houses in the country part of the townland, which present the appearance of whiteness. The houses in the country part appear more comfortable than those of Curragh, Ballynacross or Slaghtyboggy. The houses of the village are built of stone, except a few which are of brick, and tolerably comfortable. The townland in general is more wealthy and the soil (particularly of the arable part of the Hillhead) of a superior quality. The townland in general produces good wheat.

The Cavins who reside at the Hillhead are the most wealthy and obtained their land by purchase, the year after the rebellion of '98, from Doctor Martin, who fled from this county for being a United Irishman. The rent of the freehold from 2s 6d to 5s per acre, the undertenants from 30s to 35s per acre. Since the year '98 the townland has increased in wealth, those in the country by farming and those in the town by dealing and farming, except one who obtained a legacy. From John Downing, applotter of county cess, James Mewhinny, publican and farmer, George Marlin, Samuel Cavin, Richard Cavin and James McClelland.

The townland of Curran contains 16 farmers, freeholders. The following are their names: Samuel and Richard Cavin, 28 acres of arable, John Downing, 6 acres 2 roods, George Patterson, 7 acres, James McClelland, non-resident, 14 acres, James McClelland Junior, 7 acres, George Marlin, 6 acres, James Mewhinny, publican, 10 acres 2 roods, Robert James, John and George Stones 4 acres, Robert Stones Junior, 3 acres, Edward Stones, 7 acres, James Falls, non-resident, 12 acres, Henry Harbeson and William Johnstone, 7 acres, Robert Henry, non-resident, 8 acres 3 roods, George Marlin, 2 acres 2 roods. 8 of the above live in the country parts of the townland.

There are 10 undertenants, 6 of which live in the country parts of the townland, and 7 cottiers who live in the country parts of the townland. There are 3 freehold cottiers who live in the town (but none who live free in the country) and 17 cottiers who pay rent in the town. There is only *one* 2-storey house in the country parts of the townland, which is slated and occupied by Richard Cavin. 12 January 1837.

Drumlamph Townland

The townland of Drumlamph is undoubtedly the richest townland in the parish. Mr [blank] Henry, who occupies the 2-storey house near the road at Shellgrove, is the richest man in the townland. David Henderson is also what the people call a rich man.

Drumard Townland

The townland of Drumard is the poorest in the parish. It contains 81 farmhouses but no cottiers, as the agent, John Stevenson Esquire of Knockan, parish Banagher, will not allow a cottier to reside in the townland on account of the scarcity of bog. The houses are all built of stone and thatched, but very badly. The front of the houses are not kept clean, as the people retain the old custom of making manure in large piles at the doors of the dwelling houses. There are very few of the houses whitewashed. The farms are all small: there is only one 15 acre farm, the rest are on an average 6 acre farms, small farms. With indolence as the chief cause of their poverty, the average rent is 25s per acre. John Nesbitt Downing Esquire is the proprietor. From John Downing, Bernard McPeake, Peter Convery, Doctor Grey and Robert Elliott, farmers.

Ballynahone and Kilcronaghan

The tenants of the Ballynahone side of the Moyola <Myola>, parish of Maghera, have gained about 5 acres of arable land from the Kilcronaghan side

Parish of Maghera

of the river, which is the property of John Stevenson Esquire of Fortwilliam, and to whom they pay rent for it. In all about 10 acres have been added to the Ballynahone side of the river, but 5 acres are sandy and remain in the width of the river, and no rent is paid for it as it is not arable. Rev. J. Spencer Knox is the proprietor of Ballynahone. In 1835 and 1836 Mr Stevenson made very high bankments on his side [of] the river which prevents the river from encroaching on his side of the river. Information obtained from John Stevenson Esquire, Doctor Barr and Robert Martin. 23 January 1837.

ANCIENT TOPOGRAPHY

Old Church of Maghera

[Remainder of Memoir by Thomas Fagan] Local tradition does not support the existence of any other church in Maghera previous to the old one, a large portion of which at present stands. Tradition says that the old church of Maghera was built 11 years subsequent to the ancient cathedral of Armagh. The draft cut in freestone on the right of the door entering into the body of the old church of Maghera is locally said to represent St Peter, chief of the apostles, and formerly Bishop of Rome.

Termon Lands

Termon was a tract of land laid out as a foundation for a seminary or school to educate youth in the elements of letters and religion and to shelter and relieve the poor, the traveller and the orphan. These places were exempt from rent, taxes and all imposts. The termunach was the bishop's proctor and steward <stewart> in these lands. Informants Denis Roe McKenna and Francis Diamond.

Old Abbey of Maghera

The old abbey of Maghera is locally said to stand 104 feet in length by 20 feet wide and to accommodate 50 monks, which is the number said to be always under the superintendence of the abbot. Part of the foundation of the abbey was raised in sinking a grave on the site about 50 years ago.

SOCIAL ECONOMY

Area for Horses: Gort

Gort is locally said to be the name anciently given to a free space of ground set apart, enclosed by stakes, interwoven with small brambles in the neighbourhood of churches, for the safety and grazing accommodation of horses belonging to the clergy and parishioners who came to worship on Sundays. Information obtained from Denis Roe McKenna and Francis Diamond. 14 January 1837.

Emigration in 1834 and 1835

The following are the persons who have emigrated from the above parish in 1834 and 1835.

1834: males under 10 years 9, females 8; males under 20 years 19, females 9; males under 30 years 29, females 16; males under 40 years 7, females 1; males under 50 years 3, females 1; males under 60 years 4, females 1; total 107.

1835: males under 20 years 5, females 4; males under 30 years 9, females 11; males under 40 years 5, females 2; males under 50 years 1; males under 70 years 1, females 1; total 39. Written 16th January 1837.

Causes of Emigration

The following are the causes locally assigned for emigration from the above parish having prevailed to a greater extent in 1834 than in 1835. In 1834 the linen trade was very dull, the prices low and the encouragement for weavers limited; besides, the accounts from America by former emigrants was tolerably good. Also, several landholders sold their farms to emigrate, being flattered by the fair prospects held out by many who emigrated in preceding years. Together with the above causes, supply of vessels at Derry etc. was unlimited, the passage moderate and best accomodation promised by emigration merchants.

In 1835 the linen trade looked better: the demand was brisk and prices advanced, all which gave the most constant employ to a very large number of persons who, in the absence of such employment, would be obliged to emigrate and migrate to other countries to seek support. Also the accounts generally had from America were very unfavourable, which greatly retarded the progress of emigration. Besides, the supply of vessels at Derry was limited and the passage of emigrants was somewhat higher than in 1834. Besides the aforesaid, many of the working class who would have emigrated are obliged to remain at home for want of means to get out. Informants Peter Gucking, Patt Gormly and many others. 17 January 1837.

Maghera Manor Court

There is a manor court held monthly in the town of Maghera. The largest sum that this court has power to recover is 5 pounds Irish currency and the gross cost of recovering this sum is 5s 6d. The average number of summonses issued for each court day is 40. Information obtained from James Shannon, clerk of the above court. 14 February 1837.

Fair Sheets by J. Bleakly, June 1836

NATURAL STATE

Parish of Maghera

The parish of Maghera is divided into 42 townlands and contains a population of 14,091, viz. 1,255 of the Established Church, 3,030 Presbyterians, 8,715 Roman Catholics and 1,091 of other denominations. The parish is well supplied with good bog, good accommodation of roads and excellent spring water. Almost every townland in the parish contains a spring well. The Moyola is the chief river or stream, which with other smaller streams the parish is well watered.

NATURAL FEATURES

Woods

There is a wood in the townland of Drumlamph which was planted in the year 1782 by John Henderson Esquire of [blank] and consists of fir, ash, oak and some beech. Some of the ash and oak is natural growth.

There is also a wood in the townland of Ballymackpeake which was planted in the year 1781 and consists of fir, ash and oak chiefly. Previous to the above date this was a natural wood. This wood has been cut and planted 3 times. It is about 60 years since mass was celebrated at an old altar which is in this wood in the open air, before a Roman Catholic chapel was created in this end of the parish. The altar is nothing more than a few stones under the branches of an oak tree.

In the townland of Curragh there is about 2 and a half acres of a scroggy natural growth of wood, about half an acre of which has been reclaimed and made into arable by the proprietor James Anderson.

Also a growth of scroggy natural wood in the townland of Culnady near the stream and flax mill, which also can be reclaimed. There is also another piece of natural wood, chiefly hazel, white and blackthorn, in Culnady, a part of which is also reclaimed and made into arable by John McKowen.

Also a piece of natural wood in the townland of Ballymacilcur which is also reclaimed by David Clark. Information obtained from the proprietors.

There is a piece of natural wood in the townland of Dreenan on [blank] Port's farm, chiefly of hazel, oak and alder. This wood has been cut 3 times and lastly about 7 years ago. A part is also reclaimed.

Rivers

The Moyola <Myola>, which divides the parish of Maghera from Kilcronaghan, produces trout, eels and pike, the latter only a few, the trout most plentiful, all chiefly taken by nets. About 41 years ago the middle arch of the Moyola bridge was swept away by a flood from this river.

There are also other smaller streams through the parish of Maghera: the chief of the other streams proceeds from Carntogher mountain. Information obtained from David Henderson and Robert McClain.

Bogs

Drumlamph flow bog is from 2 to 14 feet deep. The imbedded timber consists chiefly of oak and fir, with some small yew sticks. The largest fir is from 18 inches to 2 feet in diameter, the oak is about 2 feet in diameter and used in making mill axles <axils>, ground joist for flooring and roofing small houses. The fir is also used in roofing houses and making furniture. The oak is frequently found near the verge of the bog and the fir near the centre, and all lying with the top east; sometimes 4 blocks of fir are found lying close together and often one across the other.

Ballymackpeake flow bog is about 9 feet deep. Very little imbedded timber is found in this bog and very little of it is cut away. A quantity of imbedded timber, chiefly oak, but now lying on the surface, all of which have the top towards the east [as] in the Drumard flow bog.

Curran flow bog is on an average 14 feet deep. The imbedded timber consists of small oak and fir, only fit for fuel and roofing small cabins.

Gulladuff and Moyagall flow bog is about 15 feet deep. At the verge of the Gulladuff side is a quantity of oak sticks, one of which is on the surface where it was found and is 27 feet long by 17 inches in diameter, with many other of smaller dimensions, and all near the clay with the top towards the east, on George Drips' farm. From David Henderson, George Drips and others.

The flow bog in Tamnymullan, Ballymacilcur and the Crew is 12 feet deep. The imbedded timber consists of oak and fir. Some of the oak is 2 feet in diameter, the top also to the east. The Tamnymullan part is 15 feet deep in the centre, viz. 5 feet deep of the top is a white moss, 5 feet deep under this moss is of decomposed branches and leaves of fir trees, and the other 5 feet is of a more black and solid nature.

Fallagloon flow bog is 8 feet deep. The imbedded timber consists of fir and oak, some of the oak so gross as to make mill axles, and also found near the clay with the top eastward.

HISTORY

See of Derry

In 597 the seat of the see of Derry was translated from Ardstraw to Maghera, and in 1158 it was removed to Derry (see Graham's *Siege*). From Alexander Falls, Henry McHenry and others. For extent of glebe lands, see *Edinburgh Review*.

ANCIENT TOPOGRAPHY

Old Church

The old church and graveyard occupies the south end of the town. Nothing remains of this old edifice (which was originally 75 by 25 feet in the clear) but the tower and part of the side walls. The tower is 14 by 11 feet in the clear with 2 outside doors each 4 feet 10 inches wide, and one inside door leading from the tower to the body of the church, which is 3 feet wide. Above this door, in emboss'd characters on cut stone, is the representation of Our Lord's crucifixion, with the 11 disciples and the 2 soldiers piercing his side. On cut stone on both sides of the door are other ornamental characters in emboss'd work. About 36 feet of the south side wall, with all the east gable, is completely demolished. There were 4 windows, 2 on each side, each 5 feet wide, and one large one on the east end. The stone tower was ornamented with a spire of wood. Under the spire was a large bell, which was broken by the falling of the spire about [blank] years ago.

On the south side of the church was a stone on which was the date of its erection in hieroglyphics, but was taken off at the building of the new church. About the year 1793 the east end was built at the expense of the parish of Killelagh, as at that time Maghera and Killelagh was a union of parishes; the separation took place in the year 1796. The roof was on the old church in 1819.

Saint Tobberlowrie's Tombstone and Well

Saint Tobberlowrie is said to have been the founder of the old church. His tombstone, which is nothing more than a common whinstone, [is] situated a short distance above the old church in the old graveyard. There are no characters on the stone more than a cross rudely cut. The stone is 2 feet high and 1 foot 3 inches broad. Lawrence Bradley was the saint's name.

The town of Maghera is supplied with excellent water from Tobberlowrie's Well, which is situated at the end of Miss Patterson's house nearly opposite the hotel.

Discoveries: Old Cot

In 1835 an old cot was discovered in a small lake in the townland of Ballymackpeake, on the property of Robert Forrister Esquire. The cot was 27 feet long by 3 and a half feet broad, cut out of the solid piece of oak, but now all destroyed except a piece which is now converted into a bedstead in the house of Henry O'Hara of Ballymackpeake, and some into rafters and ribs for the house. The cot was about 1 foot deep. The bottom was quite flat. The wood appears to be in a pretty good state of preservation.

Brass Sword, Pointed Stakes and Coins

The brass weapon now in the possession of Mr David Henderson of Drumlamph is 1 foot 3 inches long and 2 inches broad at the widest part of the hilt and three-quarters of an inch broad in the blade, and in a good state of preservation. Discovered in 1831 by William Logan, 11 feet under the surface on the clay in Drumlamph flow bog.

Near the place where this weapon was found there was a quantity of pointed stakes discovered with the points stuck in the ground, and appeared to have been regularly pointed with some edged tool.

A quantity of silver coins of Elizabeth bearing date 1575 was also discovered in a crock in the above bog in the year 1807.

Urn of Bones

Also 2 crocks full of human bones were discovered in 1832 in the verge of a flow bog in Ballynahonebeg by James Chambers, and on the farm of George Martin; none preserved. From David Henderson and Robert McClane.

Horn and Coins

There was a bullock's horn, full of old silver coins of Edward II, larger than our shilling but very thin, discovered in 1834 by James Phillips and on his farm, at a bush called the Friars' Island in Ballynahone, part of the flow bog. The horn with some of the pieces are deposited in the cabinet of the Rev. J. Spencer Knox at the Glebe.

Subterranean Pass

A pipe or subterraneous pass was discovered in 1835 in digging the foundation of the old Presbyterian meeting house. The pipe is supposed to lead from the old church to the meeting house.

Querns

Ancient <antient> querns about 6 years ago, 3 feet under the surface at a spring well which is at the verge of a small flow bog in the townland of Drumard near Denergan hill, by Alexander Downey and on his farm. The diameter of the querns is 1 foot 2 inches and 8 inches thick. The concave, which is in the under stone, is 11 inches in diameter with a small hole to let the meal through. The rim is 2 and a half inches thick. The upper stone, which is made to fill the concavity, is 9 inches in diameter and 4 inches thick. The hole in which the grain is put is 4 inches in diameter.

There is also a small hole for the pin to turn round the stone. About 2 inches of the upper stone, when placed in the concavity, is above the horizontal part of the under. The whole is of freestone supported by 3 stone feet half an inch high. From Alexander Downey and Robert McClain.

Also another ancient pair of querns 18 inches in diameter and 3 inches thick, discovered in 1834 by Edward McKane and in his possession in the townland of Drumard, and found near the rock in the rear of the house, a few inches under the surface.

Also other ancient querns of curious shape, crescent like, was discovered in a clay field 15 years ago under some small stone which appear to have been burned. These stones were put into operation by rubbing one against another, the grain being put between them, and were found by James Chambers and on his farm in the Crew, but are now deposited in Mr Knox's cabinet.

Ancient Font

Ancient font discovered 46 years ago by Doctor Barnett on the glebe farm, and is supposed to have been used in the old monastery which formerly stood where the new Presbyterian meeting house now stands. The font, which is now in the possession of John Morrisson, reedmaker in Maghera town, and is 8 inches in diameter. The concave part is 6 inches in diameter and 7 inches high, of freestone rudely cut.

Meddars

2 wooden meddars <meadars> full of butter was discovered 3 years ago in Tamnymullin flow bog, 1 foot under the surface by James Steel of the Crew. The butter when melted was used as polish for shoes.

Churns

Ancient churns, 2 of which have been discovered in 1834 3 feet under the surface of Dreenan flow bog by John Tamney, and are at present in his possession but all broken except the lid. From John Morrisson and others. These churns have been cut out of the solid piece of trees. The largest churn was 1 foot in diameter and 1 foot 1 inch deep (see specimen). The other is similar in shape but much smaller: the lid is 1 foot in diameter with a hole through which the handle of the dash passes, and 2 smaller holes in which 2 handles were put. The lid is at present in the possession of John Tamney in Dreenan. 2 handles were placed one at each side of the churn with 2 small holes in each, through which small rods as hoops were found.

Sword and Coins

Money and a *large* sword is said to have been discovered in tossing the large stone which [is] on the left side of the pass into the Dunglady Fort many years ago.

Stone Coffin

Also a stone coffin is said to have been discovered about 30 years ago by John Drips and on his farm in a field adjoining the Dunglady Fort, in a gravel hole. Nothing but ashes was in the coffin.

Urns of Bones and Stone Grave

About 40 years ago an urn of bones, human, was discovered under the large standing stone which is on Culnagrew hill. About 4 and a half feet from the above stone there is another stone in a reclined position, under which another urn of bones was found.

Also in a fort of stones 43 feet south of the large standing stone there is a stone grave regularly formed of flags, dressed and placed like a trough, 3 feet long and 2 feet broad and 2 and a half feet deep, in which also an urn of bones was found about 5 years ago by Loughlin Slaman, the proprietor. From Doctor Mooney and the above-named persons.

Brass Spur and Brass Hatchet

An ancient brass spur 18 inches long in the shank and very thick. The bow or arched part is 6 inches wide and was discovered in 1832 by Rose Bradly of Bracknagrilly in a small stream in the above townland, and now deposited in the cabinet of the Rev. J. Spencer Knox.

Also a brass hatchet which is supposed to have been used by the ancients in taking the bark off trees, and was found in Bracknagrilly by Thomas McKanna in digging a lonan or lane 12 inches under the surface. The hatchet is 6 inches long and deposited also in Mr Knox's cabinet.

Stone Crook

Also a curious stone like a crook, 1 foot long and 1 and a half inches thick was discovered in 1831 in repairing a road 3 feet under the surface in Drumconready by Patrick Convery of Bracknagrilly, and is also deposited in Mr Knox's cabinet.

Brass Spear

Discovered in a flow bog in Culnagrew, 7 feet under the surface 12 years ago by John Reynolds, the owner, a publican in Swatragh.

Copper Ladle

About 80 years ago there was a copper ladle with a chain attached discovered in an excellent spring in the rear of the hotel by John O'Neil, and is supposed to have been chained at the well for passengers to drink with. The well is long since filled up. From John Morrisson, Thomas McKenna and others.

Ancient Lakes

There is an artificial lake in the townland of Ballymacpeake, at the verge of the flow bog on the farm of Robert Forrister Esquire. In this lake is an artificial island composed of earth and moss, supported by a frame of black oak, with horizontal pieces mortised to the uprights round the edge of the island, and was 4 feet above the surface of the water. 2 foot-goes originally led into the island, viz. one from the parapet of the fort and the other from the bog at the opposite side of the lake, and were of black oak. Wildfowl used to frequent this island; many were taken by Alexander Willey. Many feet of water was taken off this island about 40 years ago. A few oak sticks appear 2 or 3 feet above the level of the island. The lake is every year becoming smaller.

There is another lake in the townland of Drumard which is much larger than the above.

Standing Stones in Swatragh

There are 2 remarkable standing stones in the village of Swatragh, in the rear of the houses on Hugh Kane's garden. These stones are 9 and a half feet asunder and each 3 and a half feet high and 1 and a half feet broad at the bottom of the north face; each stone has 4 sides. The superstitious affirm that about 80 years ago these stones were removed from the ditch where they were placed as a fence about 8 yards south of where they now stand, by some supernatural power the next morning after they were placed in the ditch.

Standing Stone in Culnagrew

There is also a remarkable standing stone in Culnagrew, about 100 perches north of the road leading from Swatragh to Kilrea and on Loughlin Slaman's farm a short distance from Swatragh, in a field which has never been tilled. The stone is 8 feet high and 2 and a half feet broad on the west side, 3 feet broad on the south side, 3 feet 4 inches on the north side and 2 feet on the east side.

Ancient Site: Stair-na-calleen

Stair-na-calleen is a large platform situated in the face of a rock in the townland of Dreenan. This platform is 5 feet broad, 10 feet long at the back and 9 feet high. From the ground to the platform is 10 feet high and is called Stair-na-callen or "the girls' chair", from 2 females named Downey who were the occupiers of this farm and who used to stand frequently on the platform. From Doctor Mooney, Loughlin Slaman and James Cassidy, schoolmaster in Dreenan.

Caves

In the townland of Drumard there is an artificial cave on Patrick Dugan's farm, of which the following is the dimensions [sketch showing shape of cave with orientation]: from a to b is the north end which is 5 feet in length; b is a stone which is placed at the entrance to this end; c is the mouth which is 3 feet wide; from d to e is 5 feet long; e is the entrance into the south end and which is 2 feet wide by 1 and a half feet high. F is the east end; from f to g is 11 feet long; f is the entrance to the east end which is also 2 feet by 1 and a half feet high; from g to h is 13 feet in length. The height of the cave is 4 feet, the width is 5 feet, total length from east to west 24 feet and from north to south entrance 10 feet. It is supposed that the above cave runs further both east and west, but the quantity of earth and stones which have fallen in at both ends obstructs the pass further.

There is another cave, artificial, in the townland of Rocktown, on the farm of Peter O'Hara which runs east, west and south, but long since closed up. The above two are the only caves in the parish of Maghera.

Rock: Clough-a-Kinney

Clough-a-Kinney is a large rock in Drumard which is 18 feet broad on the face, 11 feet high and 5 feet broad on the top.

Fairies Castle

The Fairies Castle is nothing more than a rock in which is a cliff 1 foot wide and 5 and a half feet high, situated in the townland of Craigmore, from which it is supposed the townland takes its name. From Peter O'Hara, Patrick Dugan and James Moore, farmers.

Forts

There is a fort of earth which is circular and 60 feet in diameter. The trench is 6 feet wide at the bottom and paved with stones at the inside edge of the parapet, which is 6 feet high and undisturbed, on Patrick McQuillan's farm in the townland of Moyagall.

A fort of earth in the townland of Beagh Spiritual, of which nothing remains but a small part of the north side of the parapet, on the farm of Henry Patterson.

There is also a fort of earth with stones, paved inside the parapet, in the digging of which a number of small Danes' pipes were found by Benjamin Crawford and on his farm. The above fort is long since destroyed. Information obtained from Patrick McQuillan, Henry Patterson and Benjamin Crawford, of the above townlands.

There is a fort of earth and stones in the townland of Ballymacross, on the farm of Doctor Grey. The centre is chiefly of stones, the parapet is of earth, but all nearly taken away for manure. The original diameter was 51 feet.

There is also a circular fort of earth in the townland of Toberhead, on the farm of William Badger, in which part of his house is situated, the remainder is his garden. This fort is 100 feet in diameter. The parapet at the north side is 6 feet high. On the top is a natural growth of ash and hawthorn. Part of the centre is taken away for manure and the rest laboured.

Denergan Fort is of earth and stones, situated on a hill of this name in the townland of Gulladuff, on John Downey's farm, and is nearly circular, 125 feet in diameter. The parapet is 4 feet high and undisturbed, but nothing remarkable about it.

There is another fort of earth in the townland of Drumard, on the farm of John Britan, but all demolished except a part of the parapet on the west side.

There is another fort of earth in the same townland, on Arthur Quinn's farm, but all demolished.

There is also a fort of earth on Robert Crawford's farm in Ballymacross, but all demolished.

There is a fort of earth on Patrick Higgan's farm in the townland of Moyagall, 124 feet in diameter. The inside is all ploughed up for oats. The parapet is grown over with hawthorn. The north part is taken away for manure.

There is also a fort of earth on Michael Kielt's

James II brass money

farm in the same townland, but all demolished except a part of the parapet.

There is also a fort of earth on Henry Magee's farm in Gulladuff, which is circular and 84 feet in diameter, but ploughed up in the centre. The parapet is chiefly of stones, 4 feet high, trench 6 feet broad, parapet 6 feet broad on top. Entrance at the east side is 6 feet wide.

There is also a fort of earth on James McPeak's farm in the townland of Drumard, but all demolished.

In Culnady there is a circular fort of earth 120 feet in diameter, with 2 trenches each 13 feet broad. The parapet outside is 20 feet high and 6 feet high inside. Part of the outside parapet is taken away and put inside the fort for manure. There are also 2 clumps of earth inside which appear to have been for an eminence to view from, as the fort is so well fortified. The entrance at the east side is 7 feet wide, on the farm of John Kyle.

There are 2 forts of earth in the townland of Ballymacilur, one on James Clarke's farm but all demolished; the other is on the farm of Robert Bullion but also demolished.

There is another fort of earth, one half of which is on John Paul's farm and the other half on Paul White's farm, in the townland of Tirnageeragh. The half on Paul White's farm is demolished.

There is a fort of earth and stones on a rocky hill near a stream and ancient yew tree in the townland of Dreenan. This fort is 75 feet in diameter. The parapet is of stones 3 feet high and 3 feet broad. The entrance at the east and west side is undisturbed, as so is the whole fort.

About 100 perches north of this fort, in the same townland, there is another fort of earth and stones, but demolished except a few yards of the parapet at the north west side, which is all composed of small stones and a few old hawthorn bushes. In the digging up of the trench of this fort at the north side, a human skeleton of a large size was discovered about 30 years ago by Neil Britain and dug up by Rodger Henry, on Hartfoot Downing's farm, and was deposited in the same place from whence it was taken.

Nothing remains of a fort of earth which was on James McKeown's farm in the townland of Drummuck, and which formerly had 3 trenches, but now all demolished. On the farm of Robert Wilson, in the same townland, there was another fort of earth but all demolished except part of the parapet on the west side.

Dunglady Fort

Dunglady Fort is said to be one of the highest and most beautiful fortifications in Ireland. Its diameter is 100 feet and has 3 trenches. The outside trench is 16 feet wide, the middle one is 17 feet wide and the inside one is 23 feet wide. There are 4 parapets, each about 11 feet high and 10 feet broad on the top. All the parapets and trenches are nearly covered with a natural growth of blackthorn, hawthorn and hazel. The trenches are very deep. The entrance at the east side is 6 feet wide and all regularly paved with large stones. In the centre of the fort was a draw-well, but is now 15 years closed up. The ruins of a cabin is near the entrance in one of the trenches and was inhabited about 25 years ago by Edward O'Kane, a labourer. The head of the tallest man cannot be seen when standing in the centre. A trigonometrical station is at the south side.

This fort was the burial place of the Quakers who resided in this neighbourhood. Margret Munnell was the last of the Quakers who was interred in this fort. Stillborn children were also interred here about 25 years ago. Some years ago this fort was tilled, as the ridges still appear.

Forts

On a hill called Drumglassagh in the townland of Culnady there was a fort of earth on John McKeown's farm, but all demolished.

There was another fort of earth in Upperlands on John Ardbuckle's farm, but all demolished.

Another fort of earth in the townland of Macknagh on Bernard McQuillan's farm, but all demolished except a part of the parapet.

Nothing remains of another fort of earth but a part of the parapet on Thomas Smith's farm in the same townland. This fort was originally 100 feet in diameter.

There is another fort of earth on Bernard Mellon's farm in the townland of Gorteade and is 80 feet in diameter. The parapet is 6 feet high, the centre was dug up.

In the Beagh Temporal, on Patrick O'Kane's farm, which is circular and 100 feet in diameter: the parapet is 8 feet high outside and of stones and earth. The inside is 4 feet high with a hawthorn bush and a stone in the centre. The parapet is 4 feet broad on the top and undisturbed.

There is another fort of earth on Frank Quinn's farm in the same townland, which is also circular and 112 feet in diameter and about 10 feet high outside at the east side and much higher at the north side. The parapet inside is 3 feet high, the entrance at the east side is 8 feet broad. The inside is sown with flax, the parapet is grown with hawthorn. This fort is perfect in shape.

There is another fort of earth in the Beagh Temporal, on Felix Bradly's farm, but all destroyed.

Another fort of earth but long since converted into a garden, on John Logan's farm in the townland of Macknagh.

There is another fort of earth on James Crilly's farm in the townland of Keady, circular and 62 feet in diameter. The parapet is 3 feet high, the fort is undisturbed and covered with heather.

McKeever's Fort is in Upperlands and is circular, 100 feet in diameter, all grown over with a natural growth of hawthorn, blackthorn and hazel. There are 2 trenches, each 6 feet wide. The parapet is 10 feet high outside and 4 feet broad on top, and 5 feet high inside. The entrance at the east side is 5 feet wide, all perfect and on Jacob Mooney's farm.

There is another fort of earth which is circular and 125 feet in diameter. The parapet is 4 feet high. The entrance is at the east side and 5 feet in width. All the inside is dug up. On Patrick Loan's farm in the townland of Fallagloon.

There was also a fort of earth in Bracknagrilly, on Henry O'Neil's farm, but all demolished except a part of the parapet.

There was another fort of earth on Daniel Mulholland's farm in the townland of Lisnamuck, but also demolished except a part of the parapet.

There was also another fort of earth on Denis McKenna's farm in the townland of Drumconready, but also demolished.

There is a fort of earth and stones in the townland of Ballymackpeake, about 15 yards south of the artificial lake which is in the same townland. The fort is circular and 71 feet in diameter and about 7 feet high, with a trench 3 feet broad. Part of the parapet next [to] the lake is supposed to have been taken away by the water of the lake, or to form a part of the island which is in the centre of the lake, as the parapet at that side is completely taken away. This fort appears to have been tilled as ridges are visible; on the farm of William Averin.

There was originally a cave and 2 forts in the townland of Drumlamph, but all long since demolished.

Lis-ivis-a-ladan is a fort of earth and large stones in Drumconready, on Patrick McKenna's farm, and is oval shaped, 75 by 34 feet. The largest stone is 6 and a half feet long and 4 and a half feet broad. This was standing 39 years ago. Stillborn children were interred here. From the proprietors.

There is a fort of earth and stones which is circular and 64 feet in diameter. The parapet is 5 feet high and all of stones, grown [over] with a natural growth of hawthorn and other small wood. The entrance is at the east side and 8 feet wide. There is one trench only, undisturbed, on the farm of Alexander Clark Esquire of Maghera and in the townland of Craigmore and undisturbed.

There is another fort of earth in the townland of Tamnymullan, on the farm of Cornelies O'Neil, but all demolished.

MODERN TOPOGRAPHY

Town of Maghera

The town is situated between Garvagh, Magherafelt, Castledawson and Draperstown, 8 miles from the former and 5 miles from the latter, and contains a population of 1,305 viz. 117 males of the Established Church, 143 females, 10 male servants and 7 female servants, total 277; Presbyterian males 112, females 122, male servants 9, female servants 7, total 250; Independent males 7, females 15, total 22; Roman Catholic males 311, females 370, male servants 31, female servants 44, total 756. Total houses in the town 229, 2-storey houses 76, and 153 1-storey high, houses rebuilt within the last 7 years 23; houses new within the last 5 years 13. The most respectable house is occupied by Alexander Clark Esquire and was rebuilt in 1832. The chief proprietors are Alexander Clark Esquire of Maghera, of the side of the street in which the post office is. The hotel side belongs to Rev. James Mauleverer. There is one 2-storey house in operation <opperation> at present.

Streets

The main street is 60 feet wide, the Brewery Lane is 27 feet wide, the Church Lane is 19 and a half feet wide. The streets were originally paved but are now covered with broken stones, or made as a road, except the footpath of the main street, the edge of which is flagged and the centre of paved stones, and kept in good repair at the expense of the county. About the one half of the houses of the town are slated and in good repair. The Presbyterian minister resides at the south end of the town. Opposite his door is a space in which the potato market is held on Tuesday, and is on Sir Hervey Bruce Baronet's property.

Windmills

The old windmill is situated on a rock at the Cow glen and ceased to work about 45 years ago, and was at that time used in grinding malt, chiefly for distilleries, as at that time distilleries were in

Parish of Maghera

Maghera. In 1823 it was converted into a barrack for foot soldiers, who only remained in it for a year. The windmill is 3-storey high and 15 feet in diameter inside. The walls are 3 feet thick, but now going out of repair and is at present inhabited by 8 poor females who are placed there for shelter by Mrs Clark of Maghera, wife to the proprietor.

The wind flax mill on Frank Caskey's farm in the townland of Ballymacross is of stone and lime, circular and 9 and a half feet in diameter inside and about 10 feet high, situated on a rock. It was built about 50 years ago and ceased to work about 20 years ago. At that time the roof was taken off by a blast of wind. There were 2 sets of scutchers attached. It could again be put into use with little expense. From Frank Caskey, proprietor.

Hotel

The hotel is about 22 years built; the accommodation is not of the best description. The house is 2-storey high, the proprietor is Alexander Falls.

Police Barrack

The house now occupied by the constabulary was built for such. The residence of the officer, David Patton Esquire, is in private lodgings in the town.

Original Market House

The original market house of Maghera was built of stone and lime, thatched with heather, and was accidently burned and was situated where the butter market now is held at Charles Harkin's.

Old Glebe House

The old Glebe House about 30 years ago was situated below the new, in the lane near the old church, and was of stone and lime, shingled on the roof instead of slates.

Bridge near Fortwilliam

The bridge near Fortwilliam spans the Moyola river in 4 arches, each 25 feet in the span and about 12 feet high. The walls are 5 feet high and in good repair at the expense of the county. This bridge on the top is only 13 feet 8 inches broad. About 41 years ago the middle arch was swept away by the inundation of the river. At the time of great floods the road on both sides of the bridge, for a considerable length, is covered with water, so as to render it almost impassable for foot passengers. Many of the inhabitants whose farms are on the banks of the river suffer much from these floods, which can only be prevented by making ramparts along the river edge and a wall along the road for a considerable length at the west or upper side of the bridge.

Bridges

The Milltown bridge is situated one quarter of a mile south west of Maghera in the townland of Craigadick, and on the mail coach road leading from Maghera to Tobermore <Tobbermore>. This bridge was built about 36 years ago at the expense of the county and has 2 arches, one 14 feet in the span and the other 18 feet in the span and 19 and a half feet broad on the top. The walls are 4 feet high and in good repair. In 1834 3 feet of a new top was put to the walls at the expense of the county and on a stream which proceeds from Lough Bran in the parish of Killelagh.

Also the bridge which is situated on the new road leading from Maghera to Tobermore, a quarter of a mile south west of Maghera, has 1 arch 18 feet in the span and 26 feet broad on top. 10 yards of the walls are in bad repair and 3 feet high, on the same stream, and 9 years built at the expense of the county.

The bridge which divides Culnaddy from Tirnageeragh spans a stream which proceeds from Carntogher mountain, with 4 arches. 2 of these arches are each 16 feet in the span and the other 2 are 8 feet in the span. On the top is 18 and a half feet broad. The walls were 3 feet high, but at present nearly level with the ground. Made at the expense of the county.

The bridge in the townland of Crew is 18 feet broad on the top. No arch but a small pipe. The walls are in very bad repair, at the expense of the county.

Bridge at Dreenan has 1 arch 13 feet in the span and 20 feet broad on the top. The walls are 4 feet high, all in very bad repair at the expense of the county.

The small bridge which divides Drummuck from Tirnageeragh has 3 small arches, each 12 foot in the span and 20 feet broad on the top. Walls in very bad repair, about 6 years built at the expense of the county.

The bridge at Dunglady has 4 arches, 2 of which are 17 feet in the span, the other 2 are small reserve arches. On the top is 18 feet broad. The walls are 2 feet high and in bad repair at the expense of the county.

The bridge at the beetling house near Mr Clark's of Upperlands has one arch 29 feet in the span and on the top 21 feet broad. The walls are 2 and a half feet high. All in good repair at the expense of the county.

Swatragh bridge has 2 arches, each 15 feet in the span and 18 and a half feet broad on the top, walls 3 feet high and in good repair at the expense of the county.

There is a bridge near the village of Curran which is also on the Moyola and has 4 arches, each 21 feet in the span. On the top is 14 feet broad. The walls are 3 and a half feet high and in bad repair. Also one of the pillars in the water is much shook and a part taken away by rapidity of the flood.

The bridge at the west end of the village has 5 arches, 2 of which are each 14 feet in the span, the other 3 are reserve arches, 2 of which are each 7 feet in the span; the third is a very small one, not larger than a pipe. The bridge on the top is 21 feet broad. The walls are 3 feet high but in bad repair. The stream which passes under the arches of this bridge comes from Desertmartin and falls into the Moyola a short distance below the corn mill. The stream every year overflows the bridge and covers the road for a considerable distance, which can only be prevented by making a wall along the road from the wall of the bridge.

Culnagrew bridge has 2 small arches, each 6 feet in the span and 18 feet broad on top. Walls are 3 feet high and in good repair by the county.

Also a small bridge in Fallagloon, on the road from Maghera to Ballinascreen, has one arch 10 feet in the span and 18 feet broad on top. The walls are 3 and a half feet high and in good repair, repaired last year, 1835, at the expense of the county.

Small bridge which divides the Beagh Temporal from Granaghan in parish Killelagh, has one arch 18 feet in the span, only 9 feet on top. 4 years built and cost 13 pounds, viz. 10 pounds from the Mercers' Company and 4 pounds by act of vestry, parish of Killelagh.

The Grillagh bridge has 3 arches, each 14 feet in the span. On the top is 18 feet broad. The walls on each side are 3 and a half feet high, 63 feet of which are in bad repair at the east side, on a stream called the Grillagh water.

Communications: Roads

The accommodation of roads through the parish is also very good. The leading road from Maghera to Bellaghy is 21 feet wide clear of drains and fences and in good repair, made by presentment of the grand jury. In 1831 the part of this road which passes through the townland of Beagh Spiritual at Joseph Brown's house was cut through a solid rock about 6 feet deep, at the expense of the county. The mail coach commenced travelling this road in 1832 and ceased last winter, 1835, in consequence of the bad state of the road through the bog, which is in the townland of Ballymacross. All these roads are kept in repair at present by contract for 7 years at 6d per perch, by Michael Keenan of Bellaghy.

Also the leading road from Maghera to Tobermore is 21 feet clear of drains and fences, and in good repair. Kept in repair by contract for 7 years at 8d per perch by John Kerr, farmer, of Craigadick.

The accommodation road from Gulladuff to Culnady is 15 feet wide clear of drains and fences, and in very bad repair, and was made 34 years ago by presentment of the grand jury and now kept in repair by presentment through the bog by Robert Wilson of Drummuck.

Also the by-road leading from Culnady meeting house to the corn mill is 15 feet clear of drains and fences, and in bad repair by county. From the above-named persons.

The road leading from Maghera to Portglenone through Culnady is 21 feet clear of drains and fences, and in bad repair. Made and kept in repair by presentment at the expense of the county.

The by-road leading from the main road at Tamnymullin through the flow bog to the Culnady meeting house is 15 feet clear of drains and fences, and in good repair by presentment.

Also the road leading from the Gulladuff road to Portglenone is 21 feet clear of drains and fences, and in bad repair. Kept in repair by contract for 7 years at 37 pounds from Gulladuff to Clady, by David Mulholland and Thomas McCawn. Also the road leading from this road to Tamlaght O'Crilly is 15 feet clear of drains and fences, and in bad repair; made and kept in repair as above.

Also the accommodation road leading from the Dreenan bridge to the Drumard road through Dreenan is 4 feet clear of drains and fences, but not yet finished. Made by John Downing of Gulladuff at the expense of the inhabitants and for their accommodation.

Also the road leading from Magherafelt to Kilrea is 15 feet clear of drains and fences, and in middling repair by presentment.

Also the road leading from Gulladuff through Culnady and Drummuck through the flow bog is 14 feet clear of drains and fences, and in bad repair by presentment, by Robert Wilson of Drummuck.

Also the road leading from Maghera to Portglenone through the Curragh, Drummuck

Parish of Maghera

and Dreenan is 21 feet clear of drains and made as above. From the above-named persons.

The road leading from Maghera to the Moyola bridge on the east or upper road is 21 feet clear of drains and fences, and in good repair, i.e. that part of it which passes through the parish. Made and kept in repair at the expense of the county.

Also the road leading from this road to Knockcloghrim <Knocklochram> and Castledawson is 15 feet broad clear of drains and fences, and in good repair by the county.

Also the by-road leading from the Maghera road to Falgortreevy, for the accommodation of the inhabitants to the mill and main road, is 15 feet clear of drains and fences, and in good repair by the county.

The leading road from Maghera to Kilrea through Upperlands is 21 feet clear of drains and fences, and in good repair, made by presentment of the grand jury.

Also the road leading from the Maghera and Kilrea road, leading by Mr Clark's corn mill in Tirgarvil to Culnady, for the accommodation of the inhabitants to the corn mill, was made and is kept in repair by presentment of the grand jury.

Also a new road is formed out by the Mercers' Company and at their expense, leading from the Maghera road to Swatragh, is 21 feet wide clear of drains and fences. Commenced last year, 1835, but not yet finished.

Also the road leading from O'Kane's public house in Gorteade to Dunglady and Bellaghy is 21 feet clear of drains and fences, and in middling repair by presentment. Information obtained from James McKowan, farmer and William Thompson, schoolmaster.

Roads

The road leading from the Swatragh road to Kilrea is 15 feet clear of drains and fences, and in middling repair by presentment.

Also the leading road from Swatragh to Kilrea is 21 feet clear of drains and fences, and in good repair by presentment.

The road leading from Maghera to Dungiven is 21 feet clear of drains and fences, and in good repair by contract for 7 years at 7d per perch, by Michael McKenna of Fallagloon.

Also the road leading from the Glenn Roman Catholic chapel to Ballynascreen <Ballinascreen> is 21 feet clear of drains and fences, and in good repair by contract for 7 years at 3d ha'penny per perch, and in tolerable repair by Michael McKenna of Fallagloon and James Kearney of Drumconready.

Also the road leading from Tobermore to the barony mearing is 21 feet clear of drains and fences, and in good repair by contract for 7 years at 1d 3 farthings per perch, by the above-named persons.

Also the road leading from the Moyola bridge to Dungiven is 18 feet clear of drains and fences, and in good repair by presentment.

The by-road leading from the Ballynascreen road to the mountain bog through the townland of Kirley was made by the Drapers' Company for the accommodation of their tenants, and is 15 feet clear of drains and fences and in good repair.

50 perches of the road leading from Dungiven to Knockcloghrim, with 16 perches at the march between Bracknagrilly and Fallagloon, where the hill is to be reduced, is all in bad repair and about 46 years made by presentment. One and a quarter miles of this road was repaired by the Drapers' Company.

Also another by-road leading from Dungiven road to the crossroads that leads to the Cross is 15 feet clear of drains and fences, and in middling repair, and was made by the Drapers' Company 7 years ago but now kept in repair by presentment of the county.

The old Carn road leading from Maghera to Dungiven is 21 feet clear of drains and fences, and in bad repair; made and kept in repair by presentment of the grand jury.

Also the by-road leading from the above road to Swatragh is 15 feet clear of drains and fences, and in middling repair, also by presentment.

There is also a by-road leading from the Maghera and Ballynascreen road through the bog to the Moyola bridge; is 12 feet clear of drains and fences, made by presentment. Only about 100 perches of it is finished, the rest is only formed out.

The road which branches off from the Maghera and Bellaghy road at the townland of Beagh Spiritual to Knockcloghrim was made in 18[last 2 digits blank] instead of the old road which is closed up since.

Also the road leading from the milk-house beyond the town to the Mullagh bridge is 21 feet broad.

The road leading from Knockclogchrim into the village of Curran is 21 feet clear of drains and fences, and in good repair at the expense of the county.

The road leading from Curran to Tobermore is 21 feet clear of drains and fences, and in good repair by presentment.

Social Economy and Modern Topography

Social Meeting

A social meeting is held on every Sunday evening in the schoolhouse in the townland of Crew, by the laymen of the Presbyterian congregation.

Singing School

A singing school for sacred music is only one quarter established and held in the Seceding meeting house in Culnady one evening in the week. There are at present 100 young persons who attend and are members of the congregation.

Prayer Meeting

A prayer meeting is held weekly in Swatragh by the laymen of the Presbyterian congregation, on Sunday evenings, established November 1835. From Doctor Mooney and Rev. [blank] Mulligan.

Church

The church is situated at the south end of the town opposite the Glebe House, dimensions of the church outside 67 and a half by 33 feet. The steeple is 17 by 17 feet outside, the walls are 3 feet thick with 4 Gothic windows on the south side, with metal sashes each 4 feet 7 inches wide, with cut stone window stools; east window is 6 and a half feet wide with the arched part of stained glass, with a representation of Our Lord taking the cup and other figures. There are 19 pews on the ground floor, 17 of which are double and each 10 and a half by 5 and a half feet. The other 2 are single pews, each 10 by 2 feet 8 inches, one at each side of the communion table. The aisle <isle> is flagged and 5 feet 9 inches broad. The gallery contains 8 single pews, each 3 by 11 feet 9 inches and elevated one above the other 10 inches. A seat for the clerk and singers in the front of the gallery.

There are 2 branches suspended from the ceiling; each branch contains 8 candlesticks. A baptismal font of cut stone is at the south side of the communion table, 1 foot in diameter and 6 inches deep, supported by an octagonal pillar of cut stone 3 feet 8 inches high. A stone stands in the centre of the aisle. The stairs leading to the gallery are of stone. The gallery occupies 26 feet 9 inches by 12 feet. The inside door is 3 feet 9 inches wide, the outside door is 4 feet wide. The old poor box is of copper and contains the following inscription: "The gift of Mr John Downing of Dreenan to the parish of Maghera, 1791", but now all broken and unfit for use. The vestry room is attached to the north side and is 12 by 14 feet inside, with one door outside 2 feet 8 inches wide, and a small door inside 2 feet 1 inch wide leading into the church, and also stairs leading from the vestry room into the pulpit.

The graveyard is planted with 2 rows of trees, chiefly beech and a few chestnut, planted in 1821. The wall round the yard is 5 and a half feet high and built in 1821. The gate is 8 feet wide; on the top is an arch of iron bar, in which is a place for a lamp. There is a very good bell in the tower. The top of the tower is ornamented with 4 cut stone pinnacles. On the wall above the door outside is the following inscription: [within a shield] "Erected AD 1820, Rev. I. Spencer Knox, rector, A. Sinclair and W. Miller, c[hurch]wardens." The cost of building the church is 1,500 pounds, a loan from the Board of First Fruits. Land attached or graveyard is 1 acre and 20 perches.

Income of Rector and Curate

The income of the rector, the Rev. J. Spencer Knox, 1,660 pounds viz. tithe rent 1,100 pounds, Glebe House and land 560 pounds. Income of the curate, the Rev. George Vesey, is 100 pounds paid by the rector. From the curate and the land steward.

Collections for Poor

The average collection for the poor in the church on each Sunday amounts to 5s, which sum is indiscriminately divided among 20 poor persons, whose names are registered in a book for the purpose, and 20 others whose names are not on the books.

Original Protestant Clergy

The original Protestant clergy are as follows: 1st, Rev. Bellingem Mauleverer; 2nd, Rev. [blank] Barnard; 3rd, Rev. [blank] Strangford; 4th, Rev. Henry Barnard L.L.D.; 5th, Rev. [blank] Marshall; 6th, Rev. Clotworthy Soden; 7th, Rev. J. Spencer Knox, who was appointed to the rectory of this parish in [blank].

Rector's Glebe

The Glebe House, the residence of the rector, is situated contiguous to the old church and was built in 1820, and cost 4,000 pounds, the one half of which was granted by the Board of First Fruits. There are 84 acres of excellent land attached to the glebe, 10 acres of which are under planting and consists of fir, ash, beech, sycamore, alder,

Parish of Maghera

oak and a variety of evergreens and other small trees. The most ancient trees (except a few large oaks and a few beech trees) were planted about 45 years ago and the general planting 15 years ago. The house is 3 and a half storeys high with excellent office houses and a garden, well walled, attached. The entrance is opposite the church gate, the wall at the entrance 5 feet high. William O'Farrell of Dublin was the architect. From the Rev. George Vesey and the steward.

New Presbyterian Meeting House

The new Presbyterian meeting house is built on the site of the old at the south west end of the town and was commenced last year, 1835, but is not yet finished, and measures 75 by 45 feet in the clear outside, the estimate of which is 800 pounds, built by subscription as follows: from the Honourable the Irish Society 50 pounds, from the Mercers' Company 50 pounds, from the Drapers' Company 30 pounds, from Alexander Clark Esquire, Maghera, 25 pounds, from Barre Beresford Esquire 10 pounds, from Sir Robert Bateson Baronet 10 pounds, from Captain Jones 10 pounds, from Rev. J. Spencer Knox, rector, 5 pounds, from Mr Matthew Little, Maghera, 5 pounds, from Mr James Little, farmer, 5 pounds, from Mr A.J. Campbell, merchant, Glasgow, 5 pounds, collected in Belfast by the minister of the congregation, the Rev. Charles Kennedy, 35 pounds, collected by the minister of the congregation in Glasgow 50 pounds, [total] 290 pounds, with other smaller contributions from the inhabitants of this and the adjoining parishes. The meeting house is contiguous to the old church and on the estate of Alexander Clark Esquire of Maghera, who gave the ground rent free.

Original Presbyterian Clergy

This Presbyterian congregation of this town was established about the year 1690. The first minister was the Rev. [blank] Dykes, second the Rev. [blank] Boyde, third the Rev. [blank] Smyley, fourth the Rev. [blank] Glendy, fifth the Rev. Charles Kennedy, who still continues and who commenced preaching to this congregation in the year 1800, and whose annual income is 75 pounds regium donum Irish currency and 64 pounds stipend British currency. The congregation consists of persons from the parish of Maghera, Killelagh, Termoneeny and a few from Tamlaght O'Crilly. Total families in the parish 750, total persons 3,500.

Collection for Poor

Average collection for the poor of the Presbyterian congregation amounts to 7s on each Sunday in summer and 3s 6d each Sunday in winter.

Extent of Meeting House

Since the new meeting house was commenced, which was in May 1835, the congregation assembles in the church and commences their service immediately after the church service is ended. The meeting house is now on the eve of being finished: the congregation expect to worship in it about the middle of this month, June, and [it] contains 3 aisles, each 5 feet wide and 3 rows of pews, 88 in number, 2 of which are double, each 8 feet by 5 and a half feet. The 86 single seats are each 8 feet by 2 feet 8 inches wide, each pew will accommodate 8 persons. There are 3 doors arched, viz. 2 on the west end and 1 on the east end, each 3 and a half by 8 feet. There are 8 windows arched, each 4 and a half feet wide with metal sashes. The pulpit is at the east end.

The land attached is 1 rood and 10 perches, and is situated in the townland of Largantogher. The wall round the yard is 6 feet high. The wall leading down to the meeting house is 5 and a half feet high. On each side [of] the lane there are 2 rows of trees of bush and alder planted in 1821 by Mr Knox. From the Rev. Charles Kennedy and the elders.

Benevolence of Mrs Knox and Mrs Clark

Too much praise cannot be attributed to Mrs Knox and Mrs Clark of Maghera for their unlimited attention and anxiety to relieve the wants and distresses of the poor of every denomination. A regular dinner is given by Mrs Knox at every Christmas to the female scholars of the day and Sunday schools. Premiums are also given to the deserving children according to merit, chiefly in books. Girls are apprenticed from Mrs Knox's school to dressmakers and some are sent in the capacity of servants to ladies' and gents' houses. Free houses are also given to a few poor widows who are unable to work. Mrs Clark is equally benevolent. About 4 free houses including the windmill are given to poor persons, chiefly widows, in the town and neighbourhood of Maghera. Food and clothing is also given by Mrs Clark, and on every Wednesday a ha'penny is given to each poor person who calls on Mrs Clark.

Remarkable Characters

The parish of Maghera gave birth to Sir James Murray, consulting physician to the lord lieutenant, and also to Doctor Cook in the townland of Grillagh. The house in which he was born is on the farm of Mr Isaac Flemming, but nearly in ruins. A Dominican friar named Bradley was also born in this parish.

Original Residence of Presbyterian Clergy

The house now occupied by Robert Martin, about a quarter of a mile beyond the new church, on the road leading to Bellaghy, was the former residence of 2 Presbyterian ministers. The first was Rev. [blank] Glendy. In his time the house was burned by the military in '98 for inhabiting [S.K.] Glendy, a United Irishman. The Rev. Charles Kennedy, the present minister, left it in 1821. From Rev. John McKenna P.P. and Rev. Charles Kennedy.

Moyagall Roman Catholic Chapel

The Roman Catholic chapel at Moyagall was built by subscription in the year 1802 and is 82 by 26 feet inside, all galleried except where the altar and pulpit stands. There are 8 windows on the south side, viz. 6 large oblong and 2 small Gothic windows, one at each side of the altar. There are no forms or seats in the chapel better than the steps of the gallery, which are elevated one above the other and so broad as to answer for seats and footstool without any pews. The ground floor is of earth without any seats or forms. The chapel is built of stone and lime, slated and all in good repair. A graveyard well walled except a part on the north side. The wall is 4 feet high with a good iron gate at the entrance. Kennedy Henderson Esquire of Castledawson gave 20 pounds towards building the chapel. The congregation consists of persons from the part of the parish of Maghera anciently called Lavey and Termoneeny, which was also a part of Lavey. In 1834 the congregation consisted of 1,750 persons.

Original Roman Catholic Clergy

The following are the original clergy: the first was the Rev. John Toghill, who had all the parish of Lavey and Ballyscullion; 2nd, the Rev. Patrick McFall; 3rd, Rev. [blank] McKenna; 4th, Rev. [blank] Regan; 5th, Rev. David McFall; 6th, Rev. James Murphy; 7th, Rev. John Rodger; 8th, Rev. Patrick Lynch; 9th, Rev. Charles McCann, who still continues. From the priest.

Income of Roman Catholic Clergy

The income of the Rev. Charles McCann, the parish priest of this congregation, is 110 pounds, one-third of which goes to pay the curate, the Rev. James McAleer, who is only 9 months in the parish. The parish priest is only 4 years in the parish. About 80 years ago the parish of Lavey and Ballyscullion were under one pastor. Collection for the poor 5s each Sunday.

Subscribers to Chapel in Fallagloon

The new Roman Catholic chapel is situated in the townland of Fallagloon and is commonly called the Glenn chapel; was commenced in 1825 and built by local subscription and cost 1,600 pounds.

[Insert note referring to first 3 names: These are not members of the congregation]. The Rev. J. Spencer Knox, rector of the parish, gave 10 pounds; Alexander Clark Esquire of Maghera 8 pounds; Drapers' Company 20 pounds; Captain Lamont, deceased <diseased> 12 pounds; Peter Henry Surgeon R.N. 14 pounds; Thomas McKenna publican, Maghera 16 pounds; Michael Logan, publican, Maghera 16 pounds; Alexander Falls, hotel-keeper 14 pounds; Daniel McKenna, farmer 8 pounds; John McCloskey, publican 8 pounds; Charles McKenna, farmer 8 pounds; John Kelly, blacksmith 8 pounds; Bernard Fairis, farmer 8 pounds; John McKenna, farmer 8 pounds; Neil Diamond, farmer 8 pounds; Patrick Hessan, farmer 7 pounds 10s; Patrick Henry, grocer 7 pounds 10s; Hugh Bradly, publican, 7 pounds 10s; Patrick Cassidy, farmer, 7 pounds 10s; Patrick McNamee, farmer, 7 pounds 10s; Andrew Conroy, farmer, 7 pounds 10s; James McKenna, farmer 7 pounds 10s; James Bradley, farmer 7 pounds 10s; Arthur Hessan, farmer, 7 pounds 10s; Thomas Conroy, farmer, 7 pounds 10s; John Morrisson, reedmaker 7 pounds 10s; Patrick McKenna, farmer 7 pounds 10s, with 88 others who gave each 5 pounds for their seat and others who gave smaller contributions. From the Rev. John McKenna and others.

Dimensions of Glenn Chapel

The chapel is 110 by 40 feet inside, built of stone and lime, slated. The building materials procured: stones in townland of Ballynock, parish of Killelagh; cut stone in Fallowlea, same parish; lime from Desertmartin, slates from England, timber from Belfast and Derry. There are 16 arched windows, viz. 6 on each side and 2 on each end; 2 windows, one on each side of the altar, with the glass over the doors, have each stained glass in the arched part. There are 3 doors, one on each end and one on the side, each 7 by 4 feet. The space occupied by the altar is 29 feet 4 inches by

14 and a half feet in the clear. The altar is elevated 5 feet above the surface of the floor with 9 steps and ornamented with 4 fluted columns of wood and a painting of the Crucifixion, executed by Paul Macosquin. Under the altar and partly behind it is a small room for the priest to put on his robes, with a door to enter the altar, an outer door and 2 small windows.

The chapel is all galleried except 40 feet, but the seats are not finished. The walls are 24 feet high. The floor is of clay and very rough, without seats of any kind. There is ample accommodation for 2,000 persons, which is the average attendance on each Sunday. There are in the parish of Maghera 600 families Roman Catholic, average at 5 persons to each. The congregation consists of persons from the parish of Maghera and Killelagh chiefly, and a few from Termoneeny.

There is a very good bell and belfry, with a Maltese cross on the top, at the south west end of the chapel. The bell was purchased in Church Street, Dublin and cost 50 pounds. There is a graveyard attached to the south west side; is covered with graves and many well-executed gravestones. The first corpse buried in this graveyard was Bridget Convery on the 17th December 1825. There is an iron gate 10 and a half feet wide in front.

Inscription on Glenn Chapel

The following inscription is on a cut stone above the door of the Glenn Roman Catholic chapel: [circular tablet] "Glory to God in the highest and peace on earth to men of goodwill, 1825." Information obtained from Doctor Barr, John Morrisson and many others.

Collection for the Poor

The average collection for the poor in the Glenn chapel amounts to 6s each Sunday, except on Easter and Christmas festivals when it amounts to from 3 to 4 pounds 10s.

Places of Roman Catholic Worship

Mass was originally celebrated in the old church at Maghera. The first mass house after the old church was in a cabin in Bracknagrilly. The second was also in a cabin in Fallowlea, parish Killelagh, and was built in 1782. At that time part of the 2 parishes were united and still continues. The third was on the site of the second and the present chapel is the fourth, architect Mr Robert Luske. Information obtained from the Rev. John McKenna, parish priest, Michael McKenna, schoolmaster, John McCloskey, publican and John Morrisson, reedmaker.

Original Roman Catholic Clergy

The original Roman Catholic clergy of the Glenn chapel for the last 90 years are as follows: 1st, Doctor Conway, who was pastor of this part of the parish of Maghera and Killelagh and bishop of the diocese of Derry; 2nd, Doctor O'Reilly, who was also pastor and bishop of said parishes for 6 years; 3rd, Doctor Bradley only a few years; 4th, Rev. Rodger Magilligan, pastor 6 years; 5th, Rev. Matthew McKenna for 30 years; 6th, Rev. Matthias McCosker for 28 years; 7th, Rev. John McKenna, who commenced in 1828 and still continues. Doctor O'Reilly, after his removal from Maghera, became Primate of Armagh. Doctor Conway was a native of the parish of Ballynascreen.

Income of Rev. John McKenna

The income of the Rev. John McKenna, pastor of the Glenn chapel, is 140 pounds, one-third of which goes to pay the curate the Rev. Domnick McCormick, whose residence is a private lodging at Maghera. The Rev. John McKenna resides near the Roman Catholic chapel in Fallagloon.

SOCIAL AND PRODUCTIVE ECONOMY

Superstitions of the People

Rowan <rowen> tree or mountain ash is pulled at the eve of stated seasons (chiefly May Eve) and is placed over the door or in the 4 corners of the house to prevent an evil eye, theft or any evil happening to any of the inmates or cattle, until that time 12 months. Also green rushes are pulled at Candlemas Eve and made into crosses, off which bread and butter is eaten and then placed over the door of the house, but not until the priest has blessed them.

A strone or large cake of oat bread is made the shape of the cross. The rushes are thrown on the floor and the strone placed on the rushes. All kneel round the rushes and bread, and at the end of each short prayer a piece is taken off the strone by each person and eaten. When all is eaten the crosses are made and, when blessed by the priest, are placed over the door, in hopes that they may have a plentiful supply of bread until that time 12 months, and in honour of Saint Bridget, as Saint Bridget entered the house and saluted Mary when with child of Our Lord, as did Mary to Elisabeth when with child of John the Baptist.

If a Roman Catholic dies whose sins have been

more grevious than others and from poverty unable to afford to light 12 candles, 12 rushes as a substitute for candles are lighted and held over the face of the departing sinner before life becomes extinct, and are on their knees during the time the rushes are burning, perhaps praying, which with the light of the 12 rushes to light them safe into purgatory, in commemoration of the 12 Apostles.

In 1830, as James Paul, a respectable farmer (a Seceder), was ploughing in the field in the townland of Ballynahonebeg with a pair of very fine horses, an old man begging chanced to pass by the horses, when both the horses fell as if dead in the field. The old man was pursued to a neighbouring house, brought back to bless the horses but much against his will. The horses, immediately after the old man blessed them, arose up and commenced eating. This is called blinking or an evil eye. Also if milk is blinked in churning it will have no butter until a horseshoe which was accidently found is put into the churn red hot, which will immediately produce a double quantity of butter. Also if a cow is blinked, a little straw taken from the eave <eve> of the house and burned under the nostrils of the cow will immediately restore her to her milk.

Also at May Eve a snail is picked and put into a clean metal pot and covered close during the night by the young unmarried females, chiefly Roman Catholics, who in the morning expect to see the name of the man to whom they will be married written by the trail of the snail.

As John Drips' wife was working in a field adjoining Dunglady Fort with a few others, several small stones were thrown from the fort, as they suppose, by some supernatural beings. Each stone was marked as if one stone was marked with another. Such is the superstition even of some enlightened Presbyterians. From Robert Martin, John Drips and Robert McClaine.

When a Roman Catholic priest dies, he is buried with his shoes on, and sometimes well paved with nails, in order to carry him safe through the fiery trial of purgatory, and is laid in the grave with his feet to the people's feet, in order to have a pastoral care over the ashes of his flock till the Day of Judgment.

Yarrow is a herb which is pulled at May Eve. The yarrow is only pulled by females and, while in the act of pulling, the following words are uttered:

Good morrow good yarrow,
Good morrow good thrice to thee;
I hope before this time tomorrow,
My own true love I will see."

After uttering these words they are not to speak till the morning. Also running to the door with a mantle full of cold water and listening to hear what name is mentioned by some of the inmates, and whatever Christian name is mentioned will be [the] name of the person to whom they will be married. Also a salt herring is eaten on Holy Eve night in order to create thirst, and expecting in the night to see the person to whom they will be married coming to their bedside with a drink. From Robert Martin, Henry McHenry and Miss Patterson.

Trades and Occupations in Maghera

The following are the trades and occupations: publicans 22, grocers 15, woollen drapers 4, haberdashers 9, medical repositories (apothecaries) 5, carpenters 9, shoemakers 16, tailors 6, watchmakers 2, blacksmiths 5, whitesmiths 2, coopers 2, bakers 2, butchers 4, brewers 1, stonemasons 5, wheelwrights and turners 5, painters and glaziers 3, saddlers 2, nailors 3, schoolmasters 3, schoolmistresses 1, hotel 1, dressmakers 8, dress and bonnetmakers 2, bonnetmakers 7, labourers 20, [crossed out: farmers 1], gentlemen 1, [crossed out: officers of constabulary 1], clergymen 2, [crossed out: postmasters 1, post offices 1], weighmasters 3, weighmasters and publicans 2, [crossed out: paupers who attend once a week 40], paupers resident 10, weavers 1, old clothes <cloaths> shops 2, [crossed out: lodging houses 13].

Clerks writing 2, washerwomen 3, huxters <hucksters> 7, dealers in rags, feathers and hair 1, dealers in eggs 1, flax dressers 3, [crossed out: auctioneers and weighmasters 1, Bible depository 1, poor shop 1, market houses 2], reed makers 1, hardware shops 2, [crossed out: shops in which timber is sold 6, general warehouses 5, leather stores in which are other goods 7], private houses 8, [crossed out: churches 1, meeting houses 1, sleigh <slea> drivers 2, carmen 4, cartmen 10, constabulary 9, dispensary 1, gentlemen's servants 3, servants in public houses 19, servants in private houses 31], basket makers 1, [crossed out: magistrates 1], delph shops 4, [crossed out: general warehouses 5, schoolhouses 3], skinners 1, [crossed out: medical men 7, rope makers 1], brewery 1, houses unoccupied 3.

Fairs

There is a fair held on the last Tuesday of every month for the sale of cows, horses, sheep, pigs, yarn, flax, beef, mutton, potatoes, pork, herrings, eggs, butter, crocks, delph, hardware of all sorts,

Parish of Maghera

soft goods, cakes, dulse, beans, peas, cheese, bacon, fruit and other trees in the season.

Markets

A grain market is held on every Friday, established in 1816. The house is at the upper end of the town in the rear <rere> of the houses and is 2-storey high, 20 by 30 feet in the clear, built 12 years ago by Alexander Clark Esquire of Upperlands and cost 300 pounds. The upper storey is fitted up for a special sessions room and is held once a fortnight on Saturdays.

Also a new market house for the sale of butter, beef, flax and mutton at the lower end of the town, built in 1832 by Alexander Clark Esquire of Upperlands and cost 300 pounds, and is 23 by 28 and a half feet in the clear outside and 22 feet high, with 2 doors, each 8 feet 9 inches wide with 2 good iron gates and 2 cranes to weigh the goods. There is a general market held on every Tuesday. From Charles Harkin, auctioneer and weighmaster and John McCloskey, weighmaster.

Eggs are sold (i.e.) duck eggs at 4d per dozen, bacon 6d per lb, beef 4d per lb, mutton 6d per lb, hen eggs 3d per dozen, butter 8d per lb, pork 3d to 3d ha'penny per lb, new milk 2d per quart, skim milk 1d per quart, buttermilk a ha'penny per quart.

Dairies

The only dairy in the town is kept at the rector's house. There is another dairy a short distance from the town [kept] by farmer named Robert Martin. Another dairy was held at the small house which is at the crossroads beyond the church about 20 perches, on the farm of White William Clark Esquire of Rockfield, parish Killelagh. This dairy ceased about 12 years ago.

Eggs

Eggs are bought for export by persons sent through the country, who receive each a ha'penny per dozen for gathering them and purchase them at 4d per dozen i.e. duck eggs and hen eggs at 3d per dozen, and sold in Belfast at 6d per dozen for export.

Post Office

The post office, which is also a spirit store, is in the centre of the town and was established in 1805. Samuel McDowell was then postmaster. This is a daily post, arrivals from Dublin at 12 o'clock, from Derry and Coleraine at 1 o'clock by the car, and from Dublin by the coach, delay only while changing horses.

Conveyances

There are 5 post cars or cars for hire and 1 chaise, viz. 2 cars and a chaise at the hotel with 4 horses, the other 3 cars are with publicans. There are 2 cars and 2 coaches passing through Maghera each day. The above are for public conveyance. There are also 12 private cars in the town.

Constabulary and Revenue Police

Maghera became a station for constabulary in 1825. There are at present 8 men and a chief constable, and became a station for revenue police in 18[remaining figures blank]. At that time there were [blank] men and a lieutenant, and ceased to be a station for revenue in 1832, from whence they were removed to Kilrea.

There is no custom paid in the town of Maghera since 1833: the inhabitants of the town purchased it from Alexander Clark Esquire of Upperlands.

Cloth Market

There was also a cloth market held in Maghera, which ceased about 20 years ago in consequence of a disturbance which broke out among the weavers and buyers, and by rescuing a fradulent web from the inspector and also throwing vitriol on the clothes of the merchants and buyers, which prevented their returning to the market. Chiefly fine webs were sold in Maghera.

Party Fights

On the 12th June 1823 an attack on the Protestants, which occasioned a party fight, took place at the June fair of Maghera, commenced by a man named Dellagan, who purchased from David Kennedy, a grocer, 1 oz. of tobacco and would not pay for it. 4 men were killed and 17 severely wounded. A few days after this fight the military force, consisting of foot and horse, was stationed in Maghera, the foot in the windmill and the horse at billets through the town, only for a short time. Many more is said to have been killed but taken off in secret.

Also on the 12th July 1830 a preparation for a party fight took place in the townland of Drumard, but was prevented by the military force of Dragoons. All Roman Catholics assembled from all parts of the country with provisions and made preparation to encamp at a gravel hole near the road leading from Maghera to Bellaghy, in order to prevent the Orange party from walking in possession. The Orange party were at the public house near the church at Knockcloghrim but, from the interference of the rector, the Rev. J. Spencer Knox, Alexander Forrister Esquire and Sandy Clark Esquire, J.P., the parties were prevented from meeting; but in the evening the Orange party was waylaid returning to Bellaghy and a number wounded, but none killed. A challenge previous to this was given by the Roman Catholics, which was the occasion of their assembling on that day. From David Henderson, Drumlamph, Rev. Charles Kennedy, Doctor Barr, Robert Martin and others.

Poor Shop

There is a poor shop established in 1824 through the instrumentality of Mrs Knox and superintended by her. Goods are given out on every Tuesday only, to the amount of from 5s to 1 pound in clothes, only to persons recommended and by ticket only, which sums are paid in weekly instalments of 1d to the shilling (see printed ticket) to persons from the following parishes: Maghera, Kilcronaghan, Termoneeny and Killelagh. Held in a room fitted up for the purpose in the Church Lane.

The following persons gave donations towards its establishment: the late Bishop of Derry gave 5 pounds, Rev. J. Spencer Knox 5 pounds, Captain Bruce R.N. 5 pounds 8s, Sir Robert Staples Baronet 5 pounds, Drapers' Company 10 pounds, [blank] Stewart of Ards, county Donegal, 5 pounds.

Bible Depository

The bible depository was established in 1831 through the instrumentality of Mrs Knox and Mrs Clark, and conducted by a committee of 3 ladies who meet on the first Monday of every month at 2 o'clock p.m. at the Glebe. Patroness Mrs Knox, secretary Miss Clark, treasurer and agent Miss Washington Patterson. [Conducted] at present by a committee of 9 clergymen of the Established Church, Rev. George Vesey, secretary, and supported by voluntary contribution. The following gave donations: from Mrs Knox 1 pound, Mrs Clark 1 pound, Miss Patterson 15s, Miss Inch 10s, Miss Crossley 10s, Miss Beresford 5s, Miss Clark, Rockfield, 10s. The books are deposited in the house of Miss Patterson, Maghera. From Rev. George Vesey, curate and Miss Patterson.

Spinning Fund

The spinning fund is also held in the same house with the bible depository, and was established in 1831 through the instrumentality of Mrs Knox, who is the sole patroness, and is supported by subscription. The following gave donations: Mrs Knox 10 pounds, Lord Strangford 2 pounds, Sir James Bruce Baronet 2 pounds, Miss Knox, late of Derry, 1 pound 1s. The Rev. J. Spencer Knox the second year gave 12 pounds worth of flax. At its commencement there were 30 spinners, poor housekeepers, employed. At present only 12 are employed. One spangle must be spun each week, for which the spinner receives 1s. The flax is purchased by the cwt of 6 score, in a rough state. The poor are employed to clove it at a ha'penny per lb. The hackler who is a poor female receives a ha'penny per lb for hackling. The tow is sold to the poor at the lowest market price. This is a perfect sinking fund, supported by the entire industry of Mrs Knox.

The following are the rules: 1st, the yarn must be spun to the grist of warp yarn; 2nd, for each ounce wanting or over the spinner is fined 1d; 3rd, that each hank is to be the same weight; 4th, that wanting one thread in the cut a fine of 1d, for 2 threads 2d and no more flax given; 5th, the yarn to be the proper length; 6th, no money is paid until the yarn is spun; 7th, that Mondays and Tuesdays in each week to be the days for giving out flax and taking in yarn. From Miss Patterson, agent.

Charity: Lying-inn Basket

The lying-inn basket for respectable, poor, lying-inn married females, established by Mrs Knox in 1825, being sole patroness and conductor and at her sole expense: the basket contains an entire bed and body linen, 2 changes for each woman, and 2 entire suits with every other necessary to each child. The poor woman has the entire use of the above articles for one month, which when returned clean, the child receives as a gift a new suit. The basket is confined only to the parish of Maghera and Kilcronaghan. Information obtained from Miss Patterson, Doctor Barr and the Rev. George Vesey.

Jewish Church Missionary Society

There is also a Jewish church missionary society held quarterly in the new market house and is 7 years established and patronised by Mrs Knox.

Temperance Society and Clock Clubs

There is also a temperance society established in Maghera in 1832 and consists of at present 145 members. Established through the instrumentality of Mr James Lyttle and Mr Samuel Moore, shopkeepers.

Parish of Maghera

There are also 2 watch and clock clubs established in Maghera.

Provision for the Poor

On every Wednesday the poor assemble in the town of Maghera and are relieved either in money or goods indiscriminately by the householders.

Amusements

On Easter Monday a field is given by some of the respectable inhabitants (generally the Rev. J. Spencer Knox or Mr Clark), in which all the young people assemble and where the greater part of the day is spent in a play called "wink and follow" or "touch and follow." A ring is formed by both sexes, when a young man will wink at a female and immediately run and touch the female, who will immediately run after him till taken, when both will mutually return and place their foot on a stone called the priest and mutually kiss each other. After other amusements such as skying or playing pitch-and-toss, they repair to the public houses, where the remainder of the night is spent in dancing and drinking whiskey and where many clandestine marriages take place, chiefly among the Roman Catholics.

Cock-fighting is also practised in the remote part of the parish. Common playing at Christmas is also practised. A play called "bullet" is also practised in the summer season of the year. The bullet is of lead, from 1 and three-quarters to 2 lbs weight, which is hurled along a level road for a wager of either money or whiskey for the best throw. Ball playing is also practised.

Birthplace of Doctor Adam Clarke

The birthplace of Doctor Adam Clarke, of which nothing remains but 16 feet of the east wall which is 3 feet high, and was originally 35 by 16 feet in the clear and situated a quarter of a mile south east of Maghera, in the townland of Moneymore, 15 perches west of the leading road from Maghera to Bellaghy, on the farm of James Parkes. 6 yards east of the ruins is an ancient hawthorn. 18 years ago the venerable doctor visited the ruins of his birthplace. Nothing at present remarkable about it. From Rev. Charles Kennedy and Rev. John McKenna.

MODERN TOPOGRAPHY

Bleach Green

The only bleach green in the parish is that of Alexander Clark Esquire of Upperlands. The bleach house was established in [blank] by the proprietor and cost 400 pounds. The beetling house at the road was erected in 1824 by the proprietor and cost 1,000 pounds. The other beetling house near the dwelling house is the oldest in the county.

2-Storey Houses

The 2-storey house in Grillagh was built in 1824 and cost 900 pounds.

The 2-storey house in the townland of Slaghtyboggy, on the leading road from Bellaghy to Maghera, was built in 1833 by Robert Johnston, now deceased. There is another 2-storey house in the townland of Curragh, [built] by James Anderson in 1833. The planting round this house consists of fir and ash, about half an acre, planted in 1820.

Also the trees planted at John Downing's house in Dreenan were planted in 1817 and registered by the proprietor John Downing. The planting on the side of the road beyond Dunglady Fort in the same townland of Dunglady are 14 years planted by James Anderson of the Curragh and consists of fir and alder, on the Mercers' estate.

Also the planting at townland Gorteade, at James McKowen's house, was planted 15 years ago by the proprietors and consists of fir, ash and beech.

The 2-storey house which is situated on the leading road from Maghera to Garvagh, in the townland of Grillagh, was built by the proprietor Mr Isaac Flemming in 1824 and cost 900 pounds. Information obtained from Alexander Clark Esquire, Isaac Flemming and John Downing.

Cottage at Grillagh Bridge

The cottage at Grillagh bridge occupied by Mrs Patterson is said to be on the site of an old monastery which is said to have been originally erected there, as the ancient name of the townland is Monastera Grilla. The walls round the garden at the road is about 30 years built by the proprietor Mr Robert Patterson, now deceased 6 years. Gracefield is the name given to it by the proprietor.

Planting at House of Alexander Clark

The planting round the house of Alexander Clark Esquire of Upperlands chiefly consists of fir and was planted (i.e. the oldest) 26 years ago and the general planting 16 years.

Social Economy

Remarkable Circumstances

McKeever was a chieftain of the United Irishmen in '98, for which he fled from the country. His residence was near his fort in Upperlands. Watty Graham, his companion, was taken and hanged on the market house at the new market house at Charles Harkin's of Maghera, for being a United Irishman.

About 34 years ago Ellen McKenna of Bracknagrilly was delivered of 3 children at one birth, viz. 2 sons and 1 daughter, but all died. From Hugh McKenna.

Clothing of Inhabitants of the Glenn

The clothing of the inhabitants of the Glenn consists chiefly of drugget gowns and petticoats, with printed linen handkerchiefs (i.e.) the women at work, no caps or shoes. Of the men, coarse grey coats and corduroy breeches with Kilmarnock <Kilmarnick> caps. From Michail McKenna.

Prevailing Names

The most prevailing in the Glenn part of the parish are McKenna, Bradley and McWilliams. The Converys are numerous in Gulladuff and the Lyttles in Falgortreevy. The McKeevers of this parish were originally Campbells, but as so many of them were United Irishmen in the year '98, they thought proper to change their names.

Productive and Social Economy and Modern Topography

Ironworks and Charcoal Clumps

About 100 years ago, on the brink of the Moyola in the townland of Drumconready, a forge for making iron was erected by [blank] Rennie, a celebrated inventor of machinery. The iron mine was discovered at the top of the townland of Fallagloon, joining Glenshane mountain, and worked by charcoal produced from black oak found in the bogs. Some of the charcoal may be seen to this day in the banks of clay in the townland of Bracknagrilly, near the road at Hugh McKenna's house. Also a number of small clumps or hillocks resembling the clump at the roots of trees, all of charcoal in small lumps, on the right of the road leading from Gulladuff to Portglenone, in the townland of Dreenan. The place appears to have been a natural wood which appear to have been burned in these small piles. Convenient to these clumps, at the opposite side of the river, there is an ancient yew tree which is supposed to have been the last of the trees with which this place was originally planted. The tree is 10 feet in circumference round the trunk.

Hand Scutch Mill

There is a flax hand scutch mill in William Clark's house near Dunglady Fort, made by Thomas Wilson, carpenter. The mill is turned by 2 men, with one man to hold the flax. The rim of the wheel is of cast iron and 8 feet in diameter, 1 scutcher with 4 arms attached, of wood; put up in 1835.

New Schoolhouse

New schoolhouse on the mail coach road from Maghera to Derry, about a quarter of a mile from Maghera, is now in operation and intended for a national school. It measures 34 and a half by 21 feet in the clear outside, with 4 windows, 2 on each side and the door on the end. Built by subscription and cost [blank] pounds.

Social Meeting in Beagh Spiritual

There is a social meeting held in the neighbouring houses of the Beagh Spiritual, established through the instrumentality of the teachers of the Sunday school, and for their benefit. It consists at present of 25 members, chiefly adults, and held on Sunday evening in the day schoolhouse from 6 o'clock till 9 p.m. Commences with singing and prayer and concludes with the same by one of the members. From John Downing and James McQuillan, publicans.

Village of Curran

Curran is a small village situated at the south end of the parish and contains 31 houses, 4 of which are 2-storey high, the other 27 are 1-storey high. The following are the trades and occupations: publicans 3, publicans and grocers 1, grocers 3, shoemakers 1, tailors 1, carpenters 1, hacklers 1, wheelwrights 1, weavers 16, stonemasons 1, pedlars 1, dealers in rags, flax, eggs and feathers 1, widows 1, farmers 1, millers 1, kiln man 1, schoolhouse 1, labourers who hold an acre of land and a cow's grass 16.

The 2 latest and best houses are those at the head of the street and built in 1823 and 1824. One is occupied by Mr John Downing, farmer and the other by Mr James Mewhinney, publican.

Parish of Maghera

Fairs in Curran

There are 2 fairs held in Curran, viz. one on the 22nd November and the other on the 23rd June, for the sale of cows, pigs, sheep, goats, yarn, soft goods and hardware. There is a regular patent for these fairs. From John Downing and others.

Curran Seceding Congregation

There is a Seceding congregation in the village of Curran, which was established in January 1836 and meets in the barn of George Rodgers. About 120 persons attend. There is no stationed minister, but are supplied from the presbytery of the Seceding Synod and conducted by a committee of 12 members. No income at present for the minister. The barn in which the congregation meets is in very bad repair and too small, only 24 by 14 and a half feet inside, with no other accommodation than rough temporary forms and a rough temporary pulpit. Service commences at 12 o'clock a.m. and at 5 o'clock p.m. Congregation consists of persons from the parish of Maghera, Termoneeny and Magherafelt. A regular meeting house will be erected if the proprietor (the Right Honourable Lord Strangford) will give the ground. If not, the congregation will purchase it from some of the freeholders.

Previous to the establishment of this congregation the people worshipped at Castledawson and Magherafelt; only 2 families went to the latter. These are Burghers. The Antiburghers are those who do not receive the royal bounty.

Curran Presbyterian Congregation

Another congregation in connection with the General Synod was established about 6 weeks after the above congregation and held in the national schoolhouse, in opposition to the above and supplied by their own clergy, but not appointed by the synod. Hours 5 o'clock p.m. From George Rodgers and John Downing.

Preachers

The Rev. George Vesey <Vessey>, curate of Maghera, preaches in the barn where the Seceding congregation meets on every second Wednesday evening and also visits the schools in the village.

Also a Methodist preacher holds a meeting once a month in the house of William Henry, opposite the above barn. The class consists of 12 members and is about 8 years established.

Irish Class

An Irish class was held in Curran by the teacher of the national school last winter, but from the interference of the priests it was discontinued and does not exist.

Culnady Seceding Meeting House

The Seceding meeting house in Culnady was built in 1801 by local subscriptions and cost 350 pounds. In 1826 a new roof was put on, which cost 75 pounds; voted at a vestry of the Protestant congregation 12 pounds 10s. The pews and pulpit was put in 1830 and cost 30 pounds, by the congregation. The meeting house is 63 by 30 feet in the clear, with 2 doors, one on each end, each 7 by 4 feet, and 11 windows, 5 on one side and 6 on the other; 2 of the windows are arched. There are 34 pews, 6 of which are double, each 9 by 5 feet, and 28 single pews, each 9 by 3 feet, all in good repair. The pulpit is at the centre of the south side wall. There is a good iron gate in front, given by the proprietor Barre <Berre> Beresford Esquire and cost 5 pounds. A wall round the front and east end, 5 feet high.

This is the first Seceding congregation was ever established in this parish. From the Rev. Alexander Mulligan. Service in summer commences at half past 11 o'clock a.m. and continues till 5 o'clock p.m., with the intermission of half an hour.

The Culnady congregation is a branch of the Knockcloghrim and separated from the latter 35 years ago in consequence of a party fight or a rise of the United men. The minister of the Knockcloghrim congregation at that time was the Rev. James Harper, who was the first, and who fled from his congregation for being a United man. Collections for the poor 3s 6d per Sunday.

In Scotland, in consequence of their protesting against the errors of the General Assembly in 1738, when the 5 excommunicated brethren departed from the body, the people adhered to them and established themselves into a body called Seceders.

Income of Seceding Minister

The income of the Rev. Alexander Mulligan, Seceding minister of the Culnady congregation, is 50 pounds regium donum Irish currency and 45 pounds 10s British, stipend. His residence is in the townland of Ballymacilcur. The congregation consists of persons from the parish of Maghera, Termoneeny and Tamlaght O'Crilly.

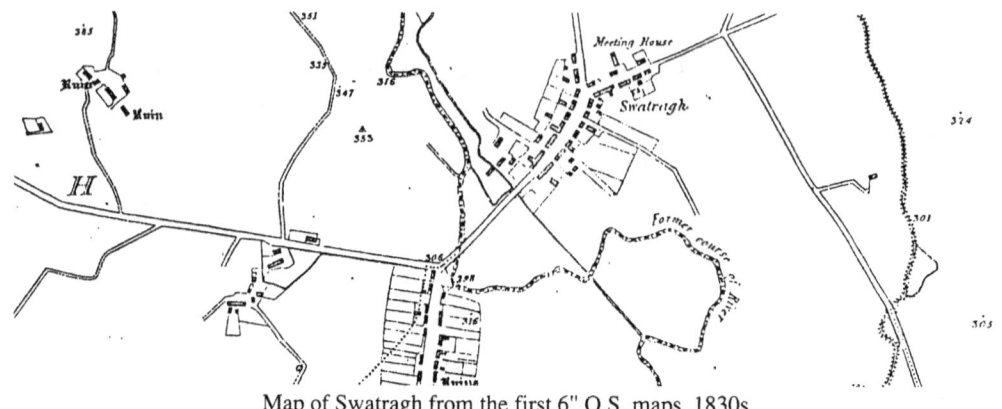
Map of Swatragh from the first 6" O.S. maps, 1830s

Planting

The trees at the Seceding meeting house in Culnady was planted 9 years ago and granted by the proprietor Barre Beresford Esquire, chiefly fir and alder. Information obtained from the minister and John Canning of Tobberhead and John Henry.

Village of Swatragh

Swatragh is a small village situated on the leading road from Maghera to Garvagh, 4 Irish miles from the latter, 4 Irish miles from Maghera and 3 Irish miles from Tamlaght O'Crilly. There are 42 houses, 37 of which are 1-storey high and 6 2-storey high. The most respectable house is the residence of the surgeon, was commenced in 1835 but not yet finished. Is of the [crossed out: [?] Ionic style] and was built at the expense of the proprietor and cost 280 pounds, with 6 large windows in front. The dispensary is held in this house.

Presbyterian Meeting House

The Presbyterian meeting house was built by subscription in 1829 and cost 260 pounds. The Mercers' Company gave 150 pounds towards finishing the meeting house, as the roof was on before the company got possession of the property. The meeting house is 52 by 21 feet inside. There are 34 pews, 4 of which are double, each 6 feet 4 inches by 8 feet long, and 30 are single, each 8 feet by 2 and a half. Each single pew would accommodate 6 persons and the double ones 12 persons. The pulpit is at the north end of the house. There are 11 windows, viz. 5 on each side and one on the north end, each 5 by 2 and a half feet. There are 2 doors, one on the north end and one on the south end, each 6 by 3 feet 3 inches. The aisle is 5 and a half feet broad, all boarded. A session room is at the north end, from which the minister can come into the pulpit. The room has 2 windows, each 3 by 3 and a half feet. The room is 16 by 10 feet 3 inches. The wall in front is 4 feet high with a good iron gate. The meeting house of stone and lime, slated and all in very good repair.

Swatragh Seceding Congregation

The congregation consists of persons from the parish of Maghera, Desertoghill, Tamlaght O'Crilly and Killelagh, and consists of 100 families, average at 5 persons to each family.

Income of Seceding Minister

The income of the Rev. James Sloan, minister of the Seceding congregation at Swatragh, is 95 pounds, viz. 50 pounds regium donum Irish and 30 pounds stipend British and 15 pounds from the Mercers' Company. His residence is in Tivaconvery, parish Tamlaght O'Crilly, and is 5 years appointed to this congregation. Average collection for the poor on each Sunday amounts only to 2s.

Constabulary

Swatragh became a station for constabulary 9 years ago and ceased to be a station in 1834. 4 men were stationed here at that time.

Fairs and Transport

There are 4 fairs held annually in Swatragh viz. one on the 5th of March, one on the 18th May and one on the 17th August, for the sale of horses, cows, pigs, sheep, goats and yarn.

The mail car passes every day through Swatragh and the coach every [crossed out: second] day.

Prayer Meeting

A prayer meeting is held on every Sunday evening

Parish of Maghera

in Swatragh by the laymen of the Presbyterian congregation, established November 1835.

Swatragh Dispensary

2 of the most respectable farmers in each townland on the Mercers' estate are furnished with a number of tickets ("to be in force for one month only") to distribute among the tenants, as occasion may require. The physician of the Kilrea dispensary is bound to attend the Swatragh dispensary on every Saturday to assist in visiting difficult cases. About 20 cases are dispensed to each day of 5 days in each week. Information obtained from Doctor Mooney, John Reynolds and Thomas Kane.

PRODUCTIVE ECONOMY

Returns from Maghera Market

The following is the quantity of grain and oatmeal sold annually in the market of Maghera for the last 10 years [insert addition: Ending 1836. From the many round numbers it will be seen that this is but an approximation].

In 1826: oatmeal, 1,400 sacks containing 4,900 cwt; barley, 600 sacks containing 16,800 stones; oats, 4,200 sacks containing 109,200 cwt; flax, 156 tons; beef, about 300 carcases annually; mutton, about 150 [carcases] annually.

In 1827: oatmeal, 1,400 sacks containing 4,900 cwt; barley, 600 sacks containing 16,800 stones; oats, 4,200 sacks containing 109,200 cwt; flax, 156 tons.

In 1828: oatmeal, 1,390 sacks containing 4,865 cwt; barley, 650 sacks containing 18,200 stones; oats, 4,260 sacks containing 110,760 stones; flax, 156 tons.

In 1829: oatmeal, 1,385 sacks containing 4,847 cwt 2 qrs; barley, 640 sacks containing 1,792 [17,920 ?] stones; oats, 4,240 sacks containing 110,240 stones; flax, 156 tons.

In 1830: oatmeal, 1,373 sacks containing 4,805 cwt 2 qrs; barley, 650 sacks containing 18,200 stones; oats, 4,250 sacks containing 110,500 cwt; flax, 156 tons.

In 1831: oatmeal 1,373 sacks containing 4,805 cwt 2 qrs; barley, 654 sacks containing 18,312 stones; oats, 4,250 sacks containing 110,500 stones; flax, 156 tons.

In 1832: oatmeal, 1,370 sacks containing 4,795 cwt; barley, 660 sacks containing 18,480 stones; oats, 4,246 sacks containing 110,396 stones; flax, 156 tons.

In 1833: oatmeal, 1,364 sacks containing 4,774 cwt; barley, 650 sacks containing 18,200 stones; oats, 4,240 sacks containing 110,240 cwt; flax, 57 tons.

In 1834: oatmeal, 1,200 sacks containing 4,200 cwt; barley, 100 sacks containing 2,800 stones; oats, 3,800 sacks containing 98,800 stones; wheat, 8 tons per annum; rye, 2 tons per annum; flax, 120 tons; butter, 400 firkins and 300 crooks.

In 1835: oatmeal, 1,200 sacks containing 4,200 cwt; barley, 100 sacks containing 2,800 stones; oats, 3,800 sacks containing 98,800 stones; wheat, 8 tons per annum; rye, 2 tons per annum; flax, 250 tons; butter, 30 cwt.

In 1836: oatmeal, 1,000 sacks; barley, 200 sacks; oats, 3,700 sacks; wheat, none; rye, none; flax, 270 tons; butter, 20 cwt.

Mutton 120 tons annually. In 1834 was the first year in which the butter market was established in Maghera.

Returns from Gulladuff Grain Market

The following is the quantity of grains sold annually in the grain market of Gulladuff for the last 7 years: [for details see Stokes].

SOCIAL ECONOMY

Emigration in 1834

List of persons who have emigrated from the parish of Maghera during the years 1834 and 1835. [Table contains the following headings: name, age, year departed, townland, religion, port to whence emigrated].

John Marlin, 38, Presbyterian, from Ballymacross to New York.

James McCahey, 28, Presbyterian, from Ballymacross to New York.

James Flemming, 17, Presbyterian, from Ballymacross to St John's.

Sarah Flemming, 15, Presbyterian, from Ballymacross to St John's.

Andrew Fleming, 24, Presbyterian, from Ballymacross to St John's.

William Barr, 20, Presbyterian, from Ballynahonebeg to Quebec.

William Martin, 20, Presbyterian, from Ballynahonebeg to Quebec.

Catherine Barr, 19, Presbyterian, from Ballynahonebeg to Quebec.

Jane Martin, 24, Presbyterian, from Ballyhonebeg to Quebec.

James Lorimar, 50, Presbyterian, from Ballynonebeg to Quebec, returned in 1835.

Robert Bradley, 36, Roman Catholic, from Ballynahonebeg to Liverpool.

Sarah McAlane, 22, Roman Catholic, from Curran to New York.
Jane McAlane, 26, Roman Catholic, from Curran to New York.
John Sturgeon, 18, Presbyterian, from Tobberhead to Quebec.
John Lee, 25, Presbyterian, from Tobberhead to Quebec.
Mary Lee, 20, Presbyterian, from Tobberhead to Quebec.
Robert Stone, 20, Presbyterian, from Tobberhead to Quebec.
Jane Stone, 24, Presbyterian, from Tobberhead to Quebec.
William Campbell, 20, Presbyterian, from Tobberhead to Quebec.
Mary Conroy, 25, Roman Catholic, from Rocktown to Philadelphia.
Sarah Millan, 20, Roman Catholic, from Rocktown to Philadelphia.
Bridget McKenna, 8, Roman Catholic, from Fallagloon to New York.
Margaret McKenna, 6, Roman Catholic, from Fallagloon to New York.
Peter McKenna, 11, Roman Catholic, from Fallagloon to New York.
John McKenna, 9, Roman Catholic, from Fallagloon to New York.
Frank Cassidy, 24, Roman Catholic, from Fallagloon to New York.
Sarah McCloskey, 26, Roman Catholic, from Fallagloon to New York.
Felix McWilliams, 25, Roman Catholic, from Fallagloon to Quebec.
Andrew McBride, 22, Roman Catholic, from Fallagloon to New York.
John Bradley, 20, Roman Catholic, from Fallagloon to Philadelphia.
Joseph Wilson, 20, Presbyterian, from Tirgarvil to Quebec.
Hannah Wilson, 19, Presbyterian, from Tirgarvil to Quebec.
Mary Wilson, 6 months, Presbyterian, from Tirgarvil to Quebec.
James Bradley, 40, Roman Catholic, from Tirgarvil to Quebec.
William Hessan, 20, Roman Catholic, from Tirgarvil to Quebec.
Nancy Hessan, 22, Roman Catholic, from Tirgarvil to Quebec.
Edward Hessan, 16, Roman Catholic, from Tirgarvil to Quebec.
John Hessan, 13, Roman Catholic, from Tirgarvil to Quebec.
Frank Hessan, 9, Roman Catholic, from Tirgarvil to Quebec.
Mary Hessan, 15, Roman Catholic, from Tirgarvil to Quebec.
Margret Hessan, 7, Roman Catholic, from Tirgarvil to Quebec.
Patrick Sweeny, 22, Roman Catholic, from Tirgarvil to Quebec.
James Toghill, 20, Roman Catholic, from Drummuck to Philadelphia.
Michael Toghill, 18, Roman Catholic, from Drummuck to Philadelphia.
Peter Toghill, 16, Roman Catholic, from Drummuck to Philadelphia.
Nancy Toghill, 14, Roman Catholic, from Drummuck to Philadelphia.
Patrick Maguigan, 30, Roman Catholic, from Drummuck to Philadelphia.
Andrew McNeil, 18, Roman Catholic, from Dunglady to Quebec.
William Kenny, 20, Roman Catholic, from Dunglady to Quebec.
John Mooney, 26, Roman Catholic, from Falgortreevy to Quebec.
John McConaghty, 26, Roman Catholic, from Craigadick to Quebec.
Neil McFlinn, 40, Roman Catholic, from Falgortreevy to Quebec.
Hugh McFlinn, 35, Roman Catholic, from Falgortreevy to Quebec.
James Donaghoe, 26, Roman Catholic, from Macknagh to Quebec.
David Mulholland, 40, Roman Catholic, from Macknagh to Quebec.
Rose McShane, 25, Roman Catholic, from Macknagh to Quebec.
James Orr, 25, Presbyterian, from Curragh to Quebec.
Robert Dysart, 19, Presbyterian, from Curragh to Quebec.
William Anderson, 30, Presbyterian, from Curragh to Quebec.
Mary Magowan, 25, Presbyterian, from Curragh to Quebec.
Elisabeth Orr, 50, Presbyterian, from Curragh to Quebec.
Mary Doherty, 26, Roman Catholic, from Fallyloon to Philadelphia.
Daniel McWilliams, 24, Roman Catholic, from Fallagloon to St John's.
Donald McWilliams, 27, Roman Catholic, from Fallagloon to Quebec.
James McKenna, 50, Roman Catholic, from Fallagloon to New York.
John McKenna, 14, Roman Catholic, from Fallagloon to New York.
Nancy McKenna, 10, Roman Catholic, from Fallagloon to New York.

Thomas Moore, 18, Presbyterian, from Fallagloon to Quebec.
Robert Huston, 19, Presbyterian, from Fallagloon to Quebec.
John Pool, 35, Presbyterian, from town of Maghera to Quebec.
Hannah Pool, 36, Presbyterian, from town of Maghera to Quebec.
James Pool, 16, Presbyterian, from town of Maghera to Quebec.
John Pool, 8, Presbyterian, from town of Maghera to Quebec.
Samuel Pool, 6, Presbyterian, from town of Maghera to Quebec.
Matthew Pool, 5, Presbyterian, from town of Maghera to Quebec.
Robert Pool, 4, Presbyterian, from town of Maghera to Quebec.
Anne Pool, 3, Presbyterian, from town of Maghera to Quebec.
Jane Pool, 1, Presbyterian, from town of Maghera to Quebec.
John Mooney, 22, Presbyterian, from town of Maghera to Quebec, returned in 1835.
Jane Mooney, 21, Presbyterian, from town of Maghera to Quebec.
John Huston, 25, Presbyterian, from Ballymacilcur to Quebec.
Henry Huston, 50, Presbyterian, from Ballymacilcur to Quebec.
William Winton, 25, Presbyterian, from Ballymacilcur to Philadelphia.
Ellen Winton, 24, Presbyterian, from Ballymacilcur to Philadelphia.
Jane Winton, 22, Presbyterian, from Ballymacilcur to Philadelphia.
Thomas Wilson, 22, Presbyterian, from Ballymacilcur to Philadelphia.
John Huston, 35, Presbyterian, from Ballymacilcur to Philadelphia.
Betty Huston, 26, Presbyterian, from Ballymacilcur to Philadelphia.
Sally Huston, 12, Presbyterian, from Ballymacilcur to Philadelphia.
Ann Jane Huston, 10, Presbyterian, from Ballymacilcur to Philadelphia.
John Huston Junior, 2, Presbyterian, from Ballymacilcur to Philadelphia.
Charles Huston, 5, Presbyterian, from Ballymacilcur to Philadelphia.
Daniel Orr, 12, Presbyterian, from Curragh to Quebec.
Mary Orr, 10, Presbyterian, from Curragh to Quebec.
Alexander Orr, 9, Presbyterian, from Curragh to Quebec.
William Orr, 7, Presbyterian, from Curragh to Quebec.
George Anderson, 50, Presbyterian, from Slaghtyboggy to Philadelphia.
Jane Anderson, 40, Presbyterian, from Slaghtyboggy to Philadelphia.
William Anderson, 14, Presbyterian, from Slaghtyboggy to Philadelphia.
David Anderson, 12, Presbyterian, from Slaghtyboggy to Philadelphia.
Martha Anderson, 10, Presbyterian, from Slaghtyboggy to Philadelphia.
Barbara Anderson, 13, Presbyterian, from Slaghtyboggy to Philadelphia.
Isabella Anderson, 8, Presbyterian, from Slaghtyboggy to Philadelphia.
Sarah Anderson, 6, Presbyterian, from Slaghtyboggy to Philadelphia.
Matthew Anderson, 16, Presbyterian, from Slaghtyboggy to Philadelphia.
Nathaniel Anderson, 21, Presbyterian, from Slaghtyboggy to Philadelphia.
Patrick Magwiggan, 22, Roman Catholic, from Drumconready to New York.

Emigration in 1835

[Table contains the following headings: name, age, year departed, townland, religion, port to whence emigrated].
John Mitchell, 35, Seceder, from Beagh Spiritual to Quebec.
Thomas Pettigrew, 30, Seceder, from Beagh Spiritual to Quebec.
Robert Pettigrew, 18, Seceder, from Beagh Spiritual to Quebec.
Sarah McCloskey, 23, Roman Catholic, from Moneymore to New York.
John McCool, 20, Presbyterian, from Tobberhead to Van Diemen's Land.
Anne Reynolds, 30, Established Church, from Tobberhead to Quebec.
Robert Henderson, 19, Presbyterian, from town of Maghera to New York.
Sarah Lagan, 25, Roman Catholic, from town of Maghera to New Orleans.
Hugh Lagan, 20, Roman Catholic, from town of Maghera to New Orleans.
Margaret McCloskey, 20, Roman Catholic, from town of Maghera to Quebec.
Jane Winton, 23, Established Church, from town of Maghera to Quebec.
Patrick Magowan, 24, Roman Catholic, from Gorteade to Quebec.
Nancy Magowan, 24, Roman Catholic, from Gorteade to Quebec.

Margaret Lafferty, 12, Roman Catholic, from Gorteade to Quebec.
Mary Lafferty, 10, Roman Catholic, from Gorteade to Quebec.
Patrick O'Kane, 22, Roman Catholic, from Gorteade to Quebec.
James McMaster, 18, Roman Catholic, from Gorteade to Quebec.
Anne McMaster, 20, Roman Catholic, from Gorteade to Quebec.
Andrew Smith, 30, Presbyterian, from Upperlands to Quebec.
Ellen Smith, 25, Presbyterian, from Upperlands to Quebec.
John Smith, 1 and three-quarter years, Presbyterian, from Upperlands to Quebec.
Catherine Fairis, 20, Presbyterian, from Upperlands to Quebec.
James Logan, 60, Presbyterian, from Upperlands to Quebec.
Margaret Logan, 60, Presbyterian, from Upperlands to Quebec.
Mary Logan, 30, Presbyterian, from Upperlands to Quebec.
Hannah Logan, 28, Presbyterian, from Upperlands to Quebec.
William Logan, 26, Presbyterian, from Upperlands to Quebec.
John Logan, 24, Presbyterian, from Upperlands to Quebec.
Nancy Logan, 22, Presbyterian, from Upperlands to Quebec.
Ellen Winton, 24, Presbyterian, from Ballymacilcur to Philadelphia.
Jane Winton, 22, Presbyterian, from Ballymacilcur to Philadelphia.
Martha Paul, 14, Presbyterian, from Crew to Philadelphia.
Jane Paul, 18, Presbyterian, from Crew to Philadelphia.
Paul Devlin, 22, Roman Catholic, from Drumconready to Van Diemen's Land.
John McKenna, 21, Roman Catholic, from Drumconready to Van Diemen's Land.
James Keilt, 42, Roman Catholic, from Lisnamuck to Philadelphia.
John Quinn, 30, Roman Catholic, from Beagh Temporal to New York.
Frank Quinn, 18, Roman Catholic, from Beagh Temporal to New York.
Alexander Hamilton, 32, Established Church, from Swatragh to New York.

Migration to Glasgow and Liverpool

List of persons who migrate annually from the parish of Maghera.

[Table contains the following headings: name, age, townland, religion (Roman Catholic unless otherwise stated), port to whence migrated (Glasgow unless otherwise stated)].

John Slaman, 35, from Tulnagrew; John Slaman Junior, 32, from Tulnagrew; Henry Slaman, 28, from Tulnagrew; Edward Kane, 30, from Tulnagrew; Felix McShane, 21, from Tulnagrew; John McLaughlin, 28, from Tulnagrew; Patrick McLaughlin, 45, from Tulnagrew; John McAtamney, 36, from Tulnagrew; Neil McAtamney, 22, from Tulnagrew; Patrick McAtamney, 20, from Tulnagrew; Bernard McLaughlin, 50, from Tulnagrew; Peter McShane, 33, from Tulnagrew; James Crilly, 23, from Tulnagrew; Michael Quinn, 20, from Tulnagrew; Patrick McKeefry, 24, from Tulnagrew; Michael McKeefry, 28, from Tulnagrew.

Edward [?] Mellor, 40, from Keady; Michael McQuillan, 25, from Keady; Joseph Loughlin, 50, from Keady; Frank O'Kane, 40, from Keady; Peter O'Kane, 35, from Keady; Peter O'Kane Junior, 30, from Keady; Thomas Magowan, 28, from Keady; Michael Magowan, 25, from Keady; Frank Doherty, 24, from Keady.

John Cassidy, 30, from Fallagloon; Thomas Maguckian, 22, from Fallagloon; John Maguckian Senior, 60, from Fallagloon; John Maguckian Junior, 18, from Fallagloon; James Sharkey, 25, from Fallagloon.

Hugh Doherty, 32, from Drummuck; John Magowan, 40, from Drummuck; William Mulholland, 25, from Drummuck; John Mulholland, 40, from Drummuck; Bernard Hegarty, 30, from Drummuck; John Millican, 40, from Drummuck; John McShane, 26, from Drummuck; William Bradley, 40, from Drummuck; Michael Devlin, 35, from Drummuck; John Maddigan Junior, 23, from Drummuck; Edward McMullan, 22, from Drummuck; Patrick McMullan, 20, from Drummuck; Frank Doherty, 40, from Drummuck; Nathaniel Clarke, 45, from Drummuck; James Clarke, 18, from Drummuck; Edward Downey, 25, from Drummuck; John Downey, 22, from Drummuck; Daniel Toghill, 20, from Drummuck; Matthew Connolly, 40, from Drummuck.

Hugh Crilly, 22, from Gorteade; James Crilly, 24, from Gorteade; Patrick Mellon, 30, from Gorteade; Michael Magowan, 26, from Gorteade; Hugh Lafferty, 21, from Gorteade; Hugh Lynn, 20, from Gorteade.

John Quigley, 26, from Drumard; Peter Convery, 28, from Drumard; Patrick Quigley, 28, from Drumard; Edward Hughs, 26, from Drumard;

Parish of Maghera

Patrick McKeigney, 22, from Drumard; Patrick Doherty, 23, from Drumard.

Peter Kelly, 45, from Gulladuff; Samuel Helferty, 44, from Gulladuff.

Charles Cassidy, 22, from Dreenan; John Connor, 40, from Dreenan; Edward Neil, 24, from Dreenan; Patrick McGoldrake, 22, from Dreenan; Bernard Henry, 26, from Dreenan; Henry Henry, 28, from Dreenan; James O'Hara, 40, from Dreenan; James McAlister, 25, from Dreenan; Henry Doherty, 24, from Dreenan; Henry Farrell, 30, from Dreenan; Edward Downey, 24, from Dreenan; Edward O'Neil, 22, from Dreenan; John Hammel, 25, from Dreenan; Patrick Hammel, 23, from Dreenan; Bernard Neil, 26, from Dreenan; Arthur Neil, 24, from Dreenan; Henry Neil, 28, from Dreenan; Patrick Henry, 27, from Dreenan; Frank Henry, 24, from Dreenan; William Hegerty, 25, from Dreenan; Thomas Henry, 40, from Dreenan; Dominick Henry, 26, from Dreenan; Neil Britain, 24, from Dreenan; Patrick Mullan, 25, from Dreenan.

Edward Donahoe, 22, from Macknagh; Andrew McShane, 25, from Macknagh; Thomas McQuillan, 25, from Macknagh; David McTamney, 25, from Macknagh; Rowley McQuillan, 25, from Macknagh.

Michael Sharkey, 30, from Fallagloon; Thomas Sharkey, 56, from Fallagloon; John Convery, 32, from Fallagloon; Michael Convery, 30, from Fallagloon; James Convery, 25, from Fallagloon; Michael Moran, 18, from Fallagloon; John Kearney, 26, from Fallagloon; Henry Johnstone, 20, Established Church, from Fallagloon; John McAlister, 24, from Fallagloon.

John Lagan, 30, from Lisnamuck to Liverpool; Thomas Lagan, 20, from Lisnamuck to Liverpool.

John McGlade, 25, from Drumconready; Rodger McCormick, 38, from Drumconready.

Jenkin McCormick, 44, from Bracknagrilly.

James Convery, 50, from Kirley to Liverpool; Hugh Convery, 25, from Kirley to Liverpool; Edward Convery, 24, from Kirley to Liverpool.

Denis McAtamney, 20, from Moyagall; Edward McAtamney, 30, from Moyagall; James McKenna, 40, from Moyagall; Henry Convery, 30, from Moyagall; James McAnally, 24, from Moyagall; James Magee, 22, from Moyagall; John Convery, 24, from Moyagall; Patrick Convery, 20, from Moyagall; John Convery Senior, 40, from Moyagall; Edward McCann, 25, from Moyagall; Neil Caldwell, 25, from Moyagall; Thomas McLarnan, 22, from Moyagall; Bernard Convery, 24, from Moyagall; John Duras, 40, from Moyagall; Edward McIlhattin, 26, from Moyagall; Patrick McIlhattin, 24, from Moyagall; Henry Convery, 24, from Moyagall; Frank Convery, 26, from Moyagall; Arthur McIntyre, 26, from Moyagall; Peter Scullion, 21, from Moyagall; John Berriman, 24, from Moyagall; John McKenna, 19, from Moyagall; Patrick McDevitt, 19, from Moyagall; John McKenna Senior, 60, from Moyagall; Nicholas Convery, 26, from Moyagall; John Convery, 35, from Moyagall; John McAtamney, 25, from Moyagall.

Hugh McKinley, 52, from Crew to Liverpool.

Edward McMullan, 24, from Drummuck; John Millican, 26, from Drummuck; John Mulholland, 30, from Drummuck; John Boyle, 25, from Drummuck; Nathaniel Boyle, 27, from Drummuck; David Mulholland, 30, from Drummuck; Stephen Boyle, 29, from Drummuck; William Convery, 26, from Drummuck; Henry Donnelly, 24, from Drummuck; Michael Montigue, 24, from Drummuck; Bernard Montigue, 26, from Drummuck; John Maddigan, 19, from Drummuck; Michael Toghill, 26, from Drummuck, William Convery, 30, from Drummuck; Daniel Boyle, 40, from Drummuck; Frank O'Neil, 35, from Drummuck; William Doherty, 34, from Drummuck.

Charles Mynogher, 20, from Dunglady to Liverpool; James Kearney, 30, from Dunglady.

Bernard McPeake, 24, from Swatragh; John Bond, 26, Established Church, from Swatragh; Arthur Crilly, 27, from Swatragh; John Crilly, 24, from Swatragh; Martha Bond, 30, Established Church, from Swatragh; John O'Kane, 38, Established Church, from Swatragh to Liverpool.

William Kennedy, 20, Presbyterian, from Culnady to Liverpool; James Williamson, 21, Presbyterian, from Culnady to Liverpool; [insert marginal note referring to previous 2 names: Tradesmen who only went twice].

John Arbuthnot, 20, Presbyterian, from Gorteade; Patrick McIlwhinney, 24, from Gorteade.

[Rough total of 167 migrants recorded by J. Stokes, from the following townlands: Culnagrew 16, Keady 9, Fallagloon 14, Drummuck 36, Gorteade 8, Drumard 6, Gulladuff 2, Dreenan 24, Macknagh 5, Lisnamuck 2, Drumconready 2, Bracknagrilly 1, Kirley 3, Moyagall 27, Crew 1, Dunglady 2, Swatragh 6, Culnady 2].

Parish of Tamlaght O'Crilly, County Londonderry

Statistical Account by Lieutenant George Dalton, 15 May 1830, with additions from Draft Memoir

NATURAL STATE

Situation

In the county Londonderry, baronies of Coleraine and Loughinsholin <Lockinsholin>, is a rectory in the province of Armagh and diocese of Derry, the right of presentation being in the bishop of the diocese. The present incumbent is the Reverend W. Napper.

Boundaries and Extent

It is bounded on the north by Desertoghill parish, on the east by Kilrea and the River Bann, on the south by Ballyscullion and Maghera, and on the west by Maghera and Desertoghill parishes. It is a large square tract of land divided into 25 townlands and containing 18,797 English acres.

Divisions

A great portion of the parish belongs to the Mercers' Company; Colonel Heyland has also several townlands and the glebes of Kilrea and Termoneeny parishes are in it.

NATURAL FEATURES

Surface

There are some high hills in the parish, particularly to the westward, the whole face of the country sloping gradually down to the valley of the River Bann.

Soil

The parish contains some very good and productive, but a far greater proportion of light and gravelly soil and reclaimed bog land, particularly to the westward where the hills are high and bleak and the country very wild and unenclosed. The bogs of this parish are very extensive and are generally of a very soft nature. [Insert addition: They are found to contain a considerable quantity of fir timber which is broken up, used as fuel].

PRODUCTIVE ECONOMY

Agriculture and Produce

No regular course of crops can be described. The small size of the farms, seldom more than 6 or 8 acres, not admitting of it. The principal are potatoes, flax, oats and wheat, which last has much increased of late. Near the River Bann are several meadows which are inundated during winter months to produce heavy crops of a coarse and bad hay. In the immediate neighbourhood of Glenone are several small nurseries and one very extensive one, which find a ready sale for small trees and shrubs to a great distance.

Manures and Turbary

Lime is procured from the neighbourhood of Desertmartin and the sides of Slieve Gallion, and is particularly useful in reclaiming the bog land, but many of the farmers and cottiers are too poor to procure it.

The parish is plentifully supplied and the bogs afford a quantity of old fir which is broken up and sold through the neighbourhood, supplying the poor with both light and heat.

MODERN TOPOGRAPHY AND PRODUCTIVE ECONOMY

Towns and Villages

There are 3 villages in the parish: Innishrush (which has a weekly corn market), Tamlaght and Glenone, which latter is merely a suburb of Portglenone, being divided from it by the River Bann. The inhabitants frequent the markets and fairs of Kilrea and Portglenone, and in some measure of Maghera. The parish church stands in the village of Tamlaght, close to the site of the former one, the ruins of which are still visible, and there is also a chapel of ease built on some rising ground near Innishrush, being a perpetual curacy now held by the Reverend M. Bloxham.

Manufactures

Linen cloth, generally of a coarse description, is made throughout the parish but for some years the demand for it has been on the decrease, and in consequence many of the looms are now idle and the poor in a very distressed state.

Roads

The parish is intersected by a great number, which

Parish of Tamlaght O'Crilly

are generally kept in very indifferent order and appear to have been laid out without any regard to the different hills. The principal one leads from Maghera to Portglenone and Ballymena, crossing the River Bann by a fine bridge at Portglenone; another from Maghera to Kilrea and Ballymoney; others again from Swatragh and Garvagh to Kilrea, and from Kilrea to Portglenone and Magherafelt along the west bank of the River Bann.

NATURAL FEATURES

Rivers

The River Bann forms the eastern boundary of the parish. This portion of it is very deep, excepting immediately above and below Portglenone bridge where it is fordable in summer. A small stream called the Inveroo [insert addition: Anvaroo] river forms the northern boundary for about a mile when it falls into the Bann, and the Clady river traverses the parish and falls also into the Bann a short distance below Portglenone bridge.

SOCIAL ECONOMY

Population Table

Inhabited houses 1,478, families 1,543, uninhabited houses 39, building 0, males 3,702, females 3,994, total 7,696. Number chiefly employed in agriculture 1,500, in trades and manufactures etc. 3,020, number occupied but not comprised in the preceding classes 475, total number occupied 4,995. Pupils: males 138, females 103, total 241.

The above table is extracted from the returns made to the House of Commons.

The county is well peopled but not so thickly as many other parts of the county Londonderry. [Signed] George Dalton, Lieutenant Royal Engineers, 15 May 1830.

Memoir by J. Stokes, 1836

MEMOIR WRITING

Memoir Writing

Received 13th December 1836.

NATURAL FEATURES

Hills

The hills of Tamlaght O'Crilly are very irregular. The country has a general fall towards the Bann. Each of the hills are small knolls of an oval form, generally with the longest axis tending north west and south east. They are tossed in irregular chains about the edges of the bogs and intersected by small valleys along sides of the streams and rivulets with which the parish is watered. Of these, the Clady river, as it is called, is the chief. It forms a valley bearing north west and south east for a half a mile of its course, south west and north east for the remainder. The highest hills are at the eastern side and are in some instances 200 feet above the level of the sea. They are in general formed by the descending features of the mountain Carntogher <Cairntogher>.

Lakes

There are several lakes but they are drying up.

In the townland of Lower Ballymacpeake there are 3 lakes. The largest of the three is called Ballymacpeake lough. It is on the southern side of the road from Maghera to Portglenone, of an oval shape and covering about 7 acres plantation measure. It is about 10 feet deep but was formerly much deeper, having been drained to a great extent about 1795 by Major Hill of Bellaghy. There is a bog on one side.

The other two are at a short distance to the south east. They are called the Bogossin loughs. The smaller one is circular, covering about 1 acre and is entirely surrounded by bog. The other is twice as large, oval shaped and bounded in the south and west by the remains of a native wood. They are both about 10 feet deep and contain springs.

In the townland of Inishrush there is the Black lough. It is near the road from Garvagh to Portglenone and is about 10 plantation acres in extent. Up to the year 1831 this extent of ground was covered with water to the average depth of 9 feet but, at that period, the occupier of the farm in which it is, drained a great part of it by making a cut to the Clady river. About 5 acres are at present undergoing irrigation and improvement. It took its name from the blackness of the bog with which it was formerly surrounded.

There is another Black lough bordering on the townland of Lisnagroat. It is oval shaped and about 20 acres in extent in the winter, but is considerably less in summer. It is from 1 to 10 feet in depth and contains some springs. The bottom is imbedded with bog timber. It is bounded on the north by bog and on the eastern side there are some traces of native wood.

In the townland of Lisnagroat, and partly in the parish of Kilrea, is Moll Reilly's lough. It occupies about 8 acres plantation measure and averages about 8 feet in depth. It is bounded on all sides by hills and has a skirting of bog round the shore.

The Green lough is in the townland of Inishrush and at a short distance east of the road from Garvagh to Portglenone. It approaches to an oval shape and occupies about 7 Irish acres. It is surrounded by high ground which had been anciently covered with oak. The above number of acres had been originally covered with water but, at some former period now forgotten, a canal 16 feet deep had been cut through the hill on the western side and into the Clady river. This had the effect of draining two-thirds of the space. The deepest part does not exceed 4 feet. Several attempts have been made since the principal one to drain the lough still further. It contains near the middle a small and insignificant island called Inisrush, for further particulars of which see Ancient Topography.

Rivers

There are 2 and a half miles statute measure of the course of the River Bann.

The Clady river rises in the centre of the eastern part of the parish of Maghera and, passing through the south of this parish, falls into the Bann near Portglenone. This stream is smooth and gliding and at Inisrush it turns some excellent mills belonging to Mr Courtnay. The floods are not injurious. The other streams are its tributaries and are small. The parish is well supplied with springs.

Bogs

In the bogs of this parish the wood found is fir, oak, yew, sally with traces of hazel. The oak is found lying at and about the edges of the bog and at or near the substratum. The fir is chiefly in the interior, disposed at different depths. The trunks that were broken off at the roots before they fell have been prostrated by a force coming from the western horizon. The trunks that have fallen with the roots still attached have been prostrated by forces coming from all points of the compass. They are always fewer and shorter than those that have lost their roots. They are not confined to any particular part of the bog.

The trunks that were broken off at the roots present a deeper charred appearance than the others. Of the timber, fir is the most charred and oak the most decayed. From 2 to 5 roots have been found resting vertically upon each other. The following account in detail of each bog will establish the above conclusions and exhibit some peculiarities in each. The plural number is used in order to include all the bog in each townland, there being generally a few small minor patches about the edges of the principal one.

Upon a small natural platform in the townland of Ballynian, at about 30 yards distant from the giant bog of that townland, there was formerly a small turf bog of about 2 acres Cunningham measure in extent. It is now entirely cut away and the surface covered with young heath. At the place John O'Crilly of Ballynian, while cutting turf in the year 1785, discovered, 4 spades deep from the surface, 14 stone steps arranged in a straight line and composed of well-shaped flat stones about 1 yard distant, one from another. They gave completely the idea, both from their size and position, of a set of stepping stones for the purpose of crossing a ford or stream. They lay upon the clay bottom and were easily removed. It is surrounded on 2 sides by a low rocky ledge rising to the elevation of 16 feet above the level of Ballynian bog and it is situated on the south eastern skirts of the bog. It is surrounded by a low declivity and has a very gentle fall from east to west. There are traces of the bed or channel in which a small stream formerly ran and fell over the ledge. It seems to have been, when running, of very trifling dimensions. It formed a very shallow pond 14 yards in breadth at the spot where the stepping stones had been and this presented a spot peculiarly adapted for the formation of bog.

The bogs of Ballymacpeake Lower, Moneystaghan Ellis, Moneystaghan McPeake and Mullaghnamoyagh are 20 feet deep in the deepest parts and contain about 400 acres. They contain oak, yew, sally and fir, the three former round the edges and at or near the clay, the latter in the interior and at various depths. Windfalls exist throughout but are only one-sixth as many as those which have no roots. The former are from 8 to 22 feet long, the latter from 12 to 44 feet. The former also have been more charred than the latter and fir more than any other kind of timber. Oak is the most decayed. The sticks are found fallen in different directions but chiefly from the north west. The windfalls lie indiscriminately.

Islands in the Bogs

Island no.1. They contain an island called the Horse Island, containing about an acre and a half. It is of natural formation. The surface is overgrown with the remains of wood and heath and there is a spring on the western side. This is in Moneystaghan McPeake.

Island no.2. Also an island called Illan-na-crieve, natural, and about 4 plantation acres in extent. It is of clay and stones, the surface hard and dry and overgrown with furze and a few ancient thorns. The summit is 8 feet higher than the level of the bog.

Island no.3. Not far from it there is a small island containing 1 rood, rising to 7 feet over the bog. It is of dark clay and small stones and could be made good arable ground. It and Illan-na-crieve are in Moneystaghan Ellis.

Island no.4. In Moneystaghan McPeake there is another called Fox Island. It is rocky and contains about 4 acres plantation. It is 6 feet above the bog and half a mile from the nearest arable ground.

Island no.5. There is one without a name near it, containing a rood and a half. It is of rich clay and could be easily reclaimed.

Island no.6. In the same townland there is another, containing half a rood, of dry black clay and stones. It is level with the surface of the bog.

Bogs

The bogs in the townland of Ballynian are about 60 acres in extent and vary in depth from 2 to 20 feet. They contain oak and fir, the former at the edges and next the clay, the latter in the interior. The number of windfalls is about a quarter that of sticks. [Insert footnote: Sticks are those trees found without roots]. The former are from 6 to 43 feet, the latter from 8 to 63 feet in length. Windfalls are not so much charred as sticks. Fir is more so than any other kind of timber. The windfalls are usually found deepest in the bog, from which the people think that they are first that fell. They lie in all directions but the sticks have fallen from the north, south and west.

The bogs of Bovedy are about 150 acres plantation measure in extent and are 20 feet deep in the deepest part. The remarks on the Ballynian bogs are every one equally applicable to these except that the windfalls have not been observed here to lie the lowest. They are here one-sixth in proportion to sticks. The latter are from 10 to 50 feet long and the former from 8 to 15 feet. The latter have fallen chiefly from the north west.

The bogs of Drumlane are about 89 acres plantation measure in extent and are 20 feet deep in the deepest part. The remarks on the Bovedy bogs are equally applicable to these. These contain, also, sally which lies at the exterior, on or near the clay. The proportion of windfalls here is the same as in Ballynian. They are from 8 to 18 feet and sticks from 10 to 75 feet. The latter have fallen from the south west. Oak is the most decayed. It contains the Wolf and Tod Islands. The former is called from the wolves that haunted it to a late date, the latter in like manner from the foxes.

[Insert footnote: Foxes are called tods in this parish]. The former is a prominent hill containing about 7 acres plantation measure. About 3 acres of it are reclaimed.

The bogs in the townland of Drumagarner contain about 95 acres plantation measure. They contain fir, oak and hazel-nuts. They are in irregular patches, of which the largest is on the eastern side of the townland. The timber is disposed in sticks, blocks and windfalls. The greater part of the sticks are found to have fallen from the north west and some from the north. The windfalls lie indiscriminately and the blocks all stand upright. In many instances 3 blocks have been found to stand one on top of the other. The oak lies along the edges of the bogs and next to the surface of the clay. It is believed to have been the first destroyed, as fir blocks have been often found on the top of oak sticks and oak blocks. Fir sticks and windfalls have been often found resting on oak sticks and blocks. Hazel-nuts are usually found in the bottom but there is no hazel. Sticks have been found from 12 to 60 feet long, windfalls from 8 to 20 feet. The largest sticks of fir and oak are found at the edges of the bog. The timber of all kinds is more decayed there than in the interior, but fir is less decayed on the north east and south east sides than on the south west or north west. The fir has a deeper charred appearance than any other kind. All the timber but oak is scattered at irregular depths; the deepest part is 30 feet.

The bogs in the townland of Drumard contain about 128 acres plantation measure. They contain oak, yew and fir, the two former at the edges and near the clay, the latter in the interior and at various depths. There are about one-third as many windfalls as sticks. The former are from 6 to 25 feet in length, the latter from 10 to 70 feet. The former also appear more charred than the latter and fir more than any other kind of timber. It had been covered with wood formerly. Near it is Tod Island, containing about half an acre. It had been likewise formerly wooded.

Round the west and south western shores of Drumoolish bog sticks of various lengths, of oak and sally, are found on the surface of the clay bottom. The largest sticks are found to have fallen from the south west but the windfalls lie indiscriminately. Windfalls vary in length from 7 to 15 feet and sticks from 10 to 40 feet. The fir sticks have been the most charred. The oak has been the most decayed. The depth is 30 feet and the extent about 90 plantation acres. There is a small island in it composed of clay and 60 by 25 yards in extent. It is of oval form and of natural formation.

The oak that lies at the greatest depth is found to be more decayed than any other timber. There have been instances known of 5 blocks being found, the one resting on the other, each upright, and all supposed to have grown and decayed in succession. The largest stood upon the clay and the rest became gradually smaller. The oak is found chiefly in the south eastern and the fir in the northern and western parts.

The bogs of Drumnacannan contain about 120 plantation acres and are 15 feet deep. They contain fir, oak and yew. The oak is found around the edges and next the clay, the fir chiefly in the interior and at various depths. The windfalls of all are found everywhere and in every direction. The yew is also found lying in every direction and chiefly along the shores or edges. The sticks are from 12 to 40 feet long, windfalls from 6 to 20 feet. The former have been more charred than the latter and fir more than any other kind of timber. The former also have been found to have fallen chiefly from the south west. The sticks are found fallen in different directions but chiefly from the south west.

The bogs in the townland of Drumsarragh contain about 120 acres plantation measure. They contain oak, fir and yew. These are disposed in sticks and windfalls with blocks. Sticks are found from 12 to 60 feet and windfalls from 8 to 20 feet. The blocks are always upright. The oak lies always nearest the bottom and all the other timber at various depths, one over the other and irregularly mixed. 3 blocks have been often found, one resting on the top or shoulder of the other, as if produced by successive growth and destruction. Blocks have been also found resting on fir and oak sticks. Oak is confined to the edges of the bog. For 1 windfall dug up there are 4 sticks. The latter are more charred than the former and fir more than any other kind of timber. The oak is very much decayed. The sticks have fallen from north west to south east. The greatest depth of these bogs is 20 feet.

The bogs of Eden contain about 200 acres plantation measure. They contain fir, oak and yew. The sticks found here vary from 18 to 100 feet and the windfalls from 6 to 20 feet. The blocks are always upright. The oak lies along the edges and the fir principally in the interior. The yew is equally dispersed and the quantity of windfalls is nearly equal to half that of sticks. The latter has been the most charred. The yew is small and of very little value. The deepest part is 20 feet.

The bogs in the townland of Gortmacrane are about 100 acres in extent and 25 feet deep in the deepest part. They contain fir and oak, the latter chiefly confined to the edges, the former both in the interior and in the outer parts. The windfalls are about a quarter in proportion to sticks. The latter are from 12 to 90 feet long and the former from 8 to 20 feet. The latter are more charred than the former and the fir more than any other kind of timber.

The bogs in the townland of Glenone contain about 200 acres plantation measure and are 30 feet deep in the deepest part. They contain oak, fir and sally, the first and last about the edges and near the clay, the second in the interior at different depths. The quantity of windfalls is about one-sixth that of sticks. The latter are from 8 to 30 feet long, the former 7 to 15 feet. The latter are more charred than the former and fir more than any other timber. The latter have fallen chiefly from the south west, the former indiscriminately. Oak is the most decayed. It contains an island of 4 acres called the Rough Island.

That part of Drumimeric flow bog which is in the townland of Lisnagroat contains oak, fir, yew and sally. The first is chiefly found about the edges and near the clay. The largest fir trees are found at the edges but the largest quantity is further in. The yew and sally is also found in the interior. The quantity of windfalls is one-third that of sticks. The latter are from 10 to 90 feet long, the former from 8 to 22 feet. The timber is charred here in the same proportion and manner as in the preceding 2 townlands. The sticks have fallen from the north, north west and south.

The bogs in the townland of Lismoyle contain about 400 acres plantation measure. The greater part is one patch called Anaghavogy. It contains oak, sally and fir, the two former along the edges. The fir and windfalls are principally got in the interior. The quantity of windfalls found is about one-sixth that of sticks. The latter vary in length from 20 to 80 feet and the former from 7 to 15 feet. The latter have fallen generally from the west. Sticks and fir timber are the most charred. There is an island in it, of natural formation, near the centre called Annaghavoy Island. The summit of it stands about 15 feet higher than the surface of the bog. It was first occupied and a part of it reclaimed about the year 1811 by 2 families who reside on it. The soil is partly rocky and partly composed of red clay and small stones. The bog round about is very quick and soft.

The Lisgorgan and Killymuck bogs contain together about 150 acres plantation measure and are but 12 feet deep. The remarks on the Ballynian bogs are equally applicable to these except as to

Parish of Tamlaght O'Crilly

the depth of the windfalls. The windfalls are one-third the quantity of sticks. They are from 8 to 30 feet long and sticks from 12 to 70 feet. The latter are found fallen from different points but chiefly from the south west. A fir stick 40 feet long was raised out of it in 1826. It was lying horizontally, having fallen from the south west, and on top of it there rested 3 fir blocks at nearly equal distances from one another, each in an upright position and each as if it had grown and decayed in that position.

The same applies also to the Killygullib Glebe bogs. They are 40 acres in extent and are 10 feet deep. In the interior there is yew at various depths. The quantity of windfalls is about one-fourth that of sticks. The latter are from 12 to 50 feet long, the former from 8 to 22 feet. The latter have fallen from the south west.

The Inisrush bogs contain about 160 acres plantation measure and vary in depth from 2 to 20 feet. The same remarks apply to them. The windfalls are about a quarter the quantity of sticks. Sally is found about the edges near the clay. The sticks are from 10 to 30 feet long and windfalls from 10 to 20 feet. The former have fallen from the north west.

The Moneysallin bogs contain about 180 acres plantation measure and are 30 feet in the deepest part. The same remarks apply also to them. A little yew and sally is found about the edges near the clay. The oak is the most decayed. The quantity of windfalls is but one-seventh that of sticks. The latter vary in length from 12 to 65 feet and the former from 10 to 20 feet. The latter have fallen from different directions but chiefly from the west. Like the substratum of the other bogs, that of this is very variable, being sometimes gravel, sometimes clay, sometimes marl.

The Timaconway bogs contain about 50 plantation acres and are 12 feet deep in the deepest part. The same remarks apply also to them. A little yew is in the interior. The quantity of timber of any kind is scanty. The sticks vary in length from 12 to 70 feet and windfalls from 8 to 20 feet. The former have fallen from the south west, west and north west. The proportion of sticks to windfalls is not known.

The Tyanee bogs contain about 400 acres plantation measure. They are 25 feet deep in the deepest part. The same remarks apply also to them. Yew and sally are found at the edges lying near the clay. The quantity of windfalls is a quarter that of sticks. The former are from 7 to 20 feet long, the latter from 7 to 40 feet. The latter have fallen chiefly from the north west. Oak is found in the most decayed state. In every bog of the parish, blocks have been found resting one upon another.

Woods

Anaghclea old wood, in the townland of Eden, contains about 26 acres plantation measure. The large trees are all cut down and nothing remaining at present but the copse or scrog as it is called. It is entirely surrounded by bog and, the cattle being allowed to graze through it, does not increase in growth.

Drumimeric wood, in the townland of Lisnagroat, contains about 6 acres plantation measure. Some of the trees are from 12 to 15 feet high.

Rossmore wood, in the townland of Lisnagroat, contains about 5 acres plantation. Nothing remains at present but scrog. In another part of the same townland there are about 4 acres, the same measure, of old wood. Nothing remains at present but scrog.

At Inisrush House, the seat of Hercules Ellis Esquire, there are about 12 acres plantation measure of the demesne under native wood. There is 1,000 large oak trees with an underwood of hazel. This is commonly called Inisrush wood.

From the above patches being still known by particular names, it would seem that the parish was formerly filled with extensive and important forests. They are very conspicuously marked in Timaconway and Ballynian by a great number of thorn-bushes which are their most durable and lasting part.

Climate and Crops

It is considered that the neighbourhood of Hervey Hill is more free from rain than either Garvagh or Portglenone. This means the northern half of the parish. There is no meteorological register kept by the residents.

Wheat is put down from the 10th October and onwards and is ripe from the 26th August. Barley is put down from the 1st April and onwards, is ripe from 20th August. Oats are put down from the 1st April and onwards and ripen from the 1st September. Flax is put down from the 1st May and ripens from the 15th August. Clover hay, which is sown from the 7th April, is in full growth from 1st of June in the second year. Vetches are put down from the 1st March, ripen from the 10th July; peas from the 16th of March and are ripe from the 15th September. Beans are put down from 25th of February and are ripe from 20th September; turnips from the 1st July and are ripe from 1st November; red beet from 12th May and are ripe from 1st November. Rye is put down from 1st November and is ripe from 24th August in the following year. Potatoes are put down from 15th April and are dug up from 20th October.

The higher parts of the parish are from 1 to 3 weeks later in ripening the various crops than the lowland or sandy soil, although the difference in sowing does not average more than 10 days.

Modern Topography

Towns: Tamlaght

Tamlaght is a small country village on the road from Garvagh to Portglenone. It is 8 statute miles from the former and 4 and a half miles from the latter place. It is also 4 miles from Kilrea and 5 and a half miles from Maghera. It stands on the western side of one of the small hills with which the country abounds. It is called Churchtown by the landlord of the estate and Tamlaght on the Ordnance map, and is the ancient name. 4 fairs were formerly annually held in the village, the first on 12th February, the second on 15th May, the third on 24th August and the fourth on 1st November. They gradually ceased about the year 1800 in consequence of the drunken and quarrelsome disposition of the inhabitants which hindered buyers from attending it. This they still manifest, though in a diminished degree.

Buildings and Occupations in Tamlaght

It contains 27 1-storey houses and 8 2-storey. There is a church, schoolhouse and dispensary. This last is merely a cabin fitted up for the purpose. There is also 1 house of stone and brick, slated and 1-storey high with garret rooms, built by the landlord in 1833 as a rent receiver's office and dwelling house.

There are: farmers 11, labourers 4, grocers 3, spirit dealers 2, shoemakers 2, masons 2, working spinsters 2, subagent 1, carpenter 1, blacksmith 1, sexton 1, tailor 1, hosier 1, carrier 1, schoolmaster 1, total 34 in 33 occupied houses. The schoolmaster lives in lodgings. With the schoolhouse and dispensary, the above 33 makes up a total of 35 houses. There is also 1 waste and unoccupied. The building of the rent receiver's office is a great improvement to the appearance of the village.

Inisrush

Inisrush is a small country village standing close to Inisrush House. The houses are scattered rather irregularly and it is upon low ground. There is a petty sessions held in it on the first Thursday of each month. There is also a small corn market every Monday, to which cranage is given by James Courtnay Esquire. It contains 31 houses of 1-storey and 9 of 2-storeys, with 1 waste house.

There are: working spinsters 7, labourers 6, butchers 3, shoemakers 3, farmers 2, spirit dealers 2, spinning wheelwright 1, grocers 1, coopers 2, millwright 1, carpenter 1, tailor 1, blacksmith 1, total 31 in 31 houses. There is also 1 petty sessions house, 1 schoolhouse, 2 corn mills, 1 flax mill, 1 flax store house, 2 corn kilns. The houses are in good repair.

Clady

In the little clachan called Clady, situated close to Glenburn House and at the sides of the high road to Portglenone, there are 10 houses. In these there are: spirit dealers 3, grocers 2, farmers 2, coopers 1, blacksmiths 1, miller 1, total 10 in 10 houses. There are 3 houses of 2-storeys and 7 of 1-storey. There are none waste or unoccupied.

Portglenone

The following are the trades and callings, with the number and height of houses, in that part of the town of Portglenone situated within this parish: labourers 9, huxters in provisions 5, boot and shoemakers 4, workwomen at spinning 3, carpenters and cartwrights 3, grocers 2, spirit dealers 2, dealers in meal, corn, butter and pigs 2, sawyers 2, lodging-house keepers 2, pensioners 2, timber, slate and iron merchant 1, attorney 1, dressmaker 1, tailor 1, bonnetmaker 1, painter and glazier 1, nailer 1, baker 1, spinning wheelwright 1, blue dyer 1, leather cutter 1, total 47.

These trades are carried on in 47 distinct houses. There is also a schoolhouse, for particulars of which see Modern Topography for the parish at large, and a dwelling house for the accommodation of 5 constabulary police. For particulars respecting the town, see the parish of [Ahoghill] in the county of Antrim, as three-fourths of it is situated there.

Of these 47 houses, there are with the schoolhouse and police house 17 2-storey high and 32 1-storey. They constitute an irregular street and form a suburb to the rest of the town of Portglenone, with which there is a communication by a good bridge over the River Bann. Its opposite bank is well ornamented with trees. The houses of this suburb are in good repair. None of them are waste or unoccupied.

Parish of Tamlaght O'Crilly

Public Buildings: Parish Church

The parish church of Tamlaght O'Crilly is a slated rectangular building, with a 3-storey belfry at the west end ornamented at the top with Gothic pinnacles. It is situated in the village of that name and close to the old church. There are 4 Gothic windows including the eastern one. The interior is in good repair. The alley and area around the communion table is flagged with cut freestone and the pew floors boarded. The church is 54 feet by 24 feet in the clear. There is a vestry room attached to the northern side which is 9 feet 4 inches by 8 feet 1 inch. It is spacious but with no galleries. The yard is enclosed with a good wall. There are sittings for 174 adults. It was built in 1816 at the cost of 1,000 pounds Irish currency. It is not large enough for the congregation.

[Insert footnote: Accommodation is required in this church for at least 500; to acquire this, a gallery is necessary].

Chapel of Ease

Tyanee church, alias the Tamlaght O'Crilly chapel of ease, stands on an eminence in a well improved neighbourhood at the townland of that name. It is a slated, rectangular building with 4 windows, 3 in the southern wall and 1 at the eastern. The interior is in good repair; the alley and area round the communion table flagged with cut freestone and the pew floors boarded. There is a 3-storey belfry topped with Gothic pinnacles at the western end. It is 50 feet by 24 feet 3 inches in the clear. The interior is spacious and lofty but with no galleries. There are sittings for 192 adults. The yard is enclosed with a good wall having some trees at the outside. The date of its erection and cost is not known within the parish.

Presbyterian Meeting House

At the village of Tamlaght O'Crilly there is a Presbyterian meeting house in the course of being built. It will be 65 feet by 45 feet. The site has been given to the congregation by Langford Heyland Esquire. He also contributed to its erection the sum of 10 pounds, Captain Jones M.P. 10 pounds, Dr Madden of Dublin 5 pounds, total 25 pounds. The remainder of the cost will be completed by local contribution of labour and materials for the building. It will be slated and of 2-storeys with a vestibule and staircases to galleries. On 23rd January 1836 a storm occurred which brought to the ground a great portion of the wall on the southern side and materially injured the walls at present standing. [Insert footnote: Note there is a money subscription going on in the adjoining parishes, particularly in Aghadowey. It is not yet closed].

Seceding Meeting House

The Seceding meeting house in the townland of Bovedy was rebuilt [insert footnote: note the former house was attached to the Synod of Ulster] about the year 1756 by joint subscription of money, horse labour and manual labour from the congregation. The cost of erection is believed to have been 150 pounds. It is a plain rectangular building with a back aisle attached. It is thatched and 58 feet 10 inches by 21 feet at the longest aisle. The back aisle is 27 feet by 21 feet. The walls are 2 feet thick with 25 windows. The floor is of clay and the pulpit and pews are not in good repair. There are sittings for 385 adults. There is a small thatched sessions house in the yard in which also in the year 1830 burials commenced. The site was originally bestowed by [blank] Cary <Carey> Esquire, the then landlord. None of his successors changed the grant and the present one, Andrew Orr Esquire of Keely, has ornamented it by enclosing it with a fence and planting about 1 acre of ground with trees within it.

Reformed Presbyterian or Covenanting Meeting House

The Covenanting meeting house in the townland of Drumbolg is a plain rectangular building, thatched, and is 51 feet by 21 feet. The walls are 2 feet thick with 10 windows. The alley is of clay but the pew floors boarded. The pulpit, pews and seats are in good repair. There are sittings for 252 adults.

There is a small thatched sessions house in the yard which was planted in 1835 with some trees and contains a few graves. The cost was 100 Irish pounds. It was built in 1812.

Roman Catholic Chapels

The Roman Catholic chapel in the townland of Drumagarner is a slated oblong building of respectable appearance. It is a mile from Kilrea on the Maghera road. It is 83 feet by 21 feet. The walls are 2 feet thick with 4 oblong and 2 lancet-shaped windows, of which one is on each side of the altar. In the interior there are 3 galleries, one at each end and one at the side. These are lighted by 4 skylights. The galleries are one, running round 3 sides of the building. The altar stands nearly in the middle of the chapel and is enclosed by a wooden railing with a neat wooden canopy overhead. Opposite the altar in the side gallery there is a good choir-box surrounded by wainscoting and drawing curtains. The ground floor is made of a composition of lime, sand and clay. The only seats are 2 on the ground floor and 2 in the choir-box, capable in all of accommodating 26 persons. The building itself is able to hold about 700 people. It was erected in 1778. There is a vestry room attached to the north side, slated and of 1-storey, containing 3 rooms.

The whole concern is in good repair and stands on an eminence adjoining the Maghera road. The yard is enclosed with a quickset fence and some trees, with the interior greatly filled by graves which are fast increasing in number. The cost of this chapel is at present unknown. It was built by contributions of money and labour.

The Roman Catholic chapel in the townland of Greenlough is 5 miles from Kilrea and on the leading road from Garvagh to Portglenone. It is a plain rectangular building, slated and is 60 feet by 21 and a half feet. The interior contains 3 galleries, lighted by a rectangular window in each gable and a portion of 4 arched windows that are in the lower part of the chapel. The altar is at the south side and in the middle of the chapel. It stands about 4 and a half feet above the floor. It is enclosed by a railing and surmounted by a canopy in the same way as that of Drumagarner. On the side gallery opposite the altar there is also a similar choir-box. There are no seats in the building except 2 in this box capable of holding 16. The whole building is able to contain about 550 people.

It was built in 1793. The fronts of the galleries are supported on timber columns and the ground floor composed of lime, sand and clay. The exterior of the graveyard was planted with a few trees in 1833. It contains some graves. The cost of this chapel was 200 Irish pounds, including contributions of labour.

Public Buildings in the Parish

The national schoolhouse in the townland of Glenone is 2-storey high, slated and measures 31 feet by 20 feet in the clear. An 8-day clock is in the course of being erected in the southern wall opposite the bridge. The walls are built with black stone. The lower storey is for males and the upper storey for females. Its situation is near the River Bann and it was begun in 1836 but is not yet completed. The site was given in trust by Daniel Daly, merchant of Glenone, to James Daly and others for a term of 24 years and 2 lives for the benefit of the national school. The cost of erection has been 155 pounds 15s 6d.

The National Board gave 103 pounds 17s; Reverend John Rogers, parish priest of the parish, 2 pounds; Reverend John McLoughlin, Roman Catholic curate of the parish, 2 pounds; Reverend Samuel Auterson, Roman Catholic curate of the parish, 1 pound; Reverend John Lynch, parish priest of Ahoghill, 2 pounds; William Henry Holmes Esquire, Kilrea, 1 pound; Daniel Daly, Glenone, 1 pound; John Daly Senior, Portglenone, 1 pound; John Daly Junior, Portglenone, 1 pound; Dr Heany Junior, Portglenone, 1 pound; Pat Mooney Junior, Portglenone, 1 pound; John Hamil Junior, Portglenone, 1 pound; James McIntyre Junior, Portglenone, 1 pound; total 118 pounds 17s.

NB Mr Holmes subscribed as a private person, not as agent to the company of Mercers.

The remainder is yet to be made up by private subscription. Mr Daniel Daly is acting manager to the erection of the concern. It stands within a few yards of Portglenone bridge.

A good schoolhouse was erected at the Seceding meeting house in Bovedy in the year 1834. The rector contributed 4 pounds, the Reverend Adam Boyle, Seceding minister, 1 pound, Andrew Orr Esquire of Keely, the proprietor, gave 35 pounds and the surrounding farmers 8 pounds towards its erection.

Gentlemen's Seats

Inisrush House, the seat of Hercules Ellis Esquire, is on the road from Garvagh to Portglenone and in a well cultivated part of the neighbourhood. The house is 11 miles from Garvagh and 1 and three-quarters from Portglenone and 6 miles from Kilrea. It is 2-storeys high, small and rectangular. It stands on a gently sloping eminence which rises with a north eastern aspect from the little village of Inisrush at its foot. There is a spacious lawn beautifully interspersed with old trees. At a little distance to the south, and in view of the house, 12 acres of the farm are covered with a native wood of oak and hazel. The farm is bounded on the west and south west by a winding stream with a slow current called the Clady river. The present house of Inisrush was built in 1825.

Glenburn House, the seat of James Courtnay Esquire, is on the road from Garvagh to Portglenone. It stands two-thirds of a mile west of Inisrush House. It is a comfortable old-fashioned dwelling house, 2-storeys high, with a small lawn and it stands on the top of a hill over the Clady

Parish of Tamlaght O'Crilly

river. There is a good prospect of the neighbourhood of Portglenone from it. It was built about the year 1786. There is a good fruit and vegetable garden enclosed by a fence and a wall.

The Glebe House, alias Hervey Hill, at present the residence of the Reverend William M. Napper, is situated 2 and a half miles statute from Kilrea and on the high road from that town to Maghera. It stands on a gently sloping eminence at a considerable distance from the road and was built about the year 1774. In 1811 it was newly roofed and raised one storey by the late Reverend James Jones. The garret storey added by him is only 3 windows in front, leaving a whimsical contrast with the other storeys which are each 4. There is a good fruit and vegetable garden, enclosed partly by a stone and lime wall and partly by a quickset fence. The farm is large and is divided into well-arranged fields and enclosed by quickset fences with hedgerow trees.

The Glebe House of Termoneeny, at present the residence of the Reverend Charles Foster, rector of Termoneeny, is at the distance of 8 miles statute from Kilrea and on the Ballymacpeake road from Kilrea to Bellaghy. It is in the townland of Ballymacpeake. The house is slated and 2-storeys high. There is a good garden enclosed by a stone wall and a quickset fence. It was built about the year 1805. The glebe is enclosed partly by quickset fences and partly by drains. It contains some small plantations. It is on the summit of a high hill.

The Glebe House of Glenone, at present the residence of the Reverend Mark Bloxham, incumbent of the curacy of Tyance, is a small, slated 2-storey house with the interior accommodation but indifferent. It is, however, well sheltered by trees and has attached to it a good garden and a farm of 15 acres plantation measure. It is 1 and a half miles from the town of Portglenone and on the road from Kilrea to Bellaghy.

Clady Bleach Green

The bleach green at Clady, at present occupied by Mr David Cunningham of Castledawson, was formerly held by James Courtnay Esquire and gave up the bleaching of white linens in 1824. The machinery is contained in 2 slated houses, each 2-storeys high, and propelled by 2 wheels. The largest, the beetling mill wheel, is 14 feet in diameter, 6 feet 1 inch across the paddles and has a fall of 1 foot 6 inches from the trough to the buckets striking abreast. The wash mill wheel is 12 feet 4 inches in diameter, 2 feet 4 inches across the paddles and has a fall of water from the trough to the buckets of 3 feet striking abreast. The water wheels are to a great extent surrounded with wood and cannot be accurately measured. The supply of water is sufficient in all seasons of the year. The beetling engine is at present occupied by Mr Cunningham and used for beetling brown linens. The other machinery is in the act of being repaired. There are about 6 acres of ground plantation contained in the green.

Table of Mills

[Table gives situation and occupant, description of house and wheel, diameter and breadth of wheel across the paddles, description and fall of water].

Ballynian flax mill, occupied by John Crilly; unroofed and undergoing alteration.

Lismoyle flax mill, occupied by John Gilmore; thatched, 1-storey, wheel undershot, 10 feet by 2 feet 1 inch, no fall along the wheel; there is a moderate supply at all seasons.

Lisnagroat flax mill, occupied by William Campbell; thatched, 1-storey, wheel undershot, 11 feet 4 inches by 1 foot 6 inches; there is a moderate supply, except in a very hot summer, at all seasons.

Lisnagrot corn mill, occupied by Alexander Craig; thatched, 1-storey, wheel undershot, 13 feet 1 inch by 2 feet; the supply of water limited in the months of June, July and August.

Moneysallin flax mill, occupied by Andrew Bradley; thatched, of 1-storey, wheel undershot, 12 feet 2 inches by 1 foot 9 and a half inches; the supply of water limited in the months of June, July and August.

Timaconway flax mill, occupied by Robert Greer; thatched, 1-storey, wheel undershot, 11 feet 10 inches by 2 feet; the supply of water limited in the summer months.

Inisrush flax mill, occupied by James Courtnay Esquire; thatched, 1-storey, wheel undershot, 12 feet 6 inches by 2 feet 2 and a half inches; the supply is good at all seasons.

Drumnacannon corn mill, occupied by Andrew Smyth; thatched, 1-storey, wheel undershot, 13 feet 6 inches by 1 foot 10 inches; the supply is scanty for half the year.

Inisrush corn mill, occupied by James Courtnay Esquire; with a shelling mill attached, both under 1 roof, thatched and 2-storeys high, 2 undershot wheels, 14 feet is the diameter of both the grinding wheel and the shelling wheel; 2 feet 8 inches is the diameter [breadth ?] of the grinding wheel and 2 feet the diameter [breadth ?] of the shelling wheel; the water is brought in 2 wooden pipes from 1 mill-race, the water supply is good.

Clady corn mills, occupied by James Courtnay Esquire: 1st, shelling mill, slated, 3-storeys high, wheel undershot, 12 feet by 2 feet 4 inches, the supply of water is abundant at all seasons of the year, being the Clady river by which both are worked; 2nd, grinding mill, slated, 2-storeys high, wheel undershot, 12 feet 10 inches by 2 feet 6 and a half inches.

There is nothing to prevent the erection of mills and machinery.

Communications

The following main lines of road pass through the parish: from Kilrea to Maghera, 4 and a half miles statute; from Kilrea to Portglenone, 3 and a quarter miles statute; from Garvagh to Portglenone, 9 and a half miles statute; from Garvagh to Kilrea, 1 and a third miles statute.

The first is 20 feet wide at an average, clear of banks, drains or fences. With few exceptions it is at present in repair. The second is 20 feet wide and in good repair. The third is 20 feet wide and in bad repair. The fourth is of the same breadth and nearly in the same state. They are entirely repaired by presentment.

The short by-roads connecting the long lines and passing through the townlands for the accommodation of farmhouses are 16 feet wide, clear of banks, drains. One-third of them is in very bad repair. No partial alterations can be suggested that would improve any of the main lines. It would be necessary to lay out anew the whole of each.

From Clady to Portglenone the second and third main lines are identical. The first runs from north east to south west, the second from north to south nearly, the third from north west to south east, the fourth nearly from east to west.

Bridges

The bridge over the Clady river in the townland of Inisrush has 5 arches. The span of the 4 eastern arches is 15 feet and that of the western is but 12. The roadway is 21 and a half feet broad with parapets 3 and a half feet high. All is in good repair.

The bridge in the townland of Drumnacannon, on the leading road from the village of Tamlaght to Bellaghy through Eden, has 4 arches. The span of the 2 most northern is 12 feet; of the 2 southern the one at the extremity of the bridge is 12 feet and the other 21 feet. The roadway is 18 feet with parapets 3 and a half feet high. All is in good repair.

The bridge in the townland of Moneysallin, on the by-road leading from Drumagarner to Portglenone, has 1 arch 15 feet 4 inches in span. The roadway is 17 feet broad with parapets 2 feet 6 inches high. All is in good repair.

The bridge in the townland of Lisnagroat, on the high road from Kilrea to Inisrush, has 2 arches, the span of each 10 feet. There is a roadway of 20 feet with parapets 2 feet high. They are not in good repair.

A bridge in the same townland, and on a by-road from Drumagarner to Portglenone, has 2 arches, the eastern 10 and a half feet and the western 11 feet wide. There is a roadway 19 feet wide with parapets 2 and a half feet high. All is in good repair.

The bridge in Killygullib Glebe has 1 arch 9 feet in span. The roadway is 18 feet with parapets 2 and a half feet high. They are not in good order.

Inverroe bridge is at the parish boundary and on the road from Clady to Kilrea. It has 3 arches, the span of each 13 and a half feet. The roadway is 18 feet with parapets 2 and a half feet high. All is in good repair. It is in the townland of Tyanee.

Hervey Hill bridge is in the townland of Killygullib, on the road from Kilrea to Swatragh. It has 1 arch 9 feet in span. The breadth of the road is 18 feet and the parapets are 1 and a half feet high.

The bridge at Portglenone has 7 arches, half in the county of Antrim, they being over the Bann. The span of each arch is 27 feet, the breadth of the roadway is 21 feet and the average height of the parapets 3 and a half feet. All is in good repair at present. The parapets are topped with cut freestone.

There is nothing to prevent the erection of bridges or the improvement in communications.

Ancient Topography

Old Church in Tamlaght O'Crilly

[The] drawing exhibits a view of the old church. The ruin is 56 feet 10 inches by 22 feet 9 inches in the clear. The average thickness of the walls is 2 feet 10 inches. The gable is from 15 feet to 18 feet high. Half the northern wall is 13 feet and the remainder 5 feet at an average. The broken part in the drawing marked "A" is where the skulls <sculls> had been found; see "Remarkable Events." The stones of the building are not carefully fitted. Some are large and some small.

The following names appear in the tombstones of the yard: Roe, Witherhoe, Hammond,

Church of Tamlaght O'Crilly

Hametion, McCartney, O'Crilly (Phelimy, 1738), Woodfall, Boylan, O'Neill, McCloy, Morell, Garnet, Caskey, McLaughlin, Molloy, Rigs, McTamney, McKee, McPeak, Walkenshaw, Crilly (Francis, 1800), Mulholland, Barber, Keenan, York, Simms, Rea.

The whole building appears to have been erected at the same time. It also seems modern from the inferior quality of the mortar, but as there is an authentic tradition that it was built by the Abbot Laurence O'Crilly in the 7th century, it is possible that it stands on the foundations of an older edifice which had been destroyed, perhaps in the troubles of 1641.

Holy Well

In the townland of Drumlane there is a holy well but the name of the saint is lost.

Military: Knockenhead

On a hill called Knockenhead, in the townland of Glenone and holding of William Clements, there are a few traces of entrenchments on the south western side. The tradition relating to these is that at some former period the site was chosen by some general, now forgotten, as a fit site for an encampment. One of the contending parties was stationed on it and the other on Knocknabrock, a hill on the other side of the Bann. It seems that after some daylight skirmishing, the party east of the Bann crossed over by night and took the Knockenhead party by surprise, and that a deadly combat then ensued in which many of both were slain. After it was over, a Captain Magill and some other officers were buried in the immediate neighbourhood of the hill.

In William Clements' garden, which is but a few yards distant from the summit, a quantity of human bones have been found. Small cannon-balls and musket balls have been also dug up from time to time, the former most frequently in the south western side and the latter on the eastern. Dr Madden of Portglenone has at present one of the cannon-balls found in 1833. There is on the same farm a hollow place called the Kiln Pot, said to have been filled with the dead bodies of the slain after the battle was over.

Eden Castle

In the townland of Eden there is an eminence called Knockbane, said to be the site of the ancient castle of Eden. It was the seat of Sir Hugh O'Neill. Some foundations with arches have been found at the place. It is at present entirely under tillage.

In the townland of Drumagarner, and holding of Miss Hutcheson, there is an eminence called the Church hill. It is near the high road from Maghera to Kilrea. It is so called from a burial ground having been on it at some former period. There is not a vestige of it to be seen at present as the site is altogether under tillage, but the late Thomas Hutcheson, when demolishing and tilling it, found from time to time within the last 60 years several graves containing skulls and various other human bones, and also a stone waterfont. From the name and the circumstance of the find it is more than probable that a church once stood here.

Name: Tamlaght

It is believed that the spot most properly called Tamlaght is the farm of Mr Andrew Smyth, situated near the end of the village. This is also believed to have been the locality of the farm or piece of ground allotted to the priest for the "milk of his 2 cows." The word tamlaght is said to be a corruption of the Irish for "2 cows' milk." The tenant of the place always calls his residence Tamlaght, it being the name that has been transmitted to him. He is ignorant of the tradition. He has never found in any of his fields, nor has he ever heard of, any foundations of ancient buildings or giant's graves having been formerly in his land.

Inisrush Island and Castle

About the middle of the Green lough there is the remains of an island called Inisrush and from which the village and townland of Inisrush have been called. The remains of the island are at present oblong, about 8 yards by 7 yards and about 4 feet above the surface of the water. There are a few apple and sycamore trees on it.

It was formerly much larger than it is at present and is locally believed to stand upon oak piles of unknown dimensions constructed some hundreds of years ago by a Ross MacGuinness, who then erected a castle on it. After his death there was no heir to inherit or inhabit it and it consequently soon fell to ruin. It was afterwards rebuilt and again inhabited by a near relation of Sir Phelimy Roe O'Neill, whose name was Bryan Carrah O'Neill. He lived in it for a number of years and is said to have expired on the site of the Roman Catholic chapel of Greenlough, on a bed brought there from the castle by his orders and placed behind a thicket of bushes that stood on the ground. This was in consequence of a vow made by himself that he would never die in the Green lough. He was also said to have been buried on the top of the Gallows hill, a small gravelly knoll that stands west and within about 20 yards of the lough, and which is so called from its having been the hill on which he himself had a gallows erected when in full possession of his wealth and power. On it he hung all persons who were in any way obnoxious to him. Graves are still visible on it.

Another tradition, most probably the truest, implies that he did not die so peacefully as in the above-mentioned one. It is said that he was a great oppressor of the inhabitants of a large and neighbouring district, and that in revenge for it, his castle was besieged by the oppressed and himself and his 2 sons taken, hanged upon his own gallows and buried at the foot of it.

Tradition also says that he was reared up with his uncle, Sir Hugh O'Neill of the castle of Eden, and that at last, in consequence of some dispute, he defeated his uncle in a skirmish, besieged him in his castle and burned him to death in it. His castle or house was composed of oak bound together with mortices. There have been large quantities of the wood raised from time to time within the last 80 years out of the lough, and it is of so good a quality that many houses in the neighbourhood have been roofed with it. There is some of it at present in the dwelling houses of John Henry and Henry McLoughlin in the townland of Inisrush. Before the year 1775 the body and the roof of the building were destroyed and carried away.

In the bottom of the lake there was once found a shirt of mail, supposed to have belonged to Bryan Carrah O'Neill, as well as some knives and forks and a quantity of what was conjectured to be stable dung. The passage to the castle is believed to have been by a drawbridge over the northern side. In digging the precincts of the Gallows hill there was found, about the year 1786, a human skull with various other human bones at a short distance below the surface.

The Green lough is supposed to have obtained its name from the green valley that skirted it all round.

Eminence: Knockarig

In the townland of Eden there is an eminence called Knock Phelim Roe, from its having been a place selected by Sir Phelimy Roe O'Neill for encamping on. From it he also defeated his oppo-

Parish of Tamlaght O'Crilly

nents who occupied another hill that stands about 700 yards distance to the east. It is still called Knockarig or the "hill of anger."

Forts

In the townland of Ballynian, and holding of Michael Moran, there are the remains of a fort or rath of ordinary form. It was 30 yards in diameter. It is at present under tillage. Within the last 5 years the above-named farmer found, from time to time while cultivating it, a pipe or gullet 2 feet broad and a foot and a half high which went across, from side to side, a second pipe of the same dimensions running in a concentric manner round half the outside of the parapet. In the interior a grave 6 feet long containing rich soil and particles of a coffin, an earthen crock containing ashes deposited in a stone cell, oblong sharpening stones, beads, a coin and an iron axe. He has some of the sharpening stones still.

In the townland of Lismoyle, and holding of Samuel Bolton, in a fort 29 yards by 25 yards there was formerly a very deep draw-well on the northern side. It was closed up in consequence of an ox having fallen into it.

In the townland of Killymuck, and holding of John Diamond, there is a fort 30 yards in diameter with 2 parapets. In demolishing part of it in 1812 a cask apparently composed of the bark of a tree was found beneath the surface of the interior. It was at the south west and at the foot of the parapet. It contained some powder, useless by time, with flints of a large size.

In the townland of Eden, and holding of Bernard Mulholland, and in a fort 35 yards in diameter there was found in 1829, by him, 2 quern-stones about 1 foot under the surface.

Old Corn Mill

The Reverend James Alexander Smyth, in making a cut from the Black lough in the townland of Inisrush, found in the year 1831, at about 70 yards distance on the western side, the remains of an old corn mill. It was constructed in an oblong black oak frame, bound together by pins of forest oak and had dimensions of about 4 feet broad and 8 feet long. In this there was one of the grinding stones, supposed to be the upper one. It was 2 feet 5 inches in diameter and 7 inches thick and had a groove in the centre round about the hole thus: [drawing, cuciform shape, with hole in the centre]. The hole in the centre was about 2 and a half inches in diameter.

Mr Smyth believes the grinding stone to be of a species of quartz which could not be procured nearer to its site than the west of the county Donegal. Part of a horn spoon was found with it. Half of it is at present in a fire hearth in Mr Smyth's house, in which also there is a portion of the black oak frame made into kitchen stools. A quantity of cinders and some oak logs were found, the former within a few yards, the latter at the site. From the former it is supposed that the rest of the mill and machinery were burned. The whole was found 6 feet or thereabouts under the surface while sinking the above canal or cut which Mr Smyth made upon the traces of an old one, now thought to have been a water cut originally made to convey water from the lough to the mill.

Iron Manufactory

Near the Black lough, alias the Forge lough near Kilrea, an old iron manufactory worked by the smith Mayberry (see parish of Kilrea), stood in the townland of Lisnagrot. Charcoal and fragments of iron have been found round about. One of the pieces of iron is at present in the corn mill of that townland. It weighs 17 stones.

Traces of an ancient forge have been also found in Eden.

Old Iron Foundry

In the townland of Timaconway, and holding of Bernard McAlary, there formerly stood an iron foundry. 2 of the moulds supposed to have been used for casting cannon-balls are at present lying beneath the surface on the site. There is a hole in each, large enough to form a 5-pounder. There is also a great deal of scoriae on the place.

Human Bones

The late John Neely, in demolishing a giant's grave in his holding in the same townland, found human bones. He buried them in the same place.

Coat of Mail

Major Hill of Bellaghy, when attempting to drain a small lake in the townland of Ballymacpeake, found on the bottom a coat of mail. The links were of steel and very small.

Vessels of Bark

A circular cask, about 9 inches in diameter and made of the bark of a tree, was found by John Patton of Drumnacannon in tilling the remains of a bog. It contained old butter but mouldered away after being taken up. The same substance was, in

1833, found in the townland of Lisnagroat, 3 feet under the surface by John McCann. It was also in a vessel of bark. The same was also found in the townland of Lismoyle, in the bog in 1815. The vessel was circular and in one hollow piece resembling bark.

Wooden Vessel

An oval wooden vessel 3 and a half feet by 2 and a half feet and 9 inches deep, with a handle at each end, was found 5 feet under the original surface of a bog in the townland of Tyanee in the year 1825.

Amber Beads

A great number of amber beads were found 8 feet below the surface of Moneysallin bog in 1828 by Andrew Bradley. They are still in his possession.

Ancient Spade

In 1828 an ancient spade was found in a turf bank in Timaconway. It was standing upright and is still in the possession of Alexander Tombs of that townland: it is represented in drawing[s]. In the same townland an iron ball was found, represented in drawing[s].

5 caves and 2 earthen crocks with ashes have been found in the parish from time to time. All were destroyed.

MODERN TOPOGRAPHY

General Appearance and Scenery

[The] drawing [see Drawings of Antiquities] is a specimen of the general appearance and scenery at the western end of the parish. The small hills of the country are there often arranged in the most favourable manner for the production of picturesque landscapes which, though on a minor scale, are still pleasing from their pastoral character, the great number of neat-looking houses and the many old thorn trees everywhere seen. The 2 last features prevail to a great extent. From 3 to 14 dwellings are constantly within sight upon the foreground of the picture, that is within a quarter of an hour's walk, and the thorn trees are sometimes so numerous as to have an important share in the beauty of the whole prospect. Many are clustered around the houses and most of them preserved with reverential care.

That of the arable ground on the eastern side has the same character as [the] drawing, except that the hills are larger and bolder and thorn trees comparatively rare. As is the case on the eastern side also, the pedestrian meets a constant variety in walking over them: swelling hills with a broad prospect of the country round, small secluded ravines fringed with furze or the remains of ancient wood, a grouping of hill, dale and farmhouses and then perhaps a dismal expanse of bog of some hundred or two of acres present themselves in succession to his view. But he has occasion to lament the absence of large hedgerow trees in the peculiar fitness which the country appears to possess for that kind of ornament.

The little vale of Inisrush is very well set off by the venerable trees of Inisrush demesne, the church of Tyanee and the plantations of Glenburn House, Mr Courtnay's residence. The scenery of the Bann is nothing particular.

SOCIAL ECONOMY

Early Improvements

The wars of 1641 and 1688 tended in this parish to confirm the plantation settlers still more in their possessions. The settlement of James I is the foundation of its present state and condition. There is a mixture of many names, both Scottish and English, so much so that it is difficult to determine which is the most prevalent. There is a remarkable one, O'Crilly, the origin of the name of the parish. It still exists as the posterity of the abbot or priest who built a church at Tamlaght O'Crilly and they hope, in case of any civil commotion, to regain the churchlands which had once been in the possession of their ancestors.

In the wars of James II, Nicholas O'Crilly, the representative of the name, is said to have refused to take the oath of allegiance to William III. He was consequently deprived of his estate, the townland of Eden and, after some time, went to France and served in the continental wars. He at length returned and lived in a cabin in Eden as a poor cottier.

The efforts of proprietors have never been much directed to the improvement of the district. The rector has exerted himself to supply its medical wants, both by vaccinations and by the establishment of a dispensary. The different temperance and religious societies have been also useful.

There are no cattle shows or premiums for improved agricultural instruments. The parishioners have a ready vent for their produce in the markets of Kilrea, Portglenone or Maghera. They are in a state of slow but progressive improvement in things both spiritual and temporal.

Obstructions to Improvement

The greatest obstruction to improvement in this

Parish of Tamlaght O'Crilly

parish is the smallness of the farms, the great number of cottiers and the system of rundale, that is of holding 5 or 6 small patches (dispersed in different directions and containing each at an average but half a rood) as 1 single farm. The consequence of this system is to be seen in the absurdly small size of the fields and the great extent of ground consumed in fences.

These features are very conspicuous in the townland of Gortmacrane, a long barren tract of churchland situated in the northern extremity of the parish. It is remarkable that 20 out of the 84 persons who are in the habit of migrating annually from the whole district to the English and Scotch harvests are inhabitants of this townland. 16 other townlands send the remaining 64, so that this one thus sends 5 times as much as any of the rest. In it, upon 768 acres statute measure, there are 120 families. The system of rundale is increased by the desire each landholder has of possessing more land. If he has a field of good ground, those whose land is inferior come and offer him 2 roods of bad for 1 of good land. Thus this field becomes split into 10 to 12 "divides" as they are called. Bad ground is portioned out in this same manner and on the same principle, and it is not uncommon for a divide to be no broader than 2 ridges of potatoes. Three-fourths of the tenants in Gortmacrane hold their farms in this manner.

Local Government: Kilrea Petty Sessions

List of criminal offences from the parish of Tamlaght O'Crilly, decided on from August 1832 to March 1836 by the magistrates of Kilrea petty sessions.

[Table lists date of information, offence, townland in which the defendant resides].

1832: August 3rd, assault, Drumean.

September 10, threatening, Drumard; September 27, assault, Lisnagroat.

October 2, assault, Drumlane; October 7, assault, Ballynian; October 11, waylaying and assault, Drumlane.

November 17, assault, 3 from Gortmacrane; November 22, assault, Killymuck; November 30, assault, Ballynian.

December 17, assault, Killygullib; rescue, Drumoolish.

1833: January 30, assault, Drumean.

March 30, assault, Moneysallin.

April 4, destroying a will, Drumbane; April 5, assault, Bovedy; April 27, rioting, Moneysallin.

May 9, assault, Bovedy.

June 16, assault, Timaconway; June 27, assault, Drumean.

July 10, assault, Drumean.

August 28, taking the door off a house, Drumlane; assault, Gortmacrane.

November 5, assault, Moneysallin; November 11, assault, Bovedy; November 13, assault, Bovedy; November 27, rescue, from a civil bill, Gortmacrane; November 27, decree, assault, Gortmacrane.

December 16, assault, Tyanee; December 26, assault, Drumean; December 31, assault, Drumean.

1834: January 4, assault, Gortmacrane; January 10, rescue, Killygullib.

February 17, rescue, Drumnacannon; February 28, assault, Moneysallin.

April 17, assault, Drumean.

June 4, assault, Lisnagroat; June 10, assault, Killygullib; June 12, stealing turf, Killygullib; June 25, assault, Lisnagroat.

July 29, assault, Drumsarragh.

September 8, stealing turf, Bovedy; September 27, assault, Drumagarner.

October 3, assault, Bovedy.

November 26, passing base coin, Killygullib.

1835: January 7, breaking windows, Drumard; January 28, rescue, Killygullib.

April 2, breaking a door, Drumlane.

March 18, assault, Ballynian; March 19, assault, Lisnagroat.

April 13, assault, Drumard.

May 11, assault, Lisgorgan; May 13, assault, Killymuck; May 18, assault, Drumean.

June 11, assault, Gortmacrane; June 13, assault, Gortmacrane; June 24, assault, Drumard.

August 28, assault, Lismoyle.

September 30, assault, Killymuck.

October 7, assault, Lisnagroat.

November 25, assault, Drumsarragh.

1836: January 6, robbery, Drumard; January 23, riotous drunkenness, Drumean.

February 11, maliciously damaging yarn, Gortmacrane.

March 3, assault, Lisnagroat; March 26, rescue, Killymuck.

Local Government: Inisrush Petty Sessions

List of criminal offences from the parish of Tamlaght O'Crilly, decided on from May 1834 to March 1836 by the magistrates of Inisrush petty sessions.

[Table lists date of information, offence, townland in which the defendant resides].

1834: May 15, assault, Inisrush; May 31, assault, Eden.

June 2, assault, Tyanee; June 3, assault, Ballymacpeake; June 4, assault, Eden.

July 1 1834, forcible entry, Tyanee; July 21, assault, Moneystaghan; assault, Eden; assault, Eden.

August 7, assault, Eden; August 14, assault, Tyanee; assault, Tyanee; August 28, malicious riot and forcibly taking a horse, 7 from Moneystaghan.

November 3, assault and threats, Ballymacpeake; forcibly taking a window, Inisrush; November 22, assault, 10 from Moneystaghan.

December 2, injuring a pig, Eden.

1835: January 28, assault, Drumard.

April 16, assault, Glenone; April 17, burglary, Glenone.

May 2, assault, Eden.

June 29, assault, Moneystaghan.

July 1, rioting, Ballymacpeake; July 8, assault and malicious destruction of turf, Inisrush; July 22, attacking a house, 5 from Tyanee.

October 8, riot and challenge to fight, 5 from Inisrush.

November 2, assault, Moneystaghan; November 10, assault, Ballymacpeake; November 19, stealing salmon, Glenone.

December 17, riotous drunkenness, 17 from Moneystaghan.

1836: January 9, burglary, Drumean.

March 10, breaking a fence, Drumoolish.

From 1st September 1834 to 16th April 1836 84 civil bills about trespass, nuisances and wages were decided on. The fines were all below a pound and very trifling.

The townland in which the defendant resided is not mentioned in the books of Inisrush until the date of information at which this list begins. The magistrates who attend at these sessions are Hercules Ellis Esquire of Inisrush and whatever stipendiary magistrate is stationed at the time being in the town of Portglenone. There is no police force of any kind resident within the parish, nor are there any manor courts. There is no illicit distillation.

Establishments for Mental and Bodily Diseases

Tamlaght O'Crilly dispensary: management by a committee of 5 subscribers appointed to meet every 3 months; number relieved from August 1 1835 to May 10 1836, 2,176 in all, partly at Hervey Hill and partly at the dispensary; funds from public bodies: 33 pounds 18s from the grand jury for 1835, the same from private individuals; 35 pounds from the grand jury for 1836, the same from private individuals; annual expense of management: house rent 2 pounds annually, salaries none; annual expenses of patients: 20 pounds expenses of medicines, bandages, wines etc.; founded August 1835. Dr Edward Nevill attends at the dispensary every Monday and Friday from 10 to 12 o'clock in the morning. Those only who attend at it are entered, as to their cases, in the books.

List of Diseases

Abscess 16, anasarca 6, asthma 5, aphonia 1, amaurosis 1, amenorrhoea 10, bronchitis 9, bite of dog 3, burns 4, contusions 19, convulsions 2, cathar [catarrh] 1, cholera 1, contused side 1, cephalalgia 11, debility from bronchitis 1, diarrhoea 35, dyspepsia 53, diseases of heart 6, diseases of the digestive organs 47, diseases of chest 46, dropsy 1, dropsy with enlarged liver 1, erysipelas 4, epilepsy 3, eruption 16, fever 18, furmulilus [furuncolosis] 9, fractures of tibia 2, fracture of humerus 1, general decay 2, helminthea 21, hepatitis 3, haemorrhoids 6, hernia 1, hydrocephalus 1, hydrops-articuli 2, infantile fever 1, injuries 16, insomnia 3, inguinal [anginal] hernia 2, iritis 3, jaundice 2, lumbago 8, laryngitis 2, laryngitis (chronic) 2, lunacy 2, leucorrhoea 3, menorrhagia 7, morbus laxa 1, necrosis 4, old age (decay from) 10, pain of ear 5, pain of side 4, pains in limbs 5, pain of breast 1, pertussis 2, parturitions 26, paralysis 1, rheumatism 18, rubiola [rubeola] 1, sore gums 2, sore throat 2, sore eyes 17, sores 25, scrofula 5, swellings 7, scald 1, scabies 7, sprained wrist 1, syncope 1, sciatica 1, scarlatina 19, scurvy of hand 1, tabes 2, toothache and dentition 17, tonsillitis 2, variola 57, weaning 1, vomiting 4.

From June 1827 to May 1836, 1,069 cases have been vaccinated by the rector's family; of these 582 succeeded.

The following is a list of the principal diseases of the parish. It is taken from the above and is so arranged that the names succeed each other in the order of frequency with which they occur. Any name that has fewer than 10 cases opposite is not included: smallpox, dyspepsia, diseases of the digestive organs, diseases of the chest, diarrhoea, sores, helminthia, contusions, scarlatina, fever, rheumatism, sore eyes, toothache and dentition, eruptions, abscess, amenorrhoea, decay from old age.

The great number of cases of smallpox shows the necessity for this dispensary.

Schools and Morality

Schools: see tables [Fair Sheets].

Parish of Tamlaght O'Crilly

The moral habits of the people are improving but slowly. They partake of the gradual amendment that is going on in the country at large.

Poor

There is a good deal of poverty in some parts of the parish, particularly in the churchlands. There are about 100 actual paupers altogether. Pauperism appears to be stationary. None of them are badged. The residence of the rector, the Reverend William Napper, is the chief almshouse in the district, and they receive besides [blank] per annum from the poor box collection at church and Drumbolg meeting house. The last is distributed among 12 individuals of good character.

Tithe Composition

The tithe composition of this parish is 435 pounds 19s 3 farthings, with glebe yielding a rental of 285 pounds 14s 9d [blank] currency. 26 acres plantation measure is attached to the Glebe House as a farm.

Income of the Clergy

The Reverend Adam Boyle, Seceding minister, receives 24 pounds per annum stipend and 50 pounds regium donum.

The Reverend James Alexander Smyth, minister of the Reformed Presbyterian congregation, receives annual stipend 50 pounds but no regium donum.

The Reverend John Rogers is a priest of the parishes of Tamlaght O'Crilly, Kilrea and Desertoghill, from which he receives a total of 180 pounds per annum, of which sum the Roman Catholic curates of the above charge, i.e. the Reverend Samuel Auterson and the Reverend John McLoughlin, receive each a fourth part, leaving the priest 90 pounds per annum and to each of his curates 45 pounds.

Habits of the People

The general style of the cottages here appears superior to that of the dwellings in the parish of Kilrea. They are for the most part in good repair. They are of stone and thatched. The inhabitants have been for the last 50 years improving in buildings, food, clothing, morals and education. There are no remarkable instances of early marriage among them, 20 being the usual age. Their longevity is considerable. Laurence Atkinson of Timaconway lived to above 100 and Matthew McCahy of Drumanacannon to 96. Both were in full possession of their faculties and died in 1836.

The Reverend Adam Boyle, the Seceding minister, is at present (1836) 82 years of age. He preaches every Sunday and visits an extended congregation without any assistance. He has been 50 years a minister.

Dress and Amusements

The dress of the people is the same in general character as in the surrounding parishes. They are very fond of finery. Their amusements and recreations are diminishing, a thing however not to be regretted as whisky drinking appears to have been their usual accompaniment. Firing is kept up on Christmas Day by the Presbyterians and the "Round Ring" is found near Inisrush every Easter Monday, that is, a circle of males and females standing in a field joining hands and the game consists in a male and female chasing one another within and without according to certain rules and regulations.

From the strong mixture of Presbyterians and Protestants, there is not much superstitious feeling and accordingly there will soon be a total disregard of its usual objects. There are few legendary tales.

Library and Temperance Society

Their literary wants are supplied by a cheap circulating library in Portglenone and by small collections of books attached to the different religious societies. The following is an account both of them and of the temperance societies.

The Tamlaght O'Crilly Temperance Society was established in the year 1830 by the Reverend William Napper, rector, who is president and secretary. The meetings are held monthly in the schoolhouse near Hervey Hill from 7 to 9 p.m. The society consists of 263 members of both sexes, of all denominations and of various ages. Of the above number there is a juvenile association of males and females, all under 14 years of age. The present number of it is [blank].

The Drumbolg Temperance Society was established in 1830 by the Reverend James A. Smyth, who is president and secretary. The meetings are held quarterly from 4 to 6 p.m. in the meeting house at Drumbolg. The society consists of 240 members of both sexes, of all denominations and of various ages.

There is a distinct Congregational society established in 1832, consisting of 120 members of both sexes and of members of the congregation itself. There is a juvenile association of 50 members under 16.

The Bovedy Temperance Society was established in the year 1831 by the Reverend Adam Boyle, who is president and secretary. It has 79 members of all denominations, of both sexes and of various ages.

Religious Societies

The Bovedy Presbyterian Moral or Religious Society was instituted in 1823. There are 9 members, male and female, all adult. They meet twice a month at different houses. The books read are the Bible, Testament and various religious works. Each member in rotation opens and closes the meeting by singing and prayer and their hours are from 6 to 9 p.m., both summer and winter. It seems to be continued with great zeal.

The Bovedy Covenanting Religious Society was instituted in 1800. It was begun by 4 members and has since increased to 60, of both sexes and of various ages who each, according to their ability, open the meeting by singing and prayer and close it by the same. They meet monthly at Samuel Warwick's house, at which it was first established. The hours are from 2 to 6 p.m. in summer and from 1 to 4 p.m. in winter. They have divided themselves into 3 branches and hold every second week meetings in different houses from 6 to 9 p.m., observing the same forms as at the monthly meeting. They read religious books and the Bible.

The Timaconway Presbyterian Religious Society was instituted in 1834. It consists at present of 10 males, all adults. They meet twice a month at one another's houses, from 4 to 9 p.m. in summer and in winter from 6 to 10 p.m. They open and close with singing and prayer and read the Bible with religious books.

A society for religious conversation and prayer is held once a fortnight in the Drumbolg meeting house. It consists of Reformed Presbyterians or Covenanters but all denominations are admitted. An auxiliary missionary society was established in the same place in 1833. They hold quarterly meetings. The Reverend Alexander Smyth is president and Alexander Christie of Tobermore in the parish of Kilcronaghan is treasurer and secretary. A committee of 10 from the congregation receive and collect the subscriptions.

Amusements

Previous to the year 1814, the Green lough was the scene of various kinds of amusement, particularly horse-racing which was strongly supported by the gentry. They subscribed money, saddles, bridles for the Greenlough races which commenced in August and were held on Saturdays for from 4 to 6 weeks in each year. The course was round the shore of the lough, a place very well adapted for the purpose. The people who assembled in thousands from various parts of the counties of Londonderry and Antrim seated themselves on the summit of the ridge of hills by which it is surrounded, and so gave themselves a full and satisfactory view of the racing below. Many also enjoyed themselves at various other amusements among the ravines in its immediate neighbourhood. The place was also well attended by vendors of all sorts of liquor, fruit, bread, gingerbread etc. Every amusement ceased in consequence of drunkenness, quarrelling and party fighting at or about the year above mentioned.

A pleasure fair is annually held in the townland of Bovedy on Christmas Day old style. The inhabitants of the adjoining country assemble in it and devote the day with a great part of the night to sundry amusements such as shooting at marks, common playing, cock-fighting, dancing, singing and drinking. This fair is of old date and is still vigorously kept up.

Emigration in 1834 and 1835

Number of persons who emigrated in the year 1834.

Below 10 years of age: 2, 1 Presbyterian, 1 Roman Catholic, 1 male, 1 female, to New York.

Between 10 and 20 years: 3, 2 Presbyterians, 1 Roman Catholic, 2 males, 1 female, to New York.

Between 20 and 30 years: 26, 2 Protestants, 12 Presbyterians, 12 Roman Catholics, 21 males, 5 females, 3 to Quebec, 5 to St John's, 18 to New York.

Between 30 and 40 years: 3, 2 Presbyterians, 1 Roman Catholic, 2 males, 1 female, 2 to Quebec, 1 to New York.

Between 40 and 50 years: 2 Presbyterian males, to New York.

Between 50 and 60 years: 1 Presbyterian female, to New York.

Total 37, 2 Protestants, 20 Presbyterians, 15 Roman Catholics, 28 males, 9 females, 5 to Quebec, 5 to St John's, 27 to New York.

Number of persons who emigrated in the year 1835.

Below 10 years of age: 12, 8 Presbyterians, 4 Roman Catholics, 7 males, 5 females, 5 to Quebec, 7 to St John's.

Between 10 and 20 years: 1 Roman Catholic female, to Quebec.

Between 20 and 30 years: 18, 11 Presbyterians,

7 Roman Catholics, 9 males, 9 females, 6 to Quebec, 9 to St John's, 3 to New York.

Between 30 and 40 years: 7, 5 Presbyterians, 2 Roman Catholics, 6 males, 1 female, 2 to Quebec, 5 to St John's.

Between 60 and 70 years: 1 Protestant male, to St John's.

Between 70 and 80 years: 1 Protestant female, to St John's.

Total 40, 2 Protestants, 24 Presbyterians, 14 Roman Catholics, 23 males, 17 females, 14 to Quebec, 23 to St John's, 3 to New York.

Migration

24 persons are in the habit of annually migrating to the English harvests and 84 to the Scottish harvests; of the latter, 20 are from the townland of Gortmacrane.

Remarkable Events: Seceders

The Seceding meeting house in the townland of Bovedy was originally built and enjoyed by the Presbyterians of the Synod of Ulster. About the year 1770 the more respectable members, as well as the majority of the congregation, decided along with their minister and the synod upon removing the site of their meeting house to the neighbouring village of Kilrea. The minority retained possession of the old house, joined the Secession Synod, procured a minister of that persuasion and have been Seceders since. The majority, having accomplished their intention, erected a house of worship at Kilrea and have remained attached to the communion of the Presbyterian body in the General Synod of Ulster.

Remarkable Events: Old Church

In demolishing a portion of the walls of the old church of Tamlaght O'Crilly, 2 human skulls were found deposited in a small cavity in the hearth of the east gable. They were in a moderate state of preservation. One of them was of peculiar form, being long and narrow and very convex at the forehead. One of them was supposed to be male and the other female. They remained some months uninterred for the inspection of the curious but were at last buried in the interior of the old church opposite to the spot in which they were found.

The pulling down of the old church in 1815 by the Reverend Edmund Knox produced at the same time much opposition and bad feeling. It appears to have been necessary from the decayed state of the old building. It was also influenced by a wish to have a church in the centre of the district in which the congregation was located. In this, however, he was disappointed from the excess of opposition, as the new church stands immediately adjoining the old one. The Reverend James Jones, his predecessor, made the same attempt but was outvoted on the question.

Note, the following is the address voted (in the vestry of the new church) to the rector on this occasion and his reply.

Tamlaght O'Crilly, April 7th 1817.

"We, the parishioners of Tamlaght O'Crilly, assembled at vestry in the parish church this 7th day of April 1817, avail ourselves of this public opportunity to return our cordial thanks to you, Sir, as to the person whose mild but steady conduct we owe the suppression of a faction which, with equal incapacity and presumption, had attempted to assume the exclusive management of our parochial concerns. To you, Sir, we are indebted for a safe and respectable house of worship, provided on terms most highly advantageous to us, and permit us to add that your zealous and truly exemplary discharge of the ministerial duties among us has already made an indelible impression on the hearts of the parishioners of Tamlaght O'Crilly."

Answer: "My respected parishioners and friends,

With feelings of no ordinary description, I have this day received your kind address which infinitely more than counterbalances the painful sensations that accompanied a contest imposed upon me by the sense of a solemn duty and in which I never once omitted an opportunity of endeavouring to reconcile my public and personal obligations to the wishes and even prejudices of those who had placed themselves in the way to obstruct our peaceful and mutual accommodation.

We have now, my parishioners, a house of worship suited to the number and respectability of the congregation that assembles in it. Here I trust that we shall henceforward meet, animated with those feelings and affections which should ever predominate in the hearts of those who enter into the House of God, living as we are bound to do in the most amiable and endearing ties of fellow subjects and fellow Christians.

With the most ardent prayers for your present welfare and future happiness, I subscribe myself, your affectionate and faithful servant, Edmund Knox."

The writer of the above reply is now Lord Bishop of Limerick.

Rebellion of 1798

The only occurrence that happened in the parish in connection with the rebellion of 1798 was Colonel Heyland's riding through one morning with a party of yeomanry, on his way from Kilrea to Maghera to suppress a meeting of United Irishmen at the ancient fort of Dungleady.

Drawings of Antiquities

Church of Tamlaght O'Crilly, gable with doorway and gravestones in foreground.

Small hatchet found in a fort in the townland of Ballynian, side and overhead view, dimensions 8 inches by 2 and three-quarter inches by three-quarters of an inch thick.

Small stone axe found in a fort in the townland of Ballynian; side, overhead and end on views, main dimensions 2 and three-quarters inches long, 1 and a quarter inches wide, half an inch thick.

Landscape: specimen of the general appearance from half a mile north east of village of Tamlaght.

A mithoe [spearhead] found by the workmen in the draining of the Black lough, side and frontal views, shaft socket hollow and an eighth of an inch thick, total length 9 inches, shaft socket 6 inches, 1 inch wide.

Ancient spade found in a bog in the townland of Timaconway, main dimensions 20 inches long, 6 and a half inches wide, half an inch thick.

Iron ball found in the townland of Timaconway, 1 and three-quarter inches diameter, depth of hole 1 and a half inches, weight 20 oz.

A giant's chair in the townland of Timaconway, main dimensions 2 feet 8 inches by 1 foot 4 inches.

Fair Sheets by Thomas Fagan, February to May 1836

MODERN TOPOGRAPHY AND PRODUCTIVE ECONOMY

Tamlaght O'Crilly: Trades and Houses

Tamlaght O'Crilly is a small country village, stands 3 and a quarter miles from Kilrea on the leading road from Garvagh to Portglenone. The following are the occupations and trades in the village of Tamlaght, also the total number and height of houses in the village, together with the number of houses built and in the process of building from January 1834 to the present period.

Grocers 3, in 3 houses; spirit dealers 2, in 2 houses; farmers 11, in 11 houses; rent agent 1, in 1 house; sexton 1, in 1 house; masons 2, in 2 houses; carpenters 1, in 1 house; blacksmiths 1, in 1 house; shoemakers 2, in 2 houses; tailors 1, in 1 house; hosiers 1, in 1 house; carriers 1, in 1 house; labourers 4, in 4 houses; working spinsters 2, in 2 houses; schoolmasters 1; total 34 people in 33 houses.

Church 1, schoolhouse 1, dispensary 1, total 3; 2-storey houses 9, 1-storey houses 27, total 36; waste houses 1. Built by Langford Rowley Heyland Esquire, proprietor of Tamlaght O'Crilly estate, 1 house, of stone and brick, slated and stands 1-storey, to be occupied as a rent receiver's office and dwelling house.

Fairs at Tamlaght

There were 4 fairs annually held in the village of Church Town, or otherwise Tamlaght O'Crilly: first fair held on 12th February, second fair held on 15th May, third fair held on 24th August, fourth fair held on 1st November. The above fairs were established by patent but ceased about 1800 in consequence of excess of drinking and riot among the people. Informants Andrew Smyth and James Clarke.

SOCIAL ECONOMY AND MODERN TOPOGRAPHY

Seceding Minister

The Reverend Adam Boyle is pastor of Boveedy Seceding congregation for the last 54 years and the first pastor of that denomination of Presbyterians that has been ordained to the aforesaid congregation, and perhaps the oldest minister of any denomination at present officiating in the north of Ireland. He is now in the 82nd year of his age and capable of discharging all of his clerical duties in a very extensive charge. The above minister receives annual stipend 24 pounds, royal annual bounty, late currency, 50 pounds.

Seceding Meeting House

Boveedy Seceding meeting house was built about 1756 by local subscription of money, horse and manual labour from the above congregation. Cost of erection can only be conjectured at this advanced period to be 150 pounds. The site of the meeting house was originally bestowed on the congregation by [blank] Cary <Carey> of Greencastle, Esquire, then proprietor of Boveedy, nor have his successive proprietors made any alterations in the original grant. The present proprietor of Boveedy has much improved and ornamented the site of the above meeting house

Parish of Tamlaght O'Crilly

by enclosing it with a quickset fence and planting the exterior of the yard and above 1 acre of a high and rocky surface within the fence with various kinds of forest trees, in 1834. Present proprietor of Boveedy, Andrew Orr of Keely, Esquire.

Boveedy Seceding meeting house stands 2 miles from Kilrea, on the leading road from Garvagh to Portglenone. The house is oblong with a back isle <aisle> attached. It is thatched and stands 1-storey. The front or long aisle is 58 feet 10 inches by 21 feet in the clear. The back aisle is 27 feet by 21 feet in the clear. Thickness of walls is 2 feet. The meeting house has in it 4 doors, 25 windows, oblong. The floor is made with clay. Pulpit, pews and seats in very moderate state of repair. Single seats in the house 55, average length of each seat, including end seats, 10 and a half feet, and will hold persons each seat 7; total persons accommodated with seats in the entire house 385. There is a sessions house in the yard, thatched, stands 1-storey. Burials commenced in the yard in 1830.

There is a collection in the aforesaid meeting house on Sundays, the proceeds of which collection goes to defray expenses incurred by repairs on the house from time to time and part to relieve indigent poor. Information received from Reverend Adam Boyle and John McIlwrath.

Boveedy Schoolhouse

There was a good substantial schoolhouse erected at the above meeting house in 1834, to which the Reverend William Napper, rector of Tamlaght, contributed 4 pounds, the Reverend Adam Boyle, Seceding Minister, 1 pound, Andrew Orr of Keely, Esquire, proprietor of Boveedy, 35 pounds, from local farmers 8 pounds. Dimensions of the schoolhouse will be found in school tables. Informants John McIlwrath and others.

Moral Societies in Boveedy

Boveedy Presbyterian Moral or Religious Society was instituted 1823. The society meet twice a month in different houses. Books read: the Bible, Testament and other pious works. The society consists of 9 members, adults of both male and female, who each in turn open and close the meeting by singing and prayer. Hours of meeting from 6 to 9 p.m. summer and winter. The above society seems to be continued with great zeal.

Boveedy Reformant Presbyterian Moral or Religious Society was instituted in 1800. It was commenced by 4 members and has since increased to 60 members, of both sexes and of various ages, and who each, according to eligibility, open the meeting by singing and prayer and close it by singing. They meet monthly in Samuel Warwick's house, Boveedy, in which house the society was first established. They open at 2 and close at 6 p.m. in summer and from 1 to 4 p.m. in winter. Books read: the Bible, Testament and other religious books. The above society divide themselves into 3 distinct bodies and hold moral meetings in different houses alternate weeks, from 6 to 9 p.m. summer and winter, and observe the same formalities as the monthly meetings in opening and closing. Information obtained from Hugh Warwick and Robert Gilmore. 24 February 1836.

Boveedy Pleasure Fair

Boveedy pleasure fair is annually held on Christmas old style. The inhabitants of Boveedy and surrounding neighbourhood assemble in the village of Boveedy and devote the day and greater part of the night to several amusements such as shooting for bets, common playing, cock-fighting, dancing, singing and drinking. The above fair has been of an old standing and is still vigorously held up. Information obtained from Hugh [?] Keating and Hugh Warwick.

Boveedy Temperance Society

Boveedy Temperance Society is held monthly in the Seceding meeting house from 6 to 9 p.m., unless during the winter months, and is opened and closed by prayer. The Reverend Adam Boyle is president and secretary. The society was established in 1831 and consists at present of 79 members of all denominations, both sexes and various ages. The resolutions of the society are total abstinence from spiritous liquors and promote temperance. Information obtained from Reverend Adam Boyle, 29th February 1836.

Temperance and Religious Societies

Drumbolg Temperance Society was established in 1830 by the Reverend James A. Smyth, who is president and secretary. Meetings are held quarterly from 4 to 6 p.m. in Drumbolg meeting house. The society consists of 240 members of both sexes, of all denominations and of various ages. They are divided into 3 bodies, to wit: the general society established in 1830 consists of 70 members of both sexes and of all denominations; the Congregational Society established 1832 consists of 120 members of both sexes and of the Reformed Presbyterians belonging to Drumbolg congregation. This branch are of various ages also. The third branch are called the Juvenile Temperance Association, established 1832. This branch consists of 50 members under 16 years of age and are Presbyterians of all denominations, who are catechised quarterly by the Reverend Mr Smyth.

There is also held in the above meeting house, once a fortnight, a society for prayer and religious conversation. This society consists of the Reformed Presbyterians and are of both sexes. All denominations are admissible to this last-mentioned society.

There was also an auxiliary missionary society established in the above meeting house in 1833. They hold their meetings quarterly. The Reverend Mr Smyth is president and Alexander Christie of Tobermore, secretary and treasurer. There is a committee of 10 persons, members of Drumbolg congregation, who each have collecting cards and receive subscriptions or donations from benevolent persons belonging to the aforesaid and other congregations. Average annual amount paid at the aforesaid society and in the above meeting house 12 pounds, which sum goes for the benefit of missionary purposes. Informant Reverend James A Smyth. 6th April 1836.

Tamlaght O'Crilly Temperance Society no. 2 was established 1830 by the Reverend William Napper, rector of Tamlaght O'Crilly, who is president and secretary of the society. Meetings held monthly and generally in Hervey Hill schoolhouse from 7 to 9 p.m. The society consists of 263 members of both sexes, of all denominations and of various ages. Of the above number there is a juvenile association, composed of male and female, and who are all under 14 years of age. This association is 13 in number. Information from the Reverend William Napper. 8th April 1836.

Moral Society

Timaconway Presbyterian Moral or Religious Society was established in 1834. It consists at present of 10 members, male adults. They meet twice in each month in different houses, open at 4 and close at 9 p.m. in summer, and in winter open at 6 and close at 10 p.m. Books read: the Bible, Testament and other religious works. The society is opened and closed by singing and prayer. The books are procured by the members respectively. Informants Robert and William Rea.

Doctor and Dispensary

Edward Nevill Esquire, M.D. attends at Tamlaght O'Crilly dispensary on Mondays and Thursdays from 10 a.m. to 1 p.m. The above dispensary was established 1835. Information from Olover Sproul.

Church of Tamlaght O'Crilly

The church of Tamlaght O'Crilly stands 1-storey, slated, an oblong building with a belfry attached to the west end, which stands 3-storeys and topped or ornamented with 4 pinnacles <pinnicles>, pyramid <pirimid> shape, with smaller ones intervening. Entrance to the church by a door into the belfry and a second door opening into the body of the church. There is also a vestry room attached to the north side of the church, slated, and stands 1-storey. The church has 4 windows, Gothic shape, 3 on the south side and 1 on the east gable where the communion table stands. The alley and area around the communion table is floored with cut freestone. The pew floors are boarded. Pulpit, pews and seats are permanently built and in a good state of repair, though plain appearance.

Pews in the church 24, single seats 28: 17 of these seats are 9 feet 2 inches and will hold persons each seat 6, total 102. 8 of these seats are 11 feet, including the end seats, and will hold persons each seat 7, total 56. One of these seats is 12 feet and will hold 8 persons; one of these seats is 6 feet 8 inches and will hold 4 persons; one of these seats is 6 feet 6 inches and will hold 4 persons. Total persons accommodated with seats in this church 174. Length of the church in the clear 54 feet; breadth of the church in the clear 24 feet; thickness of the walls 2 feet 4 inches; vestry room in the clear 9 feet 4 inches by 8 feet 1 inch. The church is spacious, there are no galleries in it. The communion table is enclosed by timber railing. The churchyard is enclosed partly by a quickset fence and partly by a stone and lime wall, entrance by an iron gate. 25th February 1836.

The new church of Tamlaght O'Crilly was completed about 1816 at an expense of [crossed out: 1,600 pounds], together with all the building materials of the old church that could be disposed of or used in the erection of the former. The above sum was advanced by the Board of First Fruits and afterwards levied on the parish, to be paid by instalments. Information from Reverend James A. Smyth, James Clarke, Robert Workman and others.

Tyanee Church

Tamlaght O'Crilly church of ease stands in the townland of Tyanee, about 5 miles from Kilrea on the leading road from Garvagh to Portglenone. The church is an oblong building, slated and

Parish of Tamlaght O'Crilly

stands 1-storey, 50 feet by 24 feet 3 inches in the clear, walls 2 feet 9 inches thick; 1 door, 4 windows, 3 of which stand on the south side wall and 1 on the east gable, where the communion table stands. The alley is floored with cut freestone, the pews are floored with timber as is also the area round the pulpit. The communion table is enclosed by timber railing; pulpit, pews and seats permanently constructed and in moderate repair. Pews in the church 14, single seats 26, length of each seat including end seats 10 feet 10 inches, and will hold 7 persons each seat. Total persons accommodated with seats in the above pews, allowing 1 and a half feet to each person, 182. There is a seat for the singers 15 feet in length and will hold 10 persons. Total persons accommodated with seats in the church 192.

The body of the church is spacious and lofty. Attached to the west gable there is a steeple, stands 3-storeys and topped with freestone pinnacles. The yard is enclosed with a good stone and lime wall. The exterior of the yard is planted with various kinds of forest trees. There is a number of tombs and headstones in the yard; entrance by an iron gate. The church stands on an eminence in a well improved neighbourhood.

Tamlaght O'Crilly chapel of ease, locally called Tyanee church, was built about 1776 by local subscription. Cost of erection can only be conjectured at present at 800 pounds, of which sum the late Henery Ellis of Inisrush, Esquire contributed a part [crossed out: about 150 pounds]. The site of the church and burial ground was granted gratis for ever by the late Counsellor Canning, Garvagh, then proprietor of Tyanee. Information from Hercules Ellis and James Courtnay Esquires, and others.

Presbyterian Meeting House

There is in process of building a Presbyterian meeting house, to be slated and stands 2-storey, built of stone and brick. Entrance by 1 large door into a hall and 2 doors into the body of the house, lower storey, and 2 doors into the galleries, upper storey, from the same hall where the staircases will stand. The meeting house was built to the square. In January last, a violent wind storm occurred on the 23rd of the same month, which brought to the ground a great portion of the south side wall and materially injured the walls at present standing. 26th February 1836.

Roman Catholic Chapel in Drumagarner

The Roman Catholic chapel of Drumagarner stands 1 mile from Kilrea, on the leading road from Kilrea to Maghera. The chapel is an oblong building, slated and stands 1-storey, 83 feet by 21 feet in the clear, walls 2 feet thick. There are 3 galleries in the chapel, the 2 end galleries 24 feet by 21 feet each and side gallery 35 feet by 8 and a half feet. Light afforded the galleries by 4 skylights in the roof. The altar stands on the south side and in the middle of the chapel. It is enclosed by timber railing and overhung by a neat timber canopy all permanently built and in a good state of repair. Opposite the altar on the side gallery stands a neat choir <coir> box, enclosed partly by wainscotting and partly by drawing curtains. Entrance to the ground floor by 2 doors, 1 in each gable. Entrance to the galleries by 2 doors, 1 in each gable immediately over the lower doors. Access to the gallery doors by stone steps erected against the gables.

Windows in the chapel 4 oblong and 2 lancet shape, one of which stands on either side of the altar. The only seats in the chapel are 2 seats on the ground floor, enclosed by timber wainscotting and sufficient to accommodate 10 persons and 2 seats in the choir-box, 19 and a half feet long each and will accommodate a total of 26 persons. The front of the galleries are supported on timber columns. The ground floor is made with lime, sand and clay. There is a vestry room attached to the north side of the chapel, slated and stands 1-storey, 25 and a half feet by 8 feet in the clear and divided into 3 distinct apartments. The site of the chapel is adjoining the above road on an eminence. The yard or burial ground is enclosed by a quickset fence intermixed with various kinds of forest trees. The yard is also studded with a large number of handsome tombs and headstones and almost entirely occupied by graves. The chapel and galleries stands in a moderate state of repair. Entrance from the road by an iron gate.

Drumagarner Roman Catholic chapel was built first in or about 1778, by local subscription of money, horse and manual labour from the parishioners of Tamlaght O'Crilly and Kilrea. Amount of the expense of building it cannot be at present ascertained, but the chapel was maliciously burned in 1810 and re-roofed and repaired in 1812 at an expense of about 160 pounds, of which sum or expense there was 120 pounds levied on the county at the spring assizes of Londonderry in 1811 and the remaining 40 pounds raised by local subscription from the parishioners of Tamlaght O'Crilly and Kilrea. The site of the chapel was first leased to the congregation by the late Rowley Heyland Esquire at 11s 4d ha'penny per annum, secondly renewed by John Church Esquire, late of Maroe [Myroe ?], at about 1s 1d per annum, thirdly leased out at a tenure renewable forever at 1s 1d per annum by the late Reverend John Paul, late rector of Aghadowey <Aghadoey> and then proprietor of the townland of Drumagarner. The last-mentioned renewal of tenure was effected in 1808. Information obtained from Edward and Michael O'Kane and others.

Income of Roman Catholic Clergy

The Reverend John Rogers is Roman Catholic pastor of the parishes of Tamlaght O'Crilly, Kilrea and Desertoghill, and receives average annual income from the above 3 parishes 180 pounds, of which annual income the Roman Catholic curates of the above charge, to wit the Reverend Samuel Auterson and the Reverend John McLoughlin, get a fourth part each as their proportion. The aforesaid management gives the parish priest as his dividend per annum 90 pounds and to each curate as his dividend per annum 45 pounds. The Worshipful the Mercers' Company, proprietors of the Kilrea proportion, gives the above parish priest, per the hands of W.H. Holmes Esquire, an annual stipend or donation of 15 pounds, and to the Reverend Samual Auterson, senior Roman Catholic curate of the above charge, per the above Mr Holmes, an annual gift of 10 pounds. Information obtained from the Reverend Samual Auterson.

Average attendance at Drumagarner Roman Catholic chapel on Sundays [blank]; average attendance at Green lough Roman Catholic chapel on Sundays [blank].

Green Lough Roman Catholic Chapel

Green lough Roman Catholic chapel stands 5 and a quarter miles from Kilrea, on the leading road from Garvagh to Portglenone. It is an oblong building, slated and stands 1-storey, 60 feet by 21 and a half feet in the clear. There are 3 galleries in the chapel. The 2 end galleries are 20 feet by 21 and a half feet each and the side gallery is 20 feet by 9 feet. The altar stands on the south side and in the middle of the chapel. It stands about 4 and a half feet above the ground floor, tastefully constructed and enclosed by a timber railing. It is also overhung by a neat timber canopy, supported on neatly finished timber columns all painted and in good repair. In the side gallery opposite the altar stands a neat choir-box, enclosed partly by wainscotting and partly by curtains.

There are no seats in the chapel except 2 that stand in the choir-box, each 12 feet long and will accommodate a total of 16 persons. 2 doors opening to the ground floor, 1 in each gable. Entrance to one of the galleries by a door in the south side wall; access to the door by stone steps. Entrance to the other galleries by a staircase outside of the chapel. Light afforded to the galleries by an oblong window in each gable and from a portion of 4 arch windows that stands in the lower part of the chapel. The front of the galleries are supported on timber columns. The ground floor is made with lime, sand and clay. House and galleries in good repair, walls 2 feet thick. There is a stone cross erected on the east gable.

The chapel stands on an eminence adjoining the above road. Beneath it stands a small but handsome lake <leak> locally called the Green lough and from which the chapel takes its name. The yard is large and, for the greater part, enclosed by a good stone and lime wall; entrance by 2 iron gates. The exterior of the yard was planted with various kinds of forest trees in 1833. There is a number of decent <deasent> tombs and headstones in the yard.

The Roman Catholic chapel of Green lough was built about 1793 at an expense of about 200 pounds, which was contributed for the greater part in money, horse and manual labour by the Roman Catholic parishioners, and part in money from benevolent persons of all other denominations. It was repaired and re-roofed in 1825 at an expense of about 50 pounds, which sum was contributed chiefly by the Roman Catholics and part by other denominations. The site of the above chapel was leased at the first-mentioned period from Henery [insert marginal query: Henry ?] McLoughlin and company, for a term of 3 lives at 3 pounds per annum. The 3 persons whose lives were inserted in the lease are still living. Information obtained from Henery McLoughlin and John Henery. 13th April 1836.

Covenanting or Reformed Presbyterian Meeting House

Drumbolg Covenanting meeting house stands 3 and a half miles from Kilrea, and near to the village of Tamlaght O'Crilly, on the leading road from Garvagh to Portglenone. The house is an oblong building, thatched and stands 1-storey, 51 feet by 21 feet in the clear. Walls 2 feet thick, alley floor made with clay, pew floors boarded; pulpit, pews and seats in moderate repair. Entrance to the house by 2 doors. Windows in the house, 10 oblong shape. Single seats in the house, finished and unfinished, 36; length of each seat, including end seats, 10 feet and will hold 7 persons each seat: total persons accommodated with seats in

Parish of Tamlaght O'Crilly

the house 252. There is a sessions house in the yard, thatched and stands 1-storey. The yard is enclosed by a quickset fence, entrance by an iron gate. The exterior of the yard was planted in 1835 with various kinds of forest trees. There are a few graves in the yard. 1st March 1836.

Drumbolg Reformed Presbyterian meeting house was built in 1812, cost of erection 100 pounds, amount subscribed by the congregation. The site of the meeting house was at the above period purchased from the occupying farmer for an unexpired term of 16 years at 8 pounds, at the expiration of which tenure the late Rowley Heyland Esquire gave a 21 year lease of the above site renewable for ever, at 1d per annum if required. Average attendance at the above meeting house on Sundays 360, total number belonging to the congregation 728. Informant Reverend James A. Smyth. 23rd March 1836.

Reformed Presbyterian Minister

The Reverend James A. Smyth is minister of Drumbolg Reformed Presbyterian congregation and receives annual stipend 50 pounds, no royal bounty.

Charity Collection

There is a collection on Sundays in Drumbolg meeting house, the proceeds of which goes weekly to relieve the wants of an average of 12 persons of destitute poor. Informant Reverend James A. Smyth.

New Presbyterian Meeting House

The new Presbyterian meeting house at present in process of building in Tamlaght O'Crilly village stands 65 feet by 45 feet from out to out, walls 2 feet thick. There are 19 arch windows in the house. The outside of the walls are built of blackish quarry stone. The yard is enclosed by a quickset fence. The site of the meeting house was bestowed on the intended Presbyterian congregation of Tamlaght O'Crilly by Langford R. Heyland Esquire, proprietor of Tamlaght O'Crilly estate. He also contributed the sum of 10 pounds towards the erection of the house. Captain Jones M.P. contributed 10 pounds, Sir Robert Bateson M.P. 10 pounds, Dr Madden of Dublin 5 pounds. The remainder of the cost of erecting the above meeting house has been raised by local subscription of money, horse and manual labour from the intended congregation of Tamlaght, and also in money from benevolent individuals of every denomination in the above and various other parishes, last estimated at 700 pounds. The occupying tenants' tenure of the above site had to be purchased at 5 pounds. Information obtained from Joseph McKeon and David Campbell.

Hervey Hill

Hervey Hill, the seat of the Reverend William Napper, stands about 2 miles from Kilrea, on the leading road from Swatragh to Kilrea. The house is an oblong building and stands 3-storeys. The demesne consists of about 36 acres and is enclosed by quickset fences and divided into well arranged fields which are also enclosed by quickset fences and iron gates. There is a good fruit and vegetable garden enclosed partly by a stone and lime wall and partly by a quickset fence. The demesne is improved and ornamented with partial plantations of various kinds of forest trees.

The above Glebe House was built by the late Reverend Robert Torrens, formerly rector of Tamlaght O'Crilly, about 1774, and newly roofed and raised 1-storey about 1811 by the late Reverend James Jones, who was also rector of the parish for several years. Mr Napper has also expended a considerable sum of money subsequently on repairing the house, office houses and planting small plantations in various parts of the demesne. Information obtained from Francis Huston, John McReynolds and others.

The house stands on an eminence and commands delightful prospects of the surrounding neighbourhood. 1st April 1836.

Glenone Glebe

Glenone Glebe, the seat of the Reverend Mark Bloxham, incumbent, stands about 1 and a half miles from Portglenone on the leading road from Kilrea to Bellaghy. The house is an oblong building and stands 2-storey, slated. The glebe or demesne consists of 15 Irish acres and is well enclosed with quickset fences and divided into well arranged fields which are also enclosed with quickset fences. There is also a good fruit and vegetable garden enclosed by a quickset fence. The glebe is partially improved and ornamented with partial plantations of various kinds of forest trees.

The above Glebe House stands on an eminence and commands a delightful prospect of Portglenone and its well improved neighbourhood for some miles. The house was built about 1780 by the late Reverend Robert Torrens, formerly rector of Tamlaght O'Crilly. The above care or living is rather a chaplaincy to the clergy

Glenburn House

Glenburn House, the seat of James Courtnay Esquire, stands about 5 miles from Kilrea on the leading road from Garvagh to Portglenone, and in a most delightful part of the neighbourhood. The house is an oblong building, slated, and stands 2-storeys. It stands on a eminence over a beautiful glen in the neighbourhood of Clady and through which glen Clady river passes. It commands a most delightful prospect of Portglenone, its well improved neighbourhood and surrounding hills. There is a good fruit and vegetable garden enclosed partly by a stone and lime wall and partly by a quickset fence. The demesne consists of about 60 acres and is also enclosed partly by a stone and lime wall and partly by quickset fences, and divided into compact fields. It is partially studded with small plantations of various kinds of forest trees. The above house was built by the late Joseph Courtnay of Glenburn, Esquire about 1786. Information obtained from James Courtnay Esquire. 15th April 1836.

Ballymcpeake Glebe

Ballymcpeake Glebe of Termoneeny, the seat of the Reverend Charles Foster, stands 6 miles from Kilrea on the Ballymcpeake road from Kilrea to Bellaghy. The house is an oblong building, slated, and stands 2-storeys. There is a good fruit and vegetable garden, partly enclosed by a stone and lime wall and partly by a quickset fence. The demesne is about 35 acres and is enclosed partly by quickset fences and partly by drains, and partially ornamented with small plantations of various kinds of forest trees. The house stands on an eminence and was built about 1805 by the late Reverend Odley Fanning, formerly rector of Termoneeny. Informants Peter Murray and George Burt. 18th April 1836.

Inisrush House

Inisrush House, the seat of Hercules Ellis Esquire, stands about 5 miles from Kilrea on the leading road from Garvagh to Portglenone, and in a well improved part of the neighbourhood. The house is an oblong building, slated, and stands 2-storeys. It stands on an eminence commanding a delightful prospect of a large tract of the surrounding neighbourhood. There is a good fruit and vegetable garden enclosed by a quickset fence. The demesne consists of about 80 acres of good, well improved soil and is enclosed partly by a stone and lime wall and partly by quickset fences. There is a good lawn in front of the house, beautifully interspersed with large and lofty trees of various kinds.

The demesne is partly studded with small plantations of forest trees. There is about 12 acres of demesne under native wood. The wood consists of 1,000 large oak trees and the underwood of hazel, producing immense quantities of nuts in the season that are sold in Derry, Belfast. The demesne is bounded on the west and south west by a beautiful winding river locally called Clady river. Mr Ellis has put about 4 acres under plantations of various kinds of forest trees within the last 5 years, such as oak, ash, larch, Scotch firs, which greatly contributes to the other improvements on the demesne. The old house of Inisrush was much larger than the present. The present house of Inisrush was built by the late Henry Ellis of Inisrush House, Esquire about 1825, at which period he demolished the old house. Entrance to the above house opens from the village of Inisrush. Information obtained from Hercules Ellis Esquire.

Bridges

Hervey Hill bridge, on the leading road from Kilrea to Swatragh, has 1 arch, span 9 feet, height of parapets on the bridge 2 feet, thickness of parapets 1 and a half feet, breadth of the road on the bridge 18 feet. The above bridge stands in moderate repair.

Inverrue bridge, on the leading road from Clady to Kilrea, has 3 arches: span of each arch 13 feet 6 inches, average height of parapets on the bridge 2 feet 6 inches, thickness of parapets 1 foot 6 inches, breadth of road on the bridge 18 feet. The above bridge divides the parishes of Kilrea and Tamlaght O'Crilly on the last-mentioned line of road. It stands at present in a moderate state of repair.

Portglenone bridge has 7 arches, one half of which stands in the above parish and in the above county. Span of each arch 27 feet, average height of parapets on the bridge 3 feet 6 inches, thickness of parapets 1 foot 6 inches, breadth of road on the bridge 21 feet. The above bridge is built with black quarry stone and the parapets topped with cut freestone; bridge and parapets in good repair at present.

Corn Mills

Clady corn mills are occupied by James Courtnay Esquire. One of the mills is for grinding corn and

Parish of Tamlaght O'Crilly

the other for shelling corn. The corn mill or grinding water wheel is undershot, diameter 12 feet 10 inches, breadth across the wheel 2 feet 6 and a half inches, fall of water from the trough to the buckets 4 feet. The shelling mill water wheel is undershot, diameter 12 feet, breadth across the wheel 2 feet 4 inches, fall of water from the trough to the buckets 3 feet 6 inches. The shelling mill is slated, stands 2-storey. The grinding mill is slated, stands 2-storey. The supply of water is abundant at the above mills at all seasons of the year. Informants George Eavens and Robert Loughlin. 7th April 1836.

Bleach Green

Clady bleach green was latterly occupied by James Courtnay and ceased to bleach in 1824. The engine house is slated and stands 2-storey. The wash mill and all other houses belonging to the bleaching establishment are slated and stand 1-storey. The beetling engine water wheel is a breast wheel, diameter 14 feet, breadth across the wheel 6 feet 1 inch, fall of water from the trough to the buckets 1 foot 6 inches. The wash mill water wheel is a breast wheel, diameter 12 feet 4 inches, breadth across the wheel 2 feet 4 inches, fall of water from the trough to the buckets 3 feet. The above water wheels are enclosed to a great extent by timber and cannot be more accurately measured. The supply of water to the above green is sufficient all seasons of the year.

The beetling engine of Clady bleach green is at present occupied by David Cunningham of Castledawson <Castle Dawson> in beetling brown linen and the other machinery and works in process of being repaired. There was about 6 acres of ground occupied by Clady green. Informants George Eavens and Robert Loughlin.

Flax Mills

Timaconway flax mill is occupied by Robert Greer. The mill is thatched and stands 1-storey. The water wheel is undershot, diameter 11 feet 10 inches, breadth across the wheel 2 feet, fall of water 6 feet. The supply of water at the above mill is limited in the months of June, July and August. Informant Robert Greer.

Lismoyle flax mill is occupied by John Gilmore. The mill is thatched and stands 1-storey. The water wheel is undershot, diameter 10 feet, fall of water 7 feet, breadth across the wheel 2 feet 1 inch. The above mill is supplied by a current and has a moderate supply of water all seasons of the year. Informant John Crilly.

Ballynian flax mill was occupied by John Crilly 14 years. It is at present unroofed and in process of being repaired. Informant John Crilly.

Road and Bridge

That line of road leading from Kilrea to Maghera by Drumagarner chapel averages 20 feet wide clear of banks, drains or fences, all within the above parish, and with few exceptions stands at present in a moderate state of repair.

Drumnacannon bridge, on the leading road from the village of Tamlaght to Bellaghy <Ballaghy> through Eden, has 4 arches: span of the 2 north arches are each 12 feet, span of the outside south arch 12 feet, span of the inside south arch 21 feet, breadth of the road on the bridge 18 feet, average height of parapets on the bridge 3 feet 4 inches, thickness of parapets 1 foot 6 inches. The above bridge and parapets are at present in a moderate state of repair. The parapets extend 52 yards on either side of the road.

Flax Mill

Moneysallin flax mill is occupied by Andrew Bradley. The mill is thatched and stands 1-storey. The water wheel is undershot, diameter 12 feet 2 inches, breadth across the wheel 1 foot 9 and a half inches, fall of water 6 feet 6 inches. The supply of water at the above mill is limited in the months of June, July and August. Informant Andrew Bradley.

Roads

That line of road leading from Garvagh to Portglenone through the village of Tamlaght O'Crilly averages 20 feet wide clear of banks, drains or fences and stands at present in a moderate state of repair, all within the above parish.

That line of road leading from Garvagh to Kilrea through Drumane averages 20 feet wide clear of banks, drains or fences and stands at present in a moderate state of repair, all within the above parish.

That line of road leading from Swatragh <Swattra> to Kilrea averages 19 feet clear of banks and drains or fences, and is all within the above parish, in a moderate state of repair.

Bridge

Moneysallin bridge on the by-road leading from Drumagarner to Portglenone has 1 arch, span 15 feet 4 inches, height of parapets average 2 feet 6 inches, thickness of parapets 1 foot 6 inches, breadth of road on the bridge 17 feet 6 inches, bridge and parapets in good repair.

Flax Mill

Lisnagroat flax mill is occupied by William Campbell. The mill is thatched and stands 1-storey. The water wheel is undershot, diameter 11 feet 4 inches, breadth across wheel 1 foot 6 inches, fall of water 6 feet. The supply of water at the above mill is limited in the months of June, July and August. Informants Andrew Bellingham and Robert McGregor.

Corn Mill

Lisnagroat corn mill is occupied by Alexander Craig. The mill is thatched and stands 1-storey. The water wheel is undershot, diameter 13 feet 1 inch, breadth across the wheel 2 feet, fall of water 12 feet. The supply of water at the above mill is moderate at all seasons of the year except in the instance of a very hot summer. Informants Michael McErlane and Robert McGregor. 16th March 1836.

Bridges and Roads

Lisnagroat bridge on the leading road from Kilrea to Inisrush has 2 arches: span of each arch 10 feet 1 inch, average height of parapets on the bridge 2 feet, thickness of parapets 1 foot 6 inches, breadth of the road on the bridge 20 feet. The parapets are slightly dilapidated and the bridge in moderate repair.

The above line of road averages 20 feet wide, clear of banks, drains or fences, and stands in a good state of repair at present, all within the above parish.

Lisnagroat bridge on the by-road leading from Drumagarner to Portglenone has 2 arches: span of east arch 10 feet 6 inch, span of west arch 11 feet, average height of parapets on the bridge 2 feet 6 inches, thickness of parapets 1 foot 6 inches, breadth of road on the bridge 19 feet, bridge and parapets in good repair.

The last-mentioned line of by-road averages 18 feet wide, clear of banks, drains or fences and stands in several parts within the above parish in a bad state of repair.

Killygullib Glebe bridge on the leading road from Kilrea to Maghera has 1 arch, span 9 feet; average height of parapets on the bridge 2 feet 6 inches, thickness of parapets 1 foot 6 inches, breadth of road on the bridge 18 feet, parapets partly dilapidated.

Corn and Flax Mills

Drumnacanan corn mill near Tamlaght village is occupied by Andrew Smyth. The water wheel is undershot, diameter 13 feet 6 inches, breadth across the wheel 1 foot 10 inches, fall of water 13 feet. The mill is thatched and stands 1-storey. The supply of water at the mill is very limited for 7 months of the year in case of hot or dry weather. Mr Smyth has constructed a small flax mill for his own use and has it so constructed that the above water wheel works its machinery. Information obtained from Andrew Smyth.

Flax Mill

Inisrush flax mill is occupied by James Courtnay Esquire. The mill is thatched and stands 1-storey. The water wheel is undershot, diameter 12 feet 6 inches, breadth across the wheel 2 feet 2 and a half inches, fall of water 7 feet. There is a good supply of water at the above mill all seasons of the year.

Road

Michael Scullion and David Mulholland, to keep in repair for 7 years about 1,474 perches of the road leading from Clady to Cullyduff, at 3d per perch per annum. The aforesaid number of perches stands within the above parish. Informant Thomas Macaw, 25th March 1836.

That line of road leading from Kilrea to Maghera by Drumbolg meeting house averages 19 feet clear of banks, drains and fences, all within the above parish and stands at present in a moderate state of repair.

Corn Mills

Inisrush corn mills are occupied by James Courtnay Esquire; one of the mills for grinding corn and the other for shelling corn. They stand under 1 roof, thatched and stand 2-storey. The grinding mill water wheel is undershot, diameter 14 feet, breadth across the wheel 2 feet 8 inches, fall of water 6 feet; the shelling mill water wheel is undershot, diameter 14 feet, breadth across the wheel 2 feet, fall of water 8 feet. The water is conveyed to Inisrush corn and flax mills in 3 wooden pipes or troughs from 1 mill lead and is sufficient all seasons of the year to work the mills alternately. Information obtained from James Henery, Thomas Macaw.

By-roads

The by-roads leading through all parts of the above parish average 16 feet wide clear of banks, drains or fences. Two-thirds of the entire lines stand at present in a tolerable state of repair. Examined at sundry dates. 26th April 1836.

Parish of Tamlaght O'Crilly

Clady Bridge

Clady bridge near Inisrush has 5 arches; span of 4 east arches 15 feet each, span of west arch 12 feet. Average height of parapets on the bridge 3 and a half feet, breadth of road between parapets 21 and a half feet. The above bridge and parapets are in moderate repair. 3rd March 1836.

SOCIAL AND PRODUCTIVE ECONOMY

Glenone: Occupations

The following are the trades and callings, the number and height of houses in that subdivision of Portglenone locally called Glenone, west of the Bann and within the above county and parish: timber, slate and iron merchant 1, in 1 house; grocers 2, in 2 houses; publicans 2, in 2 houses; attorney 1, in 1 house; dealers in meal, corn, butter and pigs 2, in 2 houses; boot and shoemakers 4, in 4 houses; carpenters and dray makers 3, in 3 houses; sawyers 2, in 2 houses; lodgings for travelling dealers 2, in 2 houses; huxters in provisions, 5, in 5 houses; pensioners 2, in 2 houses; dressmakers 1, in 1 house; bonnet makers 1, in 1 house; painters and glaziers 1, in 1 house; nailors 1, in 1 house; bakers 1, in 1 house; spinning wheelwright 1, in 1 house; blue dyers 1, in 1 house; tailors 1, in 1 house; [parish ?] police 5; labourers 9, in 9 houses; leather cutters 1, in 1 house; workwomen at spinning 3, in 3 houses; schoolhouse 1, in 1 house; [parish ?] police office 1, in 1 house; total trades and callings 54, total houses occupied 49. Total occupied houses 49, 2-storey houses 17, 1-storey houses 32, total 49.

Glenone Schoolhouse

Glenone national schoolhouse stands 2-storey, slated and measures 31 by 20 feet in the clear; walls 1 foot 10 inches thick, 1 door, 10 windows, umbrella roof. There is an 8-day clock in process of being erected in the south side wall opposite the bridge. The walls are built with black quarry stone. The lower storey is for the males and the upper storey for the females. The schoolhouse stands in that subdivision of Portglenone locally called Glenone, west [of] and immediately adjoining the River Bann, and within the above parish. The house was erected in 1836 but not at present fully completed or occupied by the school. The site of the schoolhouse was bestowed by Daniel Daly, merchant, Glenone and given in trust to James Daly and others for a term of 24 years and 2 lives for the benefit of the national school.

Cost of erection 155 pounds 15s 6d: of the above sum the Education Board gives 103 pounds 17s, the Reverend John Rogers, parish priest of Tamlaght O'Crilly, 2 pounds; the Reverend John McLoughlin, Roman Catholic curate of Tamlaght O'Crilly, 2 pounds; the Reverend Samual Auterson, Roman Catholic curate of Tamlaght O'Crilly, 1 pound; the Reverend John Lynch, parish priest of Ahoghill, 2 pounds; W.H. Holmes Esquire, 1 pound; Daniel Daly, Glenone, 1 pound; John Daly Senior, Portglenone, 1 pound; John Daly Junior, Portglenone, 1 pound; Doctor Heany, Portglenone, 1 pound; Patt Mooney, Portglenone, 1 pound; John Hamil [insert query: Hamill ?], Portglenone, 1 pound; James McEntire, Glenone, 1 pound. The remainder, up to the full cost of erecting the above schoolhouse, was contributed by benevolent persons of all denominations, in sums equal to their circumstances. Information obtained from Mr Daniel Daly, acting manager of the above schoolhouse. 5th April 1836.

Building Materials

Prices of building materials in Glenone is as follows: Memel timber per square foot, 2s 6d; pine timber per square foot, 1s 9d; 12 feet planks per 120, 21 pounds; queen ton slates per ton, 3 pounds 3s; countesses slates per ton, 6 pounds; English iron per cwt, 12s; Swedish iron per cwt, 1 pound 5s; bricks made in the neighbourhood and sold per 1,000 at 7s 6d; lime from Moneymore, distance 12 miles, and sold per barrel at 1s; sand got in the neighbourhood, per ton 1s; building stones got in the parish and sold at 1s per ton; freestone procured from Ballynascreen <Ballinascreen> and sold at various prices. Information obtained from Daniel Daly, merchant, and others. 14th April 1836.

Clady Village

Clady is a small country village 5 miles from Kilrea, on the leading road from Garvagh to Portglenone. The following are the occupations and trades and also the number and height of houses in the village: publicans 3, in 3 houses; grocers 2, in 2 houses; millers 1, in 1 house; coopers 1, in 1 house; blacksmiths 1, in 1 house; farmers 2, in 1 house. Houses 2-storey 3, 1-storey 7, houses occupied 10. All occupations 10, total houses 10. Information obtained from Hamilton McEntire.

Inisrush Village

Inisrush is a country village 5 miles from Kilrea, on the leading road from Garvagh to Portglenone.

The following are the occupations and trades in the village, also the number and height of houses in Inisrush: publicans 2, grocers 1, farmers 2, shoemakers 3, coopers 2, butchers 3, millwrights 1, spinning wheelwrights 1, carpenters 1, tailors 1, blacksmiths 1, labourers 6, working spinsters 7, total trades and callings 31. Houses occupied by persons in trade or calling 31, petty sessions house 1, schoolhouse 1, corn mills 2, flax mill 1, flax storehouse 1, corn kilns 2. Total occupied houses 39, waste houses 1, total houses in the above village 40; 2-storey houses 9, 1-storey houses 31.

There is a petty sessions held in Inisrush on the first Thursday of each month; also a corn market on Mondays, free cranage afforded by James Courtnay Esquire. Information obtained from Thomas Macaw, rent agent.

Crops

The following are the seasons of the year that the various crops are commenced to be put down and are also ripe and fit for use in the above parish; also the difference in the sowing and ripening of crops in the mountainous and cold soil of the parish.

Wheat put down from 10th October, ripe from 28th August; barley put down from 1st April, ripe from 26th August; oats put down from 1st April, ripe from 1st September; flax put down from 1st May, ripe from 15th August; clover and hay put down from 1st April, ripe from 1st June, second year; vetches put down from 1st March, ripe from 10th July; peas put down from 16th March, ripe from 15th September; beans put down from 25th February, ripe from 20th September; turnips put down from 1st July, ripe from 1st November; rye put down from 1st November, ripe from 24th August; onions put down from 15th April, ripe from 1st September; carrots put down from 15th April, ripe from 27th November; potatoes put down from 10th April, ripe from 20th October.

The mountainous parts of the parish are from 1 to 3 weeks later in ripening the various crops in almost all seasons than the low land or sandy soil, though the difference in sowing does not average more than 10 days. Information obtained from Andrew Smyth, Thomas Macaw and other farmers.

ANCIENT TOPOGRAPHY AND NATURAL FEATURES

Fort

Gortmacrane Fort stands in the holding of Michael McGuigan and stood circular shape, 40 yards in diameter. It was surrounded by a moat and 2 parapets which are at present destroyed to a great extent. The parapets were composed of stone and clay. The existing part of the inside parapet is 18 feet in breadth, 5 feet high above the area of the fort and 10 feet above the bottom of the moat. The moat averages 10 feet in breadth. The outside parapet is nearly destroyed. There is a road and stone fence through one side of the fort and the remainder under grass.

Giant's Chair

The Giant's Chair in Gortmacrane, and holding of Daniel O'Kane, is a large stone, concave on the top. The concave forms the seat and measures 2 feet 9 inches in length and breadth and 9 inches in depth. Local tradition says that it was a giant called Cruiheen that sat on the stone and sunk the print of his seat in it as above described. The inhabitants do not wish to disturb it and still call it the Giant's Chair. Information obtained from Daniel Logue and others.

Caves

There were 2 ancient caves discovered in Gortmacrane about 1815. They were built of large rough <ruff> stones and arched with long flat stones. They have been subsequently demolished and the stones used in building houses.

Bogs

The bogs of Gortmacrane and Drumagarner are chiefly flow bogs and vary in depth from 2 to 30 feet. There was a large quantity of fir and oak trees and roots got in these bogs from time to time and in some instances 3 layers of both trees and roots one above another, and the surface of many of them burned to a great extent. The tops of the trees lay chiefly east. Informants Daniel Cassidy, John Richy and others. 7th March 1836.

Forts in Timaconway

In Timaconway, and holding of Robert Dunlop, there stands on an eminence a fort approaching to circular shape, 23 yards in diameter. It was surrounded by a moat and 2 parapets composed of stone and clay. The inside parapet averages 3 and a half feet in height above the area of the fort, 6 and a half feet above the bottom of the moat and 12 feet in breadth. The moat is 10 feet in breadth. The fort is under grazing.

In the above townland, and holding of James McDaid, there stands a fort, oblong, 22 yards by

Parish of Tamlaght O'Crilly

18 yards. It is surrounded by a moat which averages 12 feet in breadth. If there was a parapet round it at any period it was demolished. The fort is called the Fort Garden and is occupied as a vegetable garden. There are some low bushes round its exterior.

In the above townland, and holding of William Caskey and others, there stands the site of an oval fort 35 yards by 30 yards. No appearance of a parapet. The site of the fort is under grazing.

In the above townland, and holding of Bernard McAlary and others, there stands the sites of 4 forts but the forts are so totally demolished that their shape or extent cannot be at present described.

Ruins of a Foundry in Timaconway

In the above townland, and holding of Bernard McAlary, there stood an ancient metal foundry. 2 of the mould stones supposed to have been occupied for casting metal balls are at present deposited beneath the surface on the site of the foundry. There is a circular hole in each of the stones, supposed to be sufficiently large to form a 5-pounder ball. There is a large quantity of forge dross on the site of the foundry. I have procured a specimen of the dross. Informants Bernard McAlary and John Quin.

Ancient Crock and Skeleton

George Neely of Timaconway, in demolishing a stone building on his holding in the above townland about 1810, got deposited beneath a large square stone an ancient earthen crock containing a quantity of burned stones. The crock mouldered down when removed.

The late John Neely, in demolishing a giant's grave in his holding in the above townland about 1775, discovered beneath the interior of the grave a skeleton <skelleton> more than ordinary size. He buried the skeleton on the site of the aforesaid grave. Informant George Neely.

Giant's Chair in Timaconway

Giant's chair in the above townland, and holding of Bernard McAlary, is a large stone in shape resembling the ancient oak chairs. The back of the chair reclines back to a great extent and in front a seat 3 feet 5 inches by 1 foot 10 inches and 1 foot 4 inches in height above the surface on which it stands. The back of the chair stands 2 feet 8 inches higher than the seat, 2 feet 3 inches broad and varying in thickness to the top, which stands 3 feet above the surface of the field on which the chair stands. The chair does not appear to be the work of art, though its shape is very peculiar. The inhabitants would not allow it to be disturbed. Information obtained from John Quin and Bernard McAlary.

Bogs in Timaconway

The bogs of the above townland are chiefly flow and vary in depth from 2 to 12 feet. There is little timber of any kind got in these bogs. Informants Robert Greer, John Greer and others, 8th March 1836.

Discoveries in a Demolished Fort

There stands in Ballynian, and holding of Michael Moran, the ruins of a fort, circular shape, 30 yards in diameter. The parapet, which was composed of stones and clay, is demolished except 10 feet long by 9 feet broad and 3 and a half feet high. The fort is under tillage. The above Mr Moran, in labouring the fort from time to time for the last 5 years, got beneath its surface 1 pipe or gullet 2 feet broad and 1 and a half feet high and seemed to run through the fort from one side to the other, and a

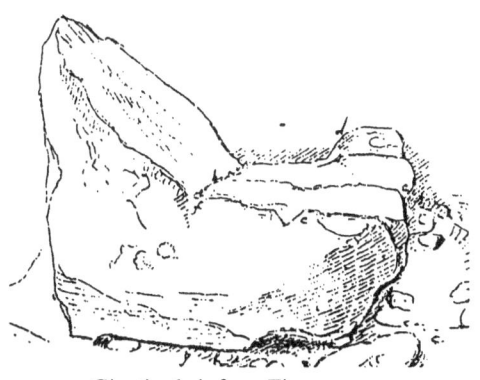

Giant's chair from Timaconway

second pipe of the aforesaid dimensions round about one half of the fort outside the parapet. He got also in the interior of the fort and about the centre a grave 6 feet long, containing rich <ritch> soil and particles of a coffin, also an earthen crock containing burned cinders or ashes deposited in a stone building, also several oblong sharpening stones of various sizes, beads, a coin and an iron battleaxe of curious shape. The axe, coin and one of the sharpening stones is at present in Mr Moran's dwelling house in the above townland. Informant Michael Moran.

In the above townland there was 4 forts at some former period. They are at present demolished and the sites under tillage. Informants John Crilly and Michael Maloy.

Bogs

Ballynian bogs are chiefly flow bogs and vary in depth from 2 to 20 feet. There was a good quantity of fir and oak trees and roots got in these bogs from time to time and in many instances layered one above another and both trees and stems burned in various parts. The trees seemed to fall from the south west. Information obtained from Joseph Quin and John Crilly.

Lismoyle Fort

Fort in Lismoyle, and holding of Samuel Bolton, is oval shape, 29 yards by 25 yards. It is surrounded by 2 moats and 3 parapets. The parapets are composed of stones and clay. The inside parapet averages 5 feet in height above the area of the fort, 11 feet above the bottom of the moat and 20 feet in breadth at the base. The middle parapet averages 5 and a half feet in height above the bottom of the moat and 15 feet in breadth. The outside parapet is partly demolished. The existing part of it averages 4 and a half feet above the bottom of the moat and 11 feet in breadth, breadth of inside moat 13 feet, breadth of outside moat 10 feet.

The fort stands on an eminence and commands a view of the surrounding neighbourhood for many miles. There was a draw-well in the north side of the fort, the depth of which well was never ascertained. It was closed at some former period in consequence of an ox being killed by falling into it. The above fort is locally called Lismoyle and gave its name to the townland. Informants Samuel Bolton and John Crilly.

The Tod Rock Fort in the above townland, and holding of William Boyd, stands on an eminence of rocky surface. It approaches to circular shape, 25 yards in diameter. The parapet was composed of stones and clay and averages 3 and a half feet in height above the area of the fort and 12 feet in breadth; no appearance of a moat. The fort is under grazing.

The Watery Fort in the above townland, and holding of Alexander Michael, was a small circular fort 15 yards in diameter. It was enclosed by a moat only. The fort and moat are at present demolished and the site under tillage.

Discoveries in a Fort

In Timaconway, and holding of James Williamson, there stands the site of a fort but so totally demolished that the shape or extent of the fort cannot be described. In demolishing the fort about 1823 there was a small grinding stone 5 inches in diameter got beneath its surface, also an oblong sharpening stone and some forge dross. Part of the last-mentioned stone is at present in Mr Williamson's dwelling house in the above townland. Informant Mrs Williamson, 9th March 1836.

Fort and Discoveries

In Killymuck, and holding of John Dimond, there stands a fort approaching to circular shape, 30 yards in diameter. It was enclosed by a moat and 2 parapets; parapets chiefly made of clay. The outside parapet, the moat and part of the inside parapet are at present demolished. The existing part averages 6 and a half feet in height above the level of the field and 24 feet in breadth at the base. It stands 2 feet higher than the area and is studded with a scrag of hawthorn and hazel <heazel> bushes. The fort is under grazing. In demolishing part of the above fort about 1812, there was a cask seemingly composed of the bark of a tree got beneath the surface of the interior of the fort, on the south west side and at the base of the parapet. The cask contained a considerable quantity of powder and flints of large size. The powder was rendered useless by time and damp and the flints subsequently destroyed. Information obtained from John Dimond.

Demolished Fort

There was a fort in Killymuck and holding of William Faulkner. It is at present totally demolished and the site under tillage. 10th March 1836.

Fort and Discoveries

Fort in Killymuck, and holding of Hugh Hamilton, is oval shaped, 22 yards by 20 yards. The

Parish of Tamlaght O'Crilly

parapet is made of stones and clay and is at present partly destroyed. The moat is also levelled. The existing part of the parapet averages 4 and a half feet in height and 15 feet in breadth at the base. There are a few ancient thorns on the parapet and the fort under tillage.

Fort in Killymuck Glebe, and holding of William McAtamney, approaches to oval shape, 35 yards by 30 yards; parapet composed chiefly of clay. It is at present partly dilapidated. It averages in height 6 feet above the level of the field, 3 feet above the area of the fort and 12 feet in breadth at the base. The moat is levelled and the fort occupied as a vegetable garden.

In demolishing the moat and labouring the interior of the fort from time to time within the last 40 years, there were graves, bones, pipes or gullets, several curious shaped stones, brass and iron articles of curious construction, forge dross and a bead of curious shape, with small stone [?] beadings, got beneath its interior and precincts. There is a brass article resembling the key of a harness saddle and a beadstone that was got in the fort at present in the above Mr McAtamney's in Killymuck. The Reverend Mr Knox of Maghera got several of the curious stones. Informants John O'Kane and William McAtamney.

Bogs

Killymuck bogs are chiefly flow bogs and vary in depth from 2 to 12 feet. There was large quantities of fir and oak trees and roots got in these bogs at some former period, but little of any value at present. Information obtained from John O'Kane and John Dimond.

Fort

Fort in Lisgorgan Glebe, and holding of Francis Quin and others, approaches to circular shape, 25 yards in diameter. The parapet is composed of stones and clay and averages in height 5 and a half feet above the bottom of the moat, 2 feet above the area of the fort and 13 feet in breadth at the base. There are a few ancient thorns round the parapet. The moat is 10 feet wide and the fort under grazing.

Ancient Coin

John O'Kane of Killymuck, on raising a stone column on his holding in 1833, discovered at its base 8 pieces of ancient silver coin, varying in size. He has subsequently sold them to a watchmaker in Kilrea. Informant John O'Kane.

Old Butter

John Patton of Drumnacannon, in labouring the remains of a bog on his holding in 1823, discovered a foot beneath the surface a circular cask, about 9 inches in diameter and composed of the bark of a tree, containing old butter. The vessel mouldered down after its being removed. Informant John Patton.

Coat of Mail

Sometime about 1795 there was an attempt made by Major Hill of Bellaghy to drain a small lake in the townland of Ballymcpeake Lower. After a quantity of the water being drawn off, there was a steel coat of mail got on the bottom of the lake. The links were very small and fastened together by rivets. The above Mr Hill had it conveyed to his dwelling at Bellaghy. Captain Heyland of Gortnamoyah got one of the sleeves. Information obtained from John and James Patton. 11th March 1836.

Fir Bog

Isaac Crockett of Drumnacannon, on raising fir roots in his bog in the above townland in 1834, cut down 3 roots that stood one on top of the other and seemed to grow in succession, and decay in the same order. After cutting and raising the lower of the roots, he discovered, lying beneath it, a tree sufficient to make a ladder. The tree lies at present in its original berth in the bog and is locally believed to have fallen previous to the growth of the aforesaid 3 roots. Informants Isaac Crockett and others. 11th March 1836.

Bogs

The bogs of Boveedy are flow and black bogs and vary in depth from 2 to 20 feet. There have been large quantities of fir and oak trees and roots got in these bogs from time to time, and in many instances layered one on top of another and burned in various parts on the surface of the trees. There have been also large quantities of hazel-nuts got in the exterior of the bogs. Informants Hugh Warwick and others.

Ancient Cave

There was an ancient cave in Gortmacrane and holding of Thomas Woods. It was built with large stones and arched with long flat stones. It is at present demolished and the stones used in other buildings. Informant Thomas Woods.

Bogs

The bogs of Drumsarragh are chiefly flow bogs and vary in depth from 2 to 30 feet. There have been a large quantity of fir and oak trees and roots got in these bogs from time to time and layered, even 3 layers one above another, and burned in various parts on the surface of the trees. The trees were found to lie indiscriminately in the bog. Informants James Johnstone and Patrick McCan. 15th March 1836.

Church Hill

The Church hill in Drumagarner, and holding of Miss Hutcheson, is an eminence nearly adjoining the leading road from Maghera to Kilrea and within about three-quarters of a mile of Kilrea. The hill is so called in consequence of a burial ground standing on it at some former period. There is not a vestige <vestage> of the burial ground to be seen but the site, which is under tillage.

The late Thomas Hutcheson of Drumagarner, in demolishing and labouring the above burial ground from time to time within the last 60 years, discovered several graves containing skulls <sculls> and various other human bones in the interior. Also a stone water font that has been for several subsequent years occupied for pounding barley in it by Thomas Woods, late of Drumane and at present of Banfield in the parish of Kilrea, and who is supposed to have it at present in his possession. Informants Edward and Michael O'Kane and others.

Fort

Fort in Killygullib Glebe, and holding of Robert Faulkner, was circular shape, 25 yards in diameter. The parapet was composed of stones and clay. It is at present greatly demolished. The existing part of it measures 5 feet in height above the level of the field on which it stands, 3 feet above the area of the fort and 13 feet in breadth at the base. The moat is levelled and the fort under tillage.

Bogs

The bogs of Moneysallin are chiefly flow bogs and vary in depth from 2 to 30 feet. There have been large quantities of fir and oak trees and roots got in the exterior of these bogs from time to time, layered one on top of another and burned on various parts of the surface. The tops of the trees were found to lie towards the east in almost all cases. Information obtained from Andrew Bradley and others.

Ancient Cave

There stands in Moneysallin, and holding of Rea Graham, an ancient cave built with large rough stones and arched with long flat stones. It was closed up by the side wall of a house built on the entrance into it in 1831. Informants James O'Neill and Robert Kirkwood.

Discoveries by Mr Bradley

Andrew Bradley of Moneysallin, in cutting turf in his bog in 1828, got 8 feet under the surface of the solid bank a fir stick about 8 feet in length and cut on one end by an axe, and lying beside it a quantity of the chips that had been cut off the stick and also a large quantity of timber cinders.

The above Mr Bradley has in his house at present a very remarkable stone, oval shape and about the size of a small hen egg, beautifully polished on the surface and a circular hole bored through the middle of it as if designed to be suspended on a ribbon. It was got in a thicket of ancient sloe bushes about 1 foot 3 inches under the surface in 1818, and in a spot supposed not to have been laboured for the last thousand years.

He has likewise in his house a set of amber beads, many of which beadstones are more than the ordinary size of modern beadstones. They were found under the surface at some former period and seem to be worthy of further notice. Information obtained from Andrew Bradley.

Fort

In Drumlane, and holding of James Armstrong, there stands a fort approaching to oval shape, 30 yards by 28 yards. It was enclosed by a moat and 2 parapets. The parapets, which were composed by stones and clay, have suffered some dilapidation. The existing part of the inside parapet averages 12 feet in height above the bottom of the moat, 5 feet above the area of the fort in some parts and 22 feet in breadth at the base. The moat averages 14 feet wide. The existing part of the outside parapet averages 5 feet in height above the bottom of the moat and varies in breadth. The existing part of both parapets is studded with a scrag of hazel, holly, oak, sloe and hawthorn bushes. The fort is under grazing and stands on a lofty eminence commanding a delightful view of the surrounding neighbourhood for many miles.

Parish of Tamlaght O'Crilly

Demolished Forts

In Lisnagroat, and holding of Joseph Murphy, there stood a fort but so demolished at present that its former shape or extent cannot be described. The site is at present under tillage.

In the last-mentioned townland, and holding of William Campbell, there stood a fort. It was so totally demolished that its former shape or extent cannot be described. The site stands on an eminence and is at present under tillage.

Bogs

Lisnagroat bogs are flow and black bogs and vary in depth from 2 to 10 feet. There have been some fir roots and trees and the same of oak got in these bogs and layered, one above another, and burned in several parts. Informants Michael McErlane and others. 16th March 1836.

Forts in Eden

Fort in Eden, and holding of John Mulholland, is at present under tillage. The moat and parapet are levelled. As near as can be at present judged, the fort stood circular shape, 35 yards in diameter. The above Mr Mulholland, in labouring the fort in 1829, got about 1 foot under the surface, in the centre of the area, 2 ancient quern stones. One of the stones is at present in his house. It is oval shape, 1 foot 6 inches by 1 foot 3 inches and a circular hole in the centre of it. Inform-ation obtained from Bernard and John Mulholland.

Fort in the above townland, and holding of James Mulholland, was oval shape, 35 yards by 30 yards. The parapet, which was composed of clay, is at present demolished almost entire. The existing part of it averages 7 feet in height above the bottom of the moat, 2 feet above the area of the fort and 13 feet in breadth at the base. The existing part of the moat averages 9 feet wide. The fort is under tillage.

Bogs

Eden bogs consist of flow and black bogs and vary in depth from 2 to 20 feet. There have been large quantities of fir and oak trees and roots got in these bogs from time to time and in various instances found 3 layers, one over another, and the surface of the trees in many instances materially injured by fire. The trees were found to lie indiscriminately in the bogs. Informants John Mulholland and others.

Demolished Fort

In Ballymcpeake Lower, and holding of Bernard McCloy, there stood a fort. There is not a vestige of it at present to be seen but an ancient haw bush, nor can its original shape or extent be described. The site is under tillage.

Curious Iron Bar

John Mulholland, Eden, in cutting turf in his bog in the above townland in 1826, got 2 feet under the surface of the bog a bar of iron of very rough shape. It was as thick in one end as a small keg and a small bar issuing from it about 6 feet in length, and seemed as if the entire of it was designed to be brought to some particular shape or purpose. The log or bar as found weighed from 60 to 70 lbs. Curiousity induced Captain Heyland of Gortnamoyah to give an equal weight of Swedish iron for the above extraordinary bar.

Ancient Wooden Dishes

The above Mr Mulholland, in cutting turf in a bog in the above townland of Eden in 1820, got about 3 feet under the surface of the bog 5 wooden dishes of rough construction, thick in substance and supposed to be made of bog sally. They varied in size and diameter. One could stand within another of the entire number so that if placed together they might appear as one dish. They were in depth about 4 inches each. They have been subsequently destroyed by pigs.

Curious Stones

The above Mr Mulholland has in his dwelling house in Eden a small stone of rather curious shape. It has caused much local conjecture concerning its original design. Nature and art might be combined in its construction. The above stone was got in breaking new land in Eden in 1832. Information obtained from John Mulholland and others.

Urns

The late John McCahy of Ballymcpeake Lower, in raising an ancient stone building on his holding in the above townland about 1780, got in its interior 2 earthen urns containing bones and ashes and a fowl's feathers, quite fresh in appearance. The urns were carved on the surface but they mouldered down on getting the air. Informants Charles McCahy and others. 18th March 1836.

Bogs

Drumard bogs are chiefly flow bogs and vary in depth from 2 to 20 feet. There have been some fir and oak trees and roots got in these bogs from time to time and layered one above another, and burned on the surface in various cases. The trees were found for the greater part to fall from the south west. Information obtained from James Magill and Thomas Armstrong.

Ancient Mill Irons

James Armstrong of Drumlane, in labouring the remains of a bog on his holding in the above townland in 1825, got about 2 feet under the surface a quantity of ancient iron mill works, 2 iron three-pronged farm forks. There is one of the forks and a portion of iron hoops, formerly used in the mill, at present in Mr Armstrong's house. They are perfectly sound but of rough construction. Informants James and Thomas Armstrong.

Bogs

The bogs of the above townland of Drumlane are flow and black bogs and vary in depth from 2 to 20 feet. There is a good quantity of fir and oak trees and roots got in these bogs, and layered one on top of another and materially injured by fire. The trees are in some cases found to fall from the north. Informants Thomas Armstrong and others.

Forts

In Drumlane, and holding of James Kelso, there stood a fort but so totally demolished at present that its original shape or extent cannot be at present described. The site is at present under tillage.

In Drumard, and holding of Andrew Smyth, there stood a fort. It was totally demolished at some former period. There is not a vestige of it at present to be seen. The site is under tillage. 19th March 1836.

Demolished Fort

Fort in Inisrush, and holding of John McLoughlin, is so demolished that its former shape or extent cannot be at present described. The site stands on an eminence and is at present under tillage.

Bog

Moneystaghan bogs are chiefly flow and vary in depth from 2 to 20 feet. There is little timber got in these bogs. Informants Patrick McErlane and John Henry.

Wooden Implement

John McCloy of Moneystaghan Mcpeake, in cutting turf in a bog on his holding in 1833, got 8 feet under the surface of the solid bog a wooden implement of so extraordinary a construction that no artisan <artizan> was able to judge for what purpose it was originally designed, though it was inspected by many. It was conveyed to the parish of Maghera where it is supposed to be at present.

Gold Hoard in Cave

The late James McCay of Ballymcpeake Lower, in demolishing an ancient cave that stood on his holding in the above townland in 1807, got in its interior a quantity of gold coin, gold bars of small size and numbered on the surface of each, and some other articles composed of stone, iron and other metals and of curious shape. The above articles were sold in Belfast. Information obtained from John Henry and John McCloy. 22nd March 1836.

Human Skull

In demolishing a portion of the walls of the old church of Tamlaght O'Crilly about 1815, there were 2 human skulls found deposited in a small recess that was constructed in the east gable. The skulls were in a moderate state of preservation. One of them differed in shape from ordinary skulls. It was long and narrow and convex on the fore part or face. One of them was supposed to be the skull of a male and the other the skull of a female. They remained some months uninterred for the inspection of the curious. They have been subsequently buried in the interior of the old church, opposite the spot in which they were found. Informants Andrew Smyth and David Campbell.

Bogs

Drumoolish bogs are chiefly flow bogs and vary in depth from 2 to 30 feet. There are large quantities of fir and oak trees and roots got in these bogs from time to time and in many instances found layered one above another, and materially injured by fire. Informants William Kelso and James Clarke.

Grey Stone

In Inisrush, and holding of Alexander McCleland, there stands an ancient stone column locally called the Grey Stone. It stands on an eminence and

Parish of Tamlaght O'Crilly

measures 3 feet 4 inches in height, 2 feet 10 inches in breadth and 1 foot 8 inches in thickness.

Bogs in Inisrush

The bogs of the above townland are chiefly flow bogs and vary in depth from 2 to 20 feet. There have been some fir and oak trees and roots got in these bogs from time to time and in some instances found layered one above another, and materially injured by fire. Informants Thomas McCaw and James Henry. 26th March 1836.

Demolished Fort

In Inisrush, and holding of Isaac McReady, there stood a fort, circular shape, 30 yards in diameter. The moat and parapet are at present demolished and the site under tillage. 28th March 1836.

Wooden Spade and Metal Ball

Alexander Tomb, in cutting turf in a bog in Timaconway in 1828, got, sunk upright in the solid turf bank, a wooden implement shaped thus: [outline of a spade]. The spade or flat part measures in length 1 foot 8 inches, breadth 6 and a half inches, thickness half an inch; the handle or shaft measures 1 foot 8 inches, breadth 1 and a half inches, thickness half an inch. There was a 3-angle knot on the end of the handle, to be held by the left or top hand when working. One half of the handle was broken off in drawing it out of the turf bank. The remaining, as shown by draft, is at present in the above Mr Tomb's house in Timaconway. The above spade is composed of a solid piece.

The above Mr Tomb has in his house at present a round metal ball a little flattened on one side, with a small hole approaching to circular and 1 and a half inches deep pierced through its centre. There is also a raised rim on the surface of the ball all round in the middle. It presents altogether a curious construction. It weighs about 20 oz. The above ball was found about 1 foot under the surface of a clay field in Timaconway in February last. Information obtained from Alexander Tomb and others.

Discoveries in New Land

John O'Neill of Ballynian, in labouring a field of new land on his holding in the last-mentioned townland in 1829, got under the surface 3 pieces of ancient silver coin, some ancient crocks containing ashes, also a stone hatchet or thunderbolt as it is locally called. The crocks and coin mouldered down subsequent to their being found. The stone hatchet is at present in his house in the above townland. Informants John O'Neill and others. 30th March 1836.

Ancient Mill Machinery

James Acheson of Timaconway, in digging a drainage moat through a bog in the above townland in 1826, got 3 feet under the surface a millstone, circular shape, 2 feet 4 inches in diameter and about 5 inches thick. There was a hole through the centre approaching to circular and 6 inches in diameter. One half of the above stone was broken off. The other half of it is at present occupied as a stepping stone at the above Mr Acheson's kitchen door. He also got in the same place a log of black oak 3 feet square, with a circular hole in each end of it as if employed in the mill machinery. The spot where the aforesaid articles have been found is locally believed to be the ruins of an ancient mill. Informants James Acheson and Henery McAlary.

Ancient Crock

Samuel Bolton of Lismoyle, in raising an ancient stone column on his holding in the last-mentioned townland in 1806, got at its base about 3 feet under the surface an ancient crock containing bones and ashes. The crock mouldered down subsequent to its being removed. Informant William Bolton. 31st March 1836.

Stone Quern

Francis Huston of Drumsarrah has in his house at present an ancient quern-stone 17 inches in diameter and 2 inches in thickness. There is a circular hole in the centre of it 2 and a half inches in diameter. It is smooth on one side and a convex on the other. There are 3 circular holes on the convex side at arranged distances one from the other and near the edge of the stone. The above quern-stone was got 2 feet under the surface in the ruins of an ancient stone building in 1811. Informant Francis Huston.

Fort Nelson

In Killygullib, and holding of John Magee, there stands a small enclosure locally called Fort Nelson. It was enclosed at some former period by the late Mrs Jones of Hervey Hill to perpetuate the memory of the late Admiral Nelson, to whose name the enclosure was dedicated. It is planted with various kinds of fruit trees and enclosed by a stone wall about 3 feet high. In the east end of the enclosure stands an ancient stone column 3 feet 10 inches high, 2 feet 3 inches broad and 1 and a half feet thick. Informant John Magee. 1st April 1836.

Black Lough

The Black lough stands in the townland of Inisrush and holdings of the Reverend James A. Smyth and others, and stands about 5 miles from Kilrea, east [of] and immediately adjoining the leading road from Garvagh to Portglenone. It occupies about 10 Irish acres and approaches to an oblong shape. It is bounded on the west and north west by an uninterrupted ridge of hills or eminences which averages about 15 feet in height above the surface of the water. It is enclosed on the east and north east by a large tract of bog which stands about 6 feet above the surface of the water. Up to 1831 the above number of acres was covered with water at an average depth of 9 feet.

At the last-mentioned period, the above-mentioned Mr Smyth sunk an old canal or water cut that lead from the lough to the Clady river that runs in a valley west of the above road and eminence. The canal was sunk about 13 feet, which gave a gradual fall to the water to the west side of the lough and had the effect of draining more than one half of the space previously covered by the water. The vacated part or remains of the aforesaid drainage is at present undergoing a process of irrigation <irragation> and improvement to a great extent by the above Mr Smyth, who has planted some thousands of various kinds of forest trees along the verge of the lough and at the base of the aforesaid ridge of hills in 1831 and subsequent springs, and which will in the course of a few years ornament the valley and remaining portion of the lough. He has also reclaimed and brought to a state of cultivation a great portion of the hills by which it is surrounded and which was previous to the above date occupied by a scrag of native wood.

Discoveries near Black Lough

The portion of the aforesaid lough at present occupied by water averages about 6 feet in depth and is partially studded with springs. It is inhabited by coots or water hens, wild ducks, bitterns <bitterins>, cormorants, cranes, snipes and wild geese occasionally. Round its precincts is also inhabited by hares and rabbits occasionally. The aforesaid Mr Smyth, in sinking the aforesaid canal in 1831, found about 70 yards west of the lough the ruins of an old corn mill. It was constructed of an oblong black oak frame <fream> which was bound together by pins of forest oak. The frame was about 8 feet long and 4 feet broad. In the frame stood one of the grinding stones, supposed to be the upper one. It was about 2 feet 5 inches in diameter and about 7 inches thick in the centre. There was a groove in the centre in which stood an iron spindle when in the process of grinding. The groove was about 6 and a half inches across thus: [diagram, cruciform shape]. The circular hole in the centre was about 2 and a half inches in diameter.

There was some portion of a horn spoon found within the mill. The grinding stone was quartz interspersed with mica, which quality of stone could not be procured nearer to the site of the aforesaid mill than west of the county of Donegal <Donagal>. One half of the grinding stone is at present in the fire hearth in a room in the above Mr Smyth's dwelling house at the Black lough. There is also in his house a portion of the black oak frame made into kitchen stools. The aforesaid portion of mill machinery was found about 6 feet under the surface in sinking the aforesaid canal. It is supposed that the rest of the mill and machinery was burned, as there was a large quantity of cinders found in the same place.

Within a few yards of it, on the east side and in the canal, under a pipe that runs across the road opposite the Black lough, there was about a bushel of living cockles got. The aforesaid canal is locally believed to be a mill lead or water cut originally made for the benefit or conveyance of water from the lough to the aforesaid mill. There is a portion of the oak logs still undisturbed in the canal on the site of the aforesaid mill.

There is pike and eel got in abundance in the Black lough in autumn.

In exploring the lough from time to time it is found to be pregnant with timber, the quality of which is not yet ascertained. But in the instance of a very dry or hot summer, a reddish scum collects on the surface of the water, which scum congeals, and when afterwards dissolved in any implement on a fire, it will make as good rushlights as any grease, and is supposed to be the resin <rozen> or essence of fir forced to the surface by intense heat. It has often procured by persons for winter light.

The Black lough is supposed to have taken its name from the blackness of the bog by which it is partly surrounded. Information obtained from the Reverend James Smyth, John Walsh and others. 11th April 1836.

Parish of Tamlaght O'Crilly

Submerged Island

Previous to draining the Black lough in 1831, there stood near the north east end of it a small circular island about 7 yards in diameter. The draining had the effect of lowering or submerging it to a great extent. Informant the Reverend James A. Smyth. 12th April 1836.

Green Lough

The Green lough stands in the townland of Inisrush and holdings of John Welsh and others, and about 5 miles from Kilrea, east of the leading road from Garvagh to Portglenone and within one half mile of the village of Inisrush. It approaches to oval shape and occupies about 7 Irish acres. It is bounded on all sides by an almost interrupted ridge of hills which averages about 20 feet in height above the surface of the water and had been formerly studded with a scrag of native oak. The above number of acres had been originally covered with one sheet of water. At some former period there was a canal cut, 16 feet in depth, through an eminence that stands west of the lough, which gave a gradual fall from the lough to Clady river that runs in a valley west of the above road. This canal had the effect of draining two-thirds of the space formerly occupied by the water. The average depth of the water in the lough at present does not exceed 6 feet, but being pregnant with springs, the actual depth of water in some parts of it was never ascertained.

It is inhabited with wildfowl such as geese, ducks, coots or water hens, cranes, cormorants, snipe and bitterns, also fish such as pike and eel which are found in great abundance in autumn. The last principal attempt to drain the lough was made about 1775. Subsequent attempts have been also made.

About 1813 there was about 10 barrels of the largest and fattest eels got in the springs of the lough. This extraordinary take on eels occurred in consequence of a severe and long-continued frost that covered the whole surface of the water with one sheet of ice, save the springs, to which it was conjectured that all the eels in the lough repaired for air. The attention of the local inhabitants was first drawn to the aforesaid springs on perceiving the heads of hundreds of eels above the water of the springs as if seeking air.

Green Lough Island and Castle

In or about the middle of the Green lough there stands an island locally called Inisrush and from which the village and townland of Inisrush took their names. The ruins of the island as it at present stands approaches to oblong, about 8 by 7 yards and stands about 4 feet above the surface of the water. There was a few apple and sycamore trees planted on it at some former period and seems to be at present in a thriving state of growth. The island was much larger at some former period than it is at present and is locally said to have stood on an oak frame, dimensions not known, but constructed some hundreds of years ago by a Ross McGuinness, a local gentleman who erected a castle on it composed of native oak and in which he lived for a series <serious> of years previous to his demise. Subsequent to the death of the above McGuinness, there was no heir of that family to inherit or inhabit the castle and the consequence was that in the course of a few after years it became a neglected pile of ruins.

At some subsequent period the castle was rebuilt and again inhabited by a prince of the Tyrone O'Neills and a near relative of Phelim Roe O'Neill called Bryan Carrah O'Neill. This chief of the O'Neills lived in the castle for a number of years and is said to have expired on the site of the Roman Catholic chapel that stands west and adjoining the Green lough, where there was a bed brought from the castle by his own orders and placed behind a thicket of bushes that stood on the above site, that he might there expire in compliance with some previous injunction or perhaps as a rash promise made by himself that he should not die in the castle or bowels of the Green lough.

He is also said to be interred on the summit of the Gallows hill, a gravelly eminence that stands west and within about 20 yards of the Green lough, so called in consequence of being the hill on which he himself had a gallows erected when in full possession of his wealth and power, and on which gallows he got executed all persons within his district who opposed his laws or neglected his mandate.

There appears at present on the summit of the Gallows hill the ruins of 3 graves, which together occupy 13 feet by 9 feet and are said to be the graves of Bryan Carrah O'Neill and his 2 sons. He is also said to lie in the middle and one of his sons on either side of him. West and at the head of the above graves stands a circular hole 8 feet in diameter and 1 and a half feet in depth, in which hole the gallows formerly stood.

Bryan Carrah O'Neill

The above Bryan Carrah O'Neill is said by some of the local inhabitants to be a great oppressor and destroyer of the lives and properties of the inhabitants of a large and neighbouring district, and that in revenge of his oppression, his castle was beseiged by the oppressed and himself and his 2 sons taken and executed on the aforesaid gallows and buried at the foot of it. Tradition also says that the above Bryan Carrah O'Neill was reared with his uncle, a Sir Hugh O'Neill, formerly of Eden Castle in the above parish, and that in consequence of some dispute between him and his uncle, he subsequently burned Eden Castle and also his uncle, who remained within its walls, after previously being defeated, himself and his forces, by Bryan and his party.

Green Lough Island and Castle

The Green Lough Island before referred to is locally said to stand on a black oak frame of unknown dimensions, but on which was placed logs of various kinds of sizes of timber and on it was afterwards raised a terrace of sand, clay and stones, sufficient for the site of the aforesaid castle. The castle was composed of native oak and bound together by mortices. There have been large quantities of the castle timber raised from time to time within the last 80 years out of the Green lough, and of so good a quality that many houses in the neighbourhood of the Green lough have been roofed with it. Parts of it are at present occupied in the dwelling houses of John Henery and Henery McLoughlin, townland of Inisrush. The upper storey or body and roof of the castle was destroyed and carried away by different persons previous to 1775.

In exploring the Green lough at some former period, there was found in its bowels a steel jacket or part of a coat composed of small steel links and supposed to belong to Bryan Carrah O'Neill; also a great number of knives and forks and a large quantity of what was conjectured to be stable dung. All the last-mentioned articles have been subsequently destroyed.

SOCIAL ECONOMY

Green Lough Races

The Green lough was for a series of years previous to 1814 the theatre of various kinds of amusement, particularly horse-races, which was strenuously supported by the local gentry of the surrounding neighbourhood by subscribing sums of money, saddles, bridles etc. The races commenced in August and were held on Saturdays from 4 to 6 weeks each year. The course was round the entire of the lough, well constructed and beautifully adapted for the purpose. The people, who assembled in thousands from various parts of the counties of Derry and Antrim, seated themselves on the summit of the ridge of hills by which the lough is surrounded and which afforded them a full and satisfactory view of the races going on round the shores of the lough.

Many also enjoyed themselves at various other amusements in the valleys in its immediate neighbourhoods. The races were also well attended by vendors of all sorts of liquors, fruit, bread, gingerbread etc. The Green lough races ceased about 1814, in consequence of tumult and quarrelling <quarling> occasioned by excess of drink and party animosities.

Supposed Derivation of Green Lough

The Green lough is supposed to have derived that name from the verdant valleys by which it is skirted all round. Information obtained from Henery, Patt and Daniel McLoughlin, William McKeon and others.

The passage into the castle of Green lough is locally believed to have been by a drawbridge on the north side. Informants above named.

ANCIENT TOPOGRAPHY AND NATURAL FEATURES

Human Bones

In labouring the precincts of the Gallows hill at the Green lough about 1876, there was a human skull with various other human bones got beneath the surface. Informants Henery McLoughlin and others.

Ruff Islands

The Ruff Islands stand nearly in the middle of a large and deep bog in the townland of Glenone. There are 4 in number and are approaching to a convex on the top of each. The summit of these islands or little hills stand from 15 to 20 feet above the surface of the bog. They vary in size and are partially studded on the surface with a scrag of native wood. The soil of which they are composed is clay, rich in appearance and quite solid on the surface, though they stand at least one-quarter of a mile from the nearest arable ground. 3 of the islands stand connected; the fourth is detached about 70 yards from the others. The space occupied by the four, including the intervening valley, might be about 4 acres. These islands are visited by swans, pheasants <phesins>, wild geese, ducks and partridge <partrige>, also by hares and rabbits.

The above islands stand about three-quarters of a mile from Portglenone and west of the Bann, and though standing in a large flat of bog, few sites command a more delightful prospect of Portglenone and its well improved neighbourhood. Information obtained from John Maloy.

Fort

In Glenone, and holding of Steel Mulholland, there stands the ruins of a fort, but so destroyed at present that its dimensions cannot be described. It stood west and on the verge of the Bann.

Brass Halbert

In sinking a water cut round the shore of the Black lough in 1831, there was discovered about 2 feet under the surface a brass halbert of curious construction. It measures 9 inches in length, including the circular void space that embraced the handle. It has 2 wings with a hole through each as if designed to be suspended by a ribbon <ribbond>. Information obtained from Reverend James Smyth, Black lough, in whose house it is at present.

Eminence: Knockenhead

Knockenhead, in the townland of Glenone and holding of William Clements, is a lofty eminence north east of and near the leading road from Garvagh to Portglenone and about 300 yards west of the Bann. It is so called in consequence of being a place selected at some former period by a general or commanding officer as a fit site for an encampment. Local tradition says that one of the contending parties were stationed on it and the other on Knocknabrock, an eminence east of the Bann, in the demesne of the Venerable Archdeacon Alexander. These hills stood contiguous <contagious> to each other and that after some combatting by day, that the party east of the Bann crossed the Bann by night and took the Knockenhead party by surprise; that a dreadful combat ensued in which many of both armies were slain. It is stated that a Captain Magill, with other officers who fell in the battle, was buried in the immediate neighbourhood of Knockenhead.

There have been a quantity of human bones found at some former period beneath the surface of Mr Clements' fruit garden that stands within a few yards of the last-mentioned hill. There have been also small cannon and musket-balls found from time to time in the precincts of Knockenhead. Dr Madden of Portglenone has at present one of the cannon-balls found in 1833. Mr Clements has also parts of others previously found. There was some of the entrenchments on Knockenhead destroyed at some former period and some traces of them still appear on the south west side of the hill, where the cannon-balls were most commonly found, and the musket balls on the east side. There is also in Mr Clements' farm a concave called the Kiln Pot, which is said to have been filled with dead bodies after the battle was over. Knockenhead is at present under a grove of fir trees. Informants Willie Clements and others.

Bog Fir

There was a fir stick raised in Drumlane bog in March last that measured 75 feet in length and about 3 feet in circumference at butt end, and got smaller in proportion to its length. It seems in a sound state except about 13 feet of the middle of the stick that is shattered and rendered of little value, perhaps occasioned by the falling of the tree. It was got about 7 feet under the surface of the original bog and about 70 yards from the arable ground. It fell from the north. There was found lying across it a stick about 13 feet long. Within about 12 feet of it on the east side stands in its growing berth, upright, the root and 5 feet in height of a fir tree. It is about 3 feet in circumference, perfectly sound and seems as if the remainder of the tree was broken off by force. There are hundreds of blocks standing upright in the above bog. This bog contains about 16 acres. There are oak sticks got in the exterior of the bog on the surface of the clay. Information obtained from John Alexander.

Oak Stick

There is an oak stick, stripped <stript> at present, in the verge of Drumoolish bog and on the holding of James Gibson, that measures 33 feet in length and 2 and a half feet across at the middle. There is 12 feet of the middle of the stick perfectly sound and the remainder partly decayed. It fell from the south west and lies on the clay 5 feet under the surface of the bog.

Ancient Vault

Robert Stewart of Ballymcpeake Lower, in demolishing an old stone building in the above townland in 1830, got beneath it an oblong enclosure about 4 by 2 feet and 12 feet in depth, and formed by well shaped flat stones set in the ground on their sides, at the ends and sides of the enclosure. It contained a quantity of calcined ashes and bones which were subsequently buried. Informants Patt McLoughlin and John O'Neill.

Dead Island

In Drumoolish bog, and holding of Robert Brown, there stands a small island composed of blackish clay. It is oval, 60 by 25 yards and approaching a convex from the base to the top, which stands about 5 feet higher than the surface of the immense tract of bog by which it is surrounded. It is partially grown over on the surface by a scrag of native wood. Round its base there are about 2 roods of a solid black heathy surface much harder than any other part of the bog. It is called the Dead Island in consequence of being a burial ground for stillborn and unbaptised children. On its summit stood for ages a large haw bush till 1818, at which period it was cut down by the late John Reid, who was immediately attacked by a cancer in the roof of the mouth which occasioned his death in the space of one year after cutting down the haw bush, to which rash act his premature death was attributed. Informants Robert Brown and others.

Timber got in Bogs

Round the west and south west shores of Drumoolish bogs there are sticks of various lengths got lying at various depths. Grey oak, which is the most numerous, is commonly found on the surface of the clay. Sally is also found in like manner. The largest trees of all kinds are found to have fallen from the south west. Windfalls are found to lie indiscriminately. Fir is more abundant in the interior than in the exterior of the bogs. Windfalls are a sixth in proportion to large sticks. The sticks found to vary in length from 10 to 40 feet. The windfalls with the roots attached vary in length from 7 to 15 feet; sally found in proportion to windfalls in lengths. The fir sticks have suffered more from burning than windfalls of any kind, and oak more decayed in some parts of bogs than any other timber. Blocks are found in various instances standing upright in their growing berths. Depth of these bogs from 2 to 30 feet. Information obtained from Robert Brown and others.

Loughs in Ballymcpeake

In Ballymcpeake Lower there are 3 lakes. The largest of these is called Ballymcpeake lough and stands south of the leading road from Maghera to Portglenone. It is oval shape and occupies about 7 acres. It is supposed to average 10 feet in depth of water. It was much deeper at some former period, but was drained to a great extent about 1795 by Major Hill of Bellaghy. It is enclosed on one side by a ridge of hills which averages about 12 feet in height above the surface of the water and by a bog on the other side. It is visited by wildfowl such as coots or water hens, ducks, teale, and inhabited by pike and eels.

South east of the above lake, and in the above townland, stand the other 2 lakes. They are called Bogossin loughs. The smaller one is circular and occupies about 1 acre, and is entirely enclosed by bog averaging about 3 feet in height above the surface of the water. These 2 loughs stand near each other and are divided by a small vein of bog. The larger of the two is oval and occupies about 2 and a half acres. It is bounded on the south and west by a ridge of hills that averages about 12 feet in height above the surface of the water and is the remains of native wood. It is bounded on the east and north by bog averaging 4 and a half feet above the surface of the water. They are encircled by an immense tract of bog and are visited by wildfowl such as geese, ducks, cranes, bitterns, teale, snipe, partridge, coots and seagulls, also hares and rabbits, and are inhabited by fish such as pike and eels which are found in abundance. These last-mentioned lakes are supposed to be from 12 to 15 feet in depth and studded with springs. They stand in the holdings of the Reverend Charles Foster and others. Informants George Burk, Peter Murray and others.

Ancient Church of Tamlaght O'Crilly

The old church of Tamlaght O'Crilly stood 56 feet 10 inches by 22 feet 9 inches in the clear; average thickness of walls 2 feet 10 inches. The east gable stands from 15 to 18 feet high and a large arch window in the centre of it. Nearly one-half of the north side wall stands about 13 feet high. The remainder of the entire walls average 5 feet in height. The interior of the church is partly occupied by graves. The yard is entirely enclosed by a good stone and lime wall. The passage into it is by a small iron gate from the new churchyard which stands detached from it. The age of the yard or burial ground, the age and respectability of the families who occupy it by burying, may be easily conjectured by viewing the almost countless and well cut headstones that stand in it. There are also many tombstones. The burials were so numerous in the yard at some former period that the church walls were absorbed by the soil to a great extent. 19th April 1836.

The old church was unroofed and disused about 1815, the year before the new church was finished. The saleable materials occupied in it were

Parish of Tamlaght O'Crilly

disposed of by the architect that built the new church. Information obtained from Robert Workman and David Campbell. 22nd April 1836.

Black Lough near Kilrea

About 1 mile south of Kilrea, and intervening between the townlands of Moneysallin, Lisnagroat and Drumane, there stands a lake called the Black lough, oval shape and occupying about 20 acres in the winter, but considerably less in summer. It varies from 1 to 10 feet in depth and is partially studded with springs and supposed to be embedded with oak, fir, yew and sally, timber supposed or found to have fallen from the west. The lough is visited by wildfowl such as swans, geese, ducks, cranes, cormorants, coots, teals, widgeon, divers, gledes <gleds>, seagulls, green and grey plover, redshanks and sand-larks, and inhabited by fish such as pike and eels.

It is bounded on the east, west and south by a ridge of hills that average 15 feet in height above the surface of the water. The hills on the east are the remains of native wood. It is bounded on the north by bog that stands about 5 feet above the surface of the water. It fills on the north side by a small river and empties on the south side by a continuation of the same river. There was a pleasure boat on the lough for a number of years but none at present.

In 1833 there was an axe of curious construction found in the lough. It was composed of iron and differed in construction from modern hatchets. It has been subsequently broken and converted to other uses. It is also said that there was a cot containing a large quantity of iron bars sunk in some part of the lough at some former period and which iron is said to have been manufactured in an old foundry that stood in Lisnagroat. There have been several pieces of iron bars and lumps of iron, not perfectly manufactured, found from time to time in the old [blank] foundry. There is one of these iron logs at present in Lisnagroat corn mill. It resembles an old anvil, weighs 17 and a half stones and is used as a weight in the mill. Informants Henery and Andrew Lenox. 20th April 1836.

Moll O'Reilly's Lough

About 1 English mile south of Kilrea, partly in the parish of Kilrea but principally in the parish of Tamlaght O'Crilly and townland of Lisnagroat, there stands a lake locally called Moll O'Reilly's lough. It approaches to oval and occupies about 8 acres and averages about 8 feet in depth. It is bounded on all sides by hills averaging about 15 feet in height above the surface of the water, with skirting of bog intervening round the shores. It is visited by wildfowl such as swans, geese, ducks, cranes, cormorants, teals, divers, widgeon, green and grey plover, gledes, seagulls, coots, redshanks, curlews, snipe, partridge, moorhens and cocks, and inhabited by fish such as pike and eels. Its precincts are also inhabited by hares, rabbits, badgers and otters. Informants Charles Neeson and John Dimond.

Native Wood

There is about 6 acres of the remains of native wood in the townland of Lisnagroat. It is locally called Drumemric wood. Some of the trees stand from 12 to 15 feet high and produce a large quantity of nuts in the season. It stands in the holding of Edward Moon. Informant Charles Neeson.

Gentle Bush

In Gortmacrane, and holding of Daniel Cassidy, there stands an ancient haw bush said to have been often seen illuminated by night and thousands of the gentry enjoying themselves at music, dancing and alternately changing stations to another haw bush that stood within 700 yards of it. In the neighbourhood of the above gentle bush a man's hair was changed from black to grey in the space of 1 night. Informant Daniel Cassidy.

Fox Island

In Drumagarner bog there stands a small island locally called the Fox Island. It is nearly oblong and occupies about 2 roods of a gravelly soil. The summit of this island stands about 6 feet higher than the large tract of bog by which it is surrounded and on its surface stands a few ancient thorns. It is called the Fox Island, in consequence of being at a former period the haunt of foxes.

Bogs in Drumagarner

Drumagarner bogs contain about 95 acres. The largest of these bogs stand on the east side of the townland. They vary in depth from 2 to 30 feet. Fir sticks, blocks and windfalls are the principal timber got in these bogs. The large trees or sticks are found for the greater part to fall from the north west. Some are also found to have fallen from the north. Windfalls lie indiscriminately and blocks stand upright, and in many instances 3 tiers of blocks stand one on top of another, as if in successive growths and destruction. The oak lies along the exterior of the bogs and on the surface of the clay in almost all cases, and is believed to have been the first destroyed as in many cases fir blocks are found on top of oak sticks and blocks and seem to have grown in that situation.

Fir sticks and windfalls are also found lying on oak sticks and blocks. Nuts are commonly found in the bottom of the bog, but the hazel altogether disappear. The largest sticks of fir and oak are found in the exterior of the bog but more decayed than in the interior; cause attributed to the lying on or near the clay soil. Fir is less decayed in the north east and south east of the bogs than in the south west or north west; cause attributed to continual damp in the former. Sticks are found from 12 to 60 feet long, windfalls from 8 to 20 feet. Fir suffered more by fire than any other timber and is found irregular and at various depths in the bog, and butter is saved in the interior of the bog from decay. Informants John Bradley and Bernard Dimond.

Bogs in Drumsarragh

Drumsarragh bogs contain about 120 acres. The largest stands on the east side of the townland. They vary in depth from 2 to 20 feet. Timber found in these bogs consists of oak, fir and yew. Oak chiefly confined to the exterior of the bogs, fir and yew found in the exterior and interior of the bogs but the proportion of windfalls found does not exceed one quarter that of sticks. Sticks found from 12 to 60 feet in length, windfalls found from 8 to 20 feet in length. Sticks have suffered more by fire than windfalls and fir has suffered more by burning than any other timber. The largest sticks lie in different directions but chiefly from north west to south east. Windfalls lie indiscriminately. Oak is found more decayed and of less value than other timber in proportion to its size. Cause assigned that it was the oldest and first that fell; also that it lies nearest the bed and rests on or near the clay or other soil not congenial to the nature of fallen timber; also that the water forcing through the soil is pernicious to timber; also that the drier the bog or other soil is, the timber of any kind decay the sooner, as the timber found in the wettest and quickest part of bogs is in the best state of preservation.

The roots or blocks of all types of timber are found upright. Oak in all cases lies nearest the surface of the clay. All other timber commonly found in bogs are found in various depths and in stratas, one over another and irregularly mixed save the blocks, that are almost in all cases found upright. There are various instances of 3 tiers of blocks or roots being found one resting on the top or shoulder of the other as if of successive growth and destruction, and blocks resting on fir and oak sticks in their growing situation as if the said had fallen and grown at successive periods. The largest blocks are found most commonly to be under the smaller. Information obtained from Francis Huston and James Johnstone.

Bogs in Gortmacrane

Gortmacrane bogs contain about 100 acres. The largest of these bogs stands in the south west side of the townland. They vary in depth from 2 to 25 feet. The timber got in these bogs consists of fir and oak. The oak is chiefly confined to the exterior of the bogs. The fir is found in the exterior and the interior. The sticks and windfalls are found in the exterior and interior, but the proportion of windfalls found does not average more than a quarter that of sticks. The sticks are found from 12 to 90 feet in length and the windfalls from 8 to 20 feet in length. The sticks have suffered more injury by fire than windfalls and fir more than any other timber. In all other respects the timber lies in these bogs as described in preceding Fair Sheets. Information obtained from Edward O'Kane and Daniel Cassidy.

Bogs in Drumane

Drumane bogs contain about 80 acres and vary in depth from 2 to 20 feet. The timber got in these bogs consists of fir and oak. The fir is principally got in the interior of these bogs. The oak and some fir is also embedded in the exterior. The windfalls are got in the exterior and interior. The quantity of windfalls got in these bogs is about one-third that of sticks. The sticks vary from 10 to 65 feet and the windfalls from 6 to 18 feet in length. The sticks are found to suffer by fire much more than windfalls and fir considerably more than oak. All other particulars connected with the timber got in these bogs is in every respect the same as described in preceding Fair Sheets. Information obtained from Bernard and John Dimond.

Bogs in Eden

Eden bogs contain about 200 acres. The largest is in the west side of the townland. The timber got in these bogs consists of oak, fir and yew. The oak lies along the exterior of the bogs chiefly, and some fir also. The fir is principally in the interior as is also the yew. Windfalls are found in the exterior and interior, and the quantity of windfalls got is nearly equal to one-half that of sticks. The sticks got in these bogs vary in length from 10 to 100 feet and windfalls from 6 to 20 feet. Sticks have suffered more by burning than windfalls and fir more than any other timber. The yew is small and of very little value. The situation of the timber found in these bogs is in all other particulars the same as in other bogs described in preceding Fair Sheets, save that the quantity and quality of the timber exceeds that found in several of the neighbouring bogs. Information obtained from Charles Duggan and John Mulholland.

Burnt Timber

In one of the above bogs that stand east of the old wood there is a large oak root with a hole burned in the middle of it, 2 and a half feet in length and breadth and 1 foot in depth. It seems evident that it occurred at or previous to the falling of the tree. I have procured a specimen of the root and also of the burned cinders. There are also in the same bogs sticks of various lengths that have fallen from south west to north east and in other directions also.

Native Wood

Anaghclea old wood in the townland of Eden contains about 26 acres. The large trees are all cut down and nothing remaining at present but the growing scrag which produce a trifling quantity of nuts in the season. It stands in the holding of David Port and is entirely enclosed by bog. There are small parcels of it reclaimed and a few cabins built on it at present. 21st April 1836.

Eminence: Krock Phelim Roe

In Eden, and holding of Thomas York and others, there stands an eminence locally called Krock Phelim Roe, so called in consequence of being a site selected by Phelim Roe O'Neill for an encampment at some former period, and on which site or hill he defeated his opponents who occupied another hill that stands about 700 yards east of the former and is locally called Krockarig or "the hill of anger or contention."

South of the above hills there stood at some former period an ancient cave but at present there is not a vestige of it to be seen. It stood on the south side of Krock Phelim Roe. Informants Thomas York and Samuel Clarke.

St Patrick's Knee Stones in Eden

In the above townland, and holding of Bernard Mulholland, there stand at present, occupied in a

Landscape view near Tamlaght

fence, 2 large whinstones with the print of a knee on the face of each and locally said to be the print of St Patrick's 2 knees, who is said to have knelt in prayer on the stones and left the above prints on them as a memorial to posterity. These stones were lying flat when discovered. The prints approach to circular and average 9 and a half inches in diameter each, and about 3 and a half inches in depth. These holes or prints are evidently the work of art.

There was an old forge or foundry stood on the site of the above stones at some former period and in the ruins of which there have been large quantities of dross found from time to time.

Krockbane: Site of Eden Ancient Castle

In the above townland, and holding of Bernard Mulholland and others, there stands an eminence called Knockbane and said to be the site of Eden ancient castle, formerly the seat of a Sir Hugh O'Neill. There was some of the ground walls and a quantity of ashes raised out of the ruins at some former period. The site is at present under tillage. Informants Henery and Bernard Mulholland.

Brass Halbert

The above [drawing] is an exact representation of an ancient brass halbert at present in Mr John Crocket's dwelling house in the townland of Drumnacannan, and said to be found under the surface at some former period in the remains of an old wood in the above townland. Information obtained from John Crocket. 22nd April 1836.

Ancient Pike Heads

James Clarke of Drumoolish, in sinking a moat in his holding in the above townland in 1823, discovered about 6 feet under the surface 2 ancient pike heads. They were composed of steel. One of them measured 1 foot 10 inches in length, the other measured 1 foot 6 inches in length. They were considered to be of very ancient date and construction. They have been subsequently left with a smith in Maghera. Informant Samuel Clarke.

Wolf Island

The Wolf Island is a high hill in the townland of Drumlane and surrounded by an immense tract of bog. It contains about 7 acres and was formerly studded with a native and lofty wood. The wood was cut down about 1813 to supply many of the neighbouring inhabitants with fuel in the absence of turf that ran scarce about that period. There is about 3 acres of the island at present reclaimed and the remainder under a scrag of wood.

Previous to the wood being cut down, the island was repaired to by hundreds of persons, of old and young, to enjoy themselves at various amusements and likewise to feast on nuts which were found in great abundance on the island in autumn. The above island stands in the holding of Mrs McAlister and is called the Wolf Island in consequence of being formerly the haunt of wolves, which are said to have remained in it longer or to a later period than in any other part of the above county.

Tod Island

In the immediate neighbourhood of the Wolf Island, and in the same bog, there stands another island which contains about half an acre. It was also covered with wood and is said to have been the haunt of foxes. It is called the Tod Island. Informants Daniel McLoughlin and Mrs McAlister and others. 22nd April 1836.

Bogs in Lisnagroat

The bogs of Lisnagroat contain above [crossed out: 400] acres. The largest of these bogs stands in the east side of the townland and is locally called Drumemric bog. They vary in depth from 2 to 30 feet. The timber got in these bogs consists of oak, fir, yew and sally. The oak is chiefly found along the exterior of the bogs and lying on the surface of the clay. The largest fir trees are also found near the exterior but the largest quantity in the interior. The yew and sally are found in the interior but of little value. Windfalls are found in the exterior and interior but not more than one-third in proportion to sticks. The sticks found in these bogs vary in length from 10 to 90 feet and windfalls from 8 to 22 feet. The sticks have suffered more injury by fire than windfalls and fir more than any other timber. The large sticks are chiefly found to fall from the north west, though many are found to fall from the north and south. The situation of timber in these bogs is in all other particulars the same as described of other bogs in preceding Fair Sheets.

The subsoil on which the above bogs rest varies: some parts of the bogs rest on blue stony clay, some on a whitish clay and stones, and other parts on a reddish gravelly soil. Information from Charles Neeson, John and James McCann and many others. 25th April 1836.

Native Wood

Rossmore native wood, in the townland of

Parish of Tamlaght O'Crilly

Lisnagroat and holding of John McCann, contains about 5 acres. Nothing remains at present but a growing scrag which is productive of a large quantity of nuts in the season. The above wood stands on an eminence nearly surrounded by bog.

In the above townland, and holding of Alexander and James Campbell, there stands about 40 acres of native wood, though nothing of it remains at present but the growing scrag. It produces a large quantity of nuts in autumn. This wood stands on a rising eminence. On either side of Inverue river there have been several iron articles such as hammers, locks, keys and chisels got beneath the surface in the interior of the wood, about 1828 and subsequently. Information from Archibald Campbell and Andrew McCann.

Old Butter in Lisnagroat

John McCann, in cutting turf in the above townland in 1833, got about 3 feet under the surface of the bog a cask of old butter. The cask resembled the bark of a tree. It was circular and composed out of a solid piece. It mouldered down shortly after being removed. The butter was useful for candles.

Iron Instruments of Defence in Lisnagroat

The above John McCann got under the surface of a clay field in the above townland in 1830 an iron instrument much resembling a halbert. It was 20 inches in length and about 4 inches broad at the hilt, and tapered to the top. Part of it was converted to other uses subsequently and the other part of it remains at present in Andrew McCann's workshop in the above townland. There was also got in the same place, and at the same period, by Henery Kerr, a steel instrument resembling a bayonet and about 2 feet in length and tapered to the top. It has been subsequently sold to an antiquarian at 4s. Each of the above instruments had an iron scabbard when found. Information from James and John McCann.

Anaghavogy Island

About the centre of that large tract of bog in the townland of Lismoyle locally called Anaghavogy there stands an island called Anaghavogy Island. The summit of it stands about 15 feet higher than the surface of the bog. It contains about 10 acres, one-half of which is under tillage and the other half under a scrag of old wood and heath. It is at least a half a mile distant from the nearest arable ground. It was first occupied, and a part of it reclaimed about 1811, by 2 families who at present reside on it in 2 small cottages built of stone and lime. The soil is partly a reddish clay and small stones, and partly a mossy rocky eminence. The bog by which it is surrounded is very quick and soft. Informants Robert and John Atkinson, residents on the island.

Bogs in Lismoyle

Lismoyle bogs are supposed to contain about 400 acres and vary in depth from 2 to 25 feet. The timber got in these bogs consists of oak, fir and sally. The oak is found along the exterior, as is also the sally. The fir and windfalls are principally got in the interior but not more than a sixth part in proportion to sticks. The sticks vary in length from 20 to 30 feet and windfalls from 7 to 15 feet. The sticks have suffered more injury by fire than windfalls and fir more than any other timber. The situation of timber found in these bogs is in all other particulars the same as in other bogs described in preceding Fair Sheets. The largest of the above bogs stands in the north side of the townland and is locally called Anaghavogy bog. Informants John Bolton Senior and Michael McCaula.

Old Butter

Samuel Taylor, in cutting turf in Lismoyle bog in 1815, found under the surface of the bog a cask of old butter. The cask was circular shape, composed out of a solid piece resembling the bark of a tree. It mouldered down subsequent to its being removed. The butter was also rendered useless by time. Informants John Bolton Senior and Michael McCaula.

Discoveries in a Bog

Michael <Michal> McCaula, in raising a fir block in Ballynian in 1822, got resting on the top of the block a powder horn supposed to be a cow horn. The bottom of the horn and the cork or stopper was wood, but completely decayed when found. The horn was in a tolerable state of preservation. He also got lying with the horn a stock and lock and a key. The timber of which the stock was composed was entirely decayed and the lock irons and the key also corroded to a great extent. These articles were found 7 feet under the surface of the original bog. They have been subsequently destroyed. Informants John O'Crilly and Michael McCaula.

Islands in a Bog

In a small bog in the west side of Ballynian there

stands 3 islands approaching to oval shape and varying in extent from 5 to 60 square perches or from one-eighth of a rood to 1 and a half roods. They are composed of large stones, gravel and clay, and vary in height from 6 to 10 feet above the surface of the bog in which they stand. They are at present nearly grown over with whins and heath. Up to about 1760 the summit of these islands were scarcely visible above the bog. Since that period there was 8 feet in depth of the bog by which they were enclosed, absorbed and cut away, which left the shape, sizes and materials of the islands exposed to view. They stand 70 yards distant one from the other. Informants Joseph Quin and John O'Crilly.

Bogs in Ballynian

Ballynian bogs contain about 60 acres and vary in depth from 2 to 20 feet. The largest of these bogs lies in the south east side of the townland. The timber got in the bogs consists of fir and oak. The oak lies in the exterior and on the surface of the clay. Fir is also found in the exterior but the greatest quantity and best quality of it is found in the interior. The windfalls are mostly found in the interior but are not more than one-quarter in proportion to sticks. The sticks found in these bogs are found to fall from the north, south and west but chiefly from south west. The windfalls lie indiscriminately. The sticks vary in length from 8 to 63 feet and windfalls from 6 to 43 feet. Sticks are most injured by burning than windfalls and fir more than any other timber. Windfalls are supposed to have fallen previous to sticks as they are commonly found lying under sticks and blocks. The situation of timber in the above bogs is in all other particulars the same as in other bogs described in preceding Fair Sheets.

Fir and Oak Sticks

There was a fir stick raised out of one of the above bogs in 1790 that measured 63 feet in length and 2 and a half feet in diameter. It was perfectly sound throughout and valued at 17 pounds Irish. It was found near the exterior of the bog and fell from the west. Informants John O'Crilly and Joseph Quin.

There stands at present in one of the above bogs in the south east of the townland an oak stick 50 feet in length and 3 feet in diameter in some parts. There was some feet in length cut off this stick at some former period or perhaps broken off in falling. One-half of its circumference is decayed and fallen off, as it is nearly flat on the top side of it. It lies in its fallen berth from north west. 27th April 1836.

Causeway

John O'Crilly of Ballynian, in cutting turf in a bog in the above townland in 1785, discovered 6 feet under the surface of the bog 14 stone steps composed of well shaped flat stones, about 1 foot in length and breadth each, and placed about 1 yard distant one from another in a straight line, as if occupied there for stepping over a ford or stream at some period previous to the formation or growth of the bog in which they were found. Informants John O'Crilly and Joseph Quin.

Bogs in Timaconway

Timaconway bogs contain about 50 acres and vary in depth from 2 to 12 feet. The largest of these bogs lies in the north side of the townland. The timber got in these bogs consists of oak, fir and yew, but very little of either kind save oak. The oak lies on or near the clay in the exterior, and fir and yew in the interior. The windfalls are found to lie indiscriminately in all directions and in the exterior and interior. The sticks vary in length from 12 to 70 feet and windfalls from 8 to 20 feet. The situation of sticks, windfalls, blocks and branches in the above bogs is in all other particulars the same as in other bogs before described. From John Quin and John Crilly.

There are several oak sticks stripped at present in the above bogs that have fallen from south west, west and north west and many of them from 12 to 26 feet in length and appear to be near the clay.

Head of a Still

James Huston of Killygullib Glebe, in sinking a moat in his holding in the above townland about 1825, found 3 feet under the surface a copper article supposed to be the head of a distilling pot or still. It is circular shape, 3 inches in diameter and depth, with a cover attached to the top of it, also round the middle of it a circular plate 1 and a half inches in breadth and inclining downwards, also across the vessel near the cover a tube having a row of oblong holes through one side of it, as if designed to convey the steam from the body of the still to the worm. It is altogether a most curious construction. Informants James and Stewart Huston.

Bogs in Killymuck and Lisgorgan

Killymuck and Lisgorgan bogs lie together and

Parish of Tamlaght O'Crilly

are supposed to contain about 150 acres. They vary in depth from 2 to 12 feet. The largest of these bogs stands in the south east of the townland. The timber got in these bogs consists of oak and fir. The oak is found to be on the surface of the clay along the exterior. The fir is found at various depths in the interior and windfalls in the interior and exterior, and lying in all directions. The sticks are found to fall from different parts but chiefly from south west. The sticks vary in length from 12 to 70 feet and windfalls from 8 to 30 feet, but not more than a third in proportion to sticks found. Sticks have suffered more injury by fire than windfalls and fir more than any other timber.

There was a fir stick 40 feet long raised out of the above bog in 1826, on the top of which stick rested 3 fir blocks at nearly equal distance one from another and seemed as if growing and decaying in that situation. The stick was got in the interior of the bog and fell from the south west. Informants Robert McCaughy and Hill Wilson.

Bogs in Killygullib Glebe

Killygullib Glebe bogs are supposed to contain about 40 acres and vary in depth from 2 to 10 feet. The largest of these bogs stands in the north west side of the townland. The timber got in these bogs consists of oak, fir and yew. The oak lies on or near the surface of the clay in the exterior and the fir and yew at various depths in the interior. The windfalls are also got in the interior and exterior, but not more than one-quarter in proportion to sticks. Sticks are found from 12 to 50 feet in length and windfalls from 8 to 22 feet. The sticks are more injured by fire than windfalls and fir more than any other timber. The sticks lie in different directions but chiefly from south west. Windfalls lie indiscriminately. In all other particulars the situation in the above bogs is the same as in the other bogs before described. Informants John Dimond and James Huston. 28th April 1836.

Drumnacannan Bog

Drumnacannan bogs are supposed to contain 120 acres and vary in depth from 2 to 15 feet. The largest of these bogs stands in the south west side of the townland. The timber got in these bogs consists of fir, oak and yew. The oak is found lying on the surface of the clay in the exterior. Fir is also got in the exterior but chiefly in the interior and at various depths. The windfalls are found in the exterior and interior and lying indiscriminately. The yew is found along the shores, nearly on the clay, and lying in different directions but limited in length. The proportion of windfalls to sticks is not more than one-fourth. Sticks from 12 to 60 feet in length, windfalls from 6 to 20 feet in length. Sticks have suffered more injury by fire than windfalls and fir more than any other timber. Sticks were found to fall from different parts but chiefly from south west. The situation of timber in the above bogs is in all other particulars the same as in other bogs before described. Informants Isaac and Archibald Crocket.

Drumoolish Bog

Drumoolish bogs contain about 90 acres and vary in depth from 2 to 30 feet. The largest of these bogs stands in the north east side of the townland. The timber found in them consists of oak and fir, the fir chiefly found in the interior of the bog and at various depths. The oak is found along the shores, lying on or near the clay. Windfalls are found in the interior and exterior but not more than one-sixth the proportion of sticks. The sticks are from 6 to 60 feet in length and windfalls from 6 to 12 feet. Sticks are more injured by fire than windfalls and fir more than any other timber. The sticks are found to fall from different parts but chief part from north west. The windfalls lie indiscriminately and the lowest, oak, is more decayed than other timber.

There are instances of 5 tiers of blocks being found in these bogs, one resting on another, upright and supposed to grow and decay in succession, the largest resting on the clay and the rest getting smaller each, to the top one which seemed of infantile growth. The oak is found in the south east side of these bogs chiefly, and the fir in the north and west sides. The situation of timber in all other cases in these bogs is the same as in other bogs before described. Informants James Clarke and Robert Brown.

Drumard Bogs

Drumard bogs contain about 128 acres and vary in depth from 2 to 20 feet. The largest of these bogs stands in the north west side of the townland. Timber got in these bogs consists of oak, fir and yew. The oak lies in the exterior on or near the clay. The yew is also got in the exterior but of very little value. The fir is got at various depths in the interior of the bogs. The windfalls are found in all parts of the bogs but not more than a third in proportion to sticks. Sticks vary from 10 to 70 feet in length and windfalls from 6 to 25 feet. Sticks have suffered more injury by fire than windfalls and fir more than any other timber. The sticks are found to fall from different parts but chiefly from the south west. The situation of timber in the above bogs is in all other particulars the same as in other bogs before described.

In 1831 Samuel McCord got, 7 feet under the surface of the above bog, a log of fir timber about 5 feet in length, 1 and a half feet in breadth and 1 foot thick. It had been dressed by some hewing axe and a square mortice in process of being cut through each end of it. It has been subsequently made into staves for some vessels by a cooper. Information from Samuel McCord and Andrew Bradley.

Fir Stick

About 1785 there was a fir stick raised out of a bog intervening between the townlands of Drumnacannan and Eden that measured about 90 feet in length. 40 feet of the butt end of it was about 4 and a half feet in diameter. It was a cause of much dispute as to which of the above townlands the stick justly belonged, as it was found on the mearings. However, it was taken by force by order of the late Rowley <Rowly> Heyland Esquire, who gave the helpers a large supply of drink on the occasion. Informant Samuel McCord. 29th April 1836.

Moneysallin Bogs

Moneysallin bogs contain about 180 acres and vary in depth from 2 to 30 feet. The largest of them stands in the south east side of the townland. The timbers got in these bogs consists of oak, fir, yew and sally. The oak lies along the exterior on or near the clay. Yew and sally are also found in the exterior, but limited in quantity. The fir is found in the interior and at various depths. Windfalls are found in the exterior and interior but limited to one-seventh the quantity of sticks. Sticks vary in length from 12 to 65 feet and windfalls from 10 to 20 feet. Sticks have suffered more injury by fire than windfalls and fir more than any other kind of timber. Sticks are found to fall from different parts but chiefly from the west. Windfalls lie indiscriminately. Oak is more decayed than other timber.

The situation of timber in all other particulars is the same in these bogs as in other bogs before described. The subsoil is also as different in these bogs as in others. In some parts of the bogs it is whitish clay and stones, in other parts blue clay and stones, other parts a gravelly reddish clay and in other parts a marly heavy clay. But the blue clay is the best clay for reclaiming. Informants Andrew Bradley and Andrew Brady. 30th April 1836.

Boveedy Bogs

Boveedy bogs contain about 150 acres and vary in depth from 2 to 20 feet. The largest of these bogs stands in the north side of the townland. The timber got in them consists of oak, fir and yew. The oak lies in the exterior of the bog at or near the clay. Yew is also got in the exterior but limited in quantity. The fir is found at various depths in the interior. Windfalls are found in the exterior and interior of the bogs but limited to one-sixth the quantity of sticks. Sticks found from 10 to 50 feet in length and windfalls from 8 to 15 feet. Sticks more injured by fire than windfalls and fir more than any other timber. Sticks are found to fall from different parts but chiefly from north west. Windfalls lie indiscriminately. In all other particulars the situation of the timber in these bogs is the same as in the other bogs before described. Informants Hugh Warwick and others. 2nd May 1836.

Inisrush Bogs

Inisrush bogs contain about 160 acres and vary in depth from 2 to 20 feet. The largest of these bogs stands in the north west side of the townland. The timber got in them consists of oak, fir and sally. The oak and sally is found in the exterior of the bogs near the clay. The sally is of little value. Fir is found at various depths in the interior. Windfalls are mostly found in the interior but limited to about one-fourth the quantity of sticks. The sticks vary in length from 10 to 30 feet and windfalls from 10 to 20 feet. Sticks lie in the different parts but chiefly from the north west. Windfalls lie indiscriminately. Oak is more decayed than other timber. Sticks are more burned than windfalls and fir more than other timber. The situation of timber is in all other particulars the same as in other bogs. Informants John and James Henery and Henery Tole. 3rd May 1836.

Bogs

The chief bogs of Ballymcpeake Lower, Moneystaghan Ellis, Moneystaghan McPeake and Mullaghnamoyagh lie together in the south side of the above townlands. They are chiefly flow and vary in depth from 2 to 20 feet. The timber got in these bogs consists of oak, fir, yew and sally. The oak, yew and sally are found in the exterior of the bogs on or near the clay. The fir is found at various depths in the interior. Windfalls are found in the exterior and interior, but limited to about

Parish of Tamlaght O'Crilly

one-sixth of the quantity of sticks. Sticks vary in length from 12 to 44 feet and windfalls from 8 to 22 feet. Sticks have suffered more injury by fire than windfalls and fir more than any other timber. Oak is more decayed than other timber. Sticks are found to fall from different parts but chiefly from north west. Windfalls lie indiscriminately. In all other particulars the situation of the timber found in these bogs is the same as in other bogs before described. The above bogs are supposed to contain between 300 and 400 acres. Information obtained from John and Francis Cassidy and Henery Tole.

Horse Island

The Horse Island in Moneystaghan McPeake bog approaches to oblong shape and contains about 1 and a half acres, and is the remains of an old wood. The summit of it stands about 6 feet higher than the level of the bog by which it is surrounded. The surface is dry and grown over with a scrag of wood and heath. On the west side of it there stands a spring well partly overhung by a protecting rock and partly by a branch of holly. On the holly branch is at present a cluster of its native berries as red and ripe as is natural in autumn. These berries have been probably nourished in their growth through winter by the heat of the above spring.

Islands in Bogs

In Moneystaghan Ellis bog there stands an island locally called Illannacrieve. It is oval shape and contains about 4 acres. The surface is quite dry and hard and is grown over with whins and a few ancient thorns. The soil is principally a blackish clay and small stones. Its summit stands about 8 feet higher than the level of the bog by which the island is entirely surrounded. Tradition says that it was partly occupied by burials at some former period. It is at present under grazing and no appearance of graves on its surface.

About 300 yards west of the above island in the same bog there stands a small island, oval shape and a convex to the top. It contains about 1 rood. The surface is dry and hard and the soil a blackish clay and small stones, and could be made good arable ground. The summit of it stands about 7 feet above the level of the bog by which it is enclosed.

In Moneystaghan McPeake bog there stands an island called the Fox Island. It is oval shape and contains about 4 acres. The surface is rocky and grown over with heath. The summit of it stands about 6 feet above the level of the bog by which it is surrounded and stands one half mile from arable ground.

Contiguous to the above island, and in the same bog, there stands a small island, oval shape, and containing about 1 and a half roods. The soil is a blackish clay which could be easily reclaimed. It is grown over on the surface with heath. Its summit stands about 8 feet above the level of the bog by which it is enclosed.

In the above bog, and about three-quarters of a mile from arable ground, there stands an island containing about half a rood of dry blackish clay and stony soil, and level with the bog. There is an ancient haw bush and a holly bush in the centre of it which is considered very gentle.

In Drumlane bog, and holding of Widow Sims, there stands an island approaching to oval shape and a convex from the base to the top. It contains about 1 acre and is grown over with a scrag of native wood and heath. The surface is quite hard and dry. The summit of the island stands about 6 feet above the level of the bog by which it is enclosed.

Bogs in Tyanee

Tyanee bogs are supposed to contain from 400 to 500 acres and vary in depth from 2 to 25 feet. The largest of them stands on the east side of the townland. The timber got in these bogs consists of oak, fir, yew and sally. The oak is found in the exterior, also the yew and sally, lying near the clay. The fir is found at various depths in the interior of the bogs. Windfalls are found in the interior and exterior but limited to about one-fourth of the quantity of sticks. Sticks vary from 7 to 40 feet in length and windfalls from 7 to 20 feet. Sticks suffered more injury by fire than windfalls and fir more than any other timber. Sticks are found to fall from different parts but chiefly from north west. Windfalls lie indiscriminately. Oak is found to be more decayed than any other timber. In all other particulars the situation of timber got in these bogs is the same as in the other bogs before described. Informants John Barclay and William Kyle.

Ancient Wooden Vessel

John O'Neill of Tyanee, in cutting turf in one of the above bogs in 1825, got 5 feet under the surface of the original bog an oval-shaped wooden vessel composed out of a solid piece of timber. It was about 3 and a half feet long, 2 and a half feet broad and about 9 inches in depth, concave to the bottom and handle attached to each end of it. It cracked and mouldered down by the air shortly after being discovered. Informants Henery and Daniel McCullagh. 4th May 1836.

Island in Bog

In Tyanee bog, east of the leading road from Kilrea to Inisrush, there stands an island approaching to oval shape and containing about 20 acres of a dry clay soil. There is about one-half of it under tillage. It is occupied by 3 farmers and inhabited by 4 cottiers who dwell in small cottages, built of stone and lime chiefly. It is entirely surrounded by bog and stands about 400 yards from arable ground. It was studded with a scrag of old wood up to 1815. Informant Henery McCullagh.

Curious Stones in Tyanee

James Witheroe of the above townland, in sinking a draw-well in his holding in 1832, got about 10 feet under the surface of a field a large quantity of polished stones of various sizes, many of which represented the shape of many objects such as cattle, fowl, fish, pistols, shoes <shews>, hammers and various other articles called Bobby Stones. Beneath the above articles was also found another strata of marly slaty soil, glittering like a silver ore and found to be most valuable manure. It is thought the above place was a continuation of the Bann at some former period, though it stands about 700 yards west of it with a deep bog intervening.

Ancient Castle

In Tyanee, and holding of James Richy, there stands the ruins of an ancient castle. It stood on an eminence one mile west of the Bann and latterly occupied by the late Squire Gage. The cellar part at present standing is 30 by 13 and a half feet in the clear. The west gable stands 5 feet high. The remainder of the cellar averages 3 feet in height above the floor. The wall averages 2 and a half feet thick. The extent of the entire house as shown, was 42 by 36 feet from out to out. There is a draw-well in the cellar but at present closed. Also in the rear of the building stands a large pump which is at present closed.

There is also one of the old office houses at present standing and besides, several square yards of a handsomely paved courtyard and avenue. There is also part of the parapet to be seen that measures 3 and a half feet in thickness. Directly opposite the castle, and across a large bog, appears the trace of a passage intended to run into the Bann. The site of the castle commands a delightful prospect of the surrounding neighbourhood and of the Bann for some miles on either side. The castle stood 2-storey, double roofed and covered with timber shingles in the absence of slates. Informants James Richy, James Witheroe and others. Gilbert Gage is supposed to be the name and surname of the above Squire Gage.

Fort

In Glenone, and holding of John McNeill Esquire, there stands the remains of a fort, square shape, 34 by 34 feet. It was demolished to a great extent. The existing part of it stands 2 and a half feet above the level of the field on which it stands. It was composed of clay. There is no appearance of a parapet having been round it at any period. There was a moat round it but it is at present levelled. There are a few haw, sloe and holly bushes on its surface. There is 15 by 10 yards of a terrace intervening between its base and the verge of the Bann. It stands about 1 foot higher than the field and appears from its situation to have been formerly attached to the fort, as it was enclosed by the moat in connection with the fort.

Bogs in Glenone

Glenone bogs contain about 200 acres and vary in depth from 2 to 30 feet. The largest of them stands in the south east side of the townland. The timber got from these bogs consists of oak, fir and sally. The oak and sally lie in the exterior of the bogs on or near the clay. The fir is found at various depths in the interior. Windfalls are found in the interior and exterior but limited to about one-sixth of the quantity of sticks. The sticks vary in length from 8 to 30 feet and windfalls from 7 to 15 feet. Sticks are found to suffer more injury by fire than windfalls and fir more than any other timber. Sticks are found to fall from different parts but chiefly from south west. Windfalls lie in all directions. Oak is found to be more decayed than other timber. The situation of the timber found in the above bogs is in all other particulars the same as in the other bogs before described. Information obtained from Peter and John McErlane and others. 5th May 1836.

Drumlane Bogs

Drumlane bogs contain about 89 acres and vary in depth from 2 to 20 feet. The largest of them stands in the north east of the townland. The timber got in these bogs consists of oak, fir and sally. Oak

Parish of Tamlaght O'Crilly

and sally is found in the exterior of the bogs, lying on or near the clay. The fir is found at various depths in the interior. Windfalls are found in the interior and exterior but limited to about one-fourth of the quantity of sticks. The sticks vary in length from 10 to 75 feet and the windfalls from 8 to 18 feet. Sticks are found to fall from various parts but chiefly from south west. Windfalls lie indiscriminately. Sticks have suffered more injury by fire than windfalls and fir more than any other timber. Oak is more decayed than other timbers. In all other particulars the situation of timber found in the above bogs is the same as in the other bogs before described. Information obtained from James Johnstone and James Marlin and others.

Holy Well

In Drumlane, and holding of John Agnew, there stands an ancient spring well locally said to be a holy well, and that it has been a practice at some former period to take sickly children and adults suffering under various disorders to this well at all seasons of the year, and some persons on their behalf performing some enjoined stations or prayers anciently recommended for the relief of the different disorders complained of; and that after the enjoined routine of prayer being gone through, the patient was washed in a stream issuing from the well and a remnant of his or her wearing apparel cut off and fastened to a bush that stood near the well, denoting that the disorder was left at the well and the patient restored to good health. Informants John Crilly and others.

The above-named well stands about 600 yards south east of the old church of Tamlaght and west of the leading road from Tamlaght to Portglenone.

Old Church of Tamlaght

Few edifices, ancient or modern, perhaps, in the north of Ireland caused so much trouble or excitement at its being disused or demolished as the old church of Tamlaght O'Crilly. About 1814, the period of its being condemned by the church valuators as being insufficient to stand, the late Reverend James Jones, then rector of Tamlaght O'Crilly, obtained the grant of getting a new church erected. He wished to have it built in Killygullib Glebe, within 2 miles of Kilrea on the leading road from Kilrea to Maghera. However, he was stiffly opposed in his project by the majority of the parishioners and chiefly by the Presbyterians, on the ground that the old church could be made sufficient at a moderate expense by rebuilding the defective parts of the walls and putting on a new roof.

The opposition embraced 2 objects: the first was to keep the old church on its original site; the second was to evade the enormous expense that the building of a church would involve the parishioners of all denominations in. The opposition rose so high that there was a vestry called in the old church and the attendance of the parishioners at large, to determine by votes if the new church was to be built as above stated or the old one repaired and let stand. The result of the vestry was that Mr Jones was outstripped by a large majority of votes by the opposition party, who were led on by the late Reverend John Smyth, the minister of the Presbyterian congregation of Kilrea. In the instance of the rector being outvoted, his adherents created some confusion in the church and the avenues leading to it, which was subsequently construed to be a premeditated riot by Mr Smyth and his party to prevent the rector's design. They were subsequently prosecuted by Mr Jones. The result of the prosecution was that Mr Smyth with 6 others were convicted. 13th May 1836.

SOCIAL ECONOMY

Illicit Distillation

Illicit distillation is so far suppressed in the above parish that there has not been an instance of it found in it for the last 2 years.

Cattle Jobbers

There is not more than 15 cattle jobbers in the above parish at present. Informants Bernard McAlary, Patt McCan and many others. [Signed] Thomas Fagan, 12th May 1836.

Census of the Population by Townlands

The census of the parish of Tamlaght O'Crilly made in September 1834.

Ballynain, 293 Roman Catholics, 1 Established Church, 10 Presbyterians, total 304.

Ballymcpeake, 266 Roman Catholics, 18 Established Church, 85 Presbyterians, total 369.

Bovedy, 29 Roman Catholics, 150 Established Church, 446 Presbyterians, total 625.

Drumlain, 28 Roman Catholics, 37 Established Church, 225 Presbyterians, total 290.

Drumnicannon, 100 Roman Catholics, 70 Established Church, 294 Presbyterians, total 464.

Drumoolish, 66 Roman Catholics, 27 Established Church, 240 Presbyterians, total 333.

Drumard, 101 Roman Catholics, 86 Established Church, 242 Presbyterians, total 429.

Drumsara, 57 Roman Catholics, 36 Established Church, 74 Presbyterians, total 167.

Drumigarner, 263 Roman Catholics, 15 Established Church, 127 Presbyterians, total 405.

Drummeen, 49 Roman Catholics, 36 Established Church, 155 Presbyterians, total 240.

Eden, 198 Roman Catholics, 121 Established Church, 39 Presbyterians, total 358.

Gortmacrane, 463 Roman Catholics, 81 Established Church, 81 Presbyterians, total 625.

Glenone, 581 Roman Catholics, 108 Established Church, 92 Presbyterians, total 781.

Inishrush, 251 Roman Catholics, 107 Established Church, 107 Presbyterians, total 465.

Killymuck, 83 Roman Catholics, 19 Established Church, 285 Presbyterians, total 387.

Killygollib, 412 Roman Catholics, 142 Established Church, 254 Presbyterians, total 808.

Liscorgan, 143 Roman Catholics, 5 Established Church, 5 Presbyterians, total 153.

Lismoile, 7 Roman Catholics, 358 Presbyterians, total 365.

Lisnagrot, 167 Roman Catholics, 109 Established Church, 129 Presbyterians, total 405.

Moneysally, 222 Roman Catholics, 55 Established Church, 93 Presbyterians, total 370.

Moneystachan, 519 Roman Catholics, 107 Established Church, 22 Presbyterians, total 648.

Tyanee, 624 Roman Catholics, 135 Established Church, 266 Presbyterians, total 1,025.

Tiveconevy, 68 Roman Catholics, 97 Established Church, 119 Presbyterians, total 284.

Total 4,990 Roman Catholics, 1,562 Established Church, 3,748 Presbyterians, [overall total] 10,300.

Kilrea parish: 2,192 Roman Catholics, 664 Established Church, 1,466 Presbyterians, [overall total] 4,322.

Desertoghill parish, 1,515 Roman Catholics, 224 Established Church, 3,161 Presbyterians, [overall total] 4,900.

Taken off a printed copy of the above census, now in the possession of the Reverend Samual Auterson, senior Roman Catholic curate of the above parishes. 14th March 1836.

Census of the Population in 1834

Census of the population as taken by Mr Thomas McCaw in 1831 and classified in 1834.

Total houses in the parish 1,904, total inhabited houses in the parish 1,837, total uninhabited houses in the parish 54, total houses in process of building 13.

Inhabited by 1,861 families, employed in agriculture of these families 1,387, employed in trade and manufacture 327, all other families not employed as above 147.

Total persons in the parish 10,069, total males in the parish 4,840, total females in the parish 5,229, total males above 20 years of age 2,339. First class farmers 65, second class farmers 1,143, labourers 511.

Manufacturers of linen 261, in retail, trade and handicraft 264, wholesale capitalists, clergy, clerks, etc. 41, labourers not employed in agriculture 5, all other males 145, male servants above 20 years of age 4, male servants under 20 years of age 68, all female servants 129.

The above taken from Mr Thomas McCaw, government enumerator's books. 9th May 1836.

Census of the Population by Denomination

Census of the population of Tamlaght O'Crilly as taken in 1834 and classified into the different religious denominations as follows: Protestants of the Church of England 1,538, Presbyterians 2,787, Roman Catholics 4,735, Seceders 865, Covenanters 298.

Congregations. The following is the average attendance at the under-mentioned house of worship on Sundays: at Tamlaght church 150, at Tyanee chapel or church of ease 70, at Drumagarner Roman Catholic chapel 1,650, at Green lough Roman Catholic chapel 1,130, at Boveedy Seceding meeting house 150, at Drumbolg Covenanting meeting house 360.

There is a new Presbyterian congregation lately formed at Tamlaght village, where they are about immediately to call a minister to reside among them. The attendance at the village of Tamlaght at present varies from 200 to 300 persons on Sundays, but the majority of the Presbyterians of the above parish worship at Kilrea Presbyterian meeting house on Sundays. Taken from the Reverend Hugh Wallace Rogers, Presbyterian minister of Kilrea's books. 11th May 1836.

Emigration to America in 1834

The following is a list of the number of persons that have emigrated to America from the above parish during the years 1834 and 1835. It will show the name, age and religion of each person, the townland in which they resided and the ports to which emigrated.

[Table lists name, age, year, townland, port emigrated to and religion].

John Quin, 22, Boveedy to New York, Presbyterian.
Margaret Gilmore, 20, Boveedy to New York, Presbyterian.
Alexander Gilmore, 22, Boveedy to New York, Presbyterian.
John Starritt, 30, Killygullib to Quebec, Presbyterian.
John McConnell, 26, Killygullib to Quebec, Roman Catholic.
James McConnell, 22, Killygullib to Quebec, Roman Catholic.
Margret McPeake, 30, Killygullib to Quebec, Roman Catholic.
Rose Maloy, 26, Ballynian to Quebec, Roman Catholic.
James Dimond, 26, Killymuck to New York, Roman Catholic.
Robert Campbell, 24, Lisnagroat to St John's, Presbyterian.
John Campbell, 25, Drumnacanon to St John's, Presbyterian.
Ann Campbell, 22, Drumnacanon to St John's, Presbyterian.
Sareah Workman, 24, Drumnacanon to St John's, Presbyterian.
Ann Workman, 21, Drumnacanon to St John's, Presbyterian.
Henery Tole, 24, Inisrush to New York, Roman Catholic.
Mary Tole, 24, Inisrush to New York, Roman Catholic.
John Tole, 1, Inisrush to New York, Roman Catholic.
Robert Hilton, 40, Ballymcpeake to New York, Presbyterian.
William Hilton, 18, Ballymcpeake to New York, Presbyterian.
John Hilton, 16, Ballymcpeake to New York, Presbyterian.
Hugh Workman, 40, Drumoolish to New York, Presbyterian.
Eliza Workman, 60, Drumoolish to New York, Presbyterian.
Paul Workman, 35, Drumoolish to New York, Presbyterian.
Mary Workman, 22, Drumoolish to New York, Presbyterian.
Robert Workman, 20, Drumoolish to New York, Presbyterian.
Margret Workman, 1, Drumoolish to New York, Presbyterian.
Thomas Neill, 20, Drumoolish to New York, Presbyterian.
Informants William Kelso, Hugh Warwick and others.

Emigration to New York in 1834

William Miller, 25, from Glenone, Established Church.
Ann Miller, 20, from Glenone, Established Church.
Robert Rainey, 22, from Glenone, Roman Catholic.
Catherine Rainey, 20, from Glenone, Roman Catholic.
Henery Henery, 21, from Glenone, Roman Catholic.
Henery Scullion, 20, from Glenone, Roman Catholic.
Ann McMullan, 19, from Glenone, Roman Catholic.
James Kane, 20, from Glenone, Roman Catholic.
William McLoughlin, 23, from Tyanee, Presbyterian.
John Madigan, 26, from Tyanee, Roman Catholic.
Information obtained from James Kelso, Hugh Warwick and others.

Emigration to America in 1835

John Quin, 30, Boveedy to St John's, Roman Catholic.
Mary Quin, 25, Boveedy to St John's, Roman Catholic.
Bridget Quin, 3, Boveedy to St John's, Roman Catholic.
Mary Jane Quin, 6 months, Boveedy to St John's, Roman Catholic.
Patrick McConnell, 24, Killygullib to Quebec, Roman Catholic.
John Quin, 30, Killygullib to Quebec, Roman Catholic.
Mary Quin, 28, Killygullib to Quebec, Roman Catholic.
Bridget Quin, 2, Killygullib to Quebec, Roman Catholic.
Mary Quin, 6 months, Killygullib to Quebec, Roman Catholic.
Patrick McLary, 23, Killygullib to Quebec, Roman Catholic.
James McCann, 20, Drumagarner to Quebec, Roman Catholic.
Patrick Bradley, 18, Drumagarner to Quebec, Roman Catholic.
Mary Crilly, 27, Ballynian to Quebec, Roman Catholic.
Catherine Crilly, 20, Ballynian to Quebec, Roman Catholic.

Robert Duncan, 26, Lismoyle to New York, Presbyterian.
Mary Duncan, 28, Lismoyle to New York, Presbyterian.
James Stewart, 30, Killymuck to Quebec, Presbyterian.
Charlot Stewart, 26, Killymuck to Quebec, Presbyterian.
John Stewart, 6, Killymuck to Quebec, Presbyterian.
Sareah Stewart, 4, Killymuck to Quebec, Presbyterian.
Mary Stewart, 2, Killymuck to Quebec, Presbyterian.
William McCollian, 30, Drumsarragh to St John's, Presbyterian.
Eliza McCollian, 26, Drumsarragh to St John's, Presbyterian.
John McCollian, 3, Drumsarragh to St John's, Presbyterian.
Andrew Graham, 30, Drumsarragh to St John's, Presbyterian.
William Douglas, 22, Drumsarragh to St John's, Presbyterian.
Margret Douglas, 25, Drumsarragh to St John's, Presbyterian.
Eliza Graham, 28, Drumsarragh to St John's, Presbyterian.
Ritchard Johnstone, 38, Drumane to St John's, Presbyterian.
Eliza Johnstone, 36, Drumane to St John's, Presbyterian.
James Johnstone, 8, Drumane to St John's, Presbyterian.
Henery Johnstone, 6, Drumane to St John's, Presbyterian.
Jane Johnstone, 4, Drumane to St John's, Presbyterian.
Ritchard Johnstone, 2, Drumane to St John's, Presbyterian.
Henery Mooney, 65, Drumane to St John's, Established Church.
Mary Mooney, 75, Drumane to St John's, Established Church.
John Kirkwood, 21, Moneysallin to St John's, Presbyterian.
William McCloy, 20, Ballymcpeake to St John's, Presbyterian.
William Campbell, 24, Drumard to St John's, Presbyterian.
Eliza Bolton, 20, Drumard to New York, Presbyterian.

Information obtained from William and James Kelso, Hugh Warwick and others. Finished 26th March 1836.

Migration to Harvest

The following is a list of the numbers of persons who annually migrate to the English and Scotch harvests from the above parish. It will show the townlands from which they migrate.
From Boveedy to Scotland 6.
From Killygullib Glebe to Scotland 6.
From Gortmacrane to Scotland 20.
From Timaconway to England 6.
From Ballynian to England 6, to Scotland 7.
From Lismoyle to Scotland 1.
From Killymuck Glebe to Scotland 2.
From Lisgorgan Glebe to Scotland 6.
From Drumane to Scotland 2.
From Eden to Scotland 6.
From Ballymcpeake Lower to Scotland 4.
From Drumard to Scotland 2.
From Moneystaghan McPeake to Scotland 6.
From Moneystaghan Ellis to England 6.
From Drumoolish to Scotland 5.
From Glenone to England 2, to Scotland 6.
From Tyanee to England 4, to Scotland 5.
Total to England 24, to Scotland 84.

Information obtained from John O'Kane, Thomas Armstrong and others.

Table of Schools

[Table contains the following headings: name, situation and description, when established, income and expenditure, physical, intellectual and moral education, number of pupils subdivided by age, sex and religion, name and religion of master or mistress].

Glenone Kildare Street Society school, about 6 miles from Kilrea on the leading road from Kilrea to Bellaghy; house slated, stands 1-storey, 36 and a half feet by 15 feet in the clear, 1 door, 3 windows, school requisites limited; established 1821; income: has received for some years from Lady Clancarthy 5 pounds, from pupils 6 pounds; intellectual education: books published by the Kildare Street Society partly, and partly by the Bible Society; moral education: visited by the parochial clergy of the Established Church; number of pupils: males, 16 under 10 years of age, 40 from 10 to 15, 4 above 15, 60 total males; females, 8 under 10 years of age, 8 from 10 to 15, 16 total females; 76 total pupils, 20 Protestants, 8 Presbyterians, 46 Roman Catholics, 2 other denominations; master John Mulholland, Roman Catholic.

Tyanee London Hibernian Society school, 5 miles from Kilrea, north west of the leading road from Kilrea to Portglenone; house thatched, stands

1-storey, 12 and a half feet by 13 and a half feet in the clear, 1 door, 2 windows, school requisites limited; established 1831; income: average annual gratuity from the London Hibernian Society 6 pounds, from pupils 6 pounds; intellectual education: books published by the London Hibernian Society; moral education: not visited by the parochial clergy, catechism of the Churches of England and Scotland taught; number of pupils: males, 9 under 10 years of age, 10 from 10 to 15, 19 total males; females, 4 under 10 years of age, 7 from 10 to 15, 11 total females; 30 total pupils, 14 Protestants, 14 Presbyterians, 2 other denominations; master Samuel Bradshaw, Presbyterian.

Killygullib London Hibernian Society school, 3 miles from Kilrea, south east of the leading road from Kilrea to Maghera; house thatched, stands 1-storey, 1 door, 2 windows, 14 feet by 13 feet in the clear, school requisites limited; established 1831, under the London Hibernian Society in 1833; income: average gratuity from the London Hibernian Society 3 pounds, from pupils 2 pounds; intellectual education: books published by the London Hibernian Society; moral education: visited by the parochial clergy of the Churches of England and Scotland, catechisms of the above churches taught; number of pupils: males, 27 under 10 years of age, 6 from 10 to 15, 1 above 15, 34 total males; females, 36 under 10 years of age, 2 from 10 to 15, 38 total females; 72 total pupils, 13 Protestants, 27 Presbyterians, 19 Roman Catholics, 13 other denominations; master Johnston McConnell, Presbyterian.

Hervey Hill London Hibernian Society school, 2 miles from Kilrea on the leading road from Swatragh to Kilrea; house thatched, stands 1-storey, 26 feet by 14 feet 8 inches in the clear, 1 door, 2 windows; school requisites limited; established 1821; income: from the Reverend William Napper, rector of Tamlaght O'Crilly, 10 pounds, from pupils 6 pounds; intellectual education: books published by the London Hibernian Society; moral education: visited by the parochial clergy of the Established Church, catechism of the above church taught after school hours; number of pupils: males, 20 under 10 years of age, 10 from 10 to 15, 30 total males; females, 16 under 10 years of age, 4 from 10 to 15, 20 total females; 50 total pupils, 12 Protestants, 10 Presbyterians, 12 Roman Catholics, 16 other denominations; master Oliver Sproul, Protestant.

Boveedy London Hibernian Society school, 2 miles from Kilrea on the leading road from Garvagh to Portglenone; house slated, stands 1-storey, 26 feet 4 inches by 15 feet 2 inches in the clear, 1 door, 5 windows, school requisites limited; established about 60 years ago, under the society 1826; income: from the Reverend William Napper, rector of Tamlaght O'Crilly, 1 pound, from the London Hibernian Society 4 pounds, from pupils 1 pound; intellectual education: books published by the London Hibernian Society; moral education: visited by the parochial clergy of the Churches of England and Scotland, no catechisms taught; number of pupils: males, 30 under 10 years of age, 20 from 10 to 15, 50 total males; females, 32 under 10 years of age, 8 from 10 to 15, 40 total females; 90 total pupils, 20 Protestants, 12 Presbyterians, 58 other denominations; master John McIlwrath, Presbyterian.

Lismoyle London Hibernian Society school, 3 miles from Kilrea and north west of the leading road from Kilrea to Swatragh; house thatched, stands 1-storey, 33 feet by 14 feet in the clear, 1 door, 5 windows, school requisites complete <compleat>; established 1832; income: from W.H. Holmes Esquire 2 pounds, average annual gratuity from London Hibernian Society 3 pounds 10s, from pupils 6 pounds; expenditure: annual rent paid for the schoolhouse by W.H. Holmes Esquire, 2 pounds 10s; intellectual education: books published by the London Hibernian Society; moral education: visited by the parochial clergy of the Churches of England and Scotland, no catechisms taught; number of pupils: males, 9 under 10 years of age, 34 from 10 to 15, 2 above 15, 45 total males; females, 14 under 10 years of age, 5 from 10 to 15, 19 total females; 64 total pupils, 16 Presbyterians, 2 Roman Catholics, 46 other denominations; master Robert Andrews, Presbyterian.

Ballynian private school, 3 and a half miles from Kilrea on the leading road from Kilrea to Swatragh; house thatched, stands 1-storey, 9 and a half feet by 9 and a half feet in the clear, 1 door, no windows, school requisites limited; established 1835; income from pupils 5 pounds; intellectual education: books read in school *Manson's Spelling books*, procured by pupils; moral education: not visited by any of the parochial clergy, Roman Catholic catechism taught; number of pupils: males, 8 under 10 years of age, 8 from 10 to 15, 16 total males; females, 8 under 10 years of age, 8 total females; 24 total pupils, all Roman Catholics; master James O'Neill, Roman Catholic.

Drumagarner London Hibernian Society school, half a mile from Kilrea, north of the leading road from Kilrea to Maghera; house thatched, stands 1-storey, 7 feet 10 inches by 14 feet in the clear, 1 door, 2 windows, school requisites limited; established 1832; income: average annual gratuity from London Hibernian Society 3 pounds, from pupils 2 pounds; intellectual education: books published by the London Hibernian Society; moral education: visited by the parochial clergy of the Established Church, no catechism taught; number of pupils: males, 34 under 10 years of age, 2 above 15, 36 total males; females, 9 under 10 years of age, 10 from 10 to 15, 6 above 15, 25 total females; 61 total pupils, 1 Protestant, 53 Presbyterians, 3 Roman Catholics, 4 other denominations; master Joseph Reid, Presbyterian.

Drumsarragh private school, 1 and a half miles from Kilrea, north of the leading road from Kilrea to Garvagh; house thatched, stands 1-storey, 13 feet by 12 and a half feet in the clear, 1 door, 2 windows, school requisites limited; established 1835; income from pupils 4 pounds; expenditure: annual house rent 1 pound 10s; intellectual education: books read in school the Bible, Testament and spelling books, all procured by the pupils; moral education: not visited by any of the parochial clergy, catechisms of the Church of England, Scotland and Roman Catholic taught; number of pupils: males, 13 under 10 years of age, 2 from 10 to 15, 15 total males; females, 7 under 10 years of age, 3 from 10 to 15, 10 total females; 25 total pupils, 6 Protestants, 12 Presbyterians, 7 Roman Catholics; master Thomas Mooney, Roman Catholic.

Gortmacrane private school, 1 mile from Kilrea, south of the leading road from Garvagh to Kilrea; house thatched, stands 1-storey, 14 feet 5 inches by 15 feet 9 inches in the clear, 1 door, 2 windows, school requisites limited; established 1830; income: from Langford Rowley Heyland Esquire 4 pounds, from pupils 5 pounds; expenditure: annual house rent 2 pounds; intellectual education: books read the Bible, Testament, *Manson's Spelling books*, partly supplied by the rector and part procured by pupils; moral education: visited by the parochial clergy of the Established Church, catechisms of the various churches taught; number of pupils: males, 15 under 10 years of age, 16 from 10 to 15, 3 above 15, 34 total males; females, 20 under 10 years of age, 12 from 10 to 15, 32 total females; 66 total pupils, 15 Protestants, 8 Presbyterians, 37 Roman Catholics, 6 other denominations; master James O'Kane, Roman Catholic.

Drumagarner private school, 1 mile from Kilrea, south of the leading road from Kilrea to Maghera; house thatched, stands 1-storey, 13 and a half feet by 12 feet in the clear, 1 door, 1 window, school requisites limited; established 1834; income from pupils 4 pounds; expenditure: annual house rent 2 pounds 6s; intellectual education: books read the Bible, Testament and *Dublin Spelling books*, all procured by pupils; moral education: not visited by the parochial clergy, Roman Catholic catechism taught; number of pupils: males, 14 under 10 years of age, 8 from 10 to 15, 22 total males; females, 6 under 10 years of age, 6 total females; 28 total pupils; mistress Mary McCotter, Roman Catholic.

Timaconway London Hibernian Society school, 3 and a half miles from Kilrea, north west of the leading road from Kilrea to Maghera; house thatched, stands 1-storey, 13 feet by 12 feet 8 inches in the clear, 1 door, 3 windows, school requisites complete; established 1832; income: average annual income from the London Hibernian Society 2 pounds, from pupils 6 pounds; expenditure: William Holmes Esquire pays 2 pounds 2s per annum for the schoolhouse; intellectual education: books published by the London Hibernian Society; moral education: visited by the parochial clergy of the Established Church, no catechism taught; number of pupils: males, 34 under 10 years of age, 9 from 10 to 15, 43 total males; females, 20 under 10 years of age, 2 from 10 to 15, 22 total females; 65 total pupils, 24 Protestants, 12 Presbyterians, 15 Roman Catholics, 14 other denominations; master James Tomb, Protestant.

Drumoolish London Hibernian Society school, 4 miles from Kilrea on the leading road from Kilrea to Maghera by Drumbolg; house thatched, 20 and a half feet by 13 and a half feet, 1 door, 2 windows, school requisites limited; established 1828; income: average annual gratuity from the London Hibernian Society 5 pounds, from pupils 5 pounds; expenditure: annual rent for schoolhouse 4 pounds; intellectual education: books published by the London Hibernian Society; moral education: visited by the parochial clergy of the Established Church, no catechism taught; number of pupils: males, 88 under 10 years of age, 12 from 10 to 15, 6 above 15, 106 total males; females, 42 under 10 years of age, 4 from 10 to 15, 4 above 15, 50 total females; 156 total pupils, 10 Protestants, 139 Presbyterians, 1 Roman Catholic, 6 other denominations; master Theophilus O'Neill, Presbyterian.

Eden London Hibernian Society school, 5 miles from Kilrea on the by-road leading from Maghera to Portglenone; house slated, stands 1-storey, 29 feet by 18 feet in the clear, 1 door, 7 windows, school requisites limited; established 1825; income: average annual gratuity from London

Hibernian Society 4 pounds, from pupils 8 pounds; intellectual education: books published by the London Hibernian Society; moral education: visited by the parochial clergy of the Established Church, no catechism taught; number of pupils: males, 44 under 10 years of age, 30 from 10 to 15, 12 above 15, 86 total males; females, 52 under 10 years of age, 25 from 10 to 15, 8 above 15, 85 total females; 171 total pupils, 37 Protestants, 27 Presbyterians, 51 Roman Catholics, 56 other denominations; master Samuel Clarke, Presbyterian.

Tyanee national school, 4 miles from Kilrea on the leading road from Clady to Kilrea; house thatched, stands 1-storey, 14 and a half feet by 13 and a half feet in the clear, 1 door, 3 windows, school requisites limited; established 1830; income: from the Education Board 8 pounds, from pupils 10 pounds; intellectual education: books published by the Education Board; moral education: visited by the Roman Catholic clergy, Roman Catholic catechism taught; number of pupils: males, 16 under 10 years of age, 6 from 10 to 15, 22 total males; females, 9 under 10 years of age, 2 from 10 to 15, 1 above 15, 12 total females; 34 total pupils, all Roman Catholics; master John Robinson, Roman Catholic.

Tyanee Presbyterian school, 4 miles from Kilrea on a by-road leading from Clady to Kilrea; house slated, stands 1-storey, 19 feet by 16 feet in the clear, 1 door, 4 windows, school requisites limited; established 1836; income: from the Presbyterian Committee of Belfast 2 pounds, from pupils 7 pounds; intellectual education: books read in the school, the Bible, Testament and spelling books, procured by pupils; moral education: visited by the Presbyterian clergy, catechisms of the Churches of England and Scotland taught; number of pupils: males, 9 under 10 years of age, 8 from 10 to 15, 1 above 15, 18 total males; females, 4 under 10 years of age, 5 from 10 to 15, 9 total females; 27 total pupils, 24 Presbyterians, 1 Roman Catholic, 2 other denominations; master James Brown, Protestant.

Greenlough national school, 6 and a half miles from Kilrea on the leading road from Garvagh to Portglenone; house thatched, stands 1-storey, 17 feet 6 inches by 13 feet 3 inches in the clear, 1 door, 4 windows, school requisites complete; established 1830, under the National Board 1834; income: from the Education Board 8 pounds, from pupils 3 pounds 10s; intellectual education: books published by the Education Board; moral education: visited by the parochial clergy of every denomination, catechisms of the above churches taught on Saturdays; number of pupils: males, 30 under 10 years of age, 44 from 10 to 15, 5 above 15, 79 total males; females, 26 under 10 years of age, 8 from 10 to 15, 2 above 15, 36 total females; 115 total pupils, 18 Protestants, 7 Presbyterians, 89 Roman Catholics, 1 other denomination; master Daniel O'Connor, Roman Catholic.

Tamlaght O'Crilly London Hibernian Society school, 3 miles from Kilrea on the leading road from Garvagh to Portglenone; house thatched, stands 1-storey, 25 feet 6 inches by 17 feet 2 inches in the clear, 1 door, 3 windows, school requisites sufficient; established 1820; income: average annual gratuity from London Hibernian Society 6 pounds, from pupils 6 pounds; intellectual education: books published by the London Hibernian Society; moral education: visited by the parochial clergy of the Established Church, no catechism taught; number of pupils: males, 22 under 10 years of age, 46 from 10 to 15, 12 above 15, 80 total males; females, 38 under 10 years of age, 20 from 10 to 15, 1 above 15, 59 total females; 139 total pupils, 20 Protestants, 30 Presbyterians, 20 Roman Catholics, 69 other denominations; mistress Constantine McRory, Roman Catholic.

Inisrush <Innasrush> London Hibernian Society school, 5 miles from Kilrea on the leading road from Garvagh to Portglenone; house thatched, stands 1-storey, 39 feet 10 inches by 16 feet 7 inches in the clear, 1 door, 6 windows, school requisites limited; established 1828; income: average annual gratuity from London Hibernian Society 4 pounds, from pupils 2 pounds; intellectual education: books published by the London Hibernian Society; moral education: visited by the parochial clergy of the Established Church, catechisms of the Churches of England and Scotland taught on Saturdays after school hours; number of pupils: males, 18 under 10 years of age, 4 from 10 to 15, 2 above 15, 24 total males; females, 11 under 10 years of age, 5 from 10 to 15, 16 total females; 40 total pupils, 12 Protestants, 15 Presbyterians, 6 Roman Catholics, 7 other denominations; master John McFarland, Presbyterian.

Lisnagroat <Lisnagrot> London Hibernian Society school, 1 and a half miles from Kilrea on the leading road from Kilrea to Inisrush; house thatched, stands 1-storey, 18 feet by 14 and a half feet, 1 door, 2 windows, school requisites limited; established 1826, under the London Hibernian Society 1828; income: annual gratuity from the London Hibernian Society 3 pounds, from the Worshipful the Mercer's Company 3 pounds, from pupils 1 pound 10s; intellectual education:

books published by the London Hibernian Society; moral education: visited by the parochial clergy of the Churches of England and Scotland, no catechism taught; number of pupils: males, 17 under 10 years of age, 13 from 10 to 15, 2 above 15, 32 total males; females, 22 under 10 years of age, 6 from 10 to 15, 28 total females; 60 total pupils, 20 Protestants, 12 Presbyterians, 28 Roman Catholics; master James McLoughlin, Roman Catholic.

Killymuck London Hibernian Society school, 3 and a quarter miles from Kilrea on the leading road to Maghera; house thatched, stands 1-storey, 12 feet by 15 feet 9 inches, 1 door, 1 window, school requisites limited; established 1832; income: average annual gratuity from London Hibernian Society 5 pounds, from pupils 5 pounds; intellectual education: books published by the London Hibernian Society; moral education: visited by the parochial clergy of the Established Church, no catechism taught; number of pupils: males, 52 under 10 years of age, 20 from 10 to 15, 2 above 15, 74 total males; females, 16 under 10 years of age, 12 from 10 to 15, 28 total females; 102 total pupils, 6 Protestants, 50 Presbyterians, 18 Roman Catholics, 28 other denominations; master William Sproul, Protestant.

Drumane private school, 3 miles from Kilrea, east of the leading road from Garvagh to Portglenone; house thatched, stands 1-storey, 15 feet by 15 feet in the clear, 1 door, 2 windows, school requisites limited; established 1807; income from pupils 2 pounds; intellectual education: books read the Bible, Testament and spelling books, procured by pupils; moral education: visited by the clergy of the Established Church, catechism of the Established Church taught; number of pupils: males, 2 under 10 years of age, 2 total males; females, 3 under 10 years of age, 3 total females; 5 total pupils, 3 Protestants, 2 Presbyterians; master Dominic Heyland, Protestant.

Sunday Schools

[Table contains the following headings: name, situation, when established, superintendents, teachers, scholars, hours of attendance, societies with which connected, observations].

Hervey <Harvey> Hill female Sunday school, held in Hervey Hill House, established 1818; superintendent Miss Nevill; teachers: 4 females, total 4; scholars: Protestants 25, Presbyterians 18, Roman Catholics 8, other denominations 9, 95 females, total 95, average 65; exclusively Sunday school scholars, average 60; hours of attendance: in summer opened from 4 to 5.30 p.m., in winter from 3 to 4.30 p.m.; societies with which connected: Sunday School Society for books; opened by prayer and ended by singing; no expenditure in the last year.

Tamlaght female Sunday school, held in Tamlaght church, established 1820; superintendent Miss Nevill; teachers: 1 male, 3 females, total 4; scholars: 46 Protestants, 34 Presbyterians, 1 Roman Catholic, 31 other denominations, 112 females, total 112; all exclusively Sunday school scholars; open from 10 to 11.30 summer and winter; societies with which connected: Sunday School Society for books; opened with prayer; no expenditure.

Tyanee Presbyterian Sunday school, held in the day schoolhouse, established 1835; superintendent Robert McCaughey; teachers: 5 males, 3 females, total 8; scholars: 2 Protestants, 61 Presbyterians, 2 Roman Catholics, 10 other denominations, 45 males, 30 females, total 75; 35 exclusively Sunday school scholars; open from 8 to 11 a.m. summer and winter; societies with which connected: Sunday School Society for books; opened and closed by singing and prayer; no expenditure.

Drumbolg Sunday school, held in Drumbolg meeting house, established 1830; superintendent Reverend James A. Smyth; teachers: 4 males, 4 females, total 8; scholars: 12 Protestants, 20 Presbyterians, 4 Roman Catholics, 27 other denominations, 30 males, 33 females, total 63; 30 exclusively Sunday school scholars; open from 9 to 11 a.m. summer and winter; societies with which connected: Sunday School Society for books; opened and closed by singing and prayer.

Glenone Sunday school, held in the day schoolhouse, established 1835; superintendent Reverend Mark Bloxham; teachers: 4 males, 2 females, total 6; scholars: 24 Protestants, 14 Presbyterians, 14 Roman Catholics, 10 other denominations, 27 males, 35 females, total 62; 36 exclusively Sunday school scholars; open from 9 to 11 a.m. summer and winter; societies with which connected: Sunday School Society for books; opened and closed by prayer and occasionally by singing.

Tyanee Sunday school, held in the day schoolhouse, established 1831; superintendent William Dool; teachers: 5 males, total 5; scholars: 30 Protestants, 23 Presbyterians, 3 Roman Catholics, 4 other denominations, 30 males, 30 females, total 60; 30 exclusively Sunday school scholars; open from 8 to 10 a.m. and from 4 to 6 p.m., in winter 9 to 11 a.m.; societies with which connected: Sunday School Society for books; opened and closed by singing and prayer; no expenditure.

Drumsarragh Sunday school, held in a farm barn 15 feet by 16 feet in the clear, established 1829; superintendent William Huston; teachers: 3 males, 2 females, total 5; scholars: 10 Protestants, 15 Presbyterians, 2 Roman Catholics, 8 other denominations, 17 males, 18 females, total 35; 31 exclusively Sunday school scholars; open from 7 to 9 a.m. and from 5 to 7 p.m., relinquished in winter; societies with which connected: Sunday School Society for books; opened and closed by singing and prayer occasionally; expenditure last year 7s 6d, contributed by superintendent, chiefly.

Hervey Hill Sunday school, held in the day schoolhouse, established 1821; superintendent Henery Neville; teachers: 3 males, total 3; scholars: 5 Protestants, 20 Presbyterians, 5 Roman Catholics, 30 males, total 30; 20 exclusively Sunday school scholars; opened from 3 to 5 p.m. summer and winter; not connected with any society; day school books read on Sundays, opened and closed by prayer; no expenditure for the last year.

Killygullib Sunday school, held in the day schoolhouse, established 1833; superintendent Johnston McConnell; teachers: 1 males, 2 females, total 3; scholars: 8 Protestants, 23 Presbyterians, 4 other denominations, 10 males, 25 females, total 35; 12 exclusively Sunday school scholars; opened from 9 to 11 a.m. summer and winter; not connected with any society; day school books read on Sundays; opened and closed by prayer and singing; no expenditure for the last year.

Boveedy Sunday school, held in the day schoolhouse, established 1816; superintendent John McIlwrath; teachers: 5 males, 2 females, total 7; scholars: 30 Protestants, 20 Presbyterians, 1 Roman Catholic, 48 other denominations, 45 males, 54 females, total 99; 91 exclusively Sunday school scholars; open 2 to 6 p.m. summer and winter; societies with which connected: Sunday School Society for books; opened and closed by prayer; no expenditure last year.

Tamlaght O'Crilly male Sunday school, held in the day schoolhouse, established 1820; superintendent Constantine McRory; teachers: 3 males, total 3; scholars: 20 Protestants, 30 Presbyterians, 50 other denominations, 100 total, all male; 60 exclusively Sunday school scholars.

Greenlough Sunday school, held in the Roman Catholic chapel, established 1825; superintendent Daniel O'Connor; teachers: 7 males, 8 females, total 15; scholars: 284 Roman Catholics, 102 males, 182 females, total 284; 185 exclusively Sunday school scholars; open from 9 to 12 a.m. alternate Sundays and from 2 to 5 p.m. alternate Sundays; not connected with any society; books read the Bible, Testament and Scripture lessons, opened and closed by prayer and singing; expenditure in last year 2 pounds 10s, raised by collection in the chapel for the purchase of books.

Inisrush Sunday school, held in the day schoolhouse, established 1831; superintendent John Orr; teachers: 6 males, 3 females, total 9; scholars: 30 Protestants, 40 Presbyterians, 4 Roman Catholics, 26 other denominations, 60 males, 40 females, total 100; 60 exclusively Sunday school scholars; open from 8 to 10 a.m. summer and winter; societies with which connected: Sunday School Society for books; opened and closed by singing and prayer; expenditure last year 15s, raised at a charity sermon in the schoolhouse.

Drumagarner Roman Catholic Sunday school, held in the Roman Catholic chapel, established 1820; superintendents: Reverend John Rodgers, parish priest, Reverend Samual Auterson, Reverend John McLoughlin, curates; teachers: 9 males, 4 females, total 13; scholars: 205 Roman Catholics, 110 males, 95 females, total 205; 100 exclusively Sunday school scholars; open 8 to 12 a.m. alternate Sundays and 12 to 4 p.m. alternate Sundays; Bible, Testament and other religious books read, all procured by pupils; no expenditure last year.

Lismoyle Sunday school, held in the day schoolhouse, established 1832; superintendent Robert Andrews; teachers: 6 males, 1 female, total 7; scholars: 24 Presbyterians, 1 Roman Catholic, 73 other denominations, 42 males, 56 females, total 98; 69 exclusively Sunday school scholars; open 6 to 9 a.m. summer and winter, as light affords; societies with which connected: Sunday School Society for books; opened and closed by prayer and singing; no expenditure.

Gortmacrane Sunday school, held in the day schoolhouse, established 1830; superintendent James O'Kane; teachers: 6 males, 4 females, total 10; scholars: 6 Protestants, 12 Presbyterians, 96 Roman Catholics, 6 other denominations, 67 males, 53 females, total 120; 80 exclusively Sunday school scholars; open 6 to 9 a.m. from March to November; societies with which connected: Sunday School Society for books; catechisms of the respective denominations taught at opening and closing the school.

Killymuck Sunday school, held in the day

schoolhouse, established 1832; superintendent William Sproul; teachers: 4 males, 1 female, total 5; scholars: 45 Presbyterians, 25 other denominations, 40 males, 30 females, total 70; 20 exclusively Sunday school scholars; open 7 to 9 a.m. from May to November, relinquished in winter; societies with which connected: Sunday School Society for books; opened and closed by singing and prayer; no expenditure.

Drumoolish Sunday school, held in the day schoolhouse, established 1831; superintendent Theophilus O'Neill; teachers: 2 males, 6 females, total 8; scholars: 12 Protestants, 112 Presbyterians, 2 Roman Catholics, 8 other denominations, 70 males, 64 females, total 134; 44 exclusively Sunday school scholars; open 5 to 8 p.m. in summer, 2 to 4 p.m. in winter; societies with which connected: Sunday School Society for books; opened and closed by singing and prayer; no expenditure.

Eden Sunday school, held in the day schoolhouse, established 1835; superintendent Samuel Clarke; teachers: 2 males, 3 females, total 5; scholars: 24 Protestants, 21 Presbyterians, 24 Roman Catholics, 61 other denominations, 65 males, 65 females, total 130; 40 exclusively Sunday school scholars; open 8 to 11 a.m. in summer, 9 to 11 a.m. in winter; societies with which connected: Sunday School Society for books; opened and closed by prayer; expenditure last year 7s 6d, defrayed by superintendent.

Notes on Drimane by T.A. Larcom, G. Dalton and J. O'Donovan, December 1836

NATURAL STATE

Notes on Drimane

There is no descriptive remark opposite Drimane townland in Tamlaght O'Crilly. Is it generally smooth (as opposite to rocky), so as to make druim min equal "smooth ridge", the probable derivation? [Signed] Thomas A. Larcom, Lieutenant Royal Engineers, 7th December 1836.

It is cultivated with a large proportion of bog. I had always thought that drum or drim equally signified "a back", the latter most generally used. Ean is, I believe, "a bird." It might also mean "a ridge of birds", or "ridge of Maon" (a family name). [Signed] G. Dalton, Lieutenant Royal Engineers, 7th December 1836.

It is spelled in Irish druim and the "i" distinctly heard. Its genitive form is droma, but the practice of writing this word drum should become general. It is to be remarked that names of places derived from this word are always written drum or drom in the Charter of Londonderry. [Signed] J. O'Donovan.

ORTHOGRAPHY OF TOWNLANDS

Notes on Townland Names

[The spelling of each townland is confirmed by the word "yes", written by Thomas Larcom [?].

Drimlane should be made Drumlane: yes.

Drimnaconan should be made Drumnacanon: yes.

Drimoolish should be made Drumoolish: yes.

Drimsaragh should be made Drumsaragh: yes.

Drimagarner should be made Drumagarner: yes.

Gortmacrane, Gurtmacrane; gort is more general: yes. The Irish "o", however, is pronounced like the "o" in mother.

www.ingramcontent.com/pod-product-compliance
Lightning Source LLC
Chambersburg PA
CBHW051211290426
44109CB00021B/2418